THE REMINISCENCES OF

Lieutenant Commander Richard A. Harralson U.S. Navy (Retired)

INTERVIEWED BY

Paul Stillwell

U.S. Naval Institute • Annapolis, Maryland

Copyright © 2000

Preface

A few years ago, I began receiving letters from Dick Harralson in which he asked for information about specific naval operations in the late 1930s because he was in the process of writing about events in which he had participated. As the correspondence progressed, he began sending me his articles about active duty service in the 1930s and 1940s. As I read his recollections, I developed a growing admiration for his ability to describe things so vividly that mental images leaped into my mind; it was almost as if I had been alongside him as he experienced the events he was telling about. Added to that was the content of the events themselves: his service in the Asiatic Fleet during its waning days just prior to World War II, and then spending more than three years of that war as a prisoner of the Japanese.

From what I read, it became apparent that the combination of subject matter and narrative ability made Mr. Harralson an ideal candidate for the oral history program. We set a date, and I flew to California to meet and interview him. He and his wife Naomi provided gracious hospitality and a sense of warmth that led to instant friendship. And I sat enthralled as he spun out stories of his time in the Navy. He is a thoroughly down-to-earth, kindly man, so it was a great pleasure to be with him for a period of three days.

In matter-of-fact language, Mr. Harralson described his life. He told of being fascinated with radio and with the sea from the time he was a boy. In the latter part of the 1930s he combined those interests when he enlisted in the Navy and became a radioman. The lure of the old China Station took him to the Far East, where he reveled in the atmosphere provided by liberty ashore in China and the Philippines. But that idyllic way of life came to an abrupt end with the beginning of war. From then on, it became a stark matter of survival. He was captured on the island of Corregidor in the spring of 1942 and then spent the remainder of the conflict as a prisoner of war. Day by day he did what he had to do in order to live until the following day. Along the way, the prisoners supported each other and provided hope in a situation that often seemed hopeless. The end of the war brought release from captivity and a sense of euphoria.

After the war, he sought again to use his skills as a radioman, but naval communications had changed a great deal during his time as a prisoner. Teletype had replaced the Morse code for most messages, and electronics in general were becoming ever more sophisticated. Through a combination of Navy schools and on-the-job training he learned the new equipment and applied his knowledge at the Navy Radio Station in Portsmouth, New Hampshire, on board the escort carrier <u>Sicily</u> during the Korean War, at the Great Lakes Naval Training Center, on a special intelligence-gathering assignment in Turkey during the Cold War, on board the former battleship <u>Mississippi</u> when she was testing guided missiles, and at the Combat Information Center in Glynco, Georgia.

Throughout the oral history, Mr. Harralson spoke often of his wife and children, because family means a great deal to them. It was a privilege to hear him talk about the people close to him and to realize the many ways in which his service contributed to the Navy.

Mrs. Debby Cutler did the initial transcription of the interview tapes. In the course of moving from that raw transcript to this final version, both Mr. Harralson and I have done some editing in the interests of accuracy, smoothness, and clarity. At times various sections of the text have been moved from one place to another in order to improve the continuity of the narrative. He made use of his personal files to track down information useful for the editing of the transcript. In addition, I have inserted footnotes to provide further information for readers who use the volume. In going through the entire process of editing and footnoting, Mr. Harralson has been most cooperative. The result is a final version that has been considerably enhanced over that in the raw initial transcripts.

Ms. Ann Hassinger of the Naval Institute's history division has made a significant contribution through her diligence in the overall process of printing, proofreading, and overseeing the binding of the completed volumes.

Paul Stillwell
Director, History Division
U.S. Naval Institute
February 2000

Richard Aymard Harralson
Lieutenant Commander, U.S. Navy (Retired)

Personal Data

Born:	8 January 1920, Visalia, California
Parents:	Henry Palmer Harralson and Martha Frost Harralson
Married:	Naomi Winkler, 20 April 1946, San Diego, California
Children:	Joseph Henry Harralson, born 30 January 1947, Kittery, Maine
	Arthur Frost Harralson, born 13 June 1949, Great Lakes, Illinois
	Helen Kay Harralson, born 11 January 1952, San Diego, California
Education:	Placer Union High School, Auburn, California; graduated in June 1937
	California State University, Sacramento, California; graduated with bachelor of arts degree in 1974

Dates of Rate and Rank:

Apprentice Seaman	8 September 1937
Seaman Second Class	January 1938
Seaman First Class	March 1939
Radioman Third Class	April 1939
Radioman Second Class	August 1940
Radioman First Class	December 1941
Chief Radioman	October 1945
Radio Electrician (W-1)	8 October 1946
Ensign	8 October 1946
Lieutenant (junior grade)	1 January 1947
Lieutenant	15 July 1951
Lieutenant Commander	1 July 1956

Decorations and Medals:

Navy Commendation Medal
Good Conduct Medal with one star
American Defense Medal
Asiatic-Pacific Campaign Medal with one star
World War II Victory Medal
Philippine Defense Medal with one star
China Service Medal (Extended)
Occupation Service Medal
National Defense Service Medal
Korean Defense Medal with three stars
United Nations Medal
Army Presidential Unit Citation with oak leaf
Navy Unit Citation
Philippine Presidential Unit Citation
Korean Presidential Unit Citation

Chronological Record of Service:

8 September 1937	Enlisted in the U.S. Navy
September 1937-December 1937	Recruit training, Naval Training Station, San Diego, California
January 1938-April 1938	Radio School, San Diego, California
May 1938-October 1938	Radio Gang, USS Saratoga (CV-3)
November 1938-August 1939	Attached to Scouting Squadron Three; detailed to flag allowance, Commander Aircraft Battle Force, embarked in USS Lexington (CV-2), from November 1938 to April 1939
August 1939-October 1939	Transportation to the Far East on board USS Henderson (AP-1)
October 1939-November 1940	Flag allowance, Commander in Chief Asiatic Fleet, embarked in USS Augusta (CA-31)
November 1940-January 1941	Flag allowance, Commander in Chief Asiatic Fleet, embarked in USS Houston (CA-30)
January 1941-December 1941	Radio gang, Navy Radio Station, Cavite, Philippines

December 1941-May 1942	Radio gang, Navy Radio Station, Corregidor, Manila Bay, Philippines
May 1942-September 1945	Prisoner of war, held in the Philippines, Formosa, and Japan
September 1945-March 1946	Post-release rehabilitation period
March 1946-June 1946	Electronics Laboratory, Point Loma, San Diego, California
July 1946-October 1946	Student, Electronics Technician School, Great Lakes, Illinois
November 1946-December 1948	Officer in charge, Navy Radio Station, Portsmouth, New Hampshire
January 1949-December 1949	Student, Electronics Maintenance School, Service Schools Command, Great Lakes, Illinois
January 1950-March 1952	Assistant electronics maintenance officer and assistant division officer, USS Sicily (CVE-118); later electronics maintenance officer and division officer
March 1952-April 1954	Instructor, Electronics Maintenance School, Service Schools Command, Great Lakes, Illinois
May 1954-February 1955	Officer in charge, Special Project X-31, Amasra, Turkey
March 1955-September 1956	Communication officer, USS Mississippi (EAG-128)
October 1956-December 1957	Electronics maintenance officer, Combat Information Center School, Glynco, Georgia
1 December 1957	Retirement from active duty

Civilian Employment:

January 1958-March 1968	Liaison engineer, Aerojet General Corporation, Sacramento, California, assigned to the Titan and Apollo programs

Authorization

The U.S. Naval Institute is hereby authorized to make available to individuals, libraries, and other repositories of its choosing the tapes and/or transcripts of three oral history interviews concerning the life and naval career of the undersigned. The interviews were recorded on 15 May 1997, 16 May 1997, and 17 May 1997 in collaboration with Paul Stillwell for the U.S. Naval Institute.

The undersigned does hereby release and assign to the U.S. Naval Institute the rights and title to these interviews, with the exception that the undersigned retains the right to use the material for his own purposes, as he sees fit. The copyright in both the oral and transcribed versions shall be the sole property of the U.S. Naval Institute. The tape recordings of the interviews are and will remain the property of the U.S. Naval Institute.

Signed and sealed this 5th day of January 1998. 1999

Richard A. Harralson
Lieutenant Commander, U.S. Navy (Retired)

Interview Number 1 with Lieutenant Commander Richard A. Harralson, U.S. Navy (Retired)

Place: Commander Harralson's home in Shingle Springs, California

Date: Thursday, 15 May 1997

Interviewer: Paul Stillwell

Paul Stillwell: Well, Mr. Harralson, it's a pleasure to have met you in person today after the correspondence we carried on for a couple of years. As I mentioned when we met at the airport, you have a gift for describing things. So I'm particularly gratified that you are willing to take part in this. Probably the best place to start is at the beginning. Please tell me when and where you were born, something about your parents, and your growing-up years.

Commander Harralson: Well, Mr. Stillwell, I certainly appreciate your interest in my sea stories. I was born in Visalia, California, January 8, 1920. I lived there for about nine years, and we moved north. My father had a good business. He built telephone lines. He would get a bunch of farmers together and enter into a contract with them to build the line into town, where he connected with the Bell Telephone Company. His biggest job was for the Forest Service, building a telephone line to General Grant National Park, which at that time was separate from Sequoia. It is now incorporated in Sequoia National Park.

The Depression of 1929 hit very hard in that part of California. This was before the stock market crash.* He had a lot of debts outstanding, and work was scarce. So we moved to greener pastures, north to the little town of Woodland, about 20 miles from Sacramento. He had a job there with the Sacramento Northern Railroad, digging post holes. He went broke because he got into some clay that he couldn't clear from his post-hole digger.

From that time on, our economic situation was downward. The Depression was full upon us. Work was scarce, and we became very hard up. We managed to eat, and he

---

* Following the crash of the New York Stock Exchange in late October 1929, the United States was plunged into the Great Depression, from which it did not recover until the nation geared up for World War II at the beginning of the 1940s. The Depression was marked by high unemployment and many business failures.

managed to keep us in a house. We moved to Sacramento, where we spent about three years. Then he got a job with the Forest Service, and we moved up to Applegate, which is up in the mountains, in the Sierra Nevadas, about 2,000-feet elevation. To me, that was the best possible thing that could happen.

I went to Placer Union High School, in Auburn, California, for three years, and graduated--just barely. And, of course, I'd been reading a lot of books about the Navy.

Paul Stillwell: What had stirred your interest in the Navy?

Commander Harralson: Well, I got started reading Captain Slocum's book about his cruise around the world in the Spray.[*] From there I went to Richard Dana, Two Years Before the Mast.[†] Then there was Mutiny on the Bounty, Nordhoff and Hall, and Men Against the Sea.[‡] And, of course, there were corresponding movies. The Mutiny on the Bounty that I remember was with Clark Gable and Charles Laughton. Charles Laughton was Captain Bligh. Then there was the follow-on, The Men Against the Sea, with Charles Laughton.

The Navy was popular in those days. There were quite a few movies out. The two carriers figured in several of those movies.

Paul Stillwell: There was one called Hell Divers that had Jimmy Thach in it.[§]

Commander Harralson: Is that right?

Paul Stillwell: Flying the F8C.[**] That had Clark Gable and Wallace Beery in it.

---

[*] Captain Joshua Slocum, Sailing Alone Around the World (New York: The Century Company, 1900). In 1985 the Naval Institute Press published a new edition of the book as part of its Classics of Naval Literature series and included a new introduction by Rear Admiral Robert W. McNitt, USN (Ret.).

[†] Richard H. Dana, Two Years Before the Mast: A Personal Narrative (Boston: Houghton Mifflin, 1911).

[‡] Charles Nordhoff and James Norman Hall wrote three novels known as "The Bounty Trilogy," all published by Little, Brown of Boston: Mutiny on the Bounty (1932), Men Against the Sea (1934), and Pitcairn's Island (1934).

[§] Released in 1932 by Metro-Goldwyn-Mayer, Hell Divers featured the rivalry between two carrier pilots and included footage shot on board the USS Saratoga (CV-3). Lieutenant (junior grade) John S. Thach, USN, was attached to squadron VF-1B in that ship. The oral history of Thach, who eventually retired as a four-star admiral, is in the Naval Institute collection.

[**] The Curtiss F8C Helldiver was a fleet fighter of the era.

Commander Harralson: Yes, yes, yes. Well, the Navy was a popular service in those days. There was a feeling, at least among my peers, that of the services the Navy was the one to be in.

Paul Stillwell: Why did they have that feeling?

Commander Harralson: I think it was just popular as a result of the media coverage, like we'd say today. Also, I think the Navy had some advantages that we knew about. I'm not sure it's actually true, but if you made a rate in the Navy, we were told, you kept it when you got transferred. Now, if you made a noncom rating in the Army, you would lose it if you got transferred.* I think that was basically true, but not entirely. I think our pay scale was better than the Army.

Paul Stillwell: That's surprising, because I thought they had comparable levels for all services.

Commander Harralson: I don't think they did then, Paul. Let's put it this way, we in the Navy thought we were better paid [Laughter], although it wasn't very much in those days.

Paul Stillwell: Did you have any part-time jobs during your growing-up years?

Commander Harralson: Yes, I did. I was lucky. I was able to pick pears at 25 cents an hour, nine-hour days, six days a week, which I felt was fortunate. Most of the kids in Applegate didn't have work. There wasn't much work around. That was probably a contributing factor for thinking about the Navy. Also, at that time, I was very much interested in radio. I'd started building crystal sets and one-tube radios when I was about 11 years old, and had progressed into shortwave, and was aspiring to become a ham.† I finally took the test when I was 16 years old, but flunked the code part of it because I didn't

---

*Noncom--non-commissioned officer, the equivalent of the Navy's enlisted petty officers.
†A ham, in this context, refers to a licensed amateur radio operator.

pay any attention to punctuation. I later got a ham ticket after I'd gone into the Navy, but then it didn't do me any good. [Laughter]

Paul Stillwell: Well, this is Steinbeck country. Did you see any of the conditions that he described in, say, The Grapes of Wrath?*

Commander Harralson: Oh, yes, yes.

Paul Stillwell: You saw the migrant workers from Oklahoma and so forth?

Commander Harralson: Yes, yes.

Paul Stillwell: What are your memories of that?

Commander Harralson: Oh, just the way they lived. I traveled with my father, from time to time, in the valley. And they were apparent in the orchards, their camps. But, you know, I really don't think overall there were the bad vibes that exist today. For example, I could hitchhike, if I wanted to go somewhere, and thought nothing of it. And people picked you up and thought nothing of it. The Grapes of Wrath is true, I'm sure. I read the book. Steinbeck was one of my favorite authors. I'm sure it happened. But, for the most part, I remember everybody being sort of in the same boat. I don't remember any particularly bad scenes.

Paul Stillwell: Do you remember the situation getting better after Roosevelt became President?†

---

*Author John Steinbeck (1902-1968) was a native of Salinas, California. His most famous work was The Grapes of Wrath, published in 1939, which told of the oppressive forces facing Oklahoma farmers who sought work in California during the Depression. The book won the 1940 Pulitzer Prize for literature and was made into a popular movie starring Henry Fonda.
†Franklin D. Roosevelt served as President of the United States from 4 March 1933 until his death on 12 April 1945.

Commander Harralson: Yes, I do. Yes, I do. I remember social security was coming in and my father thinking what a great thing it was. And, of course, nobody connected it with welfare; it was something entirely different from welfare. It was a forced contribution towards your retirement. My father's only problem was he didn't have any income to speak of.

Paul Stillwell: There was more of a stigma to welfare then, also.

Commander Harralson: Oh, absolutely. As I say, we were about as hard up as you could get, but I never went hungry. My mother always managed to put a meal on the table. We ate a lot of beans, but I loved them.

Paul Stillwell: It got you ready for the Navy. [Laughter]

Commander Harralson: Yes, they did. [Laughter]

Paul Stillwell: Did you have siblings?

Commander Harralson: Yes, I had two brothers. Palmer Frost Harralson was ten years older than me and known as Frost or Frosty. The other one, eight years older than me was Homer White Harralson, known as Bill. Frost joined the Marines when he was 19 and went out to the Asiatic station. He was on shipboard a lot. In fact, he was involved in coaling the old Pittsburgh that was a station ship out there.

Paul Stillwell: An old armored cruiser.

Commander Harralson: Yes, yes. He was on the Houston for a while. He also was on the Isabel. He came home after two years out there. Let's see, I would have been about 11, and he looked ten feet tall. He was a corporal. Noncoms, of course, wore a red stripe down their pants. He was an expert sharpshooter, expert rifleman, expert bayonet man, expert pistol man. He brought his foot locker and his piece, a Springfield, with him. I thought he was ten feet tall.

Paul Stillwell: Did any of his experience inspire you, as far as going into the service?

Commander Harralson: Yes, I think it had a lot to do with it. I admired his stories. I don't know what it is. When I went into the Navy, into boot camp, and I liked it right away.* It gave me structure; instead of flopping around, there was some order in my life.

Paul Stillwell: Did you have career goals at that point, or was this just a means to get a steady income?

Commander Harralson: No, I think I was like most kids; I couldn't see that far ahead, as to, "What do I want for my career?" or anything like that. I wanted to go to sea. I wanted to be a radioman, send and receive messages, and I wanted to travel. I wanted to see strange lands. And that was about the extent of it. When I got into boot camp, we heard about chief petty officers. At that time you could retire, after 20 years, into the fleet reserve with a monthly pension of $99.00. That sounded terrific. So immediately my goal was to be a 20-year man and to get a $99.00 pension.

Paul Stillwell: What was the reaction of your parents to your joining up?

Commander Harralson: Well, of course, my mother, when I told her what I was going to do, had a few tears.

Paul Stillwell: Were you still 17 then?

Commander Harralson: Yes. And my father thought it was great, all for me. He told me something which I think is true today. He said, "You know, you go in there, you do your

---

*"Boot" is a slang term for a newly enlisted sailor or Marine. Recruit training is known as boot camp.

four years or whatever, and when you come out your life's before you." He said, "You will have learned a lot. Maybe you'll know what you want to do."

Paul Stillwell: What do you remember of the other brother?

Commander Harralson: My other brother, Bill, went in the CCCs right away, and he became a quartermaster.* He earned all of $30.00 a month and sent $20.00 home.

Paul Stillwell: Plus, they got room and board.

Commander Harralson: Oh, yes, and food and everything. We were living in Sacramento in a little bitty clapboard house, and times were hard. Come Thanksgiving one year, we didn't have much going. The eve before Thanksgiving he came into the driveway--he had a car, which was exceptional, and held up a turkey. [Laughter]

Paul Stillwell: I can see why you would remember that.

Commander Harralson: Oh, yes.

Paul Stillwell: How far did you get in school, before you went into the Navy?

Commander Harralson: I graduated, barely.

Paul Stillwell: That would be a younger-than-normal age to graduate, wouldn't it, 17?

Commander Harralson: Yes. It had to do with when your birthday was. My birthday is in January, and when I was five years old in the fall, approaching January, my mother tried to

---

*CCC--Civilian Conservation Corps, which began in 1933 as an agency authorized by the U.S. Government to hire unemployed young men for public conservation work. Among other things, the men planted trees, built dams, and fought forest fires. More than two million men served in the CCC before it was abolished in 1942.

put me in school. They wouldn't let her, but then that next January I went in. I could read. So after a semester, they put me up with the ones that I would have been with.

Paul Stillwell: How would you evaluate the quality of your education?

Commander Harralson: It was good. The thing that my wife and I think about it is there were good teachers and bad teachers then too. But we got more of the essentials at home. The teachers had to struggle with less of what to do with our morality and mores and all of that; they were strictly teaching us.

Paul Stillwell: What sort of values did you get at home?

Commander Harralson: Well, both of my parents were honest. They were not church people. But they loved me. I had a strong feeling to do right; I didn't want to do things that were wrong, in their light.

Paul Stillwell: Was college even a remote possibility, or was that beyond the realm of thinking about?

Commander Harralson: I wanted to go to the state nautical school they had down there at Vallejo. They had the Golden Bear. I looked into that. The tuition, at that time, was, I think, $200.00, which was extremely high. Not only that, you had to pay for food and your own clothes and everything. So, really, that was out of the question.

I saw the Navy as a three-fold attraction. First, it was going to sea, which I wanted to do very badly. And secondly, if I could get into radio, I could satisfy that desire. I was totally involved in radio. It was a fascinating thing. And travel. Those three things were a strong attraction for me.

Paul Stillwell: Well, probably a fourth thing, whether it was conscious or not, was that you were no longer somebody that your parents had to support.

Commander Harralson: Oh, absolutely. Yes. I knew then that I had to get out of town. There wasn't any question of that. That's a very difficult period for young people. We see it all around here. I know you . . .

Paul Stillwell: [Laughter] We're going through that right now.*

Commander Harralson: [Laughter] The break from the nest.

Paul Stillwell: That's right. How hard was it to get into the Navy in 1937?

Commander Harralson: Well, it was kind of hard. I went down to Sacramento and was interviewed by Chief Torpedoman Cannon and took tests. They sent me over to the jailhouse, which was just down the street, to be fingerprinted. I came back, and they told me that I had been accepted and to go home and wait; I would get a letter. Of course, I went home, and I had to tell all my friends in Applegate. They told me I was real lucky to get in. The quota for this part of California was pretty flat.

Paul Stillwell: Did they give you aptitude tests at that point?

Commander Harralson: I suppose they were. I just remember vaguely taking tests and so forth.

Paul Stillwell: Well, I've heard of some places that had waiting lists during that period, because the Navy was so small it could afford to be very selective.

Commander Harralson: Yes, they could. And, of course, there were a lot of people trying to get in. I remember a figure of 80,000 in the Navy in 1937. Now, I don't know whether that's right or not. It might be a little skimpy. I saw another figure later on, where in 1940

---

*The interviewer's second son, Robert, graduated from high school two weeks after this interview and began college in the autumn of 1997.

they had 140,000. So that might have been pretty close. I think the Army was only around 300,000 then. And, of course, the nation, as you know, was very isolationist.

Paul Stillwell: Well, Hiram Johnson was one of the leaders in that, wasn't he, the senator from California?

Commander Harralson: Yes. I remember Hiram Johnson. I don't remember him specifically for that. But, of course, you have to know that politics was the least of my worries.

Paul Stillwell: One thing we haven't really talked about, from your pre-Navy period, is what sort of things you did for entertainment and fun. Did you have hobbies, sports, movies?

Commander Harralson: I spent hours and hours up in the attic with a little radio that I bought with money earned by working in the pears. I sent away for a kit, a two-tube short-wave receiver, with some of my pear money. It didn't come and didn't come. My mother got concerned, so she wrote a letter to the outfit in New York, saying that if she didn't get something back soon, she was going to the postal authorities. We got a letter back saying, "We're very sorry, but we were out of stock at that moment. So to compensate for your inconvenience, we're sending you a set already wired and put together." [Laughter] That made me mad. That wasn't what I wanted.

Paul Stillwell: You wanted the pleasure of putting it together.

Commander Harralson: That's right, yes.

Paul Stillwell: Well, please tell me about the capability of this set and what you did with it.

Commander Harralson: Well, radio was different then. VHF was laboratory stuff. I don't think there was UHF.* Communication frequencies went up to 30 megacycles. Everything above that was in laboratory experiments. We used that part of the spectrum up to 30 megacycles. The Navy used low frequencies in certain situations. There was the broadcast band and then above that your shortwave, as they called it. Within the shortwave band, there were ham bands and communication bands and so forth.

Your frequency had a lot to do with how far you were going to go. For example, in this little receiver that I had, the first thing I discovered, I couldn't get 20 meters. I fooled around and put in a band spreader; I put another condenser, a variable condenser, in there that literally spread out the band. I found it loaded with hams in there. Then during the summer months, when I was up in the attic, I had this thing going. Late one afternoon a Honolulu station came in and blasted my earphones off.

I thought, "Man, I've found it with this band spreader thing." That went on for about an hour. I was logging down all the K6s as they came in from Honolulu.† Then it disappeared and I wondered what happened. Then I got a station in Guam, an N station--N6, I think it was. I thought, "Gee, great." Then he disappeared. Then I heard a Chinese station. Then about 11:00 o'clock at night, here came the Australians, the VKs, loud and clear, see. That lasted for about an hour.

Of course, I was reading all the time: QST and Hugo Gernback's Shortwave Craft. I found out about the Heaviside layer.‡ The wave would go up and bounce off of the Heaviside layer and come back down. At nighttime, the Heaviside layer went up, so that meant that the signal came down farther out.

Paul Stillwell: What's the Heaviside layer composed of?

---

*VHF--very high frequency; UHF--ultra-high frequency.
†In all of the continental United States, except Alaska, amateur call signs began with the letter W, followed by a number to indicate the area. The 48 states were divided into six areas, with the number 6 being the designator for California, Oregon, and Nevada. Mr. Harralson's call sign was W6RSH. All signs outside began with the letter K. K6s were Hawaii. K7s were Alaska. Ham stations somehow affiliated with the Navy began with the letter N. There was a ham station in Guam that began with N6. Australians were designated VK1s through VK7s.
‡The Kennelly-Heaviside layer, named for two physicists, referred to a conducting layer in the upper atmosphere that prevents electromagnetic waves from spreading out into space. This layer is now commonly known as the ionosphere.

Commander Harralson: Ionized air molecules. There are different layers in it.

Paul Stillwell: Well, today, with television and satellites, we take all this for granted. But that must have been very exciting for you.

Commander Harralson: That was. That was. And it had to do with how the Navy operated, in that you had long-distance circuits. We went up in frequency in the daytime and came down at night. You could be working a station, S5 signal, both ways, no problems, and then within 15 or 20 minutes he would disappear and you would go to the next frequency, usually in a harmonic relationship. The station would come booming in. You had to do that, go up and down, in order to maintain long-distance communications.

Paul Stillwell: But just to sit in your attic and hear China would just be really wonderful.

Commander Harralson: Oh, yes, yes.

Paul Stillwell: Did you have any sending capability?

Commander Harralson: I couldn't get that until I had a ham ticket. I blew it. I learned to copy the code the hard way; I just learned the alphabet and then sat there and listened to these hams until I'd begin to pick up letters, then words and all. That's the best way to learn. But I totally ignored commas, dashes, periods, and that. So I went to San Francisco, and they flunked me. [Laughter]

Paul Stillwell: Well, these stations that you were getting from Hawaii and China and so forth--were they voice, as opposed to Morse code?

Commander Harralson: CW.* I didn't have much truck with voice.

---

*CW, or continuous wave, referred to a type of radio wave interrupted into the dots and dashes of the Morse code for the purpose of communication.

Paul Stillwell: Why not?

Commander Harralson: I don't know. It lacked something. [Laughter]

Paul Stillwell: Well, did you listen to the regular entertainment-type programs: Jack Benny, Amos 'n' Andy?

Commander Harralson: Oh, yes, sure, broadcast bands. We did get a radio, I think about 1931, an Edison console--built like a battleship. [Laughter]

Paul Stillwell: A real piece of furniture.

Commander Harralson: It was. It was. And it was built like it had to withstand heavy gunfire. [Laughter]

Paul Stillwell: Well, I wonder if your radio experience was an advantage when you went to enlist in the Navy--whether that helped you get in.

Commander Harralson: I don't think so, because I couldn't claim any credential. You know, I hadn't achieved anything that was measurable.

Paul Stillwell: What kind of enlistment was it? Was it a minority enlistment?

Commander Harralson: Yes.

Paul Stillwell: So it was due to expire the day before you turned 21.

Commander Harralson: Right.

Paul Stillwell: I presume that your parents had to sign off for you to be able to enlist at 17?

Commander Harralson: Yes.

Paul Stillwell: One of them eagerly and one reluctantly, from what you've described.

Commander Harralson: Oh, I don't think she was reluctant. She knew what had to happen. And both my older brothers had gone.

Paul Stillwell: Well, please describe the experience of getting into the Navy.

Commander Harralson: Well, they accepted me. I went home. I worked in pears again. The old guy I worked for said, "Dick, you joined the Navy. What did you do that for? You go out there, them Japs are going to get you." And I laughed at him. [Laughter]

Paul Stillwell: He was really prophetic, as it turned out.

Commander Harralson: Yes, he was. Yes, he was.

I got the letter that said to report at the Federal Building in San Francisco, on such-and-such a date--I think it was 7 September 1937--and come neatly dressed; wear a suit. I didn't have a suit, so I borrowed my older brother's. I did something I'm sure glad I did. We had two ferryboats, the Delta King and the Delta Queen.* And every night, at 6:00 o'clock, one would leave Sacramento and one would leave San Francisco, next to the Ferry Building.

Paul Stillwell: That's a real landmark in San Francisco.

Commander Harralson: Yes, the Ferry Building. It was just to the north. And, of course, they would pass in the night. Then the next night, they would do the same. So I thought if I was going to sea, I ought to go down and ride the ferryboat, which I did at 6:00 o'clock.

---
*These two ferryboats were later taken over for U.S. Navy service in San Francisco Bay during World War II.

It was a nice way to go, because you got into San Francisco early in the morning, but you didn't have to get off until 10:00 o'clock. So that gave me plenty of time getting down there. Then I reported in.

Paul Stillwell: Did they have bunks in the ferryboat?

Commander Harralson: Yes. There were little cabins. I had to share it with another guy. They were very small. When I got to the Federal Building, there were, maybe, 100 milling around. They were from all over northern California. They swore us in and read us Rocks and Shoals, the Articles of War.

They put us on a train and we went down the central valley, over the Tehachapi Mountains, and down to Los Angeles. It was a steam train, and it wasn't air-conditioned. The windows were open. Cinders and dirt came swirling in. By the time we arrived, we were coated with soot. At the station, down in south unit, we turned our clothes in. Each of us drew uniforms, a full seabag, a hammock, and mattress.

Paul Stillwell: Was this at the Recruit Training Command in San Diego?

Commander Harralson: Yes. We had to turn in our civilian clothes; they were to be sent home. They didn't want you packaging them. They had a recruit there, by the name of Abrou. Memory is a funny thing, but I remember Abrou. He had arms on him bigger than my legs. He took my brother's suit and he put it in a little package that big. [Laughter]

Paul Stillwell: Like about a six-inch cube. [Laughter]

Commander Harralson: Yes. [Laughter] My brother threw it in the trash. He never forgave me. I think I was the only one wearing a suit. I wore a tie too.

Paul Stillwell: How well did you adapt to the discipline and regimentation?

Commander Harralson: I loved it. Looking back now, I think we had an outstanding company commander, Chief Torpedoman Shapley. I don't mean he was a cream puff; he was hard-nosed as they come, but he was absolutely fair. That was very important.

Paul Stillwell: What are some examples of his fairness?

Commander Harralson: Well, I almost got in a fight. We were drilling; we hadn't gotten our pieces yet. We were marching, and I got to cracking knuckles with the guy next to me. We drilled by squads then. He rapped my knuckles, and I rapped his. He hit mine harder, then I hit his harder. The next thing, we just stopped and started flailing away. [Laughter] Chief Shapley came charging back and grabbed us each by the scruff of the neck. He said, "If you don't shape up, I'll give you something to really fight about.

Paul Stillwell: What do you remember about life in the barracks?

Commander Harralson: I liked it. I liked it. Although it was a Spartan life. We drilled a lot. We were quarantined for two weeks, or three weeks--spinal meningitis. That happens down there at San Diego every once in a while; you read it in the paper. We were quarantined, and during the quarantine, that's what we did--we drilled, drilled, drilled.

We slept in hammocks, and we lashed them up every morning with seven marlin hitches. We didn't air bedding every morning, but it was frequent. We draped our hammock, mattress, and blankets over large pipes, three or four inches in diameter, supported horizontally at a five-foot height by metal posts. The whole bedding assembly was lashed together with four turns of the hammock line. Three or four rows of these pipes ran parallel to the back of the baracks.

One day I hadn't put on a clean mattress cover, like I was supposed to. I tried to get by with the one I had used. When I aired bedding, they discovered it from rope marks on it. Chief Shapley told me to air my bedding 100 times. So I started to air the bedding. I took it off and then I put it back on. That wouldn't do; I had to take it off and back into the room, and then bring it out again. I spent the whole day airing bedding. But after that, I changed mattress covers when I was supposed to.

Paul Stillwell: Did you also have to wash your mattress covers and uniforms?

Commander Harralson: Oh, yes. I think we washed every night.

Paul Stillwell: Did you wash in buckets?

Commander Harralson: Yes, in buckets with some kind of soap. Salt water soap?

Paul Stillwell: Could be.

Commander Harralson: I know one kid who tried to wash his clothes the easy way. He found some lye, and he thought it would eliminate scrubbing. He put the lye in his bucket with the clothes and left it. When he took out his clothes, they came out in shreds.

You know, a big thing was bag inspection. We had to roll our clothes and tie them with clothes stops.* They had to be tied in square knots, with no Irish pennants.† Everything went in square bundles and was wrapped up in a cloth, so that your bag was square. That was fine, but you had to use those clothes too. It was a pain in the neck.

Paul Stillwell: Do you remember personnel inspections?

Commander Harralson: Yes, I do. I tell you one thing that I remember with great fondness was that every Thursday we had a review. All the companies would line up in formation, by squads--eight men to a squad and a squad leader. We went down a ramp, onto the big grinder that was used just for these reviews.* It had a big reviewing stand. They had VIPs up there all the time, politicians, and lots of times, movie people. We'd march down in a column of squads.

As we'd come onto the field, we'd do a column right and then march along the side. Then column left, into the center, and then stop. Then we opened ranks and did

---
*Clothes stops are short pieces of twine that can be used for hanging clothes from a line or tying them into a bundle.
†"Irish Pennant" is Navy slang for a loose piece of line left adrift. It can also be used in a figurative sense to refer to something that is sloppy because it hasn't been completed properly.

calisthenics. After the calisthenics, we laid our rifles down. We pulled little signal flags out of our leggings and went through the alphabet in semaphore. Then we closed ranks, and all the companies reported.

Then the word came to pass in review, and we did it. We'd right face, column right up to the north side, column left. Then as we came down towards the reviewing stand, we did a left-front into line. That put us in two rows. Then, as we'd come down, it was eyes right. We looked good. We were sharp as a pistol. Then it was back into a column again. As we marched up the ramp, the band was playing all of this shipping-over music.

Paul Stillwell: What is shipping-over music?[†]

Commander Harralson: Sousa marches and that kind of thing.[‡] But the greatest one was "Anchors Aweigh." That's what they played when we left the field, and I used to get chills up my spine.

Paul Stillwell: There's an amazing feeling of pride in that situation.

Commander Harralson: I had the feeling: "I belong. I belong."

Paul Stillwell: Well, that brings up the whole subject of camaraderie. What do you remember about that development in your company?

Commander Harralson: Oh, just friends, friends. I remember Lou Sorrento was a guy I liked. We talked a lot. Lou Sorrento inherited a racing horse. He used to tell me about all the ins and outs of racing that he knew.

Paul Stillwell: I remember when we washed our clothes in the evening, that would be a chance to chitchat back and forth, while we were doing that.

---

*The term grinder refers to a large paved area at a shore facility, used for parades, drills, and inspections.
†"Ship over" is a Navy term for reenlistment for further service.
‡John Philip Sousa (1854-1932), American composer and bandmaster known as the "March King." He was master of the Marine Band from 1880 to 1892 and later toured with a band of his own.

Commander Harralson: Oh, yes. We didn't get too much time to chitchat. [Laughter]

Paul Stillwell: No, that was why we valued the laundry period, because we could relax a little.

Commander Harralson: Yes.

Paul Stillwell: How harsh or strict was Chief Shapley?

Commander Harralson: Well, he'd brook no nonsense, but he wasn't so hard-nosed. When we were quarantined there, he was quarantined with us. [Laughter] He had a room up above. He used to come down and say good night to us. [Laughter] Of course, the guys would holler all kinds of insults at him.

Paul Stillwell: Did you have some in the group who were homesick?

Commander Harralson: Oh, sure. And, of course, everybody was looking forward to Christmas, because the time that we were there after completing our boot camp, everybody could go home on ten days' leave for Christmas.
    I went to Shapley and asked him about how a guy got into radio school. He was very communicative. He said, "You'll be taking a test towards the end of your session. Try to do real good in that test, and tell them that's where you want to go." And that's what I did. But I lost out on Christmas leave. I didn't get to go on that.

Paul Stillwell: Did you view boot camp as just something you had to get through till you could do what you really wanted?

Commander Harralson: No. There were interesting things. I didn't care for our week as mess cooks. I didn't particularly like the week when we had to do guard duties. But then we had seamanship; we had to learn the falls. Then there was one day when we got to go sailing in San Diego Bay, in these sailing whaleboats, standing lug rig, two masts. We sailed all around the bay one day. That was tremendous.

Then we spent a week with rifles. They had Springfield rifles with a .22-caliber bore. We fired on a short range there. We had a little bit of bayonet practice, with dummies.

Paul Stillwell: That's interesting. For landing parties, presumably?

Commander Harralson: Yes. Then we went out to the Marine rifle range, to fire.

Paul Stillwell: Where was that, at Camp Pendleton?

Commander Harralson: La Jolla. I was doing pretty good until we had to fire in a sitting position. I couldn't get my elbows right, and I lost all my good stuff.

Paul Stillwell: Did you have classroom instruction as well?

Commander Harralson: A little bit. Not very much. We tied knots, but I don't remember classroom training.

Paul Stillwell: Do you remember studying The Bluejackets' Manual, A to N?*

Commander Harralson: That came later. I don't remember studying A to N at that time. That was part of getting a promotion.

Paul Stillwell: I see. How long a training period was boot camp?

---

*The Bluejackets' Manual, which has been published by the U.S. Naval Institute in various editions over the years, has long been considered the "bible" for Navy enlisted men. It is a basic textbook and reference volume on a wide variety of naval subjects. Formerly these topics were addressed in chapters designated by letters from A to N.

Commander Harralson: It was a month in south unit, which was quarantined and we had to stay in there. Then the north unit for a while. Boot camp was more than two months, because I went in September 7, and we graduated just before Christmas.

Paul Stillwell: So about two and a half months.

Commander Harralson: Yes, something like that.

Paul Stillwell: What happened after your boot leave?

Commander Harralson: Well, I went to radio school right out of boot camp.

Paul Stillwell: Was that also in San Diego?

Commander Harralson: Yes, just right next door, actually. We used to see them coming out for personnel inspection. They were famous for their shoe shines; they had glassy shoe shines. The officer in charge of the radio school was a chief warrant officer by the name of P. A. E. Greenwell.* I wondered about how a person could have three initials. [Laughter] But he was awesome. He was a meticulous person. When he dressed up with his sword, his dress blues, and his gray gloves, he looked very impressive.

Paul Stillwell: What were some of the things that you learned in radio school?

Commander Harralson: Well, of course, the main thing was code. I think I learned something else, aside from what they taught. I could copy about 20 words a minute when I went there. I had to sit there in this class where they started us out at a very, very slow speed, and they gradually built up. But I had to sit there and turn in papers on it. So when it came to the end, the graduation, I could copy 20 words a minute, and everybody else could copy 20 words a minute. The thing that I think I learned there is if you want to

---

*Chief Radio Electrician Peter Albert Earl Greenwell, USN.

improve your code speed, you have to go after something faster than you can copy solid--trying faster and faster, that way.

Paul Stillwell: Sort of challenge yourself.

Commander Harralson: Right, exactly. And that's another part of the thing I think I learned; that applies in other endeavors too. You have to extend yourself; you can't just sit there, if you want to improve.

Paul Stillwell: That's the value of initiative.

Commander Harralson: Yes.

Paul Stillwell: Were you a good typist?

Commander Harralson: I took typing in high school. And a radioman doesn't have to type very fast.

Paul Stillwell: Why not?

Commander Harralson: Well, a good typing speed is 60 words a minute. Would you buy that?

Paul Stillwell: Yes, I would, and obviously 20 words a minute is much less than that. [Laughter]

Commander Harralson: Yes. The world's record, I think, at that time, for code speed, was held by a guy by the name of McElroy. I think he could copy 75 words per minute. Of course, the best I ever did was when I was at Cavite was 55 words per minute.* See, that's not driving you too fast on the typewriter.

---

*This is a reference to Mr. Harralson's service at the Cavite Navy Yard in the Philippines in 1941.

Paul Stillwell: Well, I notice when you send me a letter, it's typed. So that skill evidently stayed with you.

Commander Harralson: Yes.

Paul Stillwell: How much of a balance was there in the training between theory and hands-on practice?

Commander Harralson: Not much theory. There was something else, though, that we had to do; we also studied the requirements for quartermaster striker and for signalman.* So that when we graduated, we were qualified as a striker either as a radioman, quartermaster, or signalman.

Paul Stillwell: So how much navigation did you learn during that?

Commander Harralson: If we learned anything in that area, I've forgotten it. [Laughter] I can't remember. I remember signaling and semaphore. We learned flag hoists--the different meanings of them.

Paul Stillwell: In this basic radio course, how much of it had to do with, say, tuning receivers and so forth, as compared with just learning the code, per se.

Commander Harralson: There was no such thing as electronics then; it was radio materiel. You know, that's a good question. I don't remember learning very much at all, in that regard, radio material. What we studied, in addition to learning the code, was procedures. The Navy was very strict in how you operated. There was no such thing as shooting the breeze on radio. I mean, everything you sent was on a message or by what they called service signals or Z signals.

---

*A striker is a non-rated man who is in training for potential advancement to petty officer in a particular rating.

Paul Stillwell: And sometimes the procedures defied common sense. [Laughter]

Commander Harralson: [Laughter]

Paul Stillwell: You had to go through the whole formal routine instead of maybe just asking the guy, "Hey, send me that again."

Commander Harralson: Yes. You would use the procedure sign IMI, followed by what you wanted repeated.

Paul Stillwell: Did some of the people drop by the wayside in that course? Was that part of it, to see who could handle the code and who couldn't?

Commander Harralson: You know, I don't remember anybody dropping out. They could have. I don't remember anybody dropping out.

Paul Stillwell: How long did that course last?

Commander Harralson: That was four months.

Paul Stillwell: Were you a seaman second class at that point?

Commander Harralson: Yes.

Paul Stillwell: At what point did you start getting to go on liberty in San Diego?

Commander Harralson: Oh, once we got out of the south unit, the quarantine unit, we could go on liberty.

Paul Stillwell: I see. Well, please describe San Diego liberty of that period.

Commander Harralson: [Laughter] Well, we hung around at the foot of Broadway a lot. The center for boots was the YMCA, down towards the foot of Broadway.* It was kind of a rendezvous place, and it was used a great deal. One of the things I remember was a great big painting in the lobby that showed the Point Honda debacle, where seven four-pipers ran aground.† They used to have coffee and doughnuts and sing-alongs there a lot.

Around the corner was Murphy the tailor. Now, we felt that the Navy wanted you to look as terrible as possible in the regulation uniform. The jumper had to blouse over. You had to have the hat on your head square. The word went around that if you saw Murphy the tailor, he could do something about this blouse. And he really could. He was a kind old guy. For 50 cents he would take your jumper and tighten it up, make it fit you better around the middle, and guarantee it would pass inspection. One of the first things I did was go see Murphy.

Paul Stillwell: Ill bet however many times you multiply 50 cents by the jobs he did, he made a lot.

Commander Harralson: Yes, he did.

Paul Stillwell: We were talking during the ride from the airport about those merchants on Broadway. If you could describe that scene, please?

Commander Harralson: Well, we walked up Broadway, and there'd be these men standing outside of a shop. It could be a clothing store or anything else they thought they might be able to sell a sailor.

Paul Stillwell: Jewelry was popular.

---

*YMCA--Young Men's Christian Association.
†On 8 September 1923 seven ships of Destroyer Squadron 11 ran aground in heavy fog at Point Arguello, also known as Point Honda, off Santa Barbara, California. Twenty-two men were killed, and all seven ships were wrecked.

Commander Harralson: Jewelry, a lot of guitars, jackets, trousers, and all of that. You'd be walking along and hear, "Hey, Sailor. Have a book of matches," or something like that. You know, they had a spiel. I tried to go into the Paris Inn, which was a honky-tonk there, and the shore patrol grabbed me and wouldn't let me go in. [Laughter] I used to try it periodically, but it never worked.

Paul Stillwell: Nothing to lose by trying, right? [Laughter]

Commander Harralson: No. [Laughter]

Paul Stillwell: Well, the other thing we were mentioning about these merchants is that they would hook people on a time-payment plan.

Commander Harralson: Yes, they did. We had a lot of naive kids. I was one, too, but I wasn't so naive that I got caught myself. But they had some kids that got terribly in debt. They had the money taken out of their pay, which wasn't very much. Of course, before I left there, the CO of the training station came out with a bulletin that was distributed in town.* It said that the Navy would no longer consider any of these complaints.

Paul Stillwell: They wouldn't serve as a collection agency for the merchants.

Commander Harralson: Right. But also, some of the sailors, to get even with a bad experience, just before they were ready to leave, would go run up a great big bill and then go to the Philippines. [Laughter] That happened.

Paul Stillwell: How much opportunity was there to meet girls there?

Commander Harralson: That was difficult. There was a way, though I missed it. [Laughter]

---

*CO--commanding officer.

Paul Stillwell: This is something you heard about? (Laughter)

Commander Harralson: No. It didn't happen to me, but I talked to the guy that did it, and he had pictures to verify it. I think Saturday liberty was from noon to midnight, and Sunday was from noon to midnight. But, if you signed up to go to some kind of sing-along with coffee and doughnuts at the Y, there would be a bus there, and you could leave at 9:00 o'clock. So I signed up for that. I went and I drank their coffee and ate their doughnuts and was out the door, not that I had a heck of a lot to do.

I met this one guy later, over at North Island, and he knew more girls in San Diego.* Of course, we didn't believe him at first. Then he broke out pictures. He stayed around. He said, "If you go to those coffee-and-doughnut things, and then when you come out, if you stay, there are families there that invite you out to their house and to church, and then a meal afterwards." And that's where he met these girls.

Paul Stillwell: Well, there was something else that you were mentioning--about not being able to wear your uniform to visit a relative.

Commander Harralson: Yes, that was true. It wasn't that they forbade it; it was that if I showed up in uniform, they didn't like it, and they let me know it.

Paul Stillwell: Why did they have that feeling?

Commander Harralson: Because sailors in San Diego were considered a rowdy lot. And some of it was earned. I mean, they caroused a lot. There were a lot of wild things that happened there. So it was, "Sailors and dogs keep off the grass," which never bothered me. A lot of the better places you didn't enter in uniform. They wouldn't tell you at the door, "You can't come in," but they had ways of making you wish you weren't there.

Paul Stillwell: What were some of those ways?

---

*North Island Naval Air Station is on the end of the Coronado peninsula, across the harbor from San Diego.

Commander Harralson: The way the waiters acted towards you, mainly.

Paul Stillwell: They wouldn't wait on you, evidently?

Commander Harralson: Yes, they would stall around, stall around, and they were contemptuous.

There was a restaurant in San Diego called The Right Spot. It was very long and narrow. It was just wide enough for the stoves, walking space there for the waiters, the counter, and then stools. With every order, sandwich or whatever, they gave you a great big pile of the best fried potatoes I ever ate. The guys that waited on you looked like they'd been professional wrestlers or bums or something. They had cauliflower ears; great big guys, mean looking. But they said, "Yes, sir. No, sir. What can I do for you, sir?" That was a very popular place then, The Right Spot.

Paul Stillwell: Well, especially when you compare it with the treatment you received elsewhere.

Commander Harralson: Yes.

Paul Stillwell: Did you get involved with locker clubs, there in San Diego?

Commander Harralson: Yes.

Paul Stillwell: What difference did that make?

Commander Harralson: Well, that was after I'd gotten out of boot camp. I bought a pair of slacks and a shirt and a jacket. I would go over and put that on and go to the movies, meet the guys, go bowling--things like that. I found out, also, that I could walk into a bar and order a beer, which I couldn't do in uniform.

Paul Stillwell: Because the shore patrol wouldn't hassle you if you were in civvies?

Commander Harralson: Well, the bars would recognize you; you were very recognizable as a boot.

Paul Stillwell: In what way?

Commander Harralson: The way you wore your uniform, your hat. You know, a seaman second had two little white stripes.

Paul Stillwell: But if you were in civvies?

Commander Harralson: Oh, then civvies, why, I'd just walk into a bar and order.

Paul Stillwell: I take it they did not ask for proof of age, as they do today?

Commander Harralson: No, no.

Paul Stillwell: Your only qualification was that you had the price of a beer?

Commander Harralson: Right.

Paul Stillwell: And what was it, maybe a quarter?

Commander Harralson: I think it was 20 cents, something like that.

Paul Stillwell: Did you ever get up to the zoo in Balboa Park?

Commander Harralson: Oh, yes. That was a nice place. And I loved the streetcars in San Diego. You could go all over the place. They were streamlined and fast. You'd get on them, and they'd take off, and you had to hang on.

Paul Stillwell: Did you get over to North Island and Coronado at all?

Commander Harralson: Not while in boot camp or radio school. I used to see amphibian aircraft taking off in the bay there. When we were first there, they had these flying boats. They were open-cockpit biplanes with struts and wires all in there. And they had a little floats on the outer wing. The engines were strutted between the wings. That's what we first saw; they might have been PM-1s.* Then, before I left the training station, I saw the first PBY.† I thought they were the ultimate in airplanes.

Paul Stillwell: Of course, the PBYs were built right there in San Diego by Consolidated.

Commander Harralson: Yes. I began to get ideas of being a radioman in a PBY.

Paul Stillwell: Did you get over to the destroyer base and see all those destroyers that they had laid up in reserve?

Commander Harralson: No. I used to see destroyers going out. I never understood their whistles; they had a whistle that would go whoop, whoop, whoop. Monday morning you'd hear that a lot as they went steaming out.

Paul Stillwell: That's kind of the dashing destroyerman spirit, get out there.

Commander Harralson: Yes, the old four-pipers. They had, I think, about six light cruisers: the Cincinnati, the Raleigh, the Marblehead out in the Asiatics, that looked like overgrown four-pipers.

---

*The Martin-built PM-1 was a twin-engine flying boat; it was a 1930 production version of the Naval Aircraft Factory's PN-12. The PM-2 model had a wing span of 73 feet, length of 48 feet, gross weight of 16,964 pounds, and top speed of 116 miles per hour.
†The PBY Catalina was a twin-engine flying boat that performed extensive service before and during World War II. Built by Consolidated, it first entered fleet squadrons in 1936. The PBY-2 model had a wing span of 104 feet, length of 65 feet, gross weight of 28,400 pounds, and top speed of 178 miles per hour. Cruising speed was 103 mph.

Paul Stillwell: Well, they were very similar, yes. Not that I've seen them, but I've seen photos of them.

Did your liberty situation improve once you got out of boot camp and into the radio school?

Commander Harralson: Well, I didn't think I had a situation. [Laughter] I just liked to go on liberty.

Paul Stillwell: No, but I mean, was there more freedom later?

Commander Harralson: Oh, yes. I used to get so tired of salty advice. I'd be riding in a streetcar and see two old hashmark seamen sitting over there, you know.* I'd think, "They're going to do it, I know it."

Finally one would lean over and say, "Hey, still at the training station, eh? Well, you're going to do all right. Keep your nose clean." That was their standard comment, "Keep your nose clean. You'll get ahead." And here's a guy that's got two hashmarks and a watch mark, a seaman.

Paul Stillwell: The mark around his shoulder meant he was a non-rated man.

Commander Harralson: Yes. They did away with that, didn't they?

Paul Stillwell: Yes. It was red for engineers, and white for seamen.

Commander Harralson: Right. Yes, red on the left. There were left-arm rates and right-arm rates. Everything else being equal, your right-arm rate was senior. As seaman, you had this white watch mark.

Paul Stillwell: So they were just razzing you, essentially?

---

*A hashmark is a slang term for the service marks worn on the sleeves of the uniforms of Navy enlisted personnel to denote length of service. Each stripe denotes four years.

Commander Harralson: Yes.

Paul Stillwell: And evidently they had not followed their own advice, or they would have gotten more advanced. [Laughter]

Commander Harralson: Yes. I lost track of how many times I was told to keep my nose clean.

Paul Stillwell: Well, you mentioned one other incident that was memorable; that's when you saw the California trying to make a landing.*

Commander Harralson: It was going to tie up right at the foot of Broadway. Of course, as you know, those big ships move real slow. Everything looked fine to me, but they were barely moving.

Paul Stillwell: Did it have tugs alongside?

Commander Harralson: It must have; you don't mess around with those big ships without tugs. I know there was whistling and hollering and a lot going on, and I wondered what was happening. The thing just came to the base of the pier. A boardwalk went across the head of the pier there, and the ship just went into that walk. Great big planks and timbers just flew like match sticks.

Paul Stillwell: This was the bow of the California smashed in?

Commander Harralson: Yes. There's something else I remember about that. I looked it over and I saw something that looked like bedsprings up on the foremast. So I wondered what on earth are those? Later on, I ran across a radioman off the California, and I asked, "What are those bedsprings?"

---

*The battleship California (BB-44) was the flagship for Commander Battle Force, a four-star admiral. He was subordinate to Commander in Chief U.S. Fleet, whose flag was in the fleet flagship Pennsylvania (BB-38).

He said, "Oh, that's some kind of long-range tracking device they have now." It must have been radar.

Paul Stillwell: It was very hush-hush in that era, and California was one of the first ships to get it.

Commander Harralson: Is that right?

Paul Stillwell: I think she was the first to have a CIC, in fact.*

Commander Harralson: Oh?

Paul Stillwell: It's interesting what sticks in your memory.

Commander Harralson: Yes, it is. And other things I should know get real hazy. I think seeing those PBYs put me off course.

When I came back from boot leave, after radio school, into the T Unit--the transfer unit there--you were allowed to tell what kind of ship you wanted to go on. I thought, "How do you get into aviation?" So I put carrier. That's why I drew the Saratoga. I found my name on a detachment for the Saratoga. We were to go aboard the Utah for transportation, down at the foot of Broadway, Monday morning.† But for some reason, they sent us over there Saturday. We reported aboard Saturday, and they weren't ready for us. All they had for us to eat was coffee, bread, and turnips. (Laughter)

Paul Stillwell: Oh, Lord. [Laughter]

Commander Harralson: So I went out to my aunt's house, uniform and all. [Laughter] We got under way Monday morning, and it was a beautiful day. We got out to sea. You know, that was my first sea voyage. We headed for Long Beach. They had a bunch of

---

*CIC--combat information center.
†USS Utah (AG-16) was a former battleship that had been converted to a gunnery training ship.

Marine recruits aboard and a bunch of Navy. As we began to get closer to Long Beach, the wind began to pick up. By the time we were, I'd say, about five miles out, we had a full-blown Santa Ana.* We passed an old gambling ship that used to lie outside the three-mile limit. Boy, she was raring like a bucking horse. People were getting sick. But the thing I remember is more Marines got seasick than sailors, boots, none of whom had ever been to sea before.

Paul Stillwell: That's intriguing. I wonder why that was. [Laughter] What month was that when you got assigned to the Saratoga?†

Commander Harralson: It would have had to have been May 1938. They put us in an orientation division for a while. Then we went through a regular indoctrination so we could find our way. I had a choice of becoming a signalman or a radioman. We'd go up to the signal bridge, and here were these signalmen all suntanned and healthy-looking and out in the open where everything was happening. Then we'd go in the radio room, and we saw these pale, coffee-drinking, smoking radiomen. I did some heavy thinking about that for a while, but I finally asked for the radio gang and got it.

Paul Stillwell: What influenced that choice?

Commander Harralson: Well, that was my whole idea from the beginning, and I liked radio. It was, to me, very fascinating, a tremendous thing. I was awestruck by what radio was and what it did.

Paul Stillwell: So the signal bridge turned your head for only a moment?

Commander Harralson: Yes, that's true.

---

*Santa Ana is the term used for hot, dry winds that blow from the north, northeast, or east in southern California. In other words, these are winds that do not come in from the sea.
†USS Saratoga (CV-3) was commissioned 16 November 1927. She had a standard displacement of 33,000 tons, was 888 feet long, 106 feet in the beam, an extreme width of 130 feet on the flight deck, and had a draft of 24 feet. She had a top speed of 33.5 knots and could accommodate approximately 60-70 aircraft. She was originally armed with eight 8-inch guns that were later removed in World War II.

Paul Stillwell: Well, what was it like, getting aboard such a huge ship, and trying to learn your way around?

Commander Harralson: Trying to get aboard the Sara and the Lex anchored at Long Beach, inside the breakwater was hazardous.* You could look out there, and the water would be calm, serene, and those ships would rock until they dipped their boat booms. Now, the quarterdeck, of course, was about the hangar-deck level, forward of the hangar deck. To get into a boat, you went out the side. You were quite a way up, and there was a long ladder, with a small landing down there.

Paul Stillwell: The ladder was at an angle, maybe 45 degrees.

Commander Harralson: Yes, yes.

Paul Stillwell: I think it was called a gangway then.

Commander Harralson: Gangway, yes.

Paul Stillwell: Accommodation ladder was a later name for it.

Commander Harralson: Is that right?

Paul Stillwell: Yes.

Commander Harralson: Your terminology is probably a lot better than mine. I've been a landlubber here for 40 years. [Laughter] But, anyhow, when these ships rocked, that landing would go down into the water, sometimes, I would say, six feet. So to get from a boat, from a launch, onto the landing, you had to time it and catch that thing going up. You didn't want to try to get on it when it was going down. And the same way getting off,

---

*Lex was the nickname for the carrier Lexington (CV-2), sister ship of the Saratoga.

you know. You had to stay above and then time it so that you got down to the landing in time to get into the boat. It really was tricky, and I saw an awful lot of sailors--and more Marines--go up to their waists in water.

Paul Stillwell: I wonder if it was because those ships were so top-heavy that they would be susceptible to that rolling?

Commander Harralson: Well, later on I scraped the sides and the bottom and I was amazed how flat-bottomed these ships were. I mean, it's just straight across. And I don't remember seeing any bilge keels.

Paul Stillwell: That would probably, also, add to the rolling. [Laughter] Well, what about the business of learning your way around this labyrinth of metal?

Commander Harralson: Oh, well, we stuck together as a group, and they took us different places. They took us up to sick bay, and they showed us all the terrible instruments for venereal disease--scared the bejesus out of us.

I did a dumb thing. We went out to sea for battle practice. One day I stuck my head out of a porthole. Right above was the 8-incher, and it went off. I jerked my head back and hit that side of the ship, and I learned something.

Paul Stillwell: You probably had some ringing in your ears too.

Commander Harralson: I got a great, big lump on my head.

Paul Stillwell: What were the living accommodations like? Were you assigned to the radio division right away?

Commander Harralson: Yes. I think something like two weeks we were in this T division--that's what they called it--for orientation. Then I asked for the radio division and got it. They put me right to work as messenger and all the yeoman duties associated--running coffee, making message blanks.

Paul Stillwell: Did you have division messing and berthing?

Commander Harralson: No, we ate cafeteria style. The berthing was a hammock in the messing area, which was a miserable way to live. If you had the midwatch, which was from midnight to breakfast, you were supposed to be able to sleep in; but you couldn't sleep in if you slept in a hammock. They wouldn't let you. So you found a friendly radioman. Now, if you were a rated man, they had bunks in a compartment over near the uptakes, a real narrow place in there. If you had a kind radioman, a friend, he'd let you flake out on his bunk for the morning. But that was a problem when the master-at-arms came around. He knew darned well you were entitled to sleep in, but he'd roust you out. You'd tell him, "I had the midwatch."

He'd say, "Well, I had the midwatch too." But their midwatch was like 12:00 to 4:00--that sort of thing.

Paul Stillwell: So this was just for meanness, on his part?

Commander Harralson: Oh, absolutely, absolutely. So we acquired the ability to lay down anywhere and go to sleep. I found a good place in back of the transmitters, in the transmitter room.

Paul Stillwell: Please tell me about the art of sleeping in a hammock.

Commander Harralson: Yes, well, in boot camp we slept in hammocks. Spreaders were frowned upon.

Paul Stillwell: Why? Was the unmanly?

Commander Harralson: Yes, unmanly. [Laughter]

Paul Stillwell: Maybe you should explain what a spreader was and how it worked.

Commander Harralson: Oh, well, when you climbed in your hammock, the thing wrapped around you; you were like in a cocoon. In cold weather, that was fine. But in warm weather, it got a little hot. So we took bayonet scabbards or anything else available and spread the clews, which were the pieces of line that come out of each end of the canvas and tied up to the stanchions. You used a stick or something to spread them out, so that way it kept the sides away from you.

Paul Stillwell: Did you put notches in the stick for the clews to fit into?

Commander Harralson: Yes, I think so. Now, the key to sleeping in a hammock is pull it tight. It's awful hard on your back, so you pull it just as tight as you can. And if you've got spreaders in it, then it becomes very unstable. [Laughter] In boot camp we had to stand barracks watches. Of course, you know the Navy, you always stand watches. On the barracks watch, we had a rule that if somebody fell out of their hammock, there was no argument, no nothing, he went to sick bay automatically. Of course, that was a pretty good fall onto a concrete deck.

Paul Stillwell: What would you say, about four or five feet?

Commander Harralson: I'd say five feet, at least.

Paul Stillwell: Well, what about on board ship, and falling onto a steel deck?

Commander Harralson: Well, I don't know; they didn't seem to care there. [Laughter] You were supposed to know better.

Paul Stillwell: You were far enough away from mother there. (Laughter)

Commander Harralson: Yes.

Paul Stillwell: Well, did you, in fact, master it, so that you didn't fall out?

Commander Harralson: Yes, I could do all right. I don't remember ever falling out. It was kind of a nice way to sleep in cold weather.

Paul Stillwell: Well, and also, if the weather was a little rough, the ship would roll around you, and you stayed steady.

Commander Harralson: Yes.

Paul Stillwell: What do you remember about the messing? How good was the food?

Commander Harralson: Whenever you went to a new ship or station, the food was very good; it tasted good, the coffee was real good. But after you'd been there three or four months, the coffee wasn't so good, the food didn't taste so good. You got accustomed to it. But the Navy fed well.

Paul Stillwell: What do you remember about learning shipboard radio watches? I mean, did you get beyond this messenger stage and start manning a position?

Commander Harralson: Oh, yes. The idea that we all had was if you were happy as a messenger, you'd stay a messenger. Nobody was on your tail to take a test or anything; it was up to you. So what you did to improve your abilities was talk to a watch stander, on the midwatch or evening watch. You said, "Let me sit in on your circuit." If he thought you were good enough, he'd let you sit in there and get circuit time.

    I think about the first thing they'd give you was copying what they called the fox broadcast.* It was usually a low frequency, very high-powered, 300-KW broadcast to all

---

*"Fox" was the word for the letter F in the phonetic alphabet of the day. The fox schedule referred to the messages sent on the fleet broadcast.

ships and stations.* All ships had to copy it. That was usually the first good job you were assigned, copying the fox broadcast. It was made up of messages addressed to different ships and places.

After they finished the broadcast--these came on schedule--the supervisor would go over the messages and pick off those that concerned the ship. Some were addressed to the ship, either for action or info. A lot of general messages, like AlNavs, notices to mariners.†

Paul Stillwell: Well, would more than one person be copying this, just as a backup?

Commander Harralson: No. They had ways of getting a repeat, but that was an insult. You didn't want to have to do that. You'd better get it right. (Laughter)

Paul Stillwell: Where was the broadcast coming from?

Commander Harralson: Oh, San Diego. NPL was the radio San Diego. Radio Cavite was NPO. A few years later I ran the fox broadcast out there.

I had an interesting experience on the Saratoga. We were headed for San Francisco. There were other ships in the company; I can't tell you who. The chief, Mikesell, handed me a pair of phones and said, "Go up to the bridge and man the tactical circuit. It's over on the port side. There's a place where you can plug in. There's a little desk there and a key, and we'll give you a transmitter."

So I went up there and plugged in. Everything was alive; I could hear it. I wasn't there very long, because we were getting real close to San Francisco. Then here it came, a list of ships, by call sign. Saratoga was NELB; we were in it. IXIN, di-di-dah di-di-dah di-di dah-dah. "Execute to follow. Execute my corpen 085, or 095," something like that--I can't remember.

So I did the right thing. I hollered out, "Execute to follow, corpen 085." That made everybody happy out there on the bridge. I thought, "Man, I've got this."

---

*KW--kilowatt.
†AlNav is a type of message put out to all the Navy.

Paul Stillwell: You had the power!

Commander Harralson: Yes. So I sat there and pretty soon here it came, they executed: "Di-di dum di-di dum di-di dah dah daaaah." I don't know what the hell was the matter with me, I just sat there, happy. Well, the daaaah was when I should have hollered, "Execute." I looked up, and here were the captain and I don't know who else, all glaring at me, you know. [Laughter]

Paul Stillwell: They must have figured out from watching the other ships that it had been executed.

Commander Harralson: Yes. I hollered, but I was late. Actually, if you measured it in seconds, it probably wasn't very long, but in those things a second can seem like forever for the OD or whoever.*

Paul Stillwell: It was long enough to be noticed.

Commander Harralson: Yes, it was. I was off to a good start and I blew it. [Laughter]

Paul Stillwell: Well, in some ships, they had very little tolerance for mistakes like that. Was that the case in Saratoga?

Commander Harralson: Nobody bawled me out or said anything, but I knew I didn't do good. [Laughter]

Paul Stillwell: You didn't make that mistake again.

Commander Harralson: No.

---

*OD--officer of the deck.

Paul Stillwell: You mentioned your enlistment in San Francisco, and going there in your brother's suit. What was it like to come back as part of ship's company of Saratoga?

Commander Harralson: Oh, boring. I lived up in the mountains. I talked to a few kids around there, and there wasn't much doing; go to town or go to a movie, something like that. Very boring. Some good meals while I was home, and that sort of thing.

Paul Stillwell: But didn't you spend any time on liberty in San Francisco itself?

Commander Harralson: Oh, sure. Yes, I learned that it may be July in San Francisco, but take your peacoat. [Laughter]

Paul Stillwell: There's a famous Mark Twain quote about the coldest winter he'd ever had was August or something in San Francisco. [Laughter]

Commander Harralson: Yes, it's amazing; it can be 100 degrees in the valley here, and cold in San Francisco.

Paul Stillwell: Did you have some sort of a sea daddy in the radio gang who took you under his wing?

Commander Harralson: Oh, not specifically. Mikesell, I remember him. He looked out after the strikers. He wanted you to do your job, but he was reasonable. I found that the chiefs and most people were reasonable people. You did what you were supposed to and watched yourself, and you got along great. And they always seemed helpful if you had questions or anything. But if you wanted to get promoted, it was up to you to initiate it.

One of the things I hated worst of all was part of this promotion business. We had completed the qualification to be a striker and the qualification to go for third, but we also had to completed the A to N chapters. To do that, you had to be signed off by the division officer. That meant that at the end of each chapter, you had to go up there and find the division officer. And that was always a pain; I hated that.

Paul Stillwell: And then you had to recite for him all these things you'd learned?

Commander Harralson: Well, you took a test.

Paul Stillwell: I see.

Commander Harralson: They actually cut a section out of the book, and you took the test. I never understood why it was called A to N. But my son tells me that's Army to Navy or something like that. Did you ever hear?

Paul Stillwell: I think it's just the number of different topics; each one is assigned to a letter. And that's how many letters it happens to take up for that curriculum.

Commander Harralson: Nothing beginning with O or P or . . .

Paul Stillwell: Evidently all you needed to know was in A to N.

Commander Harralson: Yes. [Laughter]

Paul Stillwell: But that sounds like a terribly inefficient way to do it, rather than giving a number of people the test simultaneously.

Commander Harralson: Well, like I say, you could stay aboard there as a seaman messenger forever. That wasn't true later. I think after the war, if you hadn't made third class, you couldn't reenlist. But you used to see a lot of hashmark seamen.

    A funny thing happened. The <u>Saratoga</u> got up to Bremerton, and they took most of the radiomen over to the communications office in the shipyard.* But they left a radioman in the radio room aboard ship. His one job was to look out after things and to copy the fox broadcast. I had the watch there one night; I was there by myself. The fox started. I had

---

*Puget Sound Navy Yard, Bremerton, Washington.

no trouble with the fox broadcasts. I decided that margin adjustments on my typewriter were a little too close. So as I was copying, I tried to adjust them. But the darn thing kept hanging up, this little tab there. I kept fooling with it, and it went in and narrowed me down. I couldn't get it to go back. I went over and tried the other one, and it went in. I ended up copying the whole broadcast with about two or three words to each line. [Laughter] Well, I turned my copy in to the supervisor.

Paul Stillwell: And what was his reaction?

Commander Harralson: Well, he made a big deal out of it. I think he was laughing on the inside, but he thought I was terrible; I was ruined; I didn't have a chance if I couldn't do better.

Paul Stillwell: Well, you've talked about your skill in receiving and how that improved. How did you learn about sending, using the key?

Commander Harralson: Well, that went with it, yes. You couldn't send anywhere near as fast as you could receive. The fast stuff was either by machine tape or speed key; with a speed key you could send really fast.

Paul Stillwell: What was the difference between a speed key and a regular key?

Commander Harralson: A regular key was just a little arm and a contact, and you went up and down; that's the kind you usually see. A speed key--I have one down below--has a side movement. The dashes, you make with your finger to the left; the dots, you hit with your thumb, and it has an arm with weights and it vibrates.

Paul Stillwell: And this is a horizontal movement?

Commander Harralson: Yes. So you make dash this way; you hit with the thumb. It takes skill to get the right number of dots out of the thing. You can speed it up by moving the weights in, or slow it down by moving the weights out.

Paul Stillwell: When did you go to Bremerton?

Commander Harralson: We were up there July, August, and September--the best time.

Paul Stillwell: That is a good time to be there.

Commander Harralson: Oh, it was glorious up there.

Paul Stillwell: Well, please tell me about that.

Commander Harralson: I remember entering the Straits of Juan de Fuca. The sea was green, a beautiful green. When we came in, the sun was shining. The channel going around into Bremerton is pretty close. There were people on the beaches, swimming. They were waving and hollering. We pulled into dry dock, didn't waste any time.

Oh, we had to scrape it, and it was an all-hands job.

Paul Stillwell: Was this as the water was gradually drained?

Commander Harralson: As the water went out, yes. They had what they called camels; they were floats--three or four long timbers, lashed together. As the water was pumped down, we went down with the water, scraping and wire brushing. And the band played music. The band and the ship's cooks were the only ones excused; otherwise, it was everybody over the side. The cooks made sandwiches and coffee, and the band played shipping-over music.

We went down. It went straight down, then at the bottom it curved, then went straight across. [Laughter]

Paul Stillwell: How heavily encrusted was the hull at that point?

Commander Harralson: Well, it didn't look too bad to me. But I understand they had to do that frequently, like every ten months or so; because it had a big effect, of course, on the speed. And Sara and the Lex were fast, 32 knots, for their day.

Once we got it scraped and wire brushed, then they rigged planks along the sides, and we went down again, applying the first coat of red lead.[*] I can't remember whether we gave it two coats of red lead or just one, but we went down with red lead. Then, we no sooner got that done than we went down the side with antifoulant, which was a real heavy, viscous liquid. It was a hard, hard day for us.

Paul Stillwell: You did all that in one day?

Commander Harralson: Yes.

Paul Stillwell: My goodness. How would the red lead have a chance to dry?

Commander Harralson: Well, I think it was pretty thick. I remember us doing it in one day, but I wouldn't put a lot of money on that.

Paul Stillwell: That harks back to an earlier era, when coaling ship was an all-hands evolution.

Commander Harralson: Yes.

Paul Stillwell: Bands played the shipping-over music then too. You were lucky you didn't get involved with that. [Laughter]

Commander Harralson: Yes, I wouldn't have liked that.

---

[*] Red lead is the nickname for an orange-colored anti-corrosive primer paint applied to bare metal before the regular paint is put on.

Paul Stillwell: What were some of the liberty attractions in Puget Sound?

Commander Harralson: Well, Seattle was a lovely seaport. They had two ferry boats, the Chippewa and the Kalakala. They were streamlined. I remember riding on the Chippewa, going over to Seattle, and I was horrified by all the rattle and the shaking that went on in there. I thought, "Gee, this big streamlined thing ought to ride smooth." But it shook and vibrated and rattled.

We made one memorable trip, another guy and I. I even have some pictures of it. We went to the Y in Bremerton and put on dungaree trousers and a sweatshirt. Then we caught the ferry over to Port Orchard and then hitchhiked. Caught another ferry into Tacoma and hitchhiked through Tacoma. Then we headed for Rainier National Park. People in Tacoma were very friendly. We had a lunch there, then went out on the road. Several rides later, we found ourselves about ten miles short of the park, and it was getting dark. We didn't know what to do; there weren't any hotels or anything around there. We saw a couple of kids playing alongside the road, and we got to talking to them. They told us about a barn.

So we went over to the barn. It was full of hay, so we slept there. The problem with that was I'm bothered with hay fever. I got up the next morning, and I was all choked up. It was a beautiful day, clear and crisp. I went down to a stream and washed my head and face real good. I looked up and there was a patch of wild strawberries, about the size of the end of your little finger. They were the most delicious strawberries I ever ate. So we had a breakfast of strawberries. Then we went on, just to get inside the gate of the park. Then we turned around and came on back.

Paul Stillwell: Didn't feel like mountain climbing, I take it?

Commander Harralson: No, no.

Paul Stillwell: Did you make any liberties in downtown Bremerton?

Richard A. Harralson, Interview #1 (5/15/97) - Page 48

Commander Harralson: I don't recall any liberties in downtown Bremerton. Have you been there?

Paul Stillwell: Yes, and there is not much there. [Laughter]

Commander Harralson: But it was beautiful weather all the time. We rented a rowboat. You could get a picnic lunch from the galley if you had a chit signed by the division officer. Another guy and I got picnic lunches, and we rented a boat. They have pretty good tides there, you know. We went way up on the inlet and had lunch, but no girls.

Paul Stillwell: You mentioned in the narrative you wrote that there was goodwill toward sailors in the Tacoma area, because the Lexington had provided power there a number of years before.* How was that goodwill manifested?

Commander Harralson: Just by the friendliness and openness, in my personal experience.

Paul Stillwell: Better than you were treated in San Diego, for example?

Commander Harralson: Yes, very definitely. Another interesting thing I remember is that the flight deck officer of the Saratoga was a chief warrant, an AP. He drew within one dollar of what the CO drew in pay. Now, that's what I heard and believed way back then. Then later I thought, "Well, that's just scuttlebutt." But later I found out that that was true. There was a rule that they couldn't make more money than the captain. It came about, I guess, by his time in service, and his flight pay.

It's my understanding that warrant officers, prior to World War II, were in a special category. Their pay was very good. I don't know what it was. They had their own wardroom and their own mess. They apparently had a lot more status than they had later on. During the '60s, when I took the family down to the Naval Reserve center for new ID cards, they told me there that they had abolished the warrant officer.

---

*In December 1929 and December 1930, because of a severe drought in the Pacific Northwest, the turbo generators of the USS Lexington (CV-2) supplied electrical power to the city of Tacoma, Washington. For details see Steven A. Payne, "The Carrier That Lit Up Tacoma," Naval History, Fall 1990, pages 23-25.

Paul Stillwell: Well, just the W-1.* They still have 2, 3, and 4, but they don't have a pinstripe warrant anymore.

Commander Harralson: There was another point. I had always understood that a chief warrant officer, not a pinstripe but a chief warrant officer, was a commissioned officer that ranked with, but below, an ensign. When I was working at Aerojet, I got into an argument with a former Air Force officer that was telling me that a warrant officer is not a commissioned officer. I insisted that he was. An ex-Air Force warrant officer was sitting there next to us. He listened to our argument for a while and then said, "Hold it, hold it. You're both right. In the Army and Air Force, a warrant officer is not considered a commissioned officer. In the Navy, he is." Does that jibe with your knowledge?

Paul Stillwell: I'm not sure. That sounds reasonable.

Commander Harralson: I always understood a chief warrant officer was a commissioned officer.†

Paul Stillwell: How much relationship was there between different divisions and departments in the ship? Or did you pretty much stick to your own?

Commander Harralson: Radiomen are, pretty much, a self-contained group; we don't know many people outside of the radio shack. Oh, occasionally you'd know somebody else, but as a rule, we knew only the other radiomen.

Paul Stillwell: Well, would you meet people from other divisions in this cafeteria mess?

Commander Harralson: Oh, yes. You were all mixed up there.

---

*The Navy originally had four grades of warrant officer, W-1 through W-4. The W-1 had a narrow insignia stripe on sleeves and shoulder boards and thus was known as a "pinstripe warrant." The stripe was wider for the other three grades.
†Mr. Harralson is correct. In the U.S. Navy a chief warrant officer has commissioned status.

Paul Stillwell: What sorts of recreation did they have on board ship, like movies, acey-deucy?*

Commander Harralson: Well, I never got into acey-deucy until later. They had movies, of course; that was the big thing. They had a library. They had a gedunk stand.† I had a failing for chocolate malted milk. You'd go to the gedunk stand, and the guy would take a big paper cup. He'd put a spoonful of this, a spoonful of that powder, another spoon, another powder. Then he'd fill it full of water and put it in the beater. [Laughter]

Paul Stillwell: It must have been pretty good if you kept coming back for it?

Commander Harralson: Yes, it was.

Paul Stillwell: Somebody told me there was a design of a rooster in the linoleum of the deck near that gedunk, because the rooster was the symbol for the Saratoga.

Commander Harralson: You know, I very vaguely remember the rooster. I couldn't tell you anything about it. It sounds familiar.

Paul Stillwell: It sounds plausible, at least.

Commander Harralson: Yes.

Paul Stillwell: What do you remember about the head facilities?

Commander Harralson: Yes, I remember those. Two heads. They were big, very large, open; one on each side, aft. I believe there were two or three showers down in one corner, but everybody used a bucket. You'd go there and get a bucket full of water and put it

---

*Acey-deucy is a nautical version of the board game backgammon.
†Gedunk is a Navy slang term for candy, ice cream, and sodas--snack-type food.

under a steam vent pipe. The steam would heat it up to whatever you wanted. We washed clothes that way, although they had a laundry. But you lost a lot of things in the laundry, some because they weren't properly stenciled, or otherwise. We'd wash clothes, and you could hang them in the uptakes somewhere. But there again, somebody might borrow them. [Laughter]

Paul Stillwell: Borrow in quotes. [Laughter]

Commander Harralson: Yes. We washed a lot of our own clothes. Drying was a problem.

Paul Stillwell: I suspect privacy was almost nonexistent in the heads there.

Commander Harralson: Oh, absolutely. [Laughter] Yes.

Paul Stillwell: One thing people from destroyers in that era have talked about is that there was virtually no place to sit down. If you wanted to just sit down and write a letter, there wasn't room. Did you have facilities for that?

Commander Harralson: Yes, I remember a small library. But there weren't very many places you could sit, and it couldn't accommodate very many. They used the mess compartments. They were large. They had some benches on the side. I believe a lot of people used to sit there and read or write letters.

Paul Stillwell: What do you remember about a rivalry between the Saratoga and the Lexington?

Commander Harralson: I wasn't aware of any particular rivalry, but, of course, I was a boot. There were a lot of things that went on I didn't know about. It was a big ship. I don't ever remember seeing much of the Lexington until after I had left Saratoga.

Funny thing. One thing I remember is that they divided the personnel up into groups for abandon-ship drill. I found my name on the list for motorboat, an officers' boat, you know. I was trying to envision us getting off of the ship and into this boat for the drill. There was a fellow who was senior to me by about six months; he was still a seaman second, but he was an old-timer--he'd been there. I asked him questions about getting into the boat, and he just laughed and laughed and laughed. He thought that was the craziest thing he ever heard of, you know. But, by gosh, we did; we got in the boat. I remember sitting there looking at him and laughing. [Laughter] But that was one of the few times when they went that far.

Paul Stillwell: Well, I suspect that your general-quarters station was in the radio central.

Commander Harralson: We didn't have room enough for all the radiomen there. The radio room wasn't too big.

Paul Stillwell: I see.

Commander Harralson: Usually you were assigned somewhere as a sound-powered telephone talker. I think one time I was on a fire party or something like that. But only the best radiomen had their general quarters in the radio room.

Paul Stillwell: Recently I interviewed a man who was a radioman in the Colorado at that same time, 1938.[*] He remembers a great feeling of claustrophobia when the armored hatch was closed and people were in there smoking and a good crowd. Do you have any memories like that?

Commander Harralson: On the Saratoga and the Lex and the Sicily, the radio room was up in the island structure; we were just under the bridge.[†] There were a few portholes, and they were dogged down there, but I don't remember any claustrophobia. Now, on the Mississippi, of course, the radio room on a battleship is down below the armored deck.[‡]

---

[*]This is in the oral history of Captain Franklin F. Shellenbarger, USMS (Ret.).
[†]Harralson served in the escort carrier Sicily (CVE-118) during the Korean War.
[‡]Harralson served in the Mississippi (EAG-128), a former battleship, in the mid-1950s.

Richard A. Harralson, Interview #1 (5/15/97) - Page 53

Paul Stillwell: Well, that was the case, of course, in the Colorado.

Commander Harralson: Yes. I can understand that, because I am bothered, somewhat, by claustrophobia feelings I have to fight down.

Paul Stillwell: How much chance did you have to see air operations in the Saratoga?

Commander Harralson: Quite a bit. Quite a bit. Like I said, the radio shack was in the island structure, and there were a lot of places you could see it. In fact, at one time, I was on a fire party where we were in the nets. They had nets just off the flight deck, forward. I was there and watched them take off and land. It was exciting. I enjoyed it.

Paul Stillwell: Got any specific memories?

Commander Harralson: Yes, and I think this was a little later. They were qualifying pilots, and they would have to take off. They had sandbags as weights in the rear seat. They would take off and go around and land. I think they had to do it three times or something like that. When they got all through, then they called up six NAPs.* These were sailors in dungarees. They climbed in the cockpit, and they qualified. I was impressed by these guys. They did good.

Paul Stillwell: Same thing the officers were doing.

Commander Harralson: Oh, absolutely. I have another story, but that's farther down the line. There was a squadron of NAPs, and except for the skipper and the exec they were all chief petty officers. They were a Lexington fighter squadron.† Their logo was a hat in the ring. Some of them were gray-haired. [Laughter]

They pulled a spectacular save. It was in the papers in San Diego. I forget all the exact circumstances, but a guy making a parachute jump got hung up, and he was hanging

---

*NAP--naval aviation pilot, a term to designate an enlisted naval aviator before and during World War II.
†This was Fighting Two (VF-2), which had only about half a dozen commissioned officer pilots.

beneath the plane. This NAP from the squadron came up under him, got him in the plane, and the prop cut the shroud.

Paul Stillwell: That's remarkable.

Commander Harralson: It was quite a feat, yes.

Paul Stillwell: Do you remember instances of being out and operating with the Battle Force?

Commander Harralson: No, no, I don't. I don't recall seeing battleships very much. The battleships were ported in Long Beach, weren't they?

Paul Stillwell: Yes.

Commander Harralson: The Sara and the Lex were at Long Beach. The tin cans and submarines were at San Diego.

Paul Stillwell: You had the one story about the gangway platform dipping into the water. Do you have any other boat recollections from the Saratoga?

Commander Harralson: I remember the Pico Street landing in Long Beach. The director was usually a boatswain. They had the landing with several slips. As launches and motorboats came in from the different ships, he'd assign them slips by loudspeaker. Cruisers were in Long Beach. For example, he'd call out, "Northampton, slip one." I can remember vividly the ships that were there; the names were all familiar. "Saratoga motor launch, shove off. Carry out your orders."

Paul Stillwell: Another thing I've heard is that in fog, the individual ships would ring a bell with their hull number, to aid the coxswains in finding them.

Commander Harralson: Yes, that's right.

Paul Stillwell: Another facet is that at the end of the liberty, the behavior in the boat was probably not as good as when men were going ashore. [Laughter]

Commander Harralson: No, it wasn't. [Laughter] I didn't notice it so much in Long Beach or San Diego. But when we got down on the cruise to the Caribbean, there were some wild scenes coming back, of motor launches racing and sailors throwing bananas and coconuts at each other. [Laughter] That sort of thing. And some pretty sorry-looking sailors.

Paul Stillwell: What memories do you have of the Pike, there in Long Beach?*

Commander Harralson: Oh, I have a lot of memories of the Pike. Many times I went to Dreamland, a dance hall, and there were a lot of girls there. The chaplain warned us about buying ice cream cones for stray girls on the Pike. [Laughter]

Paul Stillwell: What could that lead to? [Laughter]

Commander Harralson: Who knows? [Laughter]

Paul Stillwell: Was this a dime-a-dance type arrangement?

Commander Harralson: No, it wasn't. They had Muscle Beach, even then. And they had a roller coaster that went out over the water.

Paul Stillwell: I've seen a picture of that; it was quite spectacular.

Commander Harralson: Yes. Oh, and the sounds: the clanging of the bells and the barkers. It was a fun place. It was hard to meet a nice girl, though. There was a typical

---

*The Pike was an amusement park on the waterfront, popular with sailors.

Long Beach sailor. He wore his jumper so tight he had to have zippers on the side. He had exaggerated bell-bottoms, 32-inch. He had a collar that was usually undersized. And a lot of them wore tailor-made hats; the brim was a little bit narrower than regular hats.

Paul Stillwell: Why would the collar be undersized?

Commander Harralson: Oh, they felt that was a better style, looked better that way. They wore their neckerchiefs like cravats.

Paul Stillwell: Just a tighter uniform, altogether.

Commander Harralson: Yes, a tight and extreme cut.

Paul Stillwell: Did you ever wear the flat hats?*

Commander Harralson: Yes.

Paul Stillwell: What would be the occasion for that?

Commander Harralson: Well, of course, when the blues were the uniform. I think I wore them when the Lexington got up to Norfolk. Of course, in those days, it was just "U.S. Navy" on the ribbons. But I heard stories about terrible fights developing when it used to be the name of your ship. In fact, it was, in the beginning. I remember, we had a Saratoga ribbon.

Paul Stillwell: So you came along right at the end of that era.

Commander Harralson: Yes. From the stories I heard, it caused a lot of fights, over in the bars and the honkytonks.

---

*The flat hats were of the style seen on the character Donald Duck in Walt Disney cartoons.

There was a radioman second that came aboard one day; he was a raconteur. He had just got back from 30 days' leave on his motorcycle. He'd been all around the United States. He had been a radioman on the Saratoga. Later he was attached to a squadron. He earned flight pay and used it to buy a Harley. He got 30 days' leave and took this trip. He told all about the things he did. That became some kind of goal for me: to get to North Island, in a squadron, draw flight pay, buy a motorcycle, and tour the United States.

Paul Stillwell: He was the role model! [Laughter]

Commander Harralson: Yes, he was. So one day up in the radio room, a message came in that said, "Transfer one radioman striker to Scouting Three."

I went to the chief: "Chief, I've got to have that. I've got to have that. I've got to have that." I got it! But I didn't read the fine print. [Laughter] Down at the bottom it said, "For flag allowance." So when I got down to the squadron, they sent me over to flag administration. The first job I got was two months' compartment cleaning. [Laughter]

I remember when Saratoga came into port. We'd gotten back from Bremerton. I'd received my orders, and I had to complete a checkoff list. The Friday before that, the ship had gone down off of Seal Beach for some kind of calibration--I can't remember what it was--and we lost the anchor and 15 fathoms of chain. The captain said, "We do not leave here until we recover the anchor and the 15 fathoms." But he couldn't carry that out because later he found out they were scheduled for the Shriners. They had a big Shriner convention in Long Beach, and there'd been arrangements made for the Shriners to visit. So he said, "We'll get under way. We'll go back up to Long Beach for the Shriners. And then we're coming back."

So that's what we did. We went up there Saturday so the Shriners could come aboard. I don't know how many; they were all over the place. That was the day I was to get checked out so I could leave. I knew I had to get checked out by a certain time, because we were going to go back to Seal Beach. The checkout sheet was a whole list of names that required signatures, so I had to go around and run these people down. Some of them were terribly hard to find. It never crossed my mind to forge anything there. The deadline was getting awful close. I remember I was trying to get my seabag--you know how they lashed the seabag?

Paul Stillwell: With the hammock around it.

Commander Harralson: Yes, around it. I was doing that, and I got a nosebleed. I had blood all over the place. I finally got everything together and caught the last boat in. I was the only sailor passenger in a whole boat load of Shriners.

Paul Stillwell: What came from that?

Commander Harralson: I made it ashore. I got transferred and reported first to the squadron. They sent me on up to the administration building, ComAirBatFor.* It's a big administration building. I think it has a tower and a lock in it.

Paul Stillwell: Right. That's on North Island.

Commander Harralson: Yes, on North Island. There was this big, brawny boatswain's mate who was the admiral's coxswain. Did you ever see a man--his arms weren't big with muscles but with big bones. I think you would call him rawboned. He had great big bones, and he looked like a real Norse seaman. He was an excellent coxswain. He was real nice about it, telling me my duties. I was dejected. You know, here I was qualified radio striker, and they were going to make me clean compartments for two months.

Paul Stillwell: Especially after you had this motorcycle program you were trying to work on.

Commander Harralson: Yes. But I stuck it out. Well, of course, I did. [Laughter] Like I had a choice! Then I got up into the radio room. It was a very busy place. Let's see, we

---

*ComAirBatFor--Commander Aircraft Battle Force, the type commander for aircraft carriers and planes attached to the Battle Force.

were D5P; that was ComAirBatFor. The chief asked me, "Do you know how to drive a motorcycle?"

I said, "No, but I can learn."

He said, "Well, it's just like an automobile. It's got a sidecar." He said, "I want you to be the messenger. You have to deliver messages to all the different squadrons out there." So I went down, and he showed me around a little bit. I got on the motorcycle, a Harley, and drove it like a car. I would take the messages I was supposed to deliver, put them on the sidecar seat, and fold the back down.

But one of the things about a motorcycle, even one with a sidecar, is you begin to get cocky; you begin to think you're in charge. You begin to feel it. So it wasn't long before I was coming into the curb and sliding in sideways, that sort of thing. When I'd go around a corner on a right turn, I'd lift the sidecar up in the air. One time it got away from me, and I went up over a big pile of dirt. My messages went all over everywhere.

Another time it had just rained, and I came up behind a flatbed truck. I hit the brakes, and it was like I didn't have any. The motorcycle slid right under the bed. I had stepped off just back of it.

Paul Stillwell: You survived somehow.

Commander Harralson: Yes. One time a warrant officer, a radio electrician, came running up. He said, "I've got to get down to VP-2 [or something like that] right away. Give me a ride." So he jumped in and I took off. He said, "We want to get there in one piece." [Laughter]

Paul Stillwell: This raises a question. What percentage of the messages in that era would you guess were classified?

Commander Harralson: I don't believe there were too many, but I have no way of judging.

Paul Stillwell: The encryption procedure was very cumbersome at that time.

Commander Harralson: Of course, I didn't know anything about that. The only encryption I knew of was with what they called a restricted cipher book. It was simple letter substitution, and it changed each day. The supervisor could encrypt the message, or decode it. The idea behind it was that it protected you for maybe 20 or 30 minutes, and whatever it was used for would have taken place by then. It would be too late in that sort of situation.

Paul Stillwell: What else was involved in your duty there?

Commander Harralson: I had interface with some chief radio electricians there on North Island. One was selling National Radio Institute correspondence courses, and the other was selling Capitol Radio Engineering Institute correspondence courses in radio materiel--National and CREI. They went to great lengths to sell you on it. It cost money. I forget what I had to pay for it. But I signed up for the CREI.

Paul Stillwell: But why would you need something beyond what the Navy training could provide?

Commander Harralson: What training did the Navy provide? Only what you were willing to do. They had a training course for third class, second class. And these you had to turn in. But, actually, it covered all aspects of radioman at that time, which included operating and materiel and so forth. But the materiel part was somewhat skimpy. It never got into an engineering level. This course that I signed up for was an engineering level course, which stood me in real good stead later on, when I went up for second class.

Paul Stillwell: Right, that would give you an advantage.

Commander Harralson: Oh, yes. But I wasn't alone, and it was all competitive. We had first class radiomen on North Island, flag radio, that were ending up with final multiples above 100. They were measuring them down to 100ths of a point, because there was a lot of competition and a lot of expertise and a lot of time in service and rate.

Paul Stillwell: And not very many openings.

Commander Harralson: That's right. It was this final multiple that determined your position on the list. Then you waited until the rates came out. Rates were assigned to different battle groups: so many here and so many there. If, say, you were fourth on the list, and three came out, why, tough luck; next time, maybe.

Paul Stillwell: Please tell me about what happened once you went on board the Lexington, as part of the AirBatFor staff.

Commander Harralson: Well, of course, being a striker, I had to work with the files and stand duty as a messenger. We were happy to find out that flag radio on the Lex was above the ship's bridge. It was on the flag bridge, and flag radio was right behind what I guess you would call flag plot. Then on up above, on the mast actually, was a small compartment. I would say it was six by six, or something like that; you couldn't stand up in it. It was our understanding, at one time, there had been a direction finder in there. That room was assigned to the striker who was in charge of making up the message blanks.

Now, the message blanks were a pretty complicated affair. They were a half-sheet. Your standard is eight by eleven; it'd be only half the length.

Paul Stillwell: Is that because messages were shorter in those days?

Commander Harralson: Right, right. But there were seven, eight, nine copies.

Paul Stillwell: Different colors of tissue?

Commander Harralson: Yes, they were flimsies, like onionskin, and, of course, the pieces of carbon paper were in there. Well, these message blanks had to be made up, and that was quite a big job. This one radio striker, Pavlevich, was a good friend of mine, and that became his domain up there. He had a wooden foot locker. That's where he sat making up these blanks, and that's where he made up the previous day's traffic that had been checked over by the chief. He put it in a book form and then filed it in the box.

When we weren't on watch, we'd go on up there with him. There was room for maybe four or five to sit in there. There was also a little deck outside; you could sit out there and hang your feet over the side. We hung out up there a lot, because you got to see a lot. There was a lot of activity down below, airplanes being moved about. I enjoyed it; it was quite a thrill. The ship danced around a couple of waterspouts that we got all excited about. They didn't want one of those hitting us with planes on deck, you know.

They did something that I'd never heard of before. They launched all the aircraft; all four squadrons were airborne. They announced over the speaker system, "Now rig ship for receiving aircraft over the bow." We could see them doing it, but I can't tell you what they did. They must have rigged arresting cables; it wouldn't have worked otherwise. But when they got all rigged, the ship swung around, stopped, and began backing into the wind. Then here came the planes. They landed all the planes safely. I thought nothing about it. It was just interesting to watch.

Paul Stillwell: Did you wonder why they were doing it?

Commander Harralson: Well, I figure that maybe it was so they could land planes in battle if something happened to the stern, or some other disabling event.

Paul Stillwell: That's the explanation I've always heard.

Commander Harralson: Yes. Years later we had friends in Rancho Cordova, next door. The man was an aeronautical engineer for Aerojet. He had a bunch of kids, about my kids' age. We were good friends. Well, he eventually ended up down in San Diego, and we went down there to see him. His son, about the age of my oldest, had become an aeronautical engineer himself and was a pilot in the Navy Reserve. He had done six years' active duty and was teaching school there. We were sitting in the living room there, talking about airplanes and ships, and I mentioned this landing over the bow. They thought that was the craziest thing they ever heard.

Paul Stillwell: That you had invented this whole thing?

Commander Harralson: Yes, and I began to doubt it myself, you know. It bothered me. Then one day, at the commissary at Mather Air Force Base, this guy in front of me wore a Lexington (CV-2) hat. So I asked him if he had ever heard of planes landing over the bow. Gee, he let out a string of cuss words, and he said, "Oh, we hated that, hated that." It was true.

Paul Stillwell: So that was the confirmation you were looking for.

Commander Harralson: Yes.

We tried to steer clear of Admiral King.* He had quite a reputation, which you well know.† One day they sent me down to get a receiver that had been repaired and take it back up to flag radio. I'd started up with the receiver. There was a ladder on the inboard side of the island structure. It was a long way up. At the top, it put you at the bridge level. I had taken just one or two steps up the ladder when I saw these feet in front of me. I looked up and here was all this gold. I started back down, which would have been four steps at the most. Admiral King turned around, and he went all the way back up. He said to me, as he started up, "Come on up, son." [Laughter]

Paul Stillwell: So he wasn't all bad.

Commander Harralson: He was like some other admirals. To lowly seamen, he was benevolent, kindly; the higher up the officer, the tougher he got.

Paul Stillwell: And you probably held him in awe.

---

*Vice Admiral Ernest J. King, USN, served as Commander Aircraft Battle Force from January 1938 to June 1939. He later served as Chief of Naval Operations and Commander in Chief U.S. Fleet during World War II.

†Admiral King had a widespread reputation for being tough and demanding. For details see Thomas B. Buell, Master of Sea Power: A Biography of Admiral Ernest J. King (Boston: Little, Brown, 1980).

Commander Harralson: Absolutely. Yes, he was a very imposing figure. I don't think he liked Captain Hoover, who was the CO of the Lexington.* Admiral King would lean over the rail and he'd say, "Hey, Hoover, come here." Hoover didn't seem too much in awe of him. [Laughter] But we didn't like Hoover.

ComAirBatFor went on a cruise to the Caribbean at almost the very beginning of January 1939.† As we were approaching the Miraflores Locks in the Panama Canal, they passed the word, "All hands will stay clear of all weather decks while transiting the canal." As strikers, we all headed for Pavlevich's place, up on the mast. The chief master-at-arms came up the flight deck; he was looking for people who weren't clear of the weather decks. They meant the sponsons, the flight deck, and the whole works. He looked up and saw that we were sitting there, happily looking down and watching things. He started yelling at us. The flag lieutenant leaned over the rail and said, "Hey, Boats, lay off. They're flag personnel." Of course, the chief master-at-arms didn't like that.

Paul Stillwell: Did he take it out on you later?

Commander Harralson: Well, that's where we were smart enough to disappear. We pulled back from the edge; he couldn't see us anymore. We had to go down there to eat and sleep.

Then, as we were going into the Miraflores Lock, there was all this scraping going on. The next thing, here came the admiral up the flight deck. He was all by himself--no orderly or anybody, just all alone. He was ranting and raving, saying, "I told the bureau not to put those platforms out there." He kept saying that. In the last shipyard availability they had mounted these decks for antiaircraft machine guns off both sides of the bow and stern. The clearance was pretty close in there, and these things were scraping and screeching.

Paul Stillwell: It must have been very unpleasant to listen to.

Commander Harralson: Yes, it sounded terrible.

---

*Captain John H. Hoover, USN, commanded the Lexington from June 1938 to June 1939.
†The Lexington, along with other ships of the Battle Force, went to the Caribbean to participate in Fleet Problem XX, a combat simulation involving two opposing teams of U.S. ships.

Paul Stillwell: Like a finger on a blackboard.

Commander Harralson: Yes.

Paul Stillwell: What uniform did you wear on board ship--undress whites or blues?

Commander Harralson: Undress whites on that cruise, yes.

Paul Stillwell: Did you ever get into dungarees?

Commander Harralson: I don't think so. I don't recall dungarees there, because of the nature of the work we did. We didn't have any other work to do, than as messengers.

Paul Stillwell: Maybe you wore them for that bottom scraping?

Commander Harralson: Oh, yes. We had dungarees. [Laughter] But I didn't like the small stores dungarees. The chambray shirts were short-sleeved, and I hated short sleeves. And the pants had no style to them. A lot of the men wore tailor-made dungarees, to look nice. I eventually got a set of them.

Paul Stillwell: Let me just bring up one other general thing from the era. What do you remember about the magazine called Our Navy?[*] Was that popular?

Commander Harralson: Yes. The "Captain and the Boot" were entertaining.

Paul Stillwell: That was a cartoon series.

Commander Harralson: Yes, I remember that.

---

[*] A collection of bound volumes of Our Navy is available for reference in the Naval Institute's reference library.

Paul Stillwell: Well, it really was a news magazine about the fleet.

Commander Harralson: That's right. And it was written for sailors, swabbies.

Paul Stillwell: What can you say about differences between the Lex and the Saratoga? You were in both so close together in time; how would you compare them?

Commander Harralson: Actually, they were very, very much alike. The big difference to me was that Saratoga had a vertical stripe on its stack, and the Lex had a horizontal one at the top.

Paul Stillwell: Right. But I mean, procedures and so forth were very similar?

Commander Harralson: Well, of course, on the Saratoga, I was in the ship's radio gang, and I did messenger work. Well, that's what I did in flag radio. And on the midwatches, I'd sit on circuits for as much time as I could get. But I can't think of much difference.

Paul Stillwell: Well, in some cases, I've heard different ships had different personalities. Maybe you just didn't notice it in that case?

Commander Harralson: I think I was too green, too uninformed, too unaware to notice things like that yet.

Paul Stillwell: How would you compare morale?

Commander Harralson: I thought it was high. I felt like it was all business, everybody doing their job as best they could. I don't recall complaints. Oh, griping about the food or something like that. But, no, thinking about flag radio there, I would say they were good radiomen. See, Navy radio communication was highly skilled; we were very good. A good Navy radioman was very good, as a maritime operator, and a lot more disciplined, certainly every bit as fast and capable. And the radiomen I knew there in flag radio were all extremely competent. I ran into some later on that I knew, and they were officers; they were lieutenant commanders.

Paul Stillwell: Well, radioman was an elite rating.

Commander Harralson: Yes, it was, yes. In fact, from time to time, you picked up a little resentment about it and snide remarks.

Paul Stillwell: Well, please tell me about that.

Commander Harralson: [Laughter] Oh, sometimes they would talk about "radio girls." [Laughter] But they certainly didn't know some of the studs we had. [Laughter]

Paul Stillwell: Well, you're suggesting it was sort of a good-natured ribbing.

Commander Harralson: Oh, yes. See, we were a left-arm rate. And the right-arm rates didn't think too much of us.*

Paul Stillwell: Well, for example, signalman also is communication. But that was a right-arm rate.

Commander Harralson: Exactly. Well, we got along fine with the signalmen. I don't recall having any static there.

Paul Stillwell: Probably more likely from the boatswain's mates. [Laughter]

---

*Before and during World War II, a few enlisted men in the Navy's seagoing specialties were distinguished by wearing their rating badges on the right sleeves of their uniform jumpers. Included were such ratings as boatswain's mate, mineman, quartermaster, signalman, gunner's mate, turret captain, torpedoman's mate, and fire controlman. Petty officers in the other ratings wore the insignia on their left sleeves.

Commander Harralson: Yes, the deck divisions were quick to point out something to us, or make some snide remark. But we were quite able to take care of ourselves. [Laughter]

Paul Stillwell: Was there a separate category for maintenance and repair, as opposed to just operating the radios?

Commander Harralson: No. You had one radioman. If you were in a squadron and had qualified in air, you were an airdale, but you were still a radioman. It was the same rate, only with "qual-air" in your record. You were supposed to be as competent in repair as you were in the transmitter room or in the operating room. But that didn't always work out too good, and you had men that were much more capable of tuning transmitters, working on transmitters, or repairing receivers, than they were operators and vice versa. But you were supposed to know it all. And also, at that time, in order to make chief you had to go through the radio school at Bellevue, Washington. That was a very, very tough course.

Paul Stillwell: But it was only later, then, that the separate electronics technician rating evolved?

Commander Harralson: Yes.* I was gone during that evolution. I was out of the Navy, for practical purposes.† That's when these changes came in.

Paul Stillwell: Well, please resume the narrative of your cruise.

Commander Harralson: Well, I thought it was interesting. When we got to Gatun Lake, the ship pulled out of the channel and anchored. It was my understanding that the fresh water in Gatun Lake killed the barnacles. It was terribly hot. Sleeping in a hammock is miserable in that kind of climate, so people were looking everywhere to hang their

---

*In 1942 the Navy established the rating of radio technician, which lasted until 1945. From 1945 to 1948 the rating was known as electronics technician's mate. From 1948 to the present it has been electronics technician.
†As this oral history goes on to describe, Mr. Harralson spent the bulk of World War II as a prisoner of the Japanese.

hammocks. The master-at-arms became a little lenient as people began swinging hammocks here and there. I found a place out on the gun sponson, and I swung it. Actually, part of me was over the water there. In the middle of the night there came a torrential downpour. I'd swung this hammock right under a scupper from the flight deck. I nearly drowned before I could get out of that thing. [Laughter]

On the Lex, my hammock space was in the scullery compartment. It was a small compartment, but it's where the mess cooks drew their cups and saucers. They were in big metal racks. The mess cooks got up earlier than we did, and they would all come there and draw their gear. They were always in a rush, and here I was, hanging up above them. So I had to heave out; and not only that, but lash up my hammock. It was a harrowing experience.

Paul Stillwell: I presume they were not very quiet about their drawing of mess gear.

Commander Harralson: No, and they had absolutely no sympathy for people still asleep. [Laughter]

Paul Stillwell: Well, what else from that cruise?

Commander Harralson: Oh, we stayed in Guantanamo Bay an awful lot, a long time.* All we could do was go ashore and drink beer. They had a great, big tin-roofed place, where they had the beer. There were baseball fields and there were a lot of baseball games going on.

We had a baseball team. I played some. Of course, everybody drank beer. They'd get a big washtub with ice and beer. It'd be sitting there, not far from home plate. People were drinking beer as they played. The first few innings were reasonable, but then it began to get sloppy. You know what beer does. I was out playing right field. I was a bad hitter, and they always stuck me in right field. There was a great, big guy there, a radioman first

---
*Guantanamo Bay, on the south coast of Cuba, near the eastern end of the island, for many years provided a fleet anchorage and training area for U.S. Navy ships.

class nicknamed Moose; he was a big, heavy fellow. We both started after a fly ball, and we had a head-on collision. I quit after that. [Laughter]

But I did have a break. I was up on watch one evening. Earlier that day they had announced that there would be a special liberty to go into Guantanamo City, which was inland 20 or 30 miles. There was a limited number allowed to go, and it was to be allocated to the different divisions and flag radio. It would be by seniority. We knew seamen didn't have a chance.

I was up in the radio room when the supervisor got a call from the personnel office that told him they hadn't received his list of people that were going to go on the liberty party. The chief looked over his list there, getting ready to send it down, and he saw he had room for one more. The people that were up there were either on the list or didn't want to go. Most of the others were down watching a movie. So he put my name down. The next morning, at 1000, they mustered the liberty party on the hangar deck and there I was, a seaman, with chiefs and first class all around me. They didn't like me being there. [Laughter] But I went anyhow. I was the last one in the last boat, and we went over to Caimanera--there's an alligator called the caiman.

Paul Stillwell: Caimanera was a popular drinking spot.

Commander Harralson: Yes. We went over there and got on a train and went up to Guantanamo City. Of course, I didn't have anybody to bum around with me; I had to steer clear of all these other guys. I wandered around a bit. They had this plaza in the center, and across from it was a delicatessen. It was a pretty nice place. I went in there and drank a Cuban beer, which was pretty potent. Then I had another one. A Cuban walked by, and I started speaking to him in Spanish. I had taken Spanish in high school. So he sat down, I bought him a beer, and we had a long conversation. He told me he had two wives, one in Jamaica and one in Cuba. He was a rum salesman. It was cheaper to have a wife in each place than it was to haul the same wife back and forth. [Laughter]

Paul Stillwell: Well, that was an interesting setup.

Commander Harralson: Yes. I was always glad I was able to make that trip.

Paul Stillwell: What do you remember about the battle problem itself?

Commander Harralson: Well, I didn't know much of what was going on, what we were trying to do or anything like that.

At the height of activity one day they assigned me to a sound-powered telephone; for what reason, I don't know. There was a portable direction finder up on the starboard side of the bow, and I was to communicate with the man up there. Nobody told me anything to say or who was going to say what or anything; I was just in communication with him. We were steaming along, and the ship started taking evasive action. That old ship heeled way over and then would go the other way. Things were happening.

I was trying to see what was going on. I had gone forward and was way up at the far end of the flag bridge. My cord was plugged in just outside the door to the radio room, and it passed right in front of the door into flag plot. Well, I was out there looking, and all of a sudden the phones went flying off of my head. I turned around and picked them up and went around to see what happened and to see if the plug was all right. There was Admiral King getting up off of the deck. I was terrified!

Paul Stillwell: Because you had tripped him.

Commander Harralson: Yes. I had dragged that cord so it was like a booby-trap, right across the door there. But, you know, he didn't say a word. He got up, and he went charging on out. We were being bombed by PBYs, and we were trying to evade them. I thought I was going to be called to account, but I never heard a word about it; no one ever said a word to me about it.

Paul Stillwell: Well, this, again, supports your idea that he was gentle on enlisted men.

Commander Harralson: Yes, that or he was so intent on what was taking place that he didn't have time to waste on bawling anybody out. Of course, I thought that was tremendous about him and the signal flags--when the Yorktown and the Enterprise and Halsey came on the scene.*

Paul Stillwell: What are you referring to there?

Commander Harralson: Oh, he got disgusted with the signalman and was up there grabbing flags out of the signal bag and throwing everything into confusion. Halsey was coming up, and they lost the end of the flag hoist. Halsey's signal flags were hanging out there like the wash, you know, blowing in the wind.

What I heard was that King was great on flag signals, but as much as he thought about flag signals, he really didn't know them. He got the poor signalmen on the bridge there completely confused by taking over and grabbing flags out of the bins there.

Paul Stillwell: What do you remember about going to Haiti?

Commander Harralson: Oh, we pulled in there, and liberty was granted for the afternoon, to expire at 1800 on the dock. It was a miserable little place, really; hardly anything there. But they were all trying to sell us beer. They had beer in washtubs, and down in the bottom was a little piece of ice. [Laughter] And there were some ponies around that you could rent. I went back to the dock. I think most of the liberty party wanted to get back to the ship in time to eat supper, so they were coming back early. But there were a lot of sailors that were really stewed. They were throwing them into the motor launch with the bananas and coconuts and pineapples.

When you go into Haiti, there's a prominence; you come in alongside these high mountains. We anchored quite a ways out from the dock, but we were fairly close to these high mountains. That night you could see fires up there, and you could hear drums.

I bought a sack of limes and kept them in my locker. After that I would take a lime and squeeze the juice in one of those Navy mugs and fill it with ice water. Then I'd get a little sugar and put it in. I was drinking lime juice all the way to Norfolk.

---

*Rear Admiral William F. Halsey, Jr., USN, was Commander Carrier Division Two in 1938-39. He later served as a fleet commander in World War II, eventually becoming a five-star admiral.

Paul Stillwell: Well, that's what the British did to fight off scurvy.

Commander Harralson: Yes. Oh, another thing that Hoover did was secure the heads. He said he did it to save water. The heads would only be open from, I think, 1600 to 1800. That was terrible. You'd get up to go on the midwatch, and there was no place to wash. I used to go stick my head under the scuttlebutt. They had an old-fashioned scuttlebutt, but I don't know how the thing worked, because the water came out ice cold. It was a big metal tank with a whole bunch of drinking fountains around it. It had a tap, or a faucet, underneath. I used to stick my head under the faucet.

Paul Stillwell: I wonder if it was a gravity flow-type deal.

Commander Harralson: I don't know. I wondered what was the mechanism that made it so cold.

Paul Stillwell: I had heard about those, and I thought they just had big blocks of ice in there.

Commander Harralson: Maybe, maybe it was. I never thought of that.

Paul Stillwell: What else do you recall from that trip?

Commander Harralson: Well, we really enjoyed our visit to Barbados. We finished the fleet problem, and then we dispersed. They assigned different ships to different places, and we drew Barbados. To get from Cuba to Barbados we dropped down below Hispaniola. There's this string of islands that go around, so we just followed these islands. Here we were, sitting way up there on the mast and sailing real close to these islands. It was like a tour. Then we got down past St. Vincent and turned left. From there it was a straight shot over to Barbados, which sits out of this string; it's about 100 miles or so east.

The people there were very, very nice. They had black policemen that wore pith helmets and had red pants and a white coat or a red coat and white pants. But they all had an Oxford accent. I liked to hear them talk. They were very polite, very cooperative. There was a ladies' auxiliary that invited the Lexington sailors to have a lemonade and sandwiches in the backyard at one of the houses. Pavlevich and I went in, and here they had these finger sandwiches--little, bitty, dainty things. We had a glass of lemonade and a handful of sandwiches. The ladies were a little bit upset by how fast their sandwiches went. [Laughter]

Paul Stillwell: You were talking about the challenge of trying to get on board this lower platform of the gangway when the ship was rolling. That must have been even more difficult when a guy who was drunk tried to come back aboard.

Commander Harralson: Definitely! [Laughter] You know, if I had been OD there, I would have worried myself sick. Here was a boatload of hollering, drunk sailors, and here was this landing going by, up and down. The platform at the bottom of the ladder couldn't have been more than four feet by four feet. Of course, there were bumpers on it, and it had rails that you could grab. It took skill. You had to step up on the gunwale, and then from there, on.

Paul Stillwell: You had another vignette, and that was going up in the forecastle and looking down.

Commander Harralson: Yes. You know, the Lexington had a clipper bow. And the hawsepipe actually was ahead of the cutwater. For some reason, I don't remember the chain. But the hawsepipe itself--there was a heavy beading around it. I found I could lie on the beading and look down and back and see the cutwater.

Paul Stillwell: Looking down through the hawsepipe?

Commander Harralson: Yes, looking down through the hawsepipe you could see the cutwater. Of course, the water there was crystal clear. You could see porpoises all the time as they were traveling along. They would dart across the bow and back, just having fun, I guess.

Paul Stillwell: What a neat memory to have.

Commander Harralson: I tell you one that's very vivid is the harbor in Panama City, where we dropped the anchor. There are some islands there. The water was absolutely flat. I had the midwatch that first night we were at anchor. There wasn't much going on. I was outside, and I could see it getting light--the sun not up yet. There was kind of a mist or fog; it was patchy. I was just admiring this beautiful quiet sight, and here came these darn pelicans. I don't know, they were above my level in the beginning, but then they dropped down and were skimming the water in a loose formation.

Paul Stillwell: What kind of relationship was there on board the Lexington between the Marines and the sailors?

Commander Harralson: Zero. We used to cheer when they got dunked on the landing. Of course, they cheered when we got dunked. [Laughter] You know, the first level noncom, corporal, has two stripes. The first level petty officer, third-class petty officer, has one stripe.

Paul Stillwell: Right.

Commander Harralson: So, you have the darn corporals trying to get in line with the second class on liberty. When we had a big liberty, they lined everybody up by rate before putting them into the launch.

Paul Stillwell: I hadn't heard that.

Commander Harralson: Well, the chiefs went in first. It's not like the captain who gets in last. The chiefs went first, filled the boat, and they were off.

Paul Stillwell: Once it filled up, off they went.

Commander Harralson: Yes. So if you were a seaman, you were way down there and hoping you were going to get to go. Well, these corporals tried to get up forward, in there with the second class. But a knowledgeable OD wouldn't let that happen.

Paul Stillwell: A knowledgeable OD knows a sailor from a Marine. [Laughter]

[Interruption to change tapes]

Paul Stillwell: Before, we were talking about your cruise in the Caribbean, and while we took a break here you mentioned an important letter-writing campaign that you conducted during that cruise in early 1939. If you could put that on the tape, please?

Commander Harralson: Well, in flag radio there was a telephone book for each of the New York boroughs. Since we were headed for New York after the battle problem was over, several of the radiomen got the idea of picking out what appeared to be a young female's name from the telephone book and writing a letter. They said something to the effect that they were sailors coming to New York for the first time, so we would like a little accompaniment, and so forth. Oh, I guess, each one sent out four, five, six letters. And they got answers! Some of them were interesting. Some said things like, "Well, I don't think I'm what you're looking for," and that sort of thing.

I had to try it myself. I wrote five letters. I got answers from each one. One explained that she was an older woman, but I was welcome to come to her house for a nice meal. But I had one that looked very promising. We exchanged letters, several letters. And they were nice, informative letters. So we had a nice time in New York planned out. We even exchanged pictures.

Well, the ship, on its way to New York, stopped off at Norfolk, Virginia. It anchored in Hampton Roads. I had ten days' leave coming, in which I was going to go to North Carolina to see some relatives, and then meet the ship in New York. But on the evening watch, the day before my leave was to begin, an important message came in. It was a message that sent the fleet back to the West Coast. Apparently, the Japanese were rattling their saber or did something over there that Washington didn't like, or the Navy didn't like. So the fleet was going back to the West Coast. I didn't get my ten days' leave, nor the trip to New York. We did exchange letters a couple times after that, but there wasn't much use in pursuing it any farther.

Paul Stillwell: Do you have any specific memories of what happened while the ship was in Hampton Roads?

Commander Harralson: No, I don't recall any singular event. I went ashore there a couple of times. I thought I learned a fact of life there. I went into a restaurant and ordered a tamale, but what I got wasn't what I knew as a tamale. It was something out of a can. I took that as a lesson, that if you're in a different land, another place, don't try to get what you had at home, but see what they have to offer there. In other words, be more broadminded. I tried to follow that where I went.

Paul Stillwell: What do you remember about the role and relationship of the white sailors, in those two carriers, with black sailors?

Commander Harralson: I have a very vivid picture of an occurrence that disturbed me a great deal. I got on the streetcar in Norfolk, and two black mess stewards got on board also. They sat about midway down the aisle. There was hardly anybody else on the streetcar, except myself. I was sitting toward the back, these two black mess stewards about midships. Then a white man, an older man, got up, came back, and made the two black sailors move to the back of the streetcar. This appalled me; I was not used to that sort of thing occurring. It was eminently unfair, unjust, unnecessary. The streetcar was virtually empty, except for the five of us.

Paul Stillwell: What was the situation on board those ships, the Lexington and Saratoga?

Commander Harralson: There was very little exchange between the black sailors and the white sailors. The black sailors were officers' stewards, mostly. I don't recall, at that time, seeing a general service or, let's say, a rated black sailor. I think there were, actually, a very few of them. I'm not sure about that.

Paul Stillwell: I think you're right. There was, sort of, a segregation by jobs, because they would all be berthed in the same place.

Commander Harralson: Right, yes.

Paul Stillwell: What was the mood throughout the Lexington when the news came that you would not be going to New York?

Commander Harralson: There were two groups, two sides. There were those like myself who wanted to go to New York and were greatly disappointed. Then there were the others, that had wives or families, and wanted to go home.

Paul Stillwell: Well, married enlisted people were relatively rare at that time, weren't they?

Commander Harralson: Yes, especially in the lower rates. In fact, the Navy wouldn't recognize you being married unless you were a second class petty officer or above. Some sailors did get married at a lesser rank, but they had to keep it quiet. There was no recognition of the fact, say, in housing or any of that. You got no more money for being married. In fact, a couple of years later I was at Cavite when they brought in an allowance for married people. I think it was $50.00 a month that they would get if they were married. We had one radioman who was married on paper, but he hadn't seen his wife for years. She was in San Diego, he thought, but he didn't know. But he got $50.00. This enraged some of the radiomen there: "He doesn't do any more than I do. I work just as hard as he does. Why should he get more money?"

Paul Stillwell: That's still the case. The Navy still pays married people more.

Commander Harralson: Yes. Well, if you're not married, then you can't understand why. If you're married, why, it's easily understandable.

Paul Stillwell: That's right. I'm married. I understand. [Laughter]
Well, what happened after the ship then left Norfolk and headed back to California?

Commander Harralson: We stopped off in Colón, on the Caribbean side. I remember going ashore there, but that was the only place. Other than that, we came on home.

A few days after we got back to North Island, we had a great, big picnic. We got a prorated cut of the ship's service profits. They threw a big picnic at some park back of San Diego. I can't name it. It was a real good one.

Then Admiral King was relieved by Admiral Blakely.[*] Captain Hoover became Admiral Blakely's chief of staff. Shortly after the change of command, Captain Hoover wandered into the radio shack, looked around, and said to the supervisor, "From now on, there will be no coffee in the radio room" or words to that effect. That hit us radiomen hard. Coffee was our life's blood, so unhappiness prevailed. Two or three days later, the admiral's orderly walked in and told the supervisor, "The admiral wants a cup of coffee." The supervisor told him there was no coffee. The orderly looked at him for a moment, did an about-face, and walked out. Five minutes later he returned and said, "The admiral says he never heard of a radio room without coffee. Someone explained to the orderly why there was no coffee. Two days later carpenters made an adjoining room into a coffee bar with a small counter in the radio room. The "no coffee" order was rescinded, and coffee once again flowed freely, as is proper in a true radio shack.

---

*Vice Admiral Charles A. Blakely, USN, served as Commander Aircraft Battle Force from June 1939 to June 1940.

It was about this time that I made third class radioman. I was third on the list, and ComAirBatFor was allotted two rates, so I missed out. I thought I was doomed, but about a month or so later, they got a kickback, which meant that there was a rate turned back because they didn't have enough people to fill it.

Paul Stillwell: That would be from some other command?

Commander Harralson: Yes, and it came back and I got it.

Paul Stillwell: In that situation would being on the staff give you an advantage over being in a ship?

Commander Harralson: Absolutely not. I felt that the Navy way of promotion was very, very fair. I never saw anything that would make me question it. They were very protective of the tests, how they gave you points. You got in line according to your ability, and that was it.

Paul Stillwell: When did you take the third-class test?

Commander Harralson: I took it when I was in the flag radio, ComAirBatFor. I had taken the test for seaman first, too, a while before.

Of course, once I got the rate, I had to leave the flag. I wasn't good enough to be one of their operators and I was too good to be a messenger. So they sent me back to Scouting Three, to which I was actually attached. One of the reasons was that the squadron did a lot of dive bombing back of San Diego, out in the desert. One of the planes augured in out there, and they were short a pilot, plane, and radioman. So I returned to VS-3.

I was all raring to go, but the fact was I was a general service radioman; I knew nothing about being an aviation radioman. I was resented by some of the strikers there because I knew nothing of their profession, and they didn't like that. Furthermore, they had only so many flight skins, and they had to share them with the mechs and the gunners and the people like that.*

We didn't have a leading chief radioman. Our leading radioman was a first class. So that made it more difficult. I think the radioman's name was Clomperins. He was a nice guy. He came around and said, "I want you to take the target tow hop."

"Okay. What do I do?"

He says, "Well, when you take off, a man will be standing down there holding the tail of the target, and the cable will be stretched out in the form of a U. Now, the plane will take off and pass him. As it passes, he will turn and let go. The plane will go into a steep climb. You turn your seat around, looking aft, and put your hand on the release for the tow and watch him. If anything's amiss, you release." He said, "When you get up in the air, to altitude, in the firing range, facing aft, you call out the runs to the pilot."

I said, "Okay. How the hell do I do that?"

He said, "Well, if he comes from 5:00 o'clock, it's one. If he comes from 10:00 o'clock, it's two. And if he comes from . . ." And he went through them just like that, see. I had him repeat it, but I couldn't remember them exactly. But I went ahead, anyhow.

I got in the plane and we took off headed for Point Loma.

Paul Stillwell: What kind of plane was this?

Commander Harralson: This was an SBC-3, a Curtiss biplane.† I was facing aft, sitting there, wondering what was going to happen. All of a sudden, whoom! A plane went by. I was looking for it and whoom, another went by. The pilot said, "Call out the runs!"

I was trying to figure out what run was what, and I couldn't even see the planes. They went by, but I didn't ever see them until they had passed. The pilot was getting mad. Pretty soon, the skipper's plane pulled up alongside, and he said, "Tell that Goddamn radioman to wake up." I didn't know what was going on. So eventually the run was over;

---

*"Flight skins" is a slang term for extra pay given to personnel in a flying status because of the hazardous duty involved.
†The Curtiss SBC Helldiver was a the last combat biplane produced in the United States. The scout-bomber first entered fleet squadrons in July 1937. The SBC-4 model had the following characteristics: length, 28 feet; wing span, 34 feet; gross weight, 7,632 pounds; top speed, 237 miles per hour. Scouting Three had SBC-2s, and Scouting Two had SBC-4s. The two models were distinguished by having different engines.

we turned and went back. Clomperins had told me, "Now, when you come back with the tow, you'll come up along the hangars here. There'll be a man down there with a red flag. You'll watch him. When he drops the flag, you'll release." And he added, "Release it good. Be sure and give it a good pull."

So we come around and I said, "I'm going to do something right." I watched that guy down there. He dropped the flag, and I pulled the thing up by the guts, and it came out, off of the plates. [Laughter]

Paul Stillwell: The whole handle came off?

Commander Harralson: Yes. Oh, there was cable hanging out. The thing got released, but I had a bunch of hardware in my hand. [Laughter] We landed. It was a total failure. I was in trouble.

A couple other things. On another trip I got all fouled up. I accidentally tripped the lanyard to my Mae West, so I was there in these straps with this darn Mae West inflated.* You know, they had the little bottles to inflate it. I was a total klutz.

So they started sending me over to base radio. This was the first voice radio I had run into, other than communicating with a pilot. I had mike fright to begin with, but I got over that. There was an emergency, a plane returning with a problem. We had a whole list of things we had to do in an emergency. By the time I got through with that episode, my mike fright was gone. But the clincher was, I got an overland flight. There was just a section of nine planes on this one. They were going up to Oakland. We were going to fly up over the world's fair on Treasure Island.†

So we took off. We got up in the air, and I was trying to communicate with the pilot. I had a mike, but he wasn't understanding me. I was talking, holding the mike horizontal. Well, it was an old carbon mike, and that's not the right way to talk into a carbon mike. So communications sort of failed there. We landed at Bakersfield and

---

*"Mae West" was the nickname for an inflatable life jacket that fit over a man's head and chest. When not in use it was rolled up into a pouch that he carried on his belt. The life jacket was named for a buxom movie actress of the period.
†Treasure Island is a man-made island in San Francisco Bay, located between San Francisco and Oakland. It served as the site of a world's fair in 1939-40, then was converted for use as a Navy base during and after World War II.

topped off in gas and took off again. We got up over Treasure Island and did a few loops and rolls, then landed at Oakland.

We landed, gassed the plane. You always gas the planes; you don't let them sit there with a partial tank. We tied down. The skipper said, "Okay, liberty expires 0800 tomorrow morning. You'd better be here; we're heading back." So all the radiomen, the rear-seat men, were there at 8:00 o'clock the next morning, but no pilots. We wandered around and drank coffee. Then, about 1:00 o'clock, here came the pilots, looking terrible. They had had one wild time.

We finally got off, up in the air, and we went out over the Golden Gate and turned south, to fly down the coast. We got up to altitude, in loose formation, and the pilot said, "Got any stick time?"

I said, "Yes, I have a little bit." I had about eight hours. I had taken lessons from a Coast Guard pilot who charged $3.00 for an hour. We'd go out to Camp Kearny and shoot landings. So I said, "Yes, I have a few hours."

He said, "Okay, you take it." We had a stick stowed over to the side, and there were pedals. I didn't have a throttle. I put the stick in and wiggled it, and the plane was mine. The pilot went to sleep up there. Here I was--flying. The planes were quite well spaced. Occasionally, he would wake up and wiggle the stick. He'd get us back up where he wanted us, and then I'd take over again. I flew that plane almost all the way back to San Diego. By then it was beginning to get dark, and he took over. I had some lights to attend to. We landed. And, again, they filled the tanks and pushed all the planes into the hangar. By the time we were all through with that, it was 9:00 o'clock, and I was dog tired.

Then I went by the bulletin board and was that I was scheduled for the 12:00 to 4:00 hangar watch. Here it was after 9:00. The barracks were some distance away. Well, I stood my watch, but I was disgusted. The next morning, at quarters, during the different announcements and directives, I heard one asking for volunteers for third-class radiomen for Asiatic duty. As soon as we were dismissed, I ran to the personnel office and said, "Put me down." The skipper of the squadron called me in and accused me of reading too many dime novels. But I think the rule was that if somebody applied, the CO couldn't technically or rightly turn him down. So that's how I got headed towards the Asiatics.

There's something else I want to tell you about, though. When I was in the flag, I found out that if you knew somebody in one of the squadrons, it was possible to catch a night flight around San Diego. Every Thursday they had night flying. The planes would take off and circle around San Diego, practicing touchdowns on a space that was lighted and marked like a carrier deck. It was boring for rear-seat men. If you went down and talked to one of these guys, he might take you up and say, "Lieutenant So-and-So, this is a friend of mine. He'd like to take a passenger hop tonight." Lots of times they'd let you go. So I tried it and had been up about three times. We'd take off and fly over San Diego and out around Point Loma and touch down, take off. Do that for about an hour or an hour and a half. I enjoyed it.

Then the word went around real quick--no more passenger hops. Planes then had emergency flotation gear. They were big balloons. You'd pull a lever, and these balloons would pop up on the wings. One of the squadrons was taking off, and in the back of one plane was a kid who didn't know anything. He was trying to close the canopy, and he pulled levers. He pulled the flotation gear, when they were about 30 feet in the air. [Laughter] Nobody got hurt, but the plane did. So that put the kibosh on passenger hops.

Paul Stillwell: So perhaps that midnight to 4:00 hangar watch that you stood is the reason you were later a guest of the Japanese for four years.

Commander Harralson: Yes, that's about it. There were other things. It was no longer a happy home like they told me it used to be, because Captain Hoover began shaking things up in the squadrons, laying down new rules and regulations. These hangar watches were rough.

Paul Stillwell: In what way?

Commander Harralson: Well, walking on your feet, up and down in front of the hangar. Another thing was that we weren't supposed to recognize anybody but the officer of the day. We had his picture. And he could authorize the junior officer of the day, but no one other than that.

Well, this one day, I had the 4:00 to 6:00; they dogged that watch.* I had just taken over, and everybody had gone off to the barracks in the truck. The CO was working in his office, and I'm sorry I don't remember his name. I guess about a half hour later, he came out and climbed into his Model T Ford roadster. Then he went putt-putting off down the road, down past the hangars. I guess it wasn't five minutes, and he came back. I stopped him, and he got mad. I just thought that I was doing absolutely right; I would not recognize him. I made him get the OOD. [Laughter] I really don't think he got mad at me. I think he thought I was doing right.

Paul Stillwell: Well, Captain Hoover's nickname was Genial John. And the reason for that is that it was the exact opposite of his personality. [Laughter]

Commander Harralson: Yes.

Paul Stillwell: Do you have any other stories on him?

Commander Harralson: No, I can't think of any; just the relationship between him and Admiral King. [Laughter] But he ended up an admiral, or a vice admiral, didn't he? I think he had one of the carrier task forces or something.

Paul Stillwell: Yes, I think he did become a three-star.
    Well, Jimmy Thach was then with VF-3 there at North Island. Did you encounter him at all during that period?

Commander Harralson: No, I didn't. The hangar next to us was VF-2, the Lex fighters. That's the squadron, the hat in the ring, with chiefs. We were the Bird Dog.
    Oh, another thing, connected with this not letting anybody in--the Marines had a post past the hangar area. It was unclear as to what to do about the Marines. Well, the

---

*Dogging a watch means splitting it in half. Instead of a watch lasting from 4:00 to 8:00 in the evening, there were two watches, 4:00 to 6:00 and 6:00 to 8:00, so watch standers would have an opportunity to get an evening meal.

Marines would go through the stop sign at 60 miles an hour. [Laughter] And that came to a halt when one of the guys on watch, with his .45, put a slug over their bow.

Paul Stillwell: That would get their attention.

Commander Harralson: Yes, it did. Furthermore, when the episode went through the colonel and around, the colonel was told off; nobody got in trouble.

I don't know how many times I had to check out with a .45. I was miserable when firing; I couldn't hit the side of a barn. But every time there was some kind of scare or a shakeup, why, everybody had to requalify with a .45. They gave us a .45 with ammo. There were some rabbits killed, and a plane ended up with a hole in it, which disturbed a lot of people. The JOOD was supposed to go around and hang sabotage tags on planes, and there were some very dicey confrontations on that respect, in the dark. This kid with a flashlight and a loaded .45, you know, catching this. [Laughter]

Paul Stillwell: So you were ready to go somewhere else.

Commander Harralson: Yes, I'd had enough of airplanes.

Paul Stillwell: How did your assignment to the Augusta come about?

Commander Harralson: Well, headed for the Asiatic station, I caught the Henderson in San Diego, rode it up to Long Beach.* My brother was in Long Beach and wanted to see me. I could go ashore, except I didn't have any money. So somebody told me that the paperboy could lend me some money. So I went to the paperboy, and the rate was $6.00 on payday for $5.00 at the time of the loan. So I got $5.00. When I went to pay the paperboy back, I think I handed him a $10.00 bill. When he reached into his pockets for change, I saw that every pocket was jammed with just big wads of money.

There was a vendor that came aboard in San Diego, with chocolate milk and regular milk and a few other things. They let him come aboard, and I bought a bottle of

---

*USS Henderson (AP-1) was a Navy transport that carried service personnel and their dependents.

something from him. When we got to Long Beach, we encountered the same paperboy and the same guy selling chocolate milk. When we got to Mare Island, they were there.[*] [Laughter]

When we got to Mare Island, there was a small job that had to be done on the ship, so I got ten days' leave and went home. Then I caught the ship when it was berthed at Fort Mason docks, San Francisco. That's where I begin my story about my Asiatic tour.

Paul Stillwell: Well, are you game to put it on tape tonight?

Commander Harralson: I'm game if you are.

Paul Stillwell: I'm game.

Commander Harralson: All right. We're on a roll.

It was September, early September 1939, when the Henderson left the Fort Mason docks in San Francisco and went out under the Golden Gate, which was only two years old.[†] I remember flocks of seagulls, just a big cloud of seagulls, following the ship out.

The messing was not very good. The chow line was along the side of the superstructure. I guess a promenade or something like that was where they served chow. Every man on going aboard was issued a metal tray and eating tools. He had to keep them and maintain them himself, for the duration of the trip. When you got through eating, there were cans for garbage and two big metal bins. The first one was full of hot, soapy water, and the second one was full of hot water for rinsing. It worked pretty good for the first few trays, and then the water got greasy, and then your tray got greasy.

Once you were served food, you could eat anywhere on the weather deck. That's why all the seagulls were following, because it was chow time as we were going under the Golden Gate Bridge. I remember eating back aft, right on the stern. My tray was on one of the bitts, and the darn seagulls would practically land on your tray and take your food.

---

[*] Mare Island Navy Yard, Vallejo, California.
[†] Construction on the Golden Gate Bridge, one of the largest and most spectacular suspension bridges in the world, began in 1933 and was completed in 1937.

My bunk was way aft, down a couple decks. Just aft of me was the room with steering machinery. All night long, you'd hear the clack, clack of relays, then the motors whining, and gears grinding. It'd go through that, stop, and then the whole sequence go again. If there was a good helmsman at the wheel, there would be long pauses between. If they had a green helmsman up there, why, it would get over one way and go back again. It was awful hard to get a good night's sleep. We were stacked four high.

Paul Stillwell: This was sort of reminiscent of when you had to sleep near the scullery on board the carrier.

Commander Harralson: Yes. By about the third morning out, most of the seagulls had left us, and left just some dark-colored birds with long, narrow wings. I guess they were albatross, and they were usually up high. Occasionally, they'd come down right over the surface. They'd go zooming up over a crest and down into a trough. You wondered where they slept and ate--if at all. [Laughter]

The first leg took us to Honolulu. We tied up at a dock not very far from the Aloha Tower.

Paul Stillwell: Was that the first time you'd been to Hawaii?

Commander Harralson: Yes. There was a whole string of hula-hula girls on the dock, and they were playing Hawaiian music. The sailors and Marines were leaning out over the rail, hollering and whooping. We had about four hours' liberty there. I went ashore and had a couple of beers. I bought a jar of French's mustard. My idea was that the mustard would cut some of the greasiness of the food. I put it on about everything. [Laughter]

Paul Stillwell: Did it work?

Commander Harralson: Yes, it helped, except pie and cake. Unfortunately, somebody stole it from me. [Laughter]

Paul Stillwell: Did you get a chance for any liberty there in Honolulu before you shoved off?

Commander Harralson: Just the four hours. I went ashore. I had a couple beers and bought the mustard. I had hoped on going ashore that I get to see the hula-hula dancers up close, but they were long gone.

About this time I began to recognize people. They seemed to coalesce into rating groups. You'd see boatswain's mates all together, and you'd see yeomen over here, and quartermasters over here, radiomen over here.

Paul Stillwell: That's interesting, because presumably they can associate with anybody they want.

Commander Harralson: Oh, sure, sure. So became friends with three other radiomen. There was Mudge, off of the Arizona.* He had a wife and baby. We didn't really understand why he was heading out, because Asiatic duty was voluntary, as far as I knew. Then there was Lauer, my good friend Lauer, who died last year.† He was an airdale. He had made the trip on the Lexington when they went looking for Amelia Earhart.‡ Now, he told me--and somebody else said it wasn't true--but he told me that Admiral King lost a son on that search.

Paul Stillwell: That's not true.

Commander Harralson: Well, Lauer was full of a lot of baloney. [Laughter] But he was a good guy; a very, very good friend.

---

*Radioman Second Class Arthur G. Mudge, USN.
†Radioman Second Class Willard L. Lauer, USN.
‡Amelia Earhart (1898-1937) became the first woman to fly across the Atlantic Ocean on 17 June 1928. She and her copilot/navigator Fred Noonan were lost in July 1937 during the course of an attempted around-the-world flight. For the recollections of one of the Lexington pilots on the search, see the Naval Institute oral history of Rear Admiral Francis D. Foley, USN (Ret.)

Then there was Hooper.* Hooper was a wild man. He had broken service. He had been out quite a while and just barely got his rate back, second class. Then myself, I was third class. We struck up a real good friendship.

The darn Marines would be in the chow line and get fed. As soon as they got their trays washed, they'd get back in the chow line for the next meal. We used to get so mad at them. There wasn't any time that there wasn't a line of Marines out there waiting for chow.

We all had cleaning stations, but they were tiny, little things. I think I had a section of brass rail that I had to keep polished, and that was it.

Paul Stillwell: Where did you keep your tray and utensils stored when you weren't at meals?

Commander Harralson: Well, the custody of those things was the problem. Most of us tried to stuff them in our seabag. Because if somebody lost his tray, he would take somebody else's. So that the missing tray would move all through the ship. [Laughter]

Paul Stillwell: Kind of a chain reaction. [Laughter]

Commander Harralson: Yes. As we headed toward Guam, which was west-southwest, we got caught in heavy weather from the east. It was a quartering sea. The way I see it, you have your normal pitch and roll, but you get a quartering sea, and it gives you a corkscrew motion. That's what begins to get me a little queasy, incipient seasickness. My remedy for that was to eat crackers. So I bummed a bunch of crackers from the galley and ate those and survived. I don't know whether it was mental, that the crackers cured me or not. My point is that whatever, mental or real, they did the job.

We came into Apra Harbor, Guam. It was beautiful: just like a picture book, with white sands and palms and this incredibly blue water. We anchored. The Gold Star was there, tied up to an old pier down the way.

Paul Stillwell: She was the station ship.

---
*Radioman Second Class Harold E. Hooper, USN.

Commander Harralson: Yes, but we called it the USS "Neversail." But she did actually get under way. Now, this is what I'm told, that she would get under way some time before Christmas, loaded with Guam personnel and dependents, and go to Hong Kong for a Christmas shopping spree.

Paul Stillwell: Well, she used to go out and pick up provisions also.

Commander Harralson: Is that so?

Paul Stillwell: Did you ever find out what happened to Mudge?

Commander Harralson: Mudge died. I think he was killed at Cavite.[*] Miller, the other guy on the land wire, was killed there.[†]

Paul Stillwell: So Mudge had an ill fate either way. If he'd stayed in the Arizona, he probably would have been blown up there.

Commander Harralson: That's right. I never thought of that.

We went ashore in what I remember as a white steam launch. They let us off on an old, rickety pier. I think there were five or six of us in that one group. We went to the head of the pier, and there was nothing there.

We were looking around and met a Guamanian, a Chamorro. We talked to him, and he said there might be a car by that would take us to Agana. It was--I don't know--four or five miles up the way, so we decided to walk. We walked to Agana. On the way we were confronted with a water buffalo, but we didn't know what it was. It was standing in the middle of the road, looking right at us. It had big horns, so we had a discussion about it. Someone said it was a plow-pulling buffalo. Somebody else said it looked like a cape buffalo, which was known to be surly. We went way around it.

---

[*]Mudge was a radioman first class while serving in the naval radio station at Cavite in the Philippines in the autumn of 1941.
[†]Radioman First Class Wilbur A. Miller, USN.

We walked into Agana, and there was hardly anything there, but we did find a cantina. We had a couple beers around and then hired a car to take us back. We were ready to go again, because there was little to do in Guam. I make this point because I came back through Guam after the war, and it wasn't the same; there were major, major changes. [Laughter]

Paul Stillwell: That was a big fleet base by then.

Commander Harralson: Yes.

We left there, heading up over the top of Luzon. At some point along the way, they started putting assignments to ships and stations up on the bulletin board. The four of us were assigned to the Augusta. A couple days later, as we were coming down the West Coast, they passed the word, by name, for the four of us to be prepared to report to the quarterdeck on notice, with a full seabag and hammock.

What we were able to learn was that the Augusta was standing out, and we were coming down the coast.* There would be a rendezvous at sea for the transfer of personnel. Sometime that morning, they passed the word, and we showed up at the quarterdeck. They gave us our file folders, and so forth. We climbed into the Augusta motor launch and were delivered to the Augusta.† We were about two miles northwest of Corregidor.‡

At the top of the ladder, we were met by a chief radioman and a yeoman. The yeoman took our papers, and the chief said, "Follow me." We went forward and down two decks to the flag radiomen compartment. It was a nice compartment. It extended side to side and had a big porthole on each side. It wasn't crowded, and it was airy. The chief assigned each of us a bunk and a locker. I was last, and when he got to me, the chief said, "I wouldn't bother unpacking. Jimmy doesn't like third-class radiomen." Before I could

---

*USS Augusta (CA-31), a Northampton-class heavy cruiser, was commissioned 30 January 1931. She had a standard displacement of 9,050 tons, was 600 feet long, 66 feet in the beam, and had a draft of 16 feet. Her top speed was 33 knots. She was armed with nine 8-inch guns and eight 5-inch guns. Because she was configured as a flagship, she frequently performed that function, both before and during World War II. She was eventually decommissioned on 16 July 1946.
†Harralson and his new shipmates reported aboard the Augusta on 6 January 1940.
‡Corregidor was an island fortress that dominated the entrance to Manila Bay.

ask him who Jimmy was, he had gone. But I found out later that it was Commander James Fernald, fleet communications officer.*

I found my name on the watch list. I was in the starboard watch, third section. In those days, you had port and starboard watches, and each watch had two sections. I think first and third were usually the starboard, and second and fourth were the port. Anyhow, I found I was in the third section, I believe, and I had the morning watch.

I reported to flag radio, and the supervisor told me to get on the press. The press was very important there. We copied stations from all over the world. We copied German, Japanese, Russian--English language--British, and stateside, of course. And they wanted it all. It was a job, but it improved my code speed. The fastest station was WSX, which was stateside. They broadcast at 35 to 40 words a minute. The British station clomped along at about 13 words a minute, and one would go to sleep trying to copy that. [Laughter]

Anyhow, after the ship got under way, we went up to Aparri, up at the north end of Luzon, to show the flag. Then we came back to Manila, where I made lots of liberties. I liked Manila. There were a lot of interesting things there. The old-timers said it couldn't compare with Shanghai; Shanghai was the queen of liberty ports.

About two blocks in from the landing at Manila was Legaspi Gardens. It was a great big building, air-conditioned, had real cold beer, a big jukebox, lots of tables and chairs, and lots of Filipina waitresses. A lot of sailors never got any farther. [Laughter] My brother Frost tells me that when he was out there, Legaspi Gardens was on a pier, adjacent to the landing. He said a lot of Marines never got any farther inland than Legaspi Gardens. [Laughter]

Paul Stillwell: What did some of these old-timers have to say about Shanghai? What were the attractions there?

Commander Harralson: Oh, everything: girls, cabarets, horse racing, jai alai, moving pictures, real nice theaters, real nice restaurants, a lot of action. It was truly an international city.

---
*Commander James M. Fernald, USN.

I think it was around January--that would be 1940--the ship got under way, headed for the southern islands, to show the flag. We went down to Iloilo, Zamboanga, Jolo.

Now Jolo's quite a place--Moros. The word was that they liked American sailors, but they became aggressive very easily and that we should be very careful in our behavior. We went ashore there. There was a policeman on every corner. They all carried sawed-off shotguns. All the Moros had black teeth from chewing betel nut. We were stopped by a Roman Catholic priest in a white frock and a hat. He was looking for somebody from Massachusetts. The poor guy was so homesick it was pitiful. We tried to think of somebody from Massachusetts.

Hooper and I walked quite a ways out of town and sat down. A Moro came by with a great big stalk of bananas, and we wanted to buy some from him. We kept pointing to a hand towards the center of the bunch; we were arguing about it when he finally he agreed for something like 20 centavos. Then he cut the whole bunch where we were pointing! We gave it back to him; we didn't want all those bananas. We just wanted a hand, about six or eight.

Commander Harralson: We were there for the winter months. The standard procedure, come early spring, was to head north for the China coast, pull into Shanghai, and stay there quite a while. Then, when the weather got too sticky and hot, they'd move up to Tsingtao. Tsingtao was, oh, about 300 or 400 miles north. It was on a peninsula that dropped down. They had a beautiful inner harbor there.

But there was an event of note that occurred. We left Jolo for Tawitawi. That island was incredible with its white beach. Did you ever see such intense blue as the south seas?

Paul Stillwell: I have not been there.

Commander Harralson: The only thing I can think of is the washing water, when my mother put blueing in it. It's just unbelievable--the sand white, and, of course, the palm trees and the foliage under them, all those different shades of green. We didn't get to go ashore there.

Then we headed north, for Palawan. We entered a cut that separated a small island from the big island--pulled in there. We passed a little island, right in the middle of the channel--a sandy island that had trees and foliage on it--and then anchored. There was no liberty there, either, but they ran a swimming party, back to this little island. Hooper and I went on the swimming party. It had a beautiful beach and about six feet of water. The water was clear, and we saw coral and little tropical fish. So we spent our time out there chasing the fish and bringing up pieces of coral. Every once in a while, we'd go back to the beach and stretch out to rest.

We came back one time, and we saw some guys playing baseball. They had a bat that looked like a human leg bone. Well, we didn't know about that. [Laughter] Then, about the next time we came back for a rest, they were playing football. And guess what the football was.

Paul Stillwell: A skull.

Commander Harralson: Exactly. Well, we returned to the ship, and the captain found out about it.* He was furious. He sent the two ensigns that were in charge of the swimming party and the football players back to straighten things out, undo the mess they made. Now, I don't know what kind of mess it was, and I didn't want to know. But the island turned out to be a burial site. Over on the main beach was a leper colony.

Well, the next morning, I had just eaten breakfast, and there were several of us down in the compartment. It must have been 7:00 or 7:30--something like that. The ship shuddered and shook, and the deck bounced. Boy, we hit something! We went tearing up to quarters, and we were halfway there when they sounded quarters. We got up there, and we could see the bridge. There was the old captain--leaning out, looking backward and forward, and giving helm and engine orders in a steady flow. We had hit a coral pinnacle. He worked us off of it and got us over to one side and anchored. They sent a diver down to assess the damage. One of the props was bent, and there was a hunk out of it. Also, the rudder had a bad tear in it.

---

*The commanding officer of the Augusta was Captain John H. Magruder, Jr., USN.

I think Puerto Princesa, on Palawan, was the name of the town where this happened. So we got under way again, doing five knots. It was announced over the speakers that we were headed for the Dewey floating dry dock moored in Subic Bay. And I'm telling you, five knots in a man-of-war was very boring. [Laughter] The guys that were involved in that football game got a lot of bad talk; it was held against them. They brought the bad luck on us. Of course, the bad luck was that our trip to Shanghai, our move north, was going to be delayed six weeks. There were threats of violence.

Paul Stillwell: What could people do at that point, though? The damage was already done.

Commander Harralson: Yes, but they shouldn't have done it!

Paul Stillwell: Well, that's true. But what good would a threat do after the fact?

Commander Harralson: They said they were going to punch them in the nose. That would make the punchers feel better.

Paul Stillwell: Who was the captain?

Commander Harralson: Magruder. We called him "Rocks" after that--Rocks Magruder. Now, I don't know how widespread that was, but that's what all of us in flag radio called him. I knew very little about him. Also, all I knew about Hart was he was a little guy; he wasn't very big.[*]

Paul Stillwell: Was Admiral Yarnell already gone by the time you arrived?[†]

---

[*] Admiral Thomas C. Hart, USN, served as Commander in Chief U.S. Asiatic Fleet from 25 July 1939 to 4 February 1942. James R. Leutze's biography of Hart is A Different Kind of Victory (Annapolis: Naval Institute Press, 1981).
[†] Admiral Harry E. Yarnell, USN, served as Commander in Chief U.S. Asiatic Fleet from 30 October 1936 to 25 July 1939.

Commander Harralson: Yes, he had gone. He had a real reputation out there. We had radiomen who had been out there for 10, 12, 14 years. They knew all about Yarnell.

Paul Stillwell: What did they say about him?

Commander Harralson: Well, I tell you, I was going to bring it up when we got up to Tsingtao. At Shanghai, we never had any trouble with the Japanese, because we stayed in the International Settlement and the Japanese everywhere else. Shanghai was occupied by Japanese by 1937, except the International Settlement. But when we got up to Tsingtao, that wasn't the case. There were two old Japanese ships there, the Iwate and the Izumo.*

I think their main job was to trail us. They weren't very fast; they weren't near as fast as we were, but somehow one or the other always seemed to be around. They went out with us when we went for battle practice. They fouled the range one time, if I remember right. But, anyhow, they were there. And, of course, there was a lot of Army there. The Japanese sailors on these two old ships used to row ashore in longboats. They ran around town together, in one big group, like Japanese tourists.

Oh, there were a lot of incidents there. For instance, I got out of a rickshaw one day and got caught up in one of these big groups. They kind of mauled me around for a while before I got through.

Paul Stillwell: Was this in Tsingtao?

Commander Harralson: Yes. I'm getting ahead of my story. I was going to tell you about Olongapo. We pulled into Subic Bay. Dewey, the old floating dry dock, was there, all ready for us. The Augusta went right in, and they hoisted us up in the air. We could see the propeller was pretty badly damaged, and also the rudder. I remember seeing that the void in the rudder was filled with wood. I was surprised at that. I didn't know they did that. Did you?

---

*These were armored cruisers, armed with 8-inch and 6-inch guns, built for the Japanese at a British shipyard. The Izumo was completed in 1900 and the Iwate in 1901. Both served in the Japanese battle fleet in the Russo-Japanese War.

Paul Stillwell: I'm surprised to hear that also. No, I didn't.

Commander Harralson: They shut all our heads, so we had to use the ones on Dewey, and they were very, very primitive. Olongapo was about the end of the road. I mean, there was hardly anything there. There was a radio station, NPT, and that was about all. There was nothing there in the way of amusement recreation. The little barrio of Olongapo--I'm telling you this because the naval base at Subic Bay was quite different when it was turned back to the Philippine Government.*

Olongapo, the barrio, was up the beach a way. The streets were unpaved, dry and dusty, and there wasn't much there. There was a pool hall. You had to be careful around the Filipino pool players; they were very good, and there were hustlers among them.

Paul Stillwell: Well, in the Vietnam War, Olongapo City was really a raunchy entertainment center for Seventh Fleet sailors.

Commander Harralson: Yes, I have heard that. There was a swimming place, farther up the beach, that had a shark net around it. We went there, went swimming once. But the shark net was full of big holes, great big, gaping holes. Subic Bay is noted for its shark population.

Paul Stillwell: I did not know that, either.

Commander Harralson: Yes. Oh, they have some enormous sharks out there. So, it looked pretty bleak. But then we discovered the Golden Gate. The Golden Gate was a honky-tonk. You'd ride a calesa east, about a half an hour, and you came to a big, low building that was all open on the sides. It had these wooden floors that were black wood and had a natural polish to them. There were tables and chairs, beer, a great big Wurlitzer

---

*Because of the Philippine Government's unwillingness to extend basing rights, the U.S. Air Force vacated Clark Air Force Base in November 1991, and the U.S. Navy left Subic Bay in the autumn of 1992. At that time the U.S. base at Subic was quite extensive, including facilities for aircraft carriers, supply center, ship repair facility, and recreational outlets.

jukebox, and lots of Filipina girls. We spent a lot of time out there. It was pleasant. We had a lot of fun.

Over on the back side, tied up to the pier, was the old Rochester.

Paul Stillwell: Spanish-American War veteran.

Commander Harralson: Yes. Some said it was a member of the Great White Fleet, but it wasn't, according to your Naval Institute book I've been reading.* It was commissioned in 1893 as the USS New York. At that time, it was the biggest ship in the Navy. That's from your book. It became a very popular ship with the public. It must have arrived in the Asiatics very early in its career, because your book shows--this is that old Steel Navy book--that's a tremendous book.

Paul Stillwell: Oh, it certainly is. I love that book.

Commander Harralson: Yes. Well, they have a picture of it in a dry dock at Yokosuka, Japan, in 1902. And along the line, it became the Saratoga, and then the Rochester. It must have been out there quite a while.

Paul Stillwell: She'd been down in the Caribbean for a while, as the flagship for the Special Service Squadron.

Commander Harralson: Oh. I think they called it an administrative flagship, towards the end. But, anyhow, it was real interesting, a real relic. And I'll tell you a story that I heard from one of the radiomen that was at Cavite.

He and another radioman went aboard one day and saw a whole bunch of brass fittings. Well, the Chinese just love to get their hands on brass and make all kinds of things out of it. So the radiomen figured if they could get it to Shanghai, they could make a lot of money from it. So they were on a submarine. So with a lot of careful planning and skullduggery and everything, they got a whole bunch of brass parts off of it and onto the

---

*John D. Alden, American Steel Navy (Annapolis: Naval Institute Press, 1972).

submarine. Eventually, when they got to Shanghai, on a real quiet afternoon, they were able to sell it to the Chinese on one of the sampans alongside. They were counting their money when the word was passed for them to report to the captain's cabin. They reported and the captain said, "All right, turn it over here. It goes into the rec fund." [Laughter] I think it's a true story, told by a man that was party to it.

Paul Stillwell: Did you get aboard the Rochester yourself?

Commander Harralson: No, I didn't. It looked pretty risky business, to get on it at the time; there wasn't any ladder or ramp.

Paul Stillwell: I think she was eventually sunk out there, wasn't she?

Commander Harralson: Yes. She was decommissioned in 1933. In 1938 she was stricken from the Navy list. After the war started, they took her out into Subic Bay and sank her, before she could be taken.

Now, somewheres in my papers, I have an article by a guy in Rochester, New York, telling about the Rochester. What he had to say checked fairly well with what I knew or thought I knew. But towards the end he talks about the Marines. When they came down from Shanghai, some of the Marines went to Olongapo--this was after the war started--and they put machine guns up in the upper part of the ship--I guess in the mast, as high as they could--and did battle with the Japanese bombers. I don't know if that is true.

Paul Stillwell: I had not heard that either.

Commander Harralson: Anyhow, it was sunk. Now, the Dewey dry dock was built in 1902 and built specifically for the Asiatic Fleet. I think they didn't get it out there until 1906. Until they had it out there, why, ships had to go to the mainland of China or Japan for dry docking. I think it was a terrific feat to get that dry dock out there at that time.

Oh, I found out something else interesting about the Rochester. It was involved in the first test of radio, with the USS Massachusetts. The Rochester at that time was still named New York. It and the Massachusetts and a New Jersey lighthouse conducted radio communications in 1899.

In the book, Steel Navy, it says that the Navy used radio to rendezvous; when they came down from Japan, part of the fleet went to Manila and part went over to China--I guess Hong Kong. They stayed there, but their rendezvous, to proceed on farther, was made timely by radio. So that's something a radioman would be interested in.[*]

Anyway, we got the propeller fixed.

Paul Stillwell: How long did that stay in dry dock take?

Commander Harralson: It was less than six weeks, I believe. They had some pretty good crews there. They had some men from the Canopus.[†] In fact, I ran into one here, several years back, that was involved in that repair. I believe they repaired it on the shaft; the same with the rudder. They didn't have a replacement propeller. I think it was, for that time, high-tech stuff, real skilled work, that they were able to do.

But we got out of there, and about a week later we headed north. One morning I had the watch when we were somewheres off the China coast. The supervisor told me, "Hey, Speed, get the Zakaway weather." I didn't like to ask questions, so I said, "Roger." I found a spare receiver and it had ZAK-WX weather on a little chart, where they listed station settings. I started tuning back and forth at the frequency listed, about three minutes ahead. At 10:00 here came a signal. It was the awfulest gibberish I ever heard, just absolutely ridiculous. I ended up with a blank paper. I give it to the chief, and he give me a blast and said I was in for trouble and not to go anywhere near Krantz, the aerographer. I'd missed their weather, so I was in the doghouse for about two days on that.

Finally, a friend called me over and said, "Okay, you've had enough. You're initiated. You're now a genuine Asiatic radioman."

Paul Stillwell: So this was a trick they played on everybody?

---

[*] For details on this test, see L. S. Howeth, History of Communications-Electronics in the United States Navy (Washington, D.C.: U.S. Government Printing Office, 1963), pages 28-33.
[†] USS Canopus (AS-9) was a submarine tender stationed in the Philippines to support Asiatic Fleet submarines.

Commander Harralson: Yes! The signal came from a station operated by Jesuit priests somewheres in China. It was just terrible stuff. They said you had to be out there ten years before you could copy it. But I didn't believe that; it was supposed to be a numbered weather code. So what's to prevent one of those old guys from sitting there and typing up a row of groups of five-digit numbers, in cahoots with Krantz, and saying that they copied it? That was my conclusion.

Paul Stillwell: Did you ever had any contact with Commander Fernald?

Commander Harralson: Well, we have to discuss contact. [Laughter] I saw an awful lot of Fernald--Jimmy, when he wasn't around. He spent all of his time in the radio room. Now, that was very unusual, because communications officers usually don't fool around in the radio room. But every morning at 8:00 o'clock he was up there. And he spent the whole morning walking around behind you, looking at the positions. At 1130, he would go below. Then at 1300, back he was. He would stay there until 1600 and go below. The good thing about it was that he could be depended upon. So that when he left and wasn't around, the whole place just relaxed. They broke out the coffee and cigarettes and pipes. [Laughter]

Paul Stillwell: He was predictable.

Commander Harralson: Yes, very predictable. He wore a pince-nez glass. He was a big man. We understood that he was a Harvard graduate and a 90-day wonder from World War I. Does that jibe?

Paul Stillwell: I don't know.

Commander Harralson: Oh, there were a lot of wild stories about him. He was an imposing person.

Paul Stillwell: Was it just because he wanted to know what was going on, or he didn't trust the radiomen? Why so much time there?

Commander Harralson: I think he just wanted to know exactly what was going on. If a radioman did something that he didn't like, he'd call the supervisor over. The only person he'd talk to was the supervisor. He'd point to the offender and say, "Relieve that man." And the guy got relieved.

One day, probably in the spring of 1940, I was copying press, WSX stateside. We were really moving along. Like I was telling you before, signals would begin to fade. It could happen real fast. Well, I was copying a story about one of our destroyers in the Atlantic. I was getting the copy, but I began to drop a word here and there. Jimmy was standing right behind me, and when he saw me lose a word, he called the supervisor over. Radiomen had a way, when they wanted to change. The other man took the phones, and he slid in real quick beside you. Well, that's what happened; the supervisor took it over. He took over and stopped--he never got another word. It's not that I was a good operator and he was not as good; it's simply that the signal just faded then.

Paul Stillwell: So you must have felt pretty good--to yourself, quietly, inwardly.

Commander Harralson: Yes, very inwardly. [Laughter] Because those old guys, like the supervisors, were tremendous. They could copy stuff you couldn't hear. That's why everybody predicted that radio teletype didn't have a chance; the first crash of static, you'd lose it, which wasn't true.

Paul Stillwell: What made them so good?

Commander Harralson: They'd done it so long; when you sat there hour after hour, you became a good operator.

There's another story. We were in Shanghai, moored in the middle of a river. A second class came aboard, and he had three hashmarks. His undress blues were all worn and frayed. He had the radiomen's pallor and maybe just a little gray hair. [Laughter] He was carrying a speed key in a little leatherette case, and he had his own coffee cup. So the supervisor put him on one of the fast circuits. We had some fast ones too. By that I mean there was a lot of traffic, and you had to be fast.

The new radioman got himself all set. He pulled out his speed key and plugged it in with the regular key there. He set his coffee cup aside, moved paper here and there. Then a station opened up with a message. On the fast circuits, they just gave your call sign, and away they went, full blast, on the message. They didn't wait to see if you were listening or not. Well, when he was fooling around adjusting things and wasn't alert, somebody threw a paper clip behind the platen roll on his typewriter. Now, that's an old, dirty trick that radiomen know.

He listened to the message coming in. You had to wait and listen, because there were two kinds of blanks you used, action or info. You couldn't tell which until they were well into the heading. So he sat there and listened, and he decided it took a blank for an action message. He reached over and tried to put in the blank. In the meantime, this message is rattling on. Being an old radioman, he knew what the problem was. So he got another paper clip, straightened it out, put a hook on the end and went fishing. He got the paper clip out okay, but about that time came the end of the message.

So he reached over to the speed key and gave the sending station a roger. Then he typed the message up!

Paul Stillwell: From memory.

Commander Harralson: Yes. That's the ultimate in copying behind.

Paul Stillwell: That is impressive.

Commander Harralson: Jimmy was behind him. Jimmy said, "Relieve that man." He was relieved, and we never saw him again.

Paul Stillwell: Why did he get rid of him?

Commander Harralson: One of the worst offenses a radioman could commit was to take a flyer. That means that if you weren't quite sure of a word or a piece, you winged it. [Laughter] That was strictly a no-no. I think Jimmy was afraid that this guy wasn't that good, that he might have been guessing. He didn't want any of that, and he wasn't going to have it. But the guy was good. It's hard for people that weren't involved in that kind of radio to really appreciate how good some of those guys were.

Paul Stillwell: That's why I'm so grateful to you for telling me. So he was kind of showing off there, but it cost him.

Commander Harralson: I don't even think he was showing off, because that really wasn't such a big deal. There were a lot of men who could do that.

Paul Stillwell: So he was just that competent?

Commander Harralson: Yes. He was just that competent. When you're sending on a fast circuit, you service it as you send it. In other words, you make a cross and put in date, the time, signature or initials, and the frequency sometimes. But it was such a service notation that showed that you had sent it. Well, they could do it with their left hand. Here the operator was batting along at 30 to 35 words per minute, which was moving if you're sending manually with a speed key, and over here on the left he was doing all of this servicing and sorting messages. All the time, he was roaring along. [Laughter]

Paul Stillwell: That's much more difficult than walking and chewing gum at the same time. [Laughter] Your mind has to be in two different areas simultaneously.

Commander Harralson: It does. See now, that's really the kind of radioman that I was aspiring to be, one of these real hotshot operators.

Paul Stillwell: How good were you?

Commander Harralson: I was getting there. I clocked at 55 words a minute at Cavite. I could copy a word behind, in plain language; two words sometimes; and maybe a code group, a five-letter code group behind. But every time I felt a little cocky, I'd sit on a circuit and get snowed. [Laughter]

Paul Stillwell: Well, you told me about your contact with Commander Fernald. What about with Captain Magruder?

Commander Harralson: No contact whatsoever. I think of him leaning out of the bridge up there, and that was about the only time I can remember seeing him.

Paul Stillwell: What about Admiral Hart? Any observations on him?

Commander Harralson: Nope. See, what I told you before--we'd steer clear of officers. The only memory I have of Admiral Hart is seeing him go ashore, or come back, sometimes.

I remember they had a big dance aft, on the fantail, under Chief Zeramby.* He had an orchestra at night. In the daytime, he had a band. They had a big affair with Japanese lanterns, and I remember watching that one time.

We just didn't have contact with officers. Well, one time in Manila, Lauer and I were getting ready to go ashore. We had a motor generator to take over to Canacao. Let me give you a little on the geography there. Cavite shipyard and the barrio of Cavite shared a small island connected to the main island by a bridge perhaps 200 feet long. The land on the main island side is Canacao, which extends out in a peninsula about a mile north of the Cavite Island.

The hospital was located on Canacao, along with Radio Cavite's transmitters, including a big 300-kilowatt, low-frequency job. Its antenna was a high tower. The radio equipment and personnel were located about the center of a large park-like area with large coconut palms. Extending east from there was a long sandy spit that formed the north side

---
*Bandmaster Sidney M. Zeramby, USN.

of Bacoor Bay, where the China Clipper landed. The south side of the bay was Cavite, and out on Sangley Point, near the end of this Canacao peninsula was PatWing 10's base.

So we were detailed to take this motor generator, which wasn't too big, and then we were free for the rest of the day. So we got a launch to take us over there. It was alongside, and this officer, a lieutenant, came up and said he had a carved chest he had bought and wanted to take over to his place, which was right next to Canacao. He wanted to know if we would do it for him. Of course, we were glad to.

We loaded it in the boat. He went along. When we got to Cavite, he was able to borrow a truck. We put it in the truck and then drove over. I don't quite understand, but his wife was there, even though all the dependents were supposed to have gone back to the States by then. But, anyhow, she was there. He gave us a real cold beer. I remember sitting in there and drinking out of a pewter mug. Then we delivered our motor generator to Canacao, and that was an experience.

We were invited to lunch. They had a nice mess hall. Canacao was a beautiful place with a big grassy stretch under coconut palms. Their quarters were there, the radiomen that ran high power. They had Filipino mess attendants--they weren't Navy, they were Filipinos--serving and doing mess duties. If you wanted the butter, all you had to do was look at the butter and the attendants would give you the butter. Good food, cold drinks. I thought, "Man, how do you get to Canacao?"

Paul Stillwell: Well, let's wind up with that thought for tonight, please, because we're right near the end of the tape.

Interview Number 2 with Lieutenant Commander Richard A. Harralson, U.S. Navy (Retired)

Place: Commander Harralson's home in Shingle Springs, California

Date: Friday, 16 May 1997

Interviewer: Paul Stillwell

Paul Stillwell: Well, please proceed. When we stopped off last night, you had us Shanghai-bound. So take the story from there.

Commander Harralson: Yes, there was a lot of excitement in the ship. It seemed like the high point of any Asiatic tour was our stay in Shanghai. The ship would go up there every year, in the spring. It was a great experience. The ship, I guess, adjusted speed during the night so we arrived at the Yangtze estuary in the early morning. The traffic was very heavy: a lot of Chinese junks, lug-rigged with split bamboo sails. Every one of them, large and small, had large eyeballs on the bow. It was very important, so that the ship could see where it was going.

We went up the estuary a ways. It was very wide and quite shallow in some spots. Then we made a left turn and entered the mouth of the Whangpoo. Greater Shanghai extends almost to the mouth of the river, but we were headed for the International Settlement that was about 15 miles upriver.

We arrived opposite the International Settlement and turned the ship around. The river's quite wide, and it was a tricky maneuver, it seemed to me, but they got it around, and they moored to buoys, fore and aft. They had the bow headed downstream, towards the open sea; I believe for practical purposes, because the war in Europe had started, and some big things were happening.*

Lauer and I wasted no time in going ashore at the first opportunity. They put us ashore on the Bund, they called it, a street that ran along the riverside. Then going inward

---

*World War II began on 1 September 1939, when German ground forces invaded Poland. Two days later Great Britain and France declared war on Germany.

from the Bund, the main street in the British concession of the international part was Bubbling Well Avenue. And it was along this street that the major activities took place.

The exchange rate there was 17 to 1, which doesn't mean anything until you start buying things and find out what you can get for it. One of the first things we did was eat a meal in the Chocolate Shop, a very, very nice British restaurant. We had linen on the table, nice silverware, excellent service. We shared a plank steak, and the whole bill came to 12 yuan. And 12 yuan, at that time, figured out at about 75 cents. So that gave you a clue as to how far your money went.

There were a lot of nice movie theaters in Shanghai. They had a racetrack, and they had a jai alai place.

Paul Stillwell: Fronton, they called it.

Commander Harralson: Fronton--that's the word I was looking for. I could never get too excited about it. There were lots of cabarets.

While we were there, I saw signs advertising John Steinbeck's Grapes of Wrath. I'd read the book; he was my favorite author in those days, and I wanted to see the movie very badly. I made plans so that I could. When the time came, I went ashore to see it. I arrived at the theater, and it wasn't showing. There wasn't a sign of The Grapes of Wrath anywhere, not on marquees. We came to find out, it had been withdrawn at the urging of the American element there, because it painted the United States in a rather negative way. We saw it two or three weeks later, when it was shown aboard ship. So it worked out all right.

On another occasion, they had a special showing of Gone With the Wind one Sunday morning, strictly for Navy personnel.

Paul Stillwell: Where was it held?

Commander Harralson: One of the movie theaters in Shanghai. Hooper and I arrived there a little bit worse for wear. We had been out the night before and had a few bar stains on our whites. When we got there, the lobby was full of brass--gold. [Laughter] So we hid in the washroom until the movie started and then went in. [Laughter] When intermission came, why, we scrunched down in our seats and stayed where we were. But we did see the movie.

Paul Stillwell: I'm guessing that you had not gone back to the ship during the night.

Commander Harralson: That's correct. [Laughter]

Paul Stillwell: Because they wouldn't have let you off again, looking like that.

Commander Harralson: No, they wouldn't. And, of course, I was young and full of oats. The cabarets were full of girls, taxi dancers. They had live bands at most of the cabarets. Some of them were very good. But the girls all sat around the dance floor in chairs--the Chinese girls on one side and the White Russian girls on the other. In between, completing the circle, would be Europeans, Eurasians, and that sort of thing.

Paul Stillwell: So they sort of segregated themselves.

Commander Harralson: That's right. The reason there were so many girls around was that--well, first of all, the White Russians were refugees from Communist, Red Russia, that came in through Harbin. They had been there for some time. And then, of course, there were a lot of European civilians in Shanghai, refugees from Europe at war. And, of course, the Chinese. Times were hard for these people. The younger women took to earning money in the dance halls. There were some very nice young women. In fact, some of the sailors married Russian girls.

What you would do was go in and get a table. Then you'd survey these girls. You'd pick out one you thought looked good, and you'd go over and invite her to dance. Then if you liked what you had there, why, you'd invite her to your table. You would buy her drinks, house drinks. We used to bring our own bottle, that we bought at the Marine club, and then just order Coca-Cola and ice. But we had to buy champagne cocktails for the girls.

Then when you broke up, we'd go up to the little ticket counter there and buy them two or three yards of tickets and drape them around their necks. Tickets were very cheap for American sailors.

Paul Stillwell: Did you run into any of the rickshaw boys?

Commander Harralson: Oh, we rode rickshaws all over the place and thought nothing of it. I used to wonder, sometimes, "There's another human being down there pulling this thing and pulling me." But that was the state of affairs, and I didn't worry about it.

Paul Stillwell: And they were doing it willingly, to get a little income.

Commander Harralson: Absolutely, absolutely. I had to marvel at them. They would have made excellent subjects for an anatomy class; there was no fat at all on them, and they had big calf muscles.

Shanghai didn't have a sewer system. All the big hotels--all the places, for that matter--the sewage went into a tank somewhere that had a door in it. In early morning, the Chinese would go around with carts that carried big wooden buckets or tanks on them. They'd pull up to these sumps, or whatever you want to call them, and with buckets on long poles, dip it into the big wooden tubs on the carts. Then they'd take the cart down to the river and dump it on a barge. When the barge had received its morning deposits, it would be towed upriver to spread the stuff in the farms as fertilizer.

Paul Stillwell: I think they called that night soil.

Commander Harralson: Yes, that's one name.

Paul Stillwell: Do you know some others? [Laughter]

Commander Harralson: Well, I was thinking about where we were moored and where this barge was kept, and the time that they took it upriver, brought the barge right by the ship about noontime, when we were eating. It was called the honey barge.

Paul Stillwell: You didn't need that odor to accompany your meal.

Commander Harralson: And, of course, as the weather got warmer and warmer, why, the stink was worse. The river was full of little sampans that were poled from behind. They had a peculiar way of moving a boat. They had a sweep, I guess you would call it, at the stern. The opposite end was tethered to the deck of the boat. Then the oarsmen stood alongside and moved it sideways, back and forth. But the rope holding the end down was pulled a certain way that feathered this big oar. They propelled tiny sampans and huge barges that way.

The huge barges had sweeps on them that had maybe six or eight men working the end. One man had the job of feathering. He would grab it in the middle of the rope and throw himself backwards, putting a bend in so that it created the proper feather. They used to propel these huge barges upriver that way. If the wind was right, they would hoist their split-bamboo sails. They scared a lot of OODs, I'm sure, because they tacked a lot. They'd go back and forth. There were always these little sampans on the river.

Men in the small sampans dredged the bottom of the river all the time. They pulled up a small dredge that would have a lot of coal and clinkers, odds and ends. And they'd pick each little piece of coal out. The Augusta used to dump the garbage down a chute at the stern, and there was always a great, big cluster of sampans there, to get this garbage.

Paul Stillwell: What did they do with it? Do you have any idea?

Commander Harralson: They took it home and ate it. I remember one time one of our bakers came out. He had a bunch of bread, stale bread. He thought rather than dumping it in the river, he would give it to them. So he tossed it to them in the boat. They took the bread, dumped it in the river, and then put it back in the sampan.

Paul Stillwell: Why?

Commander Harralson: It's your guess. I don't know. [Laughter]

I think we went out for exercise training once or twice that first stay in Shanghai. But all told, I think we were there two or three months in the spring of 1940. Then, when it got too hot and sticky there, why, we went up to Tsingtao, which had a lovely climate. It was on a peninsula with the Yellow Sea to the east and the inner harbor on the west. They had a beautiful harbor there. And, of course, at Tsingtao there was a colony of Germans that had been there, I think, since before World War I.

Paul Stillwell: Well, several of the major powers had set up their establishments in China.

Commander Harralson: Right. In fact, the International Settlement goes way back. The British started it in 1845, along in there. The French started a concession in 1860. And we had a concession there, back about 1850, or somewheres along in there. But we amalgamated--that's a word that I rarely use--amalgamated with the British to make the International Settlement. The French, of course, in true French fashion, didn't want to join. But they were considered part of the settlement. We knew a lot about the French side. They had a beautiful avenue there, Avenue Joffre, named for a World War I French general. It had real nice bars. One particular place was my special haunt.

Paul Stillwell: What was that called?

Commander Harralson: The Green Hall Bar. It had nothing to do with the Frenchmen there. The owner's nickname was Mikeski, and he wanted you to think he was a Russian, but he wasn't; he was a chief petty officer in the Navy Reserve. He had married a Russian named Nadia. He ran a nice bar. He was the principal bartender. If he liked you, he'd let you eat in his little three-booth restaurant in the rear. His wife was the cook. He served some of the best borscht, with a dollop of sour cream, and then a big steak accented with Russian pickles. That steak and those pickles made a good meal.

Paul Stillwell: Well, what made the difference in whether he liked you or not?

Commander Harralson: Oh, just personalities, you know; if you weren't a troublemaker. We all drank a lot. That was part of what we did when we went ashore, a big part of it.

Paul Stillwell: Mostly beer, or did you get into the hard stuff too?

Commander Harralson: Oh, the hard stuff, beer. I drank a lot of beer. I like beer. I tried not to let myself get too bad. I think one reason I stayed out of trouble was when I was feeling whatever I was drinking, I never got mean or surly; I became very friendly. I never got into trouble through drinking, but there were others who did.

Paul Stillwell: Did you typically go ashore with a buddy in that situation?

Commander Harralson: Yes, yes. I had Lauer and Hooper, the ones that I met on the Henderson. Mudge didn't go ashore much. Like I said, he was a married man. It was either Hooper or Lauer, sometimes others. We never planned ahead or anything. We happened to hit it, we went together.

Paul Stillwell: Was that drinking just part of the culture? Was that something you were expected to do?

Commander Harralson: Actually, yes. There was one case--I don't know whether it was indicative or not--of a young sailor that never went ashore and never went on a bust or a tear. It ended up, he killed himself up in the little direction finder house. Guys went up there and found that he had cut himself at the wrists, I guess, and bled to death. The place was full of blood.

Paul Stillwell: Would this be because he just didn't have any friends, maybe?

Commander Harralson: Yes, I think he never had any relief from the ship. You know, you have to let your hair down once in a while.

Paul Stillwell: But he wasn't being prevented from going ashore?

Commander Harralson: No, no, no. He probably had an instilled sense of morality that said he shouldn't go drink or that sort of stuff. I don't mean to say that that's all I ever did was go ashore and drink. But I did go on binges. We did a lot of sightseeing and went to a lot of movies. Actually, I enjoyed the cabarets. I tried to hold the drinking down. I liked to dance. I wasn't very good, but after a couple of drinks, you think you're pretty good. [Laughter]

But, you know, there's a kind of point you reach that's very, very difficult to maintain; you can't stay at that point. A good example was when I was on a bowling team. This was back at Great Lakes.* We had a bowling team and we were in competition. We'd go there and have a beer with the first frame. I'd roll a mediocre score. Then into my second beer, I'd loosened up. Then I could roll a 200 sometimes.

Paul Stillwell: That's interesting.

Commander Harralson: Boy, I would put them in there, but I couldn't stay there.

Paul Stillwell: Then you'd start to come back down again.

Commander Harralson: Yes. Then you went back down. So what you would have was a fairly decent score, a real good score, and a lousy score. [Laughter]

Paul Stillwell: Well, maybe the explanation for that middle, good score was that you had just enough confidence at that point.

Commander Harralson: Right.

---

*This was a tour of duty following World War II at the naval training center at Great Lakes, Illinois.

Paul Stillwell: How much interaction did you have with the Japanese there in Shanghai?

Commander Harralson: The only interaction in Shanghai was when a Japanese ship went by, and we'd exchange honors. We'd stand there and salute and glare at each other. Sometimes we were real close. But Tsingtao was different.

Paul Stillwell: What was it like in Tsingtao?

Commander Harralson: Well, they had these two ships I mentioned, the Izumo and the Iwate, so there were lots of sailors that traveled around in a big bunch. There were a lot of army men too. A lot of incidents occurred. They had an enlisted men's club over on the Yellow Sea side of town. Hooper and I found out you could go there and rent a locker, and you could go out wearing athletic gear. A sweatshirt and canvas shoes was considered athletic wear, and, of course, your white pants. We'd go over there and change clothes and check out a couple tennis rackets. Neither one of us knew how to play tennis.

We'd head out to the edge of town and end up in a little bar somewhere, drinking. There was a park out there that had a dilapidated tennis court. Once in a while, we'd go over there and bat tennis balls. The minute we got over there, here'd be a crowd of Chinese boys to shag balls for us. They kept trying to tell us we weren't playing the game right. [Laughter]

Paul Stillwell: Which you knew already. [Laughter]

Commander Harralson: Yes. But over on the opposite side of this park, many times there would be what I would estimate as a company of Japanese soldiers. They'd be going through bayonet practice, screaming and hollering. After one of these tennis games one time we got back to the enlisted man's club, and we were met by a shore patrol chief. He said, "You're now members of the shore patrol." He had issued all of his brassards and billy clubs, so he gave us each an empty beer bottle. [Laughter] He said, "Go up to Shantung Boulevard and assist the shore patrol there, as needed."

So we climbed back in our rickshaws and headed out. We got up to Shantung Boulevard, but the action was all over. We learned that the trouble had started in a barber shop. A Japanese sailor and an American sailor got into a fracas, and a shore patrol officer arrived on the scene. There was a lot of pushing and shoving, and the officer got his shoulder board torn off. It just grew from there and worked itself out in the street. There was quite a melee there for a while. Then, just all of a sudden, it just died.

Paul Stillwell: But that sounds more like just a typical barroom brawl, as opposed to international hostilities.

Commander Harralson: Oh, sure. Now, this is hearsay, but there was an effect on us; something happened. The story was that there were two sailors in a jewelry shop, and there was a Japanese officer in there too. I don't know the initial occurrence, but it grew--they took the sword away from the Japanese officer and broke it. That was the case where Admiral Hart restricted the fleet that was in Tsingtao for two weeks. That was kind of touchy. But there was a lot of grousing going on, because--as the old-timers said--"Old Yarnell wouldn't have done that."

Paul Stillwell: Interesting.

Commander Harralson: Yes. There was another case of a guy on the beach with a girlfriend. A Japanese sailor or soldier kept running by. All he had was sort of a thing like a G-string. It's a piece of cloth about eight inches wide and maybe two feet long. It's got a string across the top and you tie it around your waist, then reach down through your legs and pull the cloth up in front of you and up through the string. That constitutes underwear, I suppose, and it's kind of revealing.

Paul Stillwell: Yes. [Laughter]

Commander Harralson: The sailor didn't like it. The sailor beat the Jap up. Then, of course, there was that time when I got pummeled around, when I got caught in among some sailors.

Paul Stillwell: When was that? What was the occasion?

Commander Harralson: Well, I was riding in a rickshaw. I don't know what I was doing. I should have seen them; I didn't, though. But the rickshaw pulled up to the curb, and I got out and was facing the boy to pay him off. I turned around, and as I turned around, I stepped right in front of this group of Japanese sailors that was coming down the sidewalk. Because that's how they went around town. They rowed ashore in long boats and went around town together.

Paul Stillwell: How many in a group would you say?

Commander Harralson: Twenty. And they kept pushing and shoving me.

Paul Stillwell: That wasn't very good odds for you.

Commander Harralson: No. I eventually got out the other side. I was a little bit shaken up but not hurt.

Paul Stillwell: What was the role of the Augusta in going to these different ports?

Commander Harralson: As far as I know, to show the flag. But when you consider the size of the Asiatic Fleet and you think about the Japanese fleet, we were puny. [Laughter]

Paul Stillwell: Well, it was a misnomer to call ours a fleet.

Commander Harralson: Yes. The Augusta was the flagship, a heavy cruiser, 8-inch guns. The Marblehead was a light cruiser with 6-inch guns. They had a flotilla of destroyers,

World War I four-pipers, all in the 200 bunch.* The Paul Jones was the squadron leader. There were three divisions, 13 four-pipers all told.

Paul Stillwell: They had Stewart, the Parrott, and the John D. Edwards.

Commander Harralson: Then they had the S-boats, submarines. But I think they had a bunch of P-boats deployed out there, not too long before the war started.

Paul Stillwell: I think they were operating out of Cavite.

Commander Harralson: Yes, they were. There was a couple squadrons of PBYs, PatWing 10.† That's where my friend Lauer thought he was going, and he ended up on the Augusta. And, of course, they had a few tugs, and the Canopus and the Black Hawk. The Langley came out there; she used to be CV-1 but was now a seaplane tender.

Paul Stillwell: What do you remember about the discipline and protocol on board the Augusta?

Commander Harralson: With regards to what?

Paul Stillwell: Well, I mean, you've been in different ships, and some are more formal than others, and more shipshape, and emphasis on cleanliness.

Commander Harralson: Oh, well, the Augusta was the cleanest ship I was ever on. It was spotless. The crew was relatively small. We didn't feel crowded. Everybody wore tailor-mades and kept the regulation uniforms only for captain's inspection, which was every Saturday. When you have it every Saturday, you don't worry about it.

Paul Stillwell: You know what to expect.

---

*This means that all their hull numbers were between 200 and 299.
†PatWing 10--Patrol Wing Ten.

Commander Harralson: Right, right. They were held quickly; they weren't drawn out. And as soon as it was over, why, liberty call. We didn't mind it, except that we had to have all our different uniforms: dress blues, undress blues, dress whites, undress whites. They used to have dress whites that had a blue collar. That was done away with after a while.

Paul Stillwell: That was a sharp-looking uniform.

Commander Harralson: Yes, I liked it. We wore shorts. I hated them--shorts and our T-shirt was the working uniform of the day when it was warm.

Paul Stillwell: Why did you hate that?

Commander Harralson: Well, a radioman sits a lot, and you sweat a lot. Oh, I don't know; I just like long pants, just like I like long sleeves.

Paul Stillwell: What do you remember about one of those inspections?

Commander Harralson: I remember two officers getting into an argument about your gusset strings, which way it should be lashed up in the back of your 13-button blue pants. There gusset back there was laced up, allowing adjustment for waist sizes. The two officers argued whether the laces should be right to left or vice versa. Then they argued about our shoestrings one time.

Paul Stillwell: Well, the thing is, if you get a ship in really good appearance, then you just have to keep her that way.

Commander Harralson: That's right.

Paul Stillwell: It also helps if the crew takes great pride in that.

Commander Harralson: There was a lot of pride on the ship. It had a great spirit. When I think about the Navy and the kind of Navy I would like to be in, that's it. We had this Sid Zeramby; we called him Zambini. He was chief musician, and he was a born entertainer. He reminded me of Groucho Marx.* You know how Groucho walked kind of in a crouch?

Paul Stillwell: Yes.

Commander Harralson: Well, when he was going good out in front of his band, playing "The Monkeys Have No Tails in Zamboanga," Sid had a big cigar in his mouth. He used to hold concerts on the well deck every noon. I used to eat noon meal, climb up to the well deck, and enjoy the music as I smoked an Alhambra Corona cigar. They cost 20 centavos; that was 10 cents. All was right with the world.

Paul Stillwell: What a way to live.

Commander Harralson: I tell you, the world was rosy. I made second class. In Shanghai they let merchants come aboard at noontime. The master-at-arms would steer them back aft to the fantail, where they'd spread out with their wares.

Paul Stillwell: What were they selling?

Commander Harralson: All kinds of things: carved things, brass things, boxes. I went to one of the tailors and ordered two suits of dress blues. He measured me real carefully and said, "One week." One week later, he came aboard with them. They fit real good, and they were made of a material that would not pick up lint. They fit just right. When I went ashore wearing my new second class crow and my Russian boots, I felt on top of the world.

Paul Stillwell: Did you get the dragons embroidered inside your cuffs?

---

*Julius Henry "Groucho" Marx (1890-1977) was a member of the Marx brothers family of entertainers. Groucho, who had a long career in vaudeville, movies, and television, was noted for his cigar and bushy eyebrows and mustache.

Commander Harralson: No, I didn't. I had no tattoos, no dragons. But I had my idea of what a good sailor should look like.

Paul Stillwell: Did you have shipmates that you considered the Asiatic type?

Commander Harralson: I think we all were Asiatic. [Laughter]

Paul Stillwell: No, but I mean, some of them must have gone farther than you did.

Commander Harralson: Oh, absolutely. We had one guy who got the DTs, but that wasn't being Asiatic; that was showing he was an alcoholic. But yes, there were a lot of men aboard that had been out there practically their whole Navy time. A good friend of mine, Tony Lyons, was a first class and was one of the supervisors.[*] He married a Russian girl named Tina. When we were in Tsingtao, one day he said, "Why don't you come out this weekend?" His wife had come up from Shanghai to Tsingtao. He said they had a place and he told me how to get there.

    Well, I got out there, and it was a Russian enclave. They had bought this big old Victorian-type house. It had rooms built around two sides of the big lot. It looked like one of our early motels. Tony and Tina had one of the rooms. So I found them, and they invited me in. We sat around sipping vodka. Then it was time to eat. It was a community meal; they spread several long tables end to end out under a big tree. There were Russians all over the place. I think Tony and I were the only non-Russians.

    We sat down to the table, and it was very typical of what you see of Russians. In fact, it was sort of a stereotype. Here was a table loaded with meat and potatoes and vodka and pickles, and everybody was toasting everybody, and shouting and hollering. I was getting full of vodka. An old lady next to me kept trying to get me to drink tea with honey in it. No, I had to get out of there. [Laughter]

---

*Radioman First Class Anthony J. Lyons, USN.

Paul Stillwell: Well, you probably had a number of crew members, both in the flag allowance and the staff, who had been there for six or eight or ten years, maybe?

Commander Harralson: I think Tony had 14 years in the Navy at that time, and he bragged about being a sailor that had never seen a battleship. He had left the States and gone out there almost directly. Yes, a lot of them had been on river boats, you know, and different boats. I used to like to listen to the tales about the river gunboats. The Tutuila was based there in Shanghai at the time, and I think it was supposed to be the flagship then. The Isabel was the flagship there, for a while. The Isabel followed us up to Tsingtao. While we were there, the admiral made one of his side trips on the Isabel.

Paul Stillwell: Wasn't that more like a yacht?

Commander Harralson: It was a yacht, from World War I.* I think it was sold to the Navy for a dollar or something like that, and it had quite a story. It had a 4-inch gun up on the foredeck. When the admiral went aboard for one of these side trips--in this case he was going to Chefoo--he would take a radioman along, because there was always an increase in traffic. The Isabel had only one radioman on board, so the chief would rotate this duty among the flag radiomen. He gave me the nod for the trip to Chefoo.

I went over early afternoon. We were scheduled to get under way at 1600. I met the Isabel radioman. He showed me around the radio room and then told me I had the watch and shoved off. I was scheduled to make a frequency change at 1600. Sixteen hundred came around, and they were heaving short.† As I was tuning the transmitter, changing frequencies, dipping grids, peaking plates, I heard this announcement: "All hands on deck. All hands on deck." Well, I was a radioman, and I was busy tuning the transmitter, so I ignored it.

Pretty soon the guy went by again, and I ignored it again. The next thing I knew, here was this monstrous boatswain's mate standing there, explaining to me the meaning of

---
*The Isabel was built as a yacht in 1917 by Bath Iron Works and taken over on completion by the Navy from her owner, automobile manufacturer John North Willys. She wound up serving in the Navy during both World Wars, eventually being decommissioned in 1946.
†This meant heaving around on the anchor chain so that the anchor was just barely holding.

"All hands on deck." [Laughter] Boy, it happened fast. The next thing I knew, I was up on deck, heaving on an 8-inch line. The problem was that the anchor had come up foul. To straighten it out, they had to unshackle the anchor chain. I think the line was on the anchor, to hold the anchor. Apparently they didn't have a free windlass, or it wasn't rigged. So what they had was all hands on deck, with this line to hold the anchor until they could straighten the line out.

Paul Stillwell: That would be a job.

Commander Harralson: Oh, yes.

Paul Stillwell: Well, how was your proficiency as a radioman developing during this period?

Commander Harralson: I thought I was getting to be a damn good radioman. [Laughter] And I was interested in both the material part of it and the operator part. Most of what I did was the work of an operator. I copied an awful lot of press. That was really an interesting job. As I said before, the admiral wanted to keep abreast of things, and he just ate that stuff up. Before it went to the admiral, it had to be edited and rewritten smooth. Most of the press news was in abbreviated language, a lot of words chopped out, and just enough left in so that you could catch the meaning.

Paul Stillwell: Sort of like a Navy message?

Commander Harralson: Yes. I have a good example in "Envoy Kurusu ex Tokyo States-ward via Manila."

Paul Stillwell: It told you what you needed to know.

Commander Harralson: Yes, but you couldn't give it to the admiral that way. [Laughter] So the supervisor edited the copy as it came from the radioman.

Paul Stillwell: Fill in the missing words.

Commander Harralson: Yes, straighten it out. Then he'd toss it to somebody on watch, a particular circuit there, and they would have to type it up. What I'm getting at is that they took me off of press and put me on a circuit that wasn't very busy--just a few messages--but it had a collateral duty of typing up the smooth press. That was a terrible job, because it was a full length of paper, with eight flimsies behind it and, of course, the carbon paper. And the admiral brooked no strikeovers.

My supervisor was a radioman first by the name of Nasworthy.[*] He was a very competent radioman and supervisor, but he knew nothing about the English language. [Laughter] He'd toss the copy over to me, and it wouldn't make sense. Not that I knew a great deal--I had only high-school English to support me, but I remembered a few things. For example, if there wasn't a verb in there somewheres, it didn't sound right. [Laughter] So I'd say, "Hey, Nasworthy, this ain't right."

He'd say, "You fix it." So I'd fix it the best I could. Finally, he dumped it all on me, and I had to go from there. I hated it. You'd make a mistake, and then you had to stop and put paper in between the sheets so that you could erase it and not leave a smudge.

Paul Stillwell: Eight times.

Commander Harralson: Oh, gee, yes. So the one thing it did, it improved my typing accuracy.

Paul Stillwell: I bet it did. [Laughter]

Commander Harralson: Of course, there was a lot of duplication in the press we copied, and the supervisor would eliminate the duplication. Then selected items were sent to the ship's newspaper to publish.

---

[*]Radiioman First Class Robert W. Nasworthy, USN.

Paul Stillwell: Do you have any other examples of Admiral Hart and how demanding he was?

Commander Harralson: I wish I could give you an insight on him, but really I can't. When I tell you that we avoided officers, it's absolutely true. I had very little contact with them.

Paul Stillwell: Sounds like Jimmy Fernald was the only one.

Commander Harralson: That's right. Even when we got transferred to Cavite later, you used to see a warrant officer once in a while, and that was about it.

Paul Stillwell: Well, what do you remember about the messing and berthing conditions in the Augusta?

Commander Harralson: Well, the flag radiomen's compartment extended from side to side, athwartships. It had a porthole on each side. We had a long table, a practice oscillator over on one side, adequate lockers. There were a lot of extra bunks around. We were not crowded.

Paul Stillwell: So you didn't have to sleep in hammocks?

Commander Harralson: Oh, no, bunks. What I liked about the Augusta was the way we ate as a division. Each division had their own mess tables.

Paul Stillwell: They brought them down from the overhead, for the meals.

Commander Harralson: That's right. They had iron rods for legs, so that when they hung them up, the legs were folded up.

Paul Stillwell: They were held up against the overhead by a U-shaped metal bar.

Commander Harralson: Right, U-shaped, and they hung up there with the legs folded up. The rod that extended down and held the legs vertical then also held them folded up underneath. The benches were the same way. These big, long rods that went out to the legs came up to the center and hooked.

We had this big, fat guy, Louie Cook, who told these terrible stories.

Paul Stillwell: What do you mean, terrible stories?

Commander Harralson: He didn't know the difference between reality and imagination.

Paul Stillwell: I see, tall tales.

Commander Harralson: Tall tales, which he believed himself. They didn't want Louie to sit in the middle, because if he sat in the middle, it bowed the bench, and those hooks would come up. When the ship was rocking, the next thing you'd know, the legs would fold under, and everybody would go down. That was one of the perils of it. [Laughter] I think we had four tables and two mess cooks; each one took care of two tables. The senior man sat at the head of the table. There were five seats on each side of the table. The mess cook delivered to the senior man at the head. The junior man sat at the other end of the table. It was the job of the senior man at the table to see that the junior man didn't starve. Because lots of times the good things, like steak or ham, there wasn't much left by the time it got down to the end.

Paul Stillwell: Did you tip the mess cooks?

Commander Harralson: Yes, that was necessary, to keep his morale, because he had to fight for food, to get it out of the galley. I think each man chipped in 50 cents or something like that after a payday.

Paul Stillwell: I think that was the standard in most ships at that era.

Commander Harralson: Is that right?

Paul Stillwell: And some men really enjoyed mess cooking, because they got that extra money, and they didn't have to stand watches.

Commander Harralson: True.

Paul Stillwell: That would develop a good deal of camaraderie in the division. It was almost like a family atmosphere.

Commander Harralson: Yes, it was cohesive. A lot of give and take and banter went on at the table.

Paul Stillwell: What would you talk about at a meal?

Commander Harralson: About liberties, girls.

Paul Stillwell: Current events?

Commander Harralson: Naw. [Laughter] We were not political.

Paul Stillwell: Girls and liberty being the main topics?

Commander Harralson: That's right; the liberties you made, what you were going to do the next time you went ashore, and things like that. Or about some experience up in the radio room, some problem you had with this iron-fisted guy over on the Marblehead.

Paul Stillwell: Shop talk.

Commander Harralson: Yes.

Paul Stillwell: Please talk about that concept of the fist and how you could recognize somebody.

Commander Harralson: Well, after you do it so long, you develop a characteristic. When you listen for so many years, to sending and receiving, you become very sensitive to who's sending. Of course, there were people out there that became well known. The flag had a circuit called Five Points. It was the premium circuit in the Asiatics. If you were a five-point operator, you were at the top. That was the ultimate--to be a five-point operator. NPO Cavite was on it. Of course, in the Augusta the flag's call sign was C2P. The Fourth Marines were on it. I can't place the others. But the traffic was very heavy. In the daytime, normally, it was going one way or the other. The operator was either sending or copying. They sent them in strings, five at a time. The good operators could clear five without any breaks or requests for repeats and that sort of thing.

Paul Stillwell: Did you have any other training, besides on-the-job training, in becoming more proficient at this?

Commander Harralson: No, we got that way. Copying the press was an excellent way to build your code speed and your ability. When I first went aboard, I thought, "Gee, I can copy 30 or 35 words a minute. I'm pretty good." I got on the press, and I started copying stations like that at that speed. I found that, yes, I could copy that fast for three or four minutes. But then I'd begin to drop a word here and there. Then sometimes I'd hit a blank spot; I just couldn't understand it.

Paul Stillwell: So it's like mental fatigue?

Commander Harralson: Yes. But the more I stayed at it, the better I got, the less attention and concentration I had to give to it.

Paul Stillwell: It became automatic.

Commander Harralson: Yes, it did.

Paul Stillwell: That's like touch typing too. I mean, you don't think about each letter.

Commander Harralson: That's right. The only thing is a radioman gets corrupted, because copying radio Morse at 25-30 words a minute is a pretty good speed, but for a typing speed it's very slow. So even though I knew the touch, I did a lot of two-finger typing. I found that that's how a lot of the old radiomen typed. They got real fast with it. [Laughter]

Paul Stillwell: Did you have correspondence courses, to get you more prepared for higher rate?

Commander Harralson: That was on my own. I mentioned that I started taking a correspondence course back at North Island. I bought a course from Capitol Radio Engineering Institute, CREI, because it was engineering level. The other course, National, was more pictorial, analogous to water tanks and water flowing--that kind of approach to basic electricity. CREI approached it mathematically, which you have to do if you're going to understand electronics. It was a good course. It came in binders. I had a slide rule, Keuffler and Esser log-log duplex decitrig.

It was fate that I had just completed two lessons in the solving of complex parallel series combinations, to solve for impedance and phase angle, and I was hot. You solve them with your slide rule. It involves trigonometry. I had gotten very good at it--just finished the two chapters--and here came the test for second-class radioman. It was loaded with these complex series parallel combinations of resistance capacity and inductance, where you solve for phase angle and impedance. I ate it up. When the results came out, I was the only one out there that passed it. [Laughter] They gave the test over, but I didn't have to take it.

Paul Stillwell: So there can be a reward for individual initiative.

Commander Harralson: Yes. The only problem with it was that I kept getting these binders. I had a whole bunch of binders now. That's a problem when you get orders to a new station or ship, because you've got to pack up, and you don't have anybody helping you carry your luggage. [Laughter]

Paul Stillwell: So how did you manage that?

Commander Harralson: Well, I had a suitcase, I think, and, of course, I had collected a lot of souvenirs and things.

Paul Stillwell: Did you get increased responsibility that went along with being second class?

Commander Harralson: No, I stayed at the same two jobs. I was aboard the Augusta only a year and a half, I guess, something like that. I worked just some of the slow circuits and the rewriting of press. That was about the extent of what I had aboard ship. But I was building points with my ability to turn in a clear copy and demonstrate my proficiency with the speed key.

I wanted to tell you something about Louie Cook, this first class radioman, a great big guy, told all these tall stories. He was, in fact, an excellent radioman. One day Louie said he could send 35 words a minute with the manual key, not the speed key. Everybody laughed at him; you were doing good if you could do 20. So a big bet came out of it--everybody betting on whether Louie could do it, and most were against it. I bet on Louie. I had a hunch.

So the big day came for Louie to demonstrate. We went down to the oscillator and desk, down in our compartment. Everybody gathered around, and they gave Louie something to send. The men had their watches out to time him.

Paul Stillwell: Did they have a referee for this?

Richard A. Harralson, Interview #2 (5/16/97) – Page 132

Commander Harralson: Oh, I guess some of the senior first class were the word. Louie sat down, and he sent 35 words a minute just like a machine, didn't miss a beat. [Laughter] I guessed right.

Paul Stillwell: How did he do it? Just that good?

Commander Harralson: Just that good.

Paul Stillwell: But it sounds as if that was the upper limit, then, for a regular key?

Commander Harralson: Yes. I never knew anybody that could send that fast before, and I don't think anybody else did. He was very good.

Paul Stillwell: Did you have a growing proficiency in being able to set up circuits and patch them to wherever they needed to go and so forth?

Commander Harralson: No, not on there. I had nothing to do with tuning transmitters. They had a transmitter gang; that was shipboard personnel.

Paul Stillwell: So you had two separate radio organizations, the flag and the ship?

Commander Harralson: Yes, that's right. Flag radio was dominant to the extent that I didn't know any ship radiomen. We had one other third class aboard, and he was a baseball player. He never came near the radio room. Captain Magruder liked baseball. But, in effect, there was no ship radio room.

Paul Stillwell: Well, typically, a ship's communication department gets TAD to the flag.*

---

*TAD--temporary additional duty.

Commander Harralson: Yes. Now, on the Lex, we seemed to be more separated; we were strictly flag radio, and down below us, below the bridge, was the ship's radio. But on the Augusta, it's like there was no ship's radio gang or radio; it was all flag radio.

Paul Stillwell: So you would guard for traffic for both the flag and the ship?

Commander Harralson: Right, right. I can't think of Augusta's call sign now.

Paul Stillwell: That must be the only thing you don't remember. [Laughter]

Commander Harralson: I remember Lexington was NIKM and Saratoga was NELB. My gosh, I think the Augusta was NEBF. But the flag, CinC, was C2P.

Paul Stillwell: What was the paint scheme inside? Battleships had kind of a dark red deck, and I think they had white bulkheads.

Commander Harralson: I seem to recall a light green.

Paul Stillwell: That's been a typical Navy bulkhead color, also. What do you remember about damage control? Did you get much involved in that?

Commander Harralson: No.

Paul Stillwell: And for general quarters your station was probably essentially the same as for regular watches.

Commander Harralson: No. Like I said, for general quarters, they assigned their best radiomen, the more senior, experienced radiomen, to radio. The rest of us were assigned to various things like sound-powered telephone talkers. I think I had a sound-powered telephone way up in the foremast there somewhere. I liked it up there; I liked to go to general quarters.

Paul Stillwell: You had a great view, for one thing.

Commander Harralson: Yes. And I think some were on fire details and things like that.

Paul Stillwell: Well, damage control was considerably less sophisticated then than it became later. The war sort of woke people up.

Commander Harralson: Yes. I think the war woke a lot of people up. [Laughter]

Paul Stillwell: Well, please tell me your reaction to the gunfire when you were up there in the foretop? Did they fire the 8-inch guns?

Commander Harralson: I don't remember witnessing the firing from up there. What I remember is being on watch when they fired. Now, I don't recall that we went to general quarters for firing the big guns. I can remember having to stand up and hold this big receiver, to try to reduce the vibration, because we were right behind number two. I have difficulty, but I have to say it, number two turret.* [Laughter]

Paul Stillwell: That's what it was called. [Laughter]

Commander Harralson: Right. I just never, never thought that they were turrets.

Paul Stillwell: Were those receivers and transmitters shock mounted?

Commander Harralson: Yes.

Paul Stillwell: But they needed help?

---
*Mr. Harralson was accustomed to referring to them as gun mounts rather than turrets.

Commander Harralson: They still bounced around, yes. They were huge things. They were the RBA and the RBB. The RBA was the low-freq, and the RBB the high-freq. And they were huge things. They filled the whole area in front of you. They had cranks and dials. They had different frequency bands, and to shift from one band to the next, you had to turn cranks. As you did, whole big frames moved inside to put different coils in contact and different condensers to give you the different frequencies. That was all separate from the power supply. The power supply itself was down below the desk, and it was a huge piece of equipment itself. The Navy, as you know, likes to build things to withstand gunfire.

Paul Stillwell: And understandably. [Laughter]

Commander Harralson: Yes, but what they seem to miss is the fact that the bigger and heavier it is, the more inertia is involved, the more violence. See, these space shots--the electronics in there, of course, are solid state and tiny, and can withstand the G's.

Paul Stillwell: Did you ever run afoul of the disciplinary organization in that ship?

Commander Harralson: I was a good sailor; I never had a problem. [Laughter]

Paul Stillwell: Great.

Commander Harralson: Like I say, when I drank too much, I didn't get obnoxious; I got friendlier.

Paul Stillwell: And when your uniform got messed up, you scrunched down in your seat at the theater.

Commander Harralson: Yes. [Laughter]

Paul Stillwell: Did you have any contact with the Fourth Marines there in Shanghai?

Commander Harralson: Yes. At the Marine Club, I remember trying to get in the bar. When I had my second class crow, I tried to get into the sergeants' bar. [Laughter] As a third class, they tried to throw me out of the corporals' bar. Whenever you paid in the Marine Club, they'd give you your change in Marine Club tokens. Those tokens were good money all through the International Settlement. Rickshaw drivers loved to get Marine Club tokens. The unit of exchange, in China, was the yuan; and like I said, it was 17 to 1.

But all through China, at least the International Settlement, they had a dollar Mex. It was a silver dollar, and as best I can understand, Mexico had some kind of debt to China and paid off in silver dollars. So we used to get a lot of these silver dollars. But you had to be careful. The Chinese, being the craftsmen they are, were capable of peeling one face off, digging the silver out, filling it with pewter or something of approximate weight, and putting it back. You could see Chinese merchants counting their dollars-Mex. They had a way in which they would balance one good dollar on their finger, and with a handful of unknowns, they would flip them by, one by one, so they just touched. If they had the right ring, it was a good dollar; they'd go ping, tching, ting. Then they'd hit a leaden one that would go chunk. [Laughter]

Paul Stillwell: Did they have chit systems for paying for things in various places?

Commander Harralson: I don't remember that in China so much. But down in Cavite, that was sort of like your credit card.

Paul Stillwell: Well, that was that era's equivalent of a credit card.

Commander Harralson: Yes. And I'm telling you, after they blew up Cavite, there were a lot of happy men there.

Paul Stillwell: Because they didn't have to pay off their debts.

Commander Harralson: Yes. Some of those guys owed a year's pay. There was a bar. See, Cavite was actually an island; there was a bridge over from San Roque to the island. Of course, that had been a Spanish naval base. Half of this little island was the shipyard, and the other half was the little barrio of Cavite. In this little town there were several restaurants and, of course, bars. One bar was Fuji's. That was quite a popular place. Fuji closed up two weeks before Pearl. When the word got around that Fuji's bar had blown up, after they bombed Cavite, a big cheer went up. Because there were sailors that owed their soul to Fuji's bar.

Paul Stillwell: Well, I wonder if you've got anything else in your notes there, that we have not talked about.

Commander Harralson: Oh, I'll talk about liberty in Manila. A lot of sailors didn't care too much for Manila. I liked Manila a lot. When you learn about a place, find your away around, know where to go to get a good meal, where a good movie is, you begin to fit in. We rode around in calesas or carametas. They were two-wheeled carts: big, high wooden wheels and a little pony. Two sailors could ride in them; usually it was one. I tried to find out which was the proper name, looking it up in different books, but I never could find out whether they were really carametas or calesas. I tended to call them calesas. I rode around in those a lot.

And, of course, we had our bars and places. There was the Silver Dollar, the Poodle Dog. One place was famous for its Singapore Slings. If you could drink five Singapore Slings, the bartender gave you a medal. [Laughter]

Paul Stillwell: I suspect not many people could.

Commander Harralson: No.

In Manila you'd cross the Pasig River, over a bridge, and entered what was downtown Manila--Isaac Peral Boulevard. There was an odd-shaped little block, just to the right as you'd come over the river. That's where Tom Dixie's place was, up on the second deck. Around the bottom, on one corner was a drugstore--like an American drugstore, you know, where they sell everything. They had a soda fountain counter. I used to go there and eat mangos. The Philippines have the most delicious mangos. They're huge things--carabao mangos.

Then around the corner from that, on this same little block, was a bar, an old-style bar, a beautiful mahogany bar; no stools, just a brass foot rail. I went in there one time with Lauer. Being that kind of bar, I thought the proper drink there was a shot of whiskey. I took this shot of whiskey, and part of it went up my nose. Did you ever have . . .

Paul Stillwell: No. [Laughter]

Commander Harralson: Oh, God, I thought I was going to die, and--embarrassed; Lauer was embarrassed, I was embarrassed, the old bartender glaring at me, "What's the matter, kid?"

Paul Stillwell: And you were not yet 21, of course.

Commander Harralson: No. Then around the corner from there was a cocktail lounge. You'd go in there, and it was air-conditioned, cool. They had it very dark; you could hardly see, and music coming out of the walls. When you ordered a rum and Coke, they'd bring you a big bowl of ice, a bottle of Coke, and the rum bottle. You mixed your own. But we stayed away from there, because a couple of rum drinks in there, where you mixed it yourself. You had to fill it full of rum and a little shot of Coke--a couple of those and then you walk outside into that hot sun, and, man, that was not the way to go.

One favorite haunt there was Academa Number Two. It was upstairs, down by the Poodle Dog. They served just beer; there wasn't hard liquor there. They had all different kinds of beer. Our favorite there was Japanese, Asahi. You can buy it today, in the States. We called it Ash-hi, in typical sailor reaction. With the beer you got a big bowl of Spanish peanuts. They had a way of, I don't know, boiling them in oil or something; they were delicious. We'd sit in there and drink beer and gorge on peanuts.

Paul Stillwell: What's that Filipino beer? I can't remember the name of it. That was . . .

Commander Harralson: Oh, San Miguel.

Paul Stillwell: Right. Right

Commander Harralson: San Miguel made milk. [Laughter] They rejuvenated milk, that they sold to the Navy over at Cavite.

Paul Stillwell: From what you've talked about, in the officer-enlisted relations, it sounds as if there was just a vast gulf in the Augusta. You apparently had the minimum amount of contact when you had to have at all.

Commander Harralson: That's very true. But I think it depended, really, on your rate. Now, Chief Warrant King, as a yeoman and then a secretary for the admiral and things like that, had a lot of contact.*

Paul Stillwell: It was a necessity.

Commander Harralson: Right. Sure. That was his job. I think a quartermaster probably becomes familiar with a lot of officers. Oh, the yeomen, quartermasters--I was trying to think. I'm sure there are some other rates that come in contact with officers. But, as far as I was concerned, the people that ran the ship were chiefs.

Paul Stillwell: Well, that's always been true.

Commander Harralson: Yes. If you had something to do with an officer, it was usually something that was bothersome or troublesome.

Paul Stillwell: Right. Did you have a chief radioman in flag radio?

---

*Yeoman First Class Cecil S. King, USN, was then serving in the Asiatic Fleet allowance on board the Augusta. The oral history of King, who retired as a chief warrant officer, is in the Naval Institute collection.

Commander Harralson: Oh, yes. We had several chiefs. Some of them were supervisors. I don't remember any one particularly. It was at Cavite that I knew the chief real well, Chief Morrison.

When we got back to the Philippines in the fall of 1940, I was approaching the end of my enlistment, my 21st birthday, which was coming up in January of '41. I wanted to do another two years out there, but before they would let me do that, I had to agree to ship over.

Paul Stillwell: What made you want to stay longer?

Commander Harralson: Oh, I liked it. I was having a ball. I was getting acquainted with the places. I knew how to move, where to go, and things like that. [Laughter]

Paul Stillwell: So you didn't feel a sense of being bothered by being away from your family, I take it?

Commander Harralson: No. See, had I not extended or asked for another two years out there, I would have gone home with the Augusta.* I think that had something to do with it. The only time, I guess, I got a real lump of homesickness was when we stood at quarters while the Augusta cast off, with her homeward-bound pennant and the band playing, "California, Here I Come." I think I got a couple tears in my eyes and a lump in my throat.

Paul Stillwell: Well, I don't know whether it was from you or somebody else, but I think I heard that the homeward-bound pennant was so long that it got cut.

Commander Harralson: Yes, when the ship got under way, it was headed inland. So it had to swing a 180. It had this huge, long pennant dragging in the water. And as it made that

---

*After arriving in Manila on 21 October 1940, the Augusta was relieved as Asiatic Fleet flagship on 22 November, then left that same day for the United States.

big circle out there, it lost most of it that was in the water. But they didn't stop. [Laughter] They kept going.

Paul Stillwell: Please describe the transfer of the flag allowance from the Augusta to the Houston.

Commander Harralson: Well, I remember staying aboard the Houston for about a month, and the only thing I can remember about the transfer is a bunch of big lockers full of files and things. We all just moved over. Now, not everybody, because it depended on how much time they had on station whether they went back with the ship. A lot of sailors went back with the ship. When we went aboard the Houston, of course, we soon became very unhappy, because the Houston had received four more 5-inch antiaircraft guns. Where the crew on the Augusta was 750 or thereabouts, the Houston had over 1,100. It was crowded.

Paul Stillwell: Wartime complement.

Commander Harralson: Right. And it just wasn't as clean. When we first went aboard the Augusta, I thought, "Oh, my Lord, this thing's spotless." I figured it must be one hot ship, you know. But it wasn't. It was a happy ship.

Paul Stillwell: Hot ship is not a compliment, in that sense.

Commander Harralson: No, absolutely. What I meant by that term is very regulation.

Paul Stillwell: To the point of being obsessively so.

Commander Harralson: Right, right, obsessive. And with a four-star admiral aboard and all the hoopla that goes with that.

Paul Stillwell: Was the Houston painted that light gray when she came out, the same as the Augusta?

Commander Harralson: Yes. We called it battleship gray, I think.

Paul Stillwell: She hadn't gone to the war colors yet?

Commander Harralson: No.

Paul Stillwell: Well, you mentioned that they had the additional antiaircraft guns. Was there a comparable state of modernization in the radio? Did it have more modern equipment than the Augusta?

Commander Harralson: No. The standard shipboard installation, as far as receivers, was RBA, RBB. I don't know for sure, but there were about eight or ten of them in the radio room. All ships carried, as backup, RAK/RAL high- and low-frequency receivers that were of a different type of circuitry. We called them super bloopty-dynes, as opposed to the RBA/RBB super heterodynes. They had a feedback system in them that was great for amplification. And the reason they had them for backup was they were battery operated. They were a standby sort of thing.

They squealed. You tuned to a station that squealed, and then you had an adjustment that tuned out the squeal. At that point, where you lost the squeal, you had lots of volume. So they were very sensitive. They were good receivers. The main objection to them, as far as the Navy was concerned, was when they were squealing, they were transmitting, and might possibly violate security in that respect. But all ships, as far as I know, had them, and they were stuck in a corner.

Paul Stillwell: Well, if you had a concern about radio silence, that could be a real problem.

Commander Harralson: Yes, yes, indeed. Then, of course, there were a lot of restrictions on radios, having radios in the crew spaces; because the other radios, that didn't have that squealer, were superheterodynes, and most receivers that a crew member might try to have in their room would be superhets. But they could possibly cause emissions under certain conditions.

Paul Stillwell: Is there anything else specific about the Houston?

Commander Harralson: Well, they had jukeboxes aboard that had music that I hadn't heard yet. That's about it. The crew seemed very un-Asiatic.

Paul Stillwell: Understandably.

Commander Harralson: Yes. And there wasn't quite the relationship with the rest of the crew. Now, we talked about that before, about radiomen sticking pretty close to radio. In the Augusta there was some congeniality with the other crew members, in different situations. It wasn't quite the same on the Houston. They didn't seem to be a very pleasant bunch, for one thing.

When the time came, were very glad to get off of the Houston. When the admiral went over to the Marsman Building, part of the radiomen went there and part went to Cavite, to radio control. I was in the group that went to Cavite.*

Radio control there was an awesome place. I never knew that side of radio, what went on there, before. The building itself was cubicle in proportions, two-story. The upper deck was the radio room, where all the equipment was, where we stood our watches. Down below was where we lived, our bunks and lockers and the head. All of the Asiatic Fleet traffic, headed for the States, went through there.

Paul Stillwell: It would be like a communications station.

---

*Admiral Hart moved ashore from the Houston on 29 June 1941. He took up residence in a small apartment in the Manila Hotel, below the penthouse of General Douglas MacArthur. He moved his fleet headquarters into rented space in the Marsman Building, at the end of pier seven on the Manila waterfront. Harralson reported to the Navy radio station at Cavite on 17 March 1941, prior to Admiral Hart's transfer from the Houston to Manila.

Commander Harralson: A big communications station, yes. The transmitters were over at Canacao--high tower. We also handled State Department traffic. I can't say all of it, because they might have had other means. But I know there was an awful lot. Most of it was coded, five-letter code groups. You asked about that earlier. It's at Cavite where I begin to notice a preponderance of coded messages.

But they had a system of volume traffic handling there that I hadn't known about. It was called automatics, or MUX. That was kind of a misnomer because, actually, it was very labor intensive. They had what they called the frequency diversity system. They used three transmitters, each on a different frequency. Each had a rhombic directional antenna out over the water that gave space diversity. That's for the transmitting part. They would take a stack of messages. They used a perforator to punch holes in the tape in such an arrangement to create dots and dashes. You'd press a letter on a keyboard, and it would give you the proper combination of holes to make that letter.

You'd punch a stack of messages, and after the first one, you'd retrieve the bitter end and scotch-tape it to the outside of a Masonite box, about two by two by three feet high. Then, as you typed the messages out, the tape would flow into these boxes. When the boxes got full, you wouldn't break the tape. You would just slide it over and pull another box in, and start filling that box. You went on that way until you had several boxes full. Then, before you started a run, you would get a go-ahead from the receiving station on the service frequency. He'd set up. Then you'd take the bitter end that you'd saved and put it into a keying head. You had a leader on it that gave the call signs. When he said, "Go," you would flip the switch and the tape started through the keying head, keying three transmitters. It transmitted at about 120 words a minute.

At the receiving end, there were three receivers, one tuned to each frequency, each with its own antenna. They fed into a unit that I called a selector, and the strongest signal operated the recorder stylus, which made a blue line on a tape. A dot was a little spike, and a dash would be a little flat-topped mesa. You could adjust the sharpness of the spike and the width of the mesa by the speed of the take-up drive.

So you'd get a run started on the receiving end by starting the tape-puller. All this tape would flow into the box. You'd save the leader there. And, of course, each side had its transmitters and receivers. When they'd finish a run, you'd have these boxes full of tape; then you had to transcribe it.

You set the boxes at one end of the transcribing position. There was a foot throttle and a take-up wheel. You'd start that tape running through a slot in front of the typewriter and write up the messages manually on proper message blanks. I tried that for a while, and I didn't like it. I'd be going along there, typing up messages, and the thing would invert on me. When it did that, of course, it didn't make sense.

The first job they put me on at Cavite was frequency 500, the international calling frequency and distress frequency. And that was an insult, because usually they put third class or strikers on that. Lots of times it's left just on loudspeakers. They have silent period, in which you're supposed to listen for any distress calls. Other than that, it's a general calling frequency.

I couldn't just sit there and not pay attention, so I started listening and paying attention to what was going on. Real early one morning, I heard somebody with a five-letter call sign calling NPO. That meant it was an airplane, and the only airplane that I knew of was the China Clipper.* The Clippers landed in Bacoor Bay, right adjacent to Cavite. That was always an exciting thing. They brought mail. It cost 50 cents to send a letter back to the States, or the other way. So I hollered to the supervisor, "Give me a transmitter. Give me a transmitter." So he did and I answered the call.

The plane came back, "Good morning, OM. [That's ham talk for "old man."] This is the China Clipper. How's the weather in Cavite?" We shot the breeze. About the only time I can ever remember opening up in plain language with a Navy transmitter.

Paul Stillwell: But this was still with the key, rather than voice?

Commander Harralson: This was the key, yes. Voice played no part. We chatted a little bit, and he said, "QMO, please," which meant, "Send me MOs." MOs were used for taking radio direction-finder bearings, because M and O are two dashes and three dashes, which gives them a lot of meat to work on, as they are zeroing in on your signal. So I gave him a

---

*In the mid-1930s Pan American inaugurated a flying boat service from the West Coast of the United States to the Far East. Using a name reminiscent of the old sailing days, the airplanes were known as China Clippers.

whole string of MOs. Then he said, "Thank you very much, and I'll see you some time later." I think he said he was about 150 miles out.

That sounds like an inconsequential thing, but to me, at that time, the China Clipper was a beautiful sight. I thought it was tremendous, what it was doing, and the plane itself, actually, was quite beautiful.

Paul Stillwell: Well, there was so much glamour associated with that.

Commander Harralson: Glamour, yes, that's the word.

Paul Stillwell: That people could actually fly someplace, instead of taking a ship.

Commander Harralson: Yes. So that was kind of a high point. I was quite excited about it. But I was anxious to get off of 500. It was boring, and I knew I was capable of a lot more. So I went to work on the chief. So they had me checking out on the MUX. When you get good at that, they put "Qual-MUX in your record. Once you had that in your record, it had a lot to do with the rest of your career, because there was a whole series of stations--Guam, Honolulu, San Francisco, Washington. In some cases, say, we sent a string to Honolulu, they could key their transmitter directly, so that it didn't have to be transcribed. They had special arrangements for certain messages. But once you got qualified in MUX, you spent a lot of time at those different stations.

Of course, the premium station for duty was San Francisco. You got $4.00 a day per diem there, plus commuted rations. It was choice duty.

Paul Stillwell: Was that a goal of yours at that point?

Commander Harralson: No. I was a seagoing sailor. I didn't want that. That's part of the reason why I wasn't on MUX too long before I was asking to get off of it.

Paul Stillwell: Well, if you were a seagoing sailor, why did you agree to this thing in the Houston? I guess you didn't know then that the staff would be going ashore.

Commander Harralson: No, I didn't.

Paul Stillwell: So you had reenlisted on board the Augusta, for two years, probably in late 1940?

Commander Harralson: Yes. I'm not sure, but I think I agreed to reenlist for four years and extended my tour for another two years on the Asiatic Station.

Paul Stillwell: And at the end of the four years, the Japanese weren't particularly interested in whether you were officially a civilian or not. [Laughter]

Commander Harralson: No. [Laughter] I got off of the MUX. The chief put me on the Fox schedule. Like I was explaining, this was a broadcast--high power, low frequency, 16 kilocycles, 300-kilowatt transmitter. You punched messages out on the same kind of tape as for MUX, and then on a schedule you ran the tape through a keying head.

That was interesting for a while. I got in trouble one night, though. I had a bunch of weather reports going out on it, and the keying head broke down. I was happy about that. I wanted to show my skill, so I got my speed key and plugged it in. I was going to send the Fox schedule. They called them "bakers." It had a prefix B. I'm not sure what it stood for. Anyhow, I was going to send the bakers with my speed key to show my skill. But you can't key a 300-kilowatt, low-frequency transmitter with a speed key. It just doesn't happen that fast on there. I got all garbled up. I ended up pounding it out by hand.

Paul Stillwell: Yesterday you told me a story--when the machine wasn't running--about your friend Wimpy Anderson. Could you put that on the tape, please?

Commander Harralson: I first knew Wimpy back at ComAirBatFor, at North Island. To put it bluntly, Wimpy was as ugly as a mud fence. I hate to say that about anybody, but he wasn't very good looking. But what he lacked in looks, if anything, he made up by personality. He was a tremendous person--very, very smart and one of the best operators I ever saw. He was a second class, simply because he hadn't been around long enough. He used to be quite kind about letting strikers like me sit in on his circuit. He would come back from liberty late at night, you'd be on watch, he'd have hamburgers for everybody, things like that.

He carried in the back of his pocket a crypto magazine. You could see him, off and on, sitting in a corner somewhere, working these codes--what do they call them?

Paul Stillwell: Cryptograms?

Commander Harralson: Cryptograms, yes. Well, one of the officers on the staff noticed this. One day he asked Wimpy, "Would you like to go to Washington and learn something about it?" All we knew was that the officer was talking to him, and then Wimpy was gone. The word was he went back to Washington, something to do with cryptology.

Well, I went ashore in Manila one day and was walking down the street when here came Wimpy. And he was wearing a first class yeoman's crow. He recognized me, smiled faintly, and we stopped and exchanged a few pleasantries. He acted nervous. He wouldn't tell me anything. I asked, "Where are you stationed, what are you doing?" and that sort of thing. He was vague and didn't have much to say. We parted, and I felt a little miffed, because I'd known him as such a nice guy.

Paul Stillwell: Shipmates don't treat each other that way.

Commander Harralson: That's right. And, of course, when we got out to Corregidor, after the war had started, there was Wimpy with the FRU unit; we called them gumshoes.* They were very close-mouthed; they wouldn't give you the time of day. Their back half of the tunnel was separated from our front half; they were there first. And there was a heavy curtain that separated us. A Marine guard with a sidearm was posted at the curtain..

Paul Stillwell: Now, when was that, chronologically, that you ran into him?

---

*FRU--fleet radio unit, an outfit with the mission of intercepting Japanese radio messages and attempting to decrypt them.

Commander Harralson: That was after the Augusta had gotten back to the Philippines. Or perhaps it was after I had gone over to Cavite. It was some time along in there.

Paul Stillwell: Do you remember the point at which the dependents had to leave and go home?

Commander Harralson: It was before I got out there.

Paul Stillwell: I see.

Commander Harralson: That's why I said I didn't understand how that lieutenant had a wife over there. I wondered if she might have been a Russian. It was difficult for a sailor to get married out there, but it could be done.

Paul Stillwell: What sort of obstacles were in his way?

Commander Harralson: Oh, if he wanted to do it up right, actually get married, I think it was getting approval through the command. Truthfully, I don't know. I just know they told me it was difficult, but it could be done. I knew two guys that had Russian wives.

Paul Stillwell: But since it was tough to get married, that sort of encouraged the shack-up relationships?

Commander Harralson: Well, that's right, I think. That's where the term "shack up" originated, right there in Cavite, San Roque, and another little place there named Canacao. A lot of sailors did that. They would get a lavandera, a washer girl, there, you know, and they'd end up shacked up.

Paul Stillwell: The advantage for the washerwoman, or whatever the term, was that these men, with their Navy salaries, were more prosperous than the locals.

Commander Harralson: That's right, and they lived good. I can tell you kind of a funny story here. It might be a little derogatory. Should I proceed?

Paul Stillwell: Please, go right ahead.

Commander Harralson: There was one radioman there at Cavite--Skinhead, I'll call him--shacked up with a gal out in San Roque. So one day he said, "Why don't you come out to the house and have a few beers?" I decided to go with him. We went out to his place, and he had a fairly nice Filipino-type house, built up off the ground. We went up there, and he started looking for his gal, and she was not there. He got mad. He started swearing, "I know where she is. Come on."

So I followed him. We went down and over and back of some stores, strictly native place, and out in back to a chicken coop. Inside the chicken coop was a bunch of Filipino and Filipinas, gambling. She was in there, and he dragged her out. [Laughter]

Paul Stillwell: Oh, gee.

Commander Harralson: But there were an awful lot of cute Filipina girls, and I really liked them. They were fun. But this gal, of all the girls out there, was Lena the Hyena.* She was the ugliest looking woman. I thought to myself, "My God, Skinhead, why?"

We had some drinks, and then we had a little bit to eat, and decided to go to Dreamland. Just over the bridge, into Cavite, on the left side, was Dreamland, a dance hall. We had a half a bottle of rum. We started to cross the bridge, and she was carrying the rum. When we got to the top of the bridge, she threw the rum into the water. There was a big, ugly marital scene there. I proceeded on alone and left them arguing.

Paul Stillwell: This was just after he'd pulled her out of the chicken coop?

---

*Lena the Hyena was a character in Al Capp's comic strip L'il Abner. As Harralson described her in a letter, "She was one ugly woman with warts."

Commander Harralson: Well, no. We went back to his place and had a few drinks and something to eat.

Paul Stillwell: But it was the same day.

Commander Harralson: Yes. Later that evening, we decided to go to Dreamland. And the funny thing was, back in the States here, some time afterward, I met Skinhead and his new wife--a beautiful woman. I thought, "My Lord, I can blackmail this man." [Laughter]

Paul Stillwell: You don't seem to me like the blackmailing type?

Commander Harralson: No, I wouldn't do that. [Laughter]

Paul Stillwell: What else do you remember about that 1941 period? How long did you stay at the communication station?

Commander Harralson: Until they blew Cavite up. There was another little thing that was kind of interesting, I thought. At that station there was a 1928 Chevrolet, two-door sedan, I guess it would be. Nobody knew from whence it originally came. When the sailor that had it got orders, he sold it to another radioman, who kept it while he was there. When he got orders, he sold it. So it had passed on down. Well, shortly after we got to Cavite, my good friend Tony Lyons bought it.

Now, to own it, you didn't have to worry about a driver's license, insurance, or any other papers. You'd just give the guy 40 bucks or something like that, and the car was yours. Tony didn't know how to drive. He had grown up in Boston and was a product of a Catholic school there. He joined the Navy, and they sent him out to the Asiatics. He had about 14 years in. His wife, Tina, was able to get to the Philippines from Shanghai. She had set up housekeeping in San Roque, so he was going to use the car for commuting. So he wanted me to teach him to drive. I undertook the job, but he turned out to be a Filipino-type driver--all horn and no brakes. [Laughter]

It was pretty frightening at times, but we would go out to his place. Tina would have a lunch or a picnic. Then we'd take off for the boonies somewhere, and have a picnic and sightsee. That was a lot of fun; I enjoyed that. I enjoyed getting out into the country. And the Filipino people are real nice people. I liked them.

I used to go out to his house for dinner--palaminies and piroshkis.

Paul Stillwell: What are those?

Commander Harralson: They're Russian. The piroshkis are different versions of meat, with cabbage or dough wrapped around them. And then palaminies--I forget which was which. That was always a nice break, because the mess hall there at Cavite was terrible. They served San Miguel milk, from mechanical cows. I think they had far more garbage than what the sailors ate.

Paul Stillwell: Did you stay in the shipyard barracks?

Commander Harralson: Yes, right down below, on the first deck. I had a bunk and a big locker. Over in one corner, sort of halfway between the two, was a rec room--kind of small.

Another interesting thing that happened while I was there was that HMS Warspite, a British battleship, showed up in the harbor one day. It looked kind of weird. We didn't know what was wrong. A radioman, British, came over to see us one day, just to take a look around. We asked him a lot of questions. The ship had been very badly damaged in the Med and had come on through the Indian Ocean, this way, and was going to Bremerton.* They had liberty for the first time in a long while. I don't know when the last time was the crew had liberty, but they really went to town in Manila.

These British sailors had their liberty over there, and I guess they tried to turn the town upside down. I wasn't over there. I was due to go on watch the next morning. I

---

*On 22 May 1941, the Warspite was operating in the Kithera Channel northwest of Crete, when she was attacked by German aircraft. She received a direct hit from a 550-pound bomb that exploded in the 6-inch gun battery on the starboard side. She was damaged again the night of 23-24 June, during an air raid on Alexandria, Egypt. She was repaired at the Puget Sound Navy Yard between August and December 1941.

showed up at the desk at 8:00 o'clock. Morrison, our chief, asked, "How well do you know K. L. Harris?"[*]

I said, "We're friends."

He said, "Okay. The shore patrol's got him, and they will sign him over to a petty officer. So I want you to go over there and get him." He said, "I'll take your desk here. I'll watch your desk."

So I caught the next ferry over to Manila, the San Felipe.

Paul Stillwell: How long did it take to get there from Cavite?

Commander Harralson: I was trying to figure. I think it was about 20 minutes, 30 minutes, something like that. When I got over there, coming up to the landing, there was the most awfullest-looking sight you ever saw; beat-up, dirty, filthy sailors--British mostly. I got ashore and heard some nasty tales about some of the things that had happened.

But, anyhow, I went to the shore patrol office, and there was K. L. Harris. Now, I knew K. L. He was a nice guy, a good friend. But he was very macho. He was a strong, bullish type, very macho. I guess he tried to get macho with the shore patrol, and they beat him down to size. He was bruised and bleeding. The bleeding was all dried by then, see. So I signed for him, and we rode back on the San Felipe.

Paul Stillwell: Did he get thrown in the brig?

Commander Harralson: No. I think they took the situation into consideration, and he was now under our care.

Paul Stillwell: He'd been punished already.

Commander Harralson: Yes, he had. There were things that became legends around there before long, about some of these wild British sailors.

---

[*]Radioman First Class Kenneth L. Harris, USN.

Paul Stillwell: They do get pretty rowdy sometimes. Did you get on board the Warspite at all?

Commander Harralson: No, I didn't. I had no desire to go on her. [Laughter] It was a pretty-sorry looking ship, you know. It had really been mangled. And the sailors looked like they had been through the war.

Paul Stillwell: Well, you can understand why they'd want to let off some steam.

Commander Harralson: Absolutely. That fighting in the Mediterranean there, around Crete, was terrible.

Paul Stillwell: Well, they were in the face of land-based German aircraft.

Commander Harralson: Yes. They lost a lot.

Paul Stillwell: Did you have any personal encounters with any of the British sailors?

Commander Harralson: No. Only just the one that we talked to, that came over. We compared notes and so forth.

By that time, I was on the land-wire desk. I had been on the bakers there for a while, and the word went around that there was going to be an opening on the land wire telegraph. I decided I wanted that job, but the problem was you had to know American Morse, which was different from International Morse, partly--about 11 or 12 characters and the numbers.

It would be about a month before it would be open, so I figured out a way to punch out American Morse on tape. We had a keying head and oscillator. I punched up boxes full of practice tape in American Morse. Just punching it out helped me learn it. Then I'd run the tape through and practice that way. By the end of the month, I could handle it, and I got the job.

I really loved that job. We had five wires and only one sounder and a little row of five lights. If somebody called you, a light would flash, and then you would throw a switch, putting that line onto your sounder. Then you could work him. The busiest circuit was with the Marsman Building--the admiral's office over there--in international Morse. The second busiest was with the Bureau of Posts in Manila, and that was in American Morse. Occasionally, personal messages came over that line, but the bulk of it was State Department traffic, encoded; very, very little plain language. We were also on the wire with Army headquarters in Manila and Corregidor. We were on that. Then we had a wire with PatWing 10. Another wire was with the Bureau of Posts, right there in Cavite, for personal messages and things like that, which wasn't very often.

So it meant that I would clear traffic with the admiral in Manila, and then I'd shift over and clear traffic with the civilian operators at the Bureau of Posts. I was switching back and forth, American to international to American. It was a real good position. It wasn't like sitting in front of a receiver and tethered by the headset, see. If I had to go to the head, I just told the chief, "I'm going to the head." I could read a newspaper. I had a cup of coffee and a doughnut--that was my breakfast--and read the newspaper. Then clear some traffic and that sort of thing. It was a lot of fun.

But there was one incident. I was sitting there working one day, and the chief threw a State Department coded message on my desk. He said, "That's a hot one. Get rid of it." It was a triple priority, they called it. That was, I think, the top priority. It was to go to the Army headquarters in Manila. So I switched on to that circuit and heard Manila working Corregidor. I listened a little bit, and it sounded routine, so I broke him. You would open the circuit, and that interrupted him. Then he was supposed to close his key, so that whoever interrupted him could send him something. So I broke him, and then I said, "I've got a hot one."

He said, "Wait," and went on sending to Corregidor.

The supervisor said, "That's hot. Get rid of it." I broke him again, and the same thing happened.

Finally, I told him, "You take it or nobody sends." I left my key open. Every once in a while I'd close it. He started to tell me to get lost, and I'd open it again. We played a little game there. Finally, he gave me the go-ahead. So I sent it, with my speed key.

The Army operators weren't very good. I sent it with the chief standing right behind me. The Army man came back, on telegraph, receiving okay, and gave his sign. Then you put his sign and time on the message to show who you sent it to and when.

Paul Stillwell: That's that cross thing you were explaining about.

Commander Harralson: Yes. Right. The chief was right behind me. As soon as the Army man gave me a roger, he started back with Corregidor again. I thought there was something wrong there, because usually when I sent them messages, I'd get broken several times through the message, asking for a repeat.

It wasn't very long afterwards, I guess the next day, that tracer proceedings came in on this message. I was so happy the chief was there to back me up. Do you know what that darn guy did? This story came out later; it's what I heard. He got tired of me busting him, and let me send and didn't even bother to copy it. Then, when I was through, he said, "Okay." Then he went on with his traffic. This message concerned the Japanese Envoy Kurusu, who was leaving Tokyo for the States, but he was going unexpectedly via Manila.* There he was supposed to be met and accorded all honors appropriate to his rank, which was really high.

Paul Stillwell: Right. By MacArthur?

Commander Harralson: Yes. There was no one at the airport to meet him.

Paul Stillwell: Because they didn't listen to your message.

Commander Harralson: Exactly, yes. It caused, I guess, a wave in the diplomatic arena, because he was involved in those final negotiations before Pearl.

---

*Japanese special envoy Saburo Kurusu went to the United States in November 1941 to assist the ambassador, Admiral Kichisaburo Nomura, in his negotiations with U.S. Secretary of State Cordell Hull. The negotiations were still in progress when a Japanese carrier task force struck Pearl Harbor on 7 December.

Paul Stillwell: Well, he was then on his way to the States. Yes, you're right; it was very fortunate the chief was standing right with you.

Commander Harralson: Yes. But I can't imagine an operator being that dumb.

Paul Stillwell: And arrogant.

Commander Harralson: Yes. But, you know, there was a lot of arrogance with Army against the Navy out there. Of course, higher up, there are a couple of real incidents. But you get into the war in that.

Paul Stillwell: Did you feel an increasing sense of tension as the year 1941 moved on?

Commander Harralson: Yes, I did. It got to the point where you'd go ashore, over to Manila, and here'd be troops coming down the street. One time I went over, and here came some tanks. They weren't big Sherman-like tanks that I saw in pictures later. In fact, they looked kind of small, but they were tanks. And there seemed to always be some strange ship in the harbor--a man-of-war, one of ours--that was not part of the Asiatic Fleet.

Paul Stillwell: The Boise came out there.*

Commander Harralson: There you are. The Boise, yes, and there was another tender that came out. These sailors would go ashore in Manila and they didn't know prices. They caused inflation, and we got so mad. [Laughter]

Paul Stillwell: They ruined things for the rest of you.

Commander Harralson: Yes, they did. They started building sand-filled barricades. See, Cavite was on a sandy island, and they couldn't dig down without getting into water. So

---

*USS Boise (CL-47) was a new light cruiser, having been commissioned 12 August 1938. She was considerably more modern than the Asiatic Fleet's light cruiser Marblehead (CL-12), commissioned in 1924.

what they did was build a few--not very many--barricades. The had wood sides and were filled with sand--about four feet thick and six feet high.

Paul Stillwell: Cofferdams?

Commander Harralson: Cofferdams, I guess. But I questioned the idea of wood. I thought that wasn't too smart, you know--a long wooden box full of sand.

There was this idea that war was in the offing, but we had a real pleasant life. There were two of us on the land wire: Miller, a first class, and myself. The way we worked it, one would go on watch at 8:00 o'clock in the morning and take the watch from 8:00 to 10:00 o'clock at night. He would take off for lunch and for evening meal while the supervisor was watching the wire desk. He'd do that two days in a row and then be off two days. I had more liberty than I had money to spend on it.

Paul Stillwell: That's a typical sailor's complaint. [Laughter]

Commander Harralson: Yes. That and liberty, but no boats.

Paul Stillwell: Right. But all you had to do was read the newspapers to realize that things were getting worse.

Commander Harralson: Yes, but I didn't pay too much attention to the newspapers.

Paul Stillwell: Are you saying that you didn't feel any sense of fright or that it was something you had to get away from?

Commander Harralson: No, it was just a kind of a feeling. I'd catch a jolt in the stomach when suddenly I'd think, "You know, we could have war here." And I'd wonder what would happen and how it would take place. As much as we glared at the Japanese sailors in China, we respected them as a navy.

We were impressed by their number of ships and the way they looked. And Tony Lyons on the Augusta had been up to Tokyo a couple of years before I was out there. He was a raconteur. He used to tell about different places he had been and told us about Tokyo. But he also told us about the navy ships--the battleships and the things that he had seen. So the people out there knew well that the Japanese Navy was no cream puff or pushover. I think we knew that better than MacArthur did, and better than the people back in Washington. I really believe that.

Paul Stillwell: Well, that was a widespread feeling, that the Japanese were inferior.

Commander Harralson: Absolutely. And I'm telling you, when they hit us, we were the ones that felt inferior.

Paul Stillwell: The Augusta had been up to Vladivostok, Russia, a few years before that, also, with Admiral Yarnell on board. Did some of your shipmates talk about that?

Commander Harralson: I can't recall anything specific, but I know about the event. In fact, I read about it probably in the Naval History.*

Paul Stillwell: We did have an article on that recently.

Commander Harralson: Let's see, who was it he was confronted with up there?

Paul Stillwell: Well, the man who wrote the article was the son of the Russian officer. The officer had been hospitable to the Americans, and so the Russians got rid of him after that.

Commander Harralson: Yes, that's right. That's it. I don't remember anything specific about that. The Augusta had been into Saigon, French Indochina. It's upriver, I believe.

---

*The Augusta visited Vladivostok, Russia, in July 1937. For details we Ilya Sergievich Okunev, "Vengeance in Vladivostok," Naval History, May/June 1996, pages 43-45.

Paul Stillwell: Yes.

Commander Harralson: When they went there, they drank a lot of French wine. One of the stories was that when they finally left--got out to sea the next morning--half the crew was drunk. They held a shakedown, looking for liquor. They couldn't find any, and they finally reasoned that these sailors had gotten drunk on this wine, and they had sort of a kickback the next morning, after they drank water.

Paul Stillwell: [Laughter] That's interesting.

Commander Harralson: I guess that was quite a place to go. I wish I had been on that. I should have got out there earlier.

Paul Stillwell: Well, we get too-late smart, they say.

Commander Harralson: Yes.

[Interruption for change of tape]

Paul Stillwell: Where were we?

Commander Harralson: Oh, the ominous clouds in the offing. It's about time for the big thing.

Paul Stillwell: Right.

Commander Harralson: I went over to Manila one Sunday, for a movie and a dinner, and came back. I was due to take the watch at 8:00 o'clock Monday morning.

Paul Stillwell: Would this Sunday be December 7?

Commander Harralson: Yes. I came back and turned in. The next thing I knew, I was being shaken violently. It was the chief, and he said, "Get up there and relieve Miller. He's been up there since 3:00 o'clock." Then he went charging off. People were running by, in both directions, everywhere. So I finally collared one, and I said, "What's going on?"

"Pearl's been bombed!"

I went tearing up topside and relieved Miller. The traffic was flowing heavy. What had happened was that the supervisor had taken a turn around back of the operator positions. We had a lot of Filipino Insular Force trainees there. One of them was sitting on some circuit; I don't know which one. But the supervisor looked over the operator's shoulder, and here was a whole log sheet full of, "Pearl Harbor has been bombed by the Japanese. This is not a drill." Just over and over and over. He'd been copying that for, I don't know, a half an hour or an hour. Just sitting there. So, of course, they called everybody, and that started things going.

When I got up there and relieved Miller, there was a lot of traffic to go. But on the wall, back of the desk aways, was a TCO transceiver. Now, that was something brand new to me. It was a VHF transceiver using voice. It was stuck up there and in operation, but there didn't seem to be any person assigned to listen or guard it. It was just there and running. I hadn't been up there very long, and Clark Field came roaring out with a guy saying, "We're being bombed. We're being bombed."[*] He was describing what was going on. You could hear the bombs.

Paul Stillwell: That must have been voice.

Commander Harralson: Oh, yes, that was voice. So I figured that, "This is it." All day long we worked real hard. All kinds of rumors were flying. I think they bombed Nichols Field too.[†]

---

[*]Clark Field was a U.S. Army Air Forces base was about 50 miles north of Manila, on the island of Luzon.
[†]On the following day, 9 December, Japanese aircraft bombed Nichols Field, an Army Air Forces base on the outskirts of Manila.

That Sunday evening, we sat on a little seawall, back of the building there, and you could see over to Manila. It was supposed to be blacked out, but there were lights everywhere. And we'd see a red rocket go up in the air.

Paul Stillwell: I wonder what that was from.

Commander Harralson: We speculated, but that was all we knew. And, of course, we went over events. Fuji's Bar, closed two weeks before; Fuji is Japanese, you know. There was also a barber shop there with Japanese barbers that had closed shop two weeks before. There was a restaurant over in Manila, on Dewey Boulevard. It was The Old German restaurant until the war broke out, and they changed the name to The Old Europe. Sailors used to go there. I liked to go there. It was very good food. But we heard that that was a hot spot for espionage.

Paul Stillwell: So it was off limits?

Commander Harralson: No. This was after the war started we started hearing this. We didn't know.

There was kind of a sad story. I was sitting there next to a fellow by the name of Ernie Clark. He was a first class radioman. He was person I hadn't seen around before. I got to talking to him. He had been in the fleet reserve--a retired first class radioman--and they called him back. They called a bunch back before the war started. They had assigned him to the Federal Building in San Francisco. He hadn't been there long when they asked for a radioman volunteer for a merchant ship headed for Manila. Ernie volunteered.

The ship arrived in Manila the sixth of December. Ernie came over to the radio station to see old friends and to hang around there until the ship departed. Well, when the attack came on Pearl Harbor, the ship got under way abruptly and left Ernie there. So Ernie was stuck with us. His lot was with us. There's more to Ernie's story, later on.[*]

---

[*]The remainder of the story is covered in Commander Harralson's account of his prisoner of war experiences.

Paul Stillwell: Well, it sounds as if there was a great deal of confusion coming over the circuits in those first several hours.

Commander Harralson: Total confusion. And I'll point out here, that our air force--I think we had 60 B-17s and about 160 P-40s. They were virtually wiped out the first day, on the ground. And here's a point that baffles me: Admiral Kimmel and General Short were relieved for being caught unprepared out there.* Their careers were ruined.

Paul Stillwell: They were relieved, right.

Commander Harralson: I thought there was a movement afoot, now, to rescind that or do something with it.

Paul Stillwell: Well, the Kimmel children tried to get their father reinstated to four stars posthumously, but the Defense Department turned it down.

Commander Harralson: But compare that with MacArthur, sitting out there. He had eight hours' advance notice, and his air force was wiped out, on the ground. I think just a handful of planes ever got into the air, and I don't understand that.

Paul Stillwell: Well, apparently he had sufficient political clout that President Roosevelt didn't feel that he could get rid of MacArthur. But, more important, the public was focused on Pearl Harbor, not the Philippines. Roosevelt needed a scapegoat, or two scapegoats, to tell the American public that the fault lay elsewhere, not in Washington. And Kimmel and Short, unfortunately, bore the brunt of that.

Commander Harralson: Trying to look at it militarily, in which I've had no training

---

*Admiral Husband E. Kimmel, USN, had been Commander in Chief Pacific Fleet since 1 February 1941. He was relieved of command on 17 December in the wake of the attack earlier in the month. He was essentially forced to retire in early 1942 as a two-star admiral, his permanent rank. Lieutenant General Walter Short, USA, commander of the Army's Hawaiian Department, was also relieved on 17 December and retired in 1942. Neither was the subject of a court-martial.

whatsoever in strategy or any of that, but it just seems to me that he was a total failure at defending. He didn't use what he had properly. He was caught time and again unaware. He would not communicate with the Navy. I think Admiral Hart lost a lot of his torpedoes because MacArthur didn't tell him he was going to abandon Manila.

Paul Stillwell: MacArthur declared it an open city, as of Christmas.

Commander Harralson: Yes, right. As a result, Hart could not relocate a lot of his submarine supplies. And there's a whole bunch of things like that. MacArthur never personally went over and took a look at Bataan. He went over to Mariveles once, from Corregidor. It seemed to me that he had no idea of what the situation was on the front.

Paul Stillwell: Well, to address your perplexity, it was a political decision, rather than a military one, to keep him.

Commander Harralson: Oh, yes. [Laughter] I have yet to run across a POW that didn't hate MacArthur with a passion.

Paul Stillwell: Does that include you?

Commander Harralson: Absolutely. Even National Geographic had a big article on MacArthur. You know, they try to remain apolitical. But if you read carefully what they say, you can't help but realize that this guy was a brilliant man, but his genius lay in self-aggrandizement, or promotion. That's where his genius was.

Quezon gave to Mac--I've seen two figures--one, a million dollars and the other, $500,000.[*] He took half and split with his top staff members. Quezon gave it to MacArthur, to get Quezon out of there. I think maybe the difference in figures lies in whether we're talking in dollars or pesos. The peso was solid at two-for-one. So a million pesos would be $500,000. I read that in another book. They say it's a matter of record.

---

[*]Manuel Quezon was President of the Philippine Commonwealth from its founding in 1935 until his death in 1944.

Well now, I think that borders on some kind of criminal activity, militarily. We didn't have the Uniform Code then but against the Rocks and Shoals or the Articles of War.

Paul Stillwell: Well, taking a bribe is just against the law.

Commander Harralson: It ought to be, if it isn't. [Laughter]

Paul Stillwell: Well, what do you remember about the bombing of Cavite?

Commander Harralson: December 10 I left the desk at noon and went over to eat, and I remember going around the head of the docks area there. There were two destroyers in there and two submarines. I remember wondering, you know, where they're going to go and what they're going to do in the future, in this war.

Paul Stillwell: Sealion and Seadragon were the submarines.

Commander Harralson: Yes. Through conversation with other sailors, I learned that the two four-stack destroyers in the yard were the Peary and the Pillsbury. The Pillsbury was able to get up steam and escape. The Peary, although damaged, was rescued by the heroic efforts of the Whippoorwill. The two submarines in the yard were the Sealion and the Seadragon. The Sealion was sunk, but the Seadragon managed to escape.

Paul Stillwell: I interviewed a retired admiral named Bub Ward, who was in the Seadragon.* He described that experience. And the Peary was the destroyer that took Cecil King out of the Philippines.

Commander Harralson: That's why it's so interesting.

Paul Stillwell: You bet it is!

---

*See the Naval Institute oral history of Rear Admiral Norvell G. Ward, USN (Ret.).

Commander Harralson: I mean, talking to you. I know a little thing, and here you come along and fill in all the rest of it. That's great.

Paul Stillwell: Well, you were describing going around the head of the dock and seeing these four ships.

Commander Harralson: I ate lunch and I went back. I got back to my desk and was working, and I heard this TCO again: "Manila, Manila. There's a flight of 54 bombers headed for Manila." So on the land wire I called the Marsman Building. I knew the operator there, Dasso, from Augusta. I said, "Hey, Dasso, 54 bombers headed your way. Heads up! Good luck."*

He replied, "Thanks." Pretty soon he came back, "Hey, those 54 bombers--they're headed for Cavite. Good luck." [Laughter] He had hardly finished that and, boy, they started falling. That old building jumped and vibrated and shook. At one point, a guy standing at the window said, "Got one. They got one."

I said to Dasso, "They got one. They got one."

Dasso came back, "The admiral wants to know who got what."

[Laughter] So I said, "They got one of the Japs." But that wasn't true.

Paul Stillwell: Wishful thinking.

Commander Harralson: Wishful thinking, because we didn't have anything that could touch them. Now, I wasn't out there where I could see the planes. But I've always known that they were at high level; they didn't come down like at Pearl. Well, they had both at Pearl, didn't they? They had some that bombed from altitude, and others that came down.

Paul Stillwell: Right. But they weren't trying to torpedo the ships, as they were at Pearl. Also, they were bound to hit something if they dropped the bombs.

Commander Harralson: Yes.

---
*Radioman First class Luis A. Dasso, USN.

Paul Stillwell: What did you do? Did you hit the deck?

Commander Harralson: No, we sat there. Now, I have wondered why in the world we stayed in that building. Nobody told us to go out or go hide or anything. But that's how unprepared we were. There was nothing, as far as I know, set up in case of an air raid or anything. It was absolutely ridiculous for us to sit up there like a target, when we could have gotten down behind that seawall and been a hell of a lot safer. But we were just lucky. The building didn't take a direct hit. The bombing stopped, but the place was filling with smoke. Morrison showed up, in the smoke, and he said, "Everybody out. The building's on fire."

So I raced down below, to my locker, and I grabbed a laundry bag and threw a bunch of stuff in it--essentials like cigarettes soap, toothpaste. Then I ran out and jumped behind the seawall with the rest of them. But it was apparent we weren't going to be able to stay there. The place was going up in flames and was hotter than hell. So I got on the wharf that extended out from the radio building there and ran to the end. I took a look around and didn't like what I saw, because the fire was coming fast down the wharf. There was ammo stacked on the wharf. I got down to the end, and I looked again, and I thought, "I have to get out of here."

So I stripped down to my skivvy drawers. I put the socks in my shoes. I folded my clothes and put them in the laundry bag. Then I took the laundry bag and shoes and put them on a ledge at the end of the dock. I don't know when I was going to come back and get them. [Laughter] Then I dove into the water and started swimming. I swam and I swam and I swam. And, of course, you know this: people trying to swim away from a sinking ship just can't seem to make any distance. But somewhere, somebody had cast off a barge. It was quite a ways out, and I got out to it. It was awful hard, but with the help of the men on the barge, I was able to get up on it.

So we sat there on this barge and watched Cavite--what was left of it--go up in flames. A motor launch came and threw us a line and towed us. We saw the Whippoorwill working like mad, thrashing water--it would go ahead and back, trying to get the destroyer out of there. The launch towed us on around past the torpedo shed; a big part of it was still standing. It had a freight-type door, and there were people running around in there. Then, all of a sudden, the whole thing blew up in one mighty explosion.

Paul Stillwell: There was a ship named the Pigeon that had a role in hauling out some of the ships.*

Commander Harralson: Yes, it did. I remember the Pigeon. The Pigeon was a submarine rescue ship that had been a minesweeper before that.

Paul Stillwell: A man named Hawes was the skipper of the Pigeon.† He's got one of the ships in the current fleet named after him.

Commander Harralson: Yes. Well, didn't the skipper of the Whippoorwill get a big award of some kind?‡

Paul Stillwell: That I don't remember.

Commander Harralson: There's a book out about the Asiatic Fleet; you probably know it.§ The writer was Captain Winslow, who was on the Houston. Have you read that book, perchance?

Paul Stillwell: No. I've met Winslow and talked to him, but I haven't read the book.

Commander Harralson: Well, it's a real sad book. You know, one of the saddest things was that the torpedoes that they had out there would not detonate. And those people put

---

*For details see Anthony C. Santore, "The Mustang and the Pigeon," U.S. Naval Institute Proceedings, April 1985, pages 154-156.
†The commanding officer was Lieutenant Richard E. Hawes, USN, who was awarded the Navy Cross for his exploits on 10 December 1941. The frigate Hawes (FFG-53) was named in his honor.
‡For a description of the exploits of the minesweeper Whippoorwill (AM-35) on 10 December, see Dictionary of American Naval Fighting Ships, Volume VIII (Washington, D.C.: U.S. Government Printing Office, 1981), pages 260-261.
§Walter Winslow, The Fleet the Gods Forgot: The U.S. Asiatic Fleet in World War II (Annapolis: Naval Institute Press, 1982).

their ship, their sub, and their crew in jeopardy, to shoot a dud.

Paul Stillwell: That was a fleet-wide problem for a couple of years.

Commander Harralson: It was. But he also says in there, that back in Washington they blamed this failure--to sink a ship and to mix it up--on the command.

Paul Stillwell: The skippers.

Commander Harralson: The skippers, yes. And that it virtually ruined their careers. It took them two years to find out that the darn torpedoes weren't any good. Is that how you . . . ?

Paul Stillwell: Well, I know it took them two years. I don't think that careers were ruined. Because after a while, there was such a widespread pattern that somebody figured out it must be something else.

Commander Harralson: But that's what Winslow says in his book. And one of the most remarkable things is the Isabel did a lot of dangerous things there and survived, and finally ended up in Australia. He points out that for all of their valiant work, all the crew got was the Victory Medal and, I think, an Asiatic-Pacific War Medal--one of those. There was never any recognition for their heroics.

Paul Stillwell: That's another injustice that sometimes happens.

Commander Harralson: Well, that's the way medals are, you know. It's just one of those things.

Well, a motor launch came along and threw us a line and towed us around. It gave us a good overall view of what used to be Cavite. I had the funniest feeling, sitting there. Here I was, sopping wet, in my drawers, and I didn't have anything. I'd been cleansed, purged, and I felt good; relieved of all of this baggage I had--all of these correspondence course books, all my souvenirs removed--for a clean start. You know, it was a real happy feeling.

Paul Stillwell: That's interesting.

Commander Harralson: Yes. You know, they say you spend the first half of your life collecting things and the last half getting rid of them. Here I was, I'd been cleansed and purged, and I felt like a new man.

Paul Stillwell: I hope you didn't feel like your life was half over.

Commander Harralson: Well, no. You didn't look too far ahead.

Paul Stillwell: You couldn't.

Commander Harralson: No. This motor launch beached us, just on the San Roque side, away from Cavite, and we got off there. I didn't know what the heck to do next, see. Somebody, some other sailor, said, "Why don't you go over to the Marine barracks? I hear it's still standing. Maybe they can give you some clothes."

I thought that was a good idea, and I went over there. The fire was very close, so they were not too particular about who could draw what. I went in and found small stores, and the storekeeper gave me underwear, socks, shoes, shirt, and pants.

Paul Stillwell: Khakis?

Commander Harralson: Yes, khakis. I didn't want a hat; I didn't want some sergeant to tell me what to do. [Laughter] I always liked the Marines, but I didn't want to look like one. Then I went back to the bridge to find the rest of the bunch. I found them at the bridge, and Morrison there. He was saying, "We've got to go fight fire." It was getting dark. So I don't know what the hell they were going to fight fire for, because what was burning was rubble, busted parts. But we went back into there.

There was hardly any water pressure or any equipment that we could use. We were really just fumbling around in there. Bodies everywhere, mostly Filipino. It seemed like they were running around when they shouldn't have been. They should have gotten down, at least flat on the ground.

Paul Stillwell: Did you have any feeling of disbelief while all this was going on: "How can I be caught in something like this?"

Commander Harralson: I can't remember anything quite like that.

Paul Stillwell: Well, maybe that's because you had at least a couple days' warning, compared with what happened to the people at Pearl.

Commander Harralson: Yes, that's right. That's true. In other words, it wasn't really a surprise.

Paul Stillwell: It was a question of when.

Commander Harralson: That's right. It finally had come upon us. I remember after the first bombs dropped, I said, "Hey, I can say I'm a veteran now."

Paul Stillwell: I guess you could. [Laughter]

Commander Harralson: Fighting fires, there's something funny there I want to tell you about. We had a radioman who was real short. Com 16, Admiral Rockwell, was out there too, and they were trying to figure out how to fight the fire.[*] And this little radioman named Stoddard was trying to tell the admiral what he should do.[†] Here were these flames, and here were these two in silhouette, like Mutt and Jeff.[‡]

---

[*]Rear Admiral Francis W. Rockwell, USN, Commandant 16th Naval District.
[†]Radioman Second Class Harry G. Stoddard, USN.
[‡]Mutt and Jeff were two comic strip characters of the period; one was short, the other tall.

Paul Stillwell: Rockwell was a tall, thin man.

Commander Harralson: Yes, that's right; he was a big, tall guy.

Paul Stillwell: Was he listening?

Commander Harralson: He appeared to be. It didn't look like he was trying to ignore him or anything.

Paul Stillwell: But, as you say, it was really a futile effort, at that point.

Commander Harralson: Oh, it was. So finally Morrison said, "Well, we'll all go back to the bridge and get on a flatbed truck that will take us out somewhere so we can get some sleep." So we did. We climbed on this truck and rode out into the boondocks. We found a fairly clear place and climbed out and looked around for a place to lay down.

I found kind of a shallow ditch that seemed to fit my back, and I went to sleep. I woke up sometime during the night and lay there, sort of half awake. I saw these lights just zooming through the sky, way up there, you know. I thought, "They're airplanes fighting. But planes don't dogfight at night." I pondered that a while. Then my eyes gradually began to focus better, and it turned out to be a swarm of fireflies, about six inches above my face. [Laughter]

Paul Stillwell: You were probably not completely awake, to begin with.

Commander Harralson: Yes. We got up the next morning, daylight. Morrison was our source of information, and he told us that we were going to Corregidor. We were to get on the truck, which would take us back to Cavite. Then we'd catch the San Felipe to take us out to Corregidor.

The truck took us as close as we could get. Then we had to scramble through wreckage and carnage. We got aboard the San Felipe and headed out. It was kind of a nervous ride, because there were Japanese airplanes about. They were uncontested, flying at will. The poor PatWing 10 PBYs had a terrible time out there; they were sitting ducks.

We reached Corregidor all right. We hadn't eaten for some time, and there were two officer mess stewards that had a big box of groceries. As soon as we came aboard, you could see these mess stewards getting more and more nervous. They didn't have a chance; there were about 25 of us, I guess, at that point, and we raided their box of groceries. When they got to Corregidor, there wasn't anything in them. The only thing I got out of it was a can of fruit cocktail. I guess I wasn't quite as ravenous as some of the rest. There was bread and, I don't know, the usual foodstuffs.

Paul Stillwell: What was your reaction to seeing the corpses?

Commander Harralson: I don't know. I think the human mind has some kind of mechanism, or arrangement, that under stress, those things don't bother you.

Paul Stillwell: It's kind of filtered out?

Commander Harralson: Yes. They just, maybe, don't register fully. I do not like the sight of bloodshed. I will avoid a wreck, or anything where somebody is hurt. But at that time seeing bodies didn't bother me in the least. Believe me, I saw a lot. I'll tell you about an incident later on that was really something.

We got out to Bottomside, on Corregidor, and a sailor met us and told us that he would show us how to get out to Monkey Point. We followed him. We passed through Malinta Tunnel, and I was amazed at the size of it. It's a long tunnel, with these tremendous laterals going out on each side. We came out the other side, and we went down this road. The island was beautiful. The trees were green, the vegetation lush, birds were singing. The air was balmy. I thought, "Gee, what a nice place to fight a war." It was about, I would say, a mile maybe, out to Monkey Point.

Monkey Point sat on a bluff, about 50 feet above the ocean--beautiful site--and the entrance to the tunnel faced south. There were a few trees out there. Not too far to the west were four two-story, wooden apartment buildings where dependents had stayed. We moved in there. There wasn't any furniture, but who needs furniture? I took a bath. There was a bathtub. Of course, there wasn't any hot water or soap. But I remember taking that bath and how good it felt.

We set up operations in the front end of the tunnel. They put me on land wire. We had a wire with the Army tunnel, Malinta Tunnel. We were supposed to handle some of the Army traffic, headed for the States. There was a MUX system, not quite as elaborate as at Cavite. Our transmitters were in Queen Tunnel, which was perhaps a half a mile to the west, which was a major flaw. The lines to the transmitters were all above ground.

In that period before Christmas, things were pretty serene there. Hooper and I caught a streetcar that ran from Malinta Tunnel through Bottomside, Middleside, to Topside. The west end of the island was a mount 550 feet high, a big mound. We rode the streetcar up there. It was a beautiful place--park-like, big trees. There was a commissary, and I think there was a movie house, quarters, and all. We went in the PX there, but it had been looted, so to speak.* There wasn't anything there of real value, you know, like toothpaste, toothbrush, soap, edibles--no edibles or anything like that. So we really couldn't buy anything.

Paul Stillwell: Did you get into Navy uniforms at some point in this sequence?

Commander Harralson: I know at some point I was back into dungarees. I don't remember where I got them or just when I got them. But I still had my Marine shoes. I really don't know how I came to be in dungarees again, but I was. Somehow I had lost my khaki pants and shirt.

Christmas day, our cooks put together a real Christmas dinner in one of the apartment houses there. We had ham, I think, and sweet potatoes and holiday pickles and the usual trimmings. It was all on the table. We were maybe 10 or 15 minutes from sitting down to eat when an air raid hit us. We all beat it for low spots--to find someplace we could get down below the general level of the ground, in ditches and so forth. They hit us real hard. They destroyed everything: all the buildings and our dinner and the whole

---

*PX--post exchange.

schmear. That sort of marked the beginning of a slide downhill. It just, from there, became worse and worse.

The food became bread and coffee for breakfast. We'd eat two meals a day. We had bread and coffee for breakfast; for the evening meal we had rice and beans, for a while. Finally, that ran out, and it was spaghetti. Now, we're talking spaghetti with no meatballs, no tomato sauce, no Parmesan cheese.

Paul Stillwell: Just spaghetti.

Commander Harralson: Just spaghetti. The water became a real problem. The water came from wells at Bottomside. It was in short supply, and they were worried about purity. Our source for drinking was a very large Lister bag, hung on a tripod in the middle of our mess area in front of the tunnel. The tunnel was built up by the FR unit at the back and our unit at the front. There was very little space. So the galley was outside, and our eating facilities were outside.

Generally, except for when we were on watch, we were outside. We were left on your own as to where to bunk. I scrounged a hammock mattress and an Army blanket. I dug a long hole in the ground, because I wanted to get below the surface when I slept.

The water situation was bad. There was a short time there when we were able to take bucket baths, which sailors are well acquainted with. But restrictions reduced it down to a canteen cup bath. Then from that, to a wet-rag bath. And then forget it.

I dug a hole about 75 yards away from the entrance to the tunnel, where I could put my hammock mattress--to sleep. When I was digging the hole, there was a Marine squad out there that had an ancient-looking gun, very small, that they referred to as a one-pounder. It looked like something from, maybe, the Spanish-American War.

Paul Stillwell: Was this like a field piece?

Commander Harralson: Yes. Very small. But it overlooked a beach to the east of us. There was kind of a hook on the tail of Monkey Point. The squad leader was a Corporal York. In digging my hole, York and I came in close proximity to one another. You know, sailors don't have much to say to Marines, or vice versa. We made comments about each other, from time to time. It went on, and we began to make sarcastic comments about each other and MacArthur. After the bombs and shelling started going for good, why, we became more philosophical, and I guess we eventually became what one might call friends.

Paul Stillwell: You had a common enemy.

Commander Harralson: We did. [Laughter]

The Red Cross had tried to put together little Christmas packages, little sacks with tidbits in it. But they didn't have much to work with. One of the items--the only one thing I can remember--was a plug of chewing tobacco. So there was a lot of it around. The Navy doesn't like chewing tobacco, for good reason, but out there it didn't make any difference. So York and I started chewing tobacco and sitting on the edge of the cliff and spitting over into the ocean and telling each other sea stories and philosophizing and all.

But York didn't sleep in a hole; he didn't believe in that. So one night I had the watch, and we got word that there was a big raid coming. I thought about York out there, so I raced out to York, made a special trip out there. I shook York. I said, "York, wake up. There's big one coming."

York raised up on one elbow and said, "What the hell. I can't stop them." Then he laid down and went back to sleep. That's the kind of guy he was. A very good friend. A real Marine.

Paul Stillwell: What happened to him?

Commander Harralson: I don't know. Things kept getting worse.

I used to roam through the forest there. I found a little berry--something like a grape--and a nut that were edible. So I spent a lot of time looking for them. If a raid or a shelling came, I just found a little spot or a hole and waited it out. But the forest began to get a little broken up and messy. They started shelling us from the south shore. They had pulled up guns there, and they went to work on the small craft that was anchored below us and somewhat to the west, because the vise was closing, and to leave there was to get blown up. There was a little bit of protection there.

They shelled from the south shore. They never hit anything. We never saw a hit on one of the ships. Then they shifted to our area, for harassment; we didn't have any big guns there to speak of. They destroyed the forest around Monkey Point. You could hardly go anywhere that there wasn't a crater.

There were government mules. There was a bunch of mules on the island, and they were slaughtered. We received some of the mule meat. It tasted very good, but was very, very tough.

I talked to a soldier. He was in the construction battalion, I believe it was, and he was a draftee. At that time, draftees were not supposed to leave the States. He had been in the Philippines for a while. He had come back from the front. He described things going on up there, and they were terrible. The ration, on paper, was supposed to be 2,000 calories per day. But they didn't get anywhere near that. A truck would leave Mariveles with supplies, and by the time it got out there, it would be mostly gone, rifled. The place was swarming with civilians, understandably. I don't mean to blame the rifling of the trucks on the civilians, but food was in short supply everywhere.

They had a bad time. Malaria was rampant. There was no quinine. That's another thing critics can't understand. Here we are, not very far from the source of quinine. Nobody thought about quinine. There seemed to be no logistical thoughts. Most of the rice was left in Manila, back there. That was another big question. Here they were, supposed to get 2,000 calories a day. Probably it was more like 1,000 or 1,500, if that. A fighting soldier requires on the order of 4,000 calories a day. Then they dropped it down to 1,500 calories a day, on paper. There's no telling what they were actually getting, with all of that.

Furthermore, a big part of the line were the Filipino soldiers. Now, the Filipino soldiers were untrained. It was one of MacArthur's big ideas to have an army of 300,000 trained Filipino soldiers. So they had started towards that, but they had no officer cadre. According to Baldwin, the only thing they knew was to stand up and salute and ask,

"When do we eat?"* [Laughter] Most of them headed for the hills when the war started. And I don't feel you can blame them, because we had the Philippine Scouts that were excellent soldiers. In fact, our trained soldiers out there--this is, again, from Baldwin--we only had 21,000 American soldiers. I never realized it was that small. Our total of trained soldiers was 31,000; I think 10,000 of those were Philippine Scouts; well trained, tremendous soldiers.

A bunch of Japanese Marines tried to circumvent the end of the line by sea and come ashore. They did; they got ashore. We sent a battalion of mostly sailors up there, in whites dyed in coffee, to make them less conspicuous.

Paul Stillwell: These are Americans.

Commander Harralson: Americans. They went up there to fight these Japanese Marines, going through the woods, hollering to one another. They got really mauled. Then they sent somebody else up there, to try to get them out. It ended up they had to send the Philippine Scouts. Of course, the scouts went up there and drove the Japs into the sea, had them jumping off the cliffs and all of that.

Of course, there was also the Fourth Marines, which, according to Baldwin, was the only trained infantry on Corregidor. They were down to 1,600, actual. They were in three battalions that were supposed to be 1,000 each. The difference between the 1,600 and the 3,000 was made up of clerks, sailors, and Filipino soldiers. That's what was left to defend Corregidor, although the population of Corregidor was 10,000. Sometimes it seems to me that they could have gotten more than 3,000 soldiers out there fighting.

Paul Stillwell: What was your mental state, as these months progressed?

Commander Harralson: It was kind of a funny feeling. You know, there was fear involved, but when this situation goes on day after day, you feel like you're racing down a dead-end road to a brick wall. I don't recall being bothered much by fear.

---

*See Hanson W. Baldwin, Battles Lost and Won: Great Campaigns of World War II (New York: Harper & Row Publishers, 1966). Chapter 4, titled "The Rock," deals with Corregidor.

Paul Stillwell: Had you just accepted capture as inevitable?

Commander Harralson: Not really. I tell you, having been in China and up in Tsingtao and elsewhere, and, of course, reading Life magazine and newspapers, I knew the Japanese soldiers could be vicious, bloodthirsty. They killed Chinese without provocation. And I actually thought--my evaluation of what would happen if we fell was that, although we wouldn't be slaughtered by the numbers, we would be killed off very readily. I didn't think much of the future. Feeling that way about it, I tried not to let myself dwell on it. I took it day by day, and I had a bunch of courageous people around me. That always helped. I liked to be with York.

Paul Stillwell: After you became friends. [Laughter]

Commander Harralson: Yes. [Laughter] I'd rather sweat out a raid--bombs, shelling, or whatever--with him than anybody else.

Paul Stillwell: What was the reaction when MacArthur was evacuated?[*]

Commander Harralson: Well, like I said, we didn't like him. We felt that we really had been abandoned. The morale went down. Well, we started realizing it right after Christmas. I think we understood what had happened back at Pearl. And we understood the might of the Japanese Army and the Navy. We had seen it. We knew that it was not some small outfit, that they were big and mean and capable. I thought I was going down the tubes. But you didn't let yourself think about it too much.

There was a barge loaded with rifles and machine guns that was sunk just off Bottomside. Divers were able to recover the guns. They issued them out. I drew a Lee-Enfield. My friend Hooper drew a Springfield, .30-06. They were all saturated with

---

[*]On 11 March 1942, General Douglas MacArthur, whom President Roosevelt had personally ordered to leave the Philippines, escaped from Corregidor with his family and selected staff members on board four PT boats of Lieutenant John D. Bulkeley's Motor Torpedo Boat Squadron Three. MacArthur reached Mindanao on 14 March, then continued his journey to Darwin, Australia, by airplane on 17 March.

cosmoline.* Of course, the first thing you had to do was break the gun down and clean it. I wasn't very good at that; I didn't know much about it. I was trying to do that, and a Marine came along. He had a bunch of sarcastic comments, but he helped me. We broke the thing down, and he showed me how to get it cleaned up, and I got it working. But I didn't like the gun; the bolt action was different from the Springfield.

My friend Hooper was a gun nut; he knew a lot about guns. He had his Springfield in good shape. But he was curious about my Enfield, so we swapped. I ended up with his Springfield, and he had the Lee-Enfield. Along with that were a bunch of Marlin .30-caliber, air-cooled machine guns. The Marines got a bunch of them and went to work on cleaning them up. They had a machine there that put the ammo belts together. They test-fired the guns. They'd fire three rounds and the gun would jam, not just one, but all of them. So they had ordnance experts down there--the Army, the Navy, and the Marine Corps; they all took their turns at it. They couldn't make them work. They were useless.

Bataan fell.† They blew up a supply tunnel over there that took the whole side of the mountain. There were people getting over to Corregidor any way they could, with all kinds of terrible tales of brutalities and so forth.

Paul Stillwell: Not the sort of thing that would raise your morale, either.

Commander Harralson: Nope, not at all. That was April the ninth. The Japs no sooner had the point there, the hills above Mariveles, than they moved their big guns in and their spotters. Then they went to work on us. They raked it from one end to the other. Some of them were big. I saw all kinds of duds laying around, which I steered clear of, of course. I estimated the biggest ones to be about 250 millimeter. That's about 10 inch.

I remember the day, but Baldwin tells about it--I didn't know what day it was, but he says it was the Emperor's birthday--they raked the island with 10,000 plus; they just poured it on. Of course, when all that was going so heavy like that, why, we scrounged into the front of the tunnel there. Of course, we faced south. Now, we were getting some

---

*Cosmoline is a preservative used to prevent rust.
†Bataan is a peninsula on the west side of Manila Bay.

from the south shore, too, but nowhere like what we were getting from Bataan. We knew the final showdown was coming.

On the night of the fifth of May, the shelling, again, was very, very heavy. We were in the mouth of the tunnel. Our instructions were, in the case of assault, the section on watch would stay on watch to destroy the remaining papers and all equipment. The other two sections would man a sunken walk that was atop the tunnel, parallel to the tunnel access. That was the extent of our instructions. So about 2300, I was getting ready to go on watch at midnight. And I really wanted to go on watch; I didn't want to go out there. Then the darn shelling stopped, I guess about 2330. The silence was awesome, just this deathly silence.

Paul Stillwell: In what sense?

Commander Harralson: Well, we had been hearing these terrific explosions, and then, suddenly, just nothing. That in itself is eerie.

Paul Stillwell: Was it ominous?

Commander Harralson: Oh, yes, yes. So the chief said, "Okay. You two sections man the sunken walk up there. The watch that's on will stay to destroy equipment." So I grabbed two bandoleers of ammunition, two hand grenades, and my Springfield, and I went charging out the tunnel. I got out there, and it was like Dante's Inferno; I'll swear the ground was on fire. It was so frightening, I turned and ran back into the tunnel.

Paul Stillwell: Had they started shelling again?

Commander Harralson: No, no, no. The ground was burning.

Paul Stillwell: Oh, I see. It was the remnants of--

Commander Harralson: Yes, of the shelling. I never really understood it until I read somewhere, where it was the kind of material they were using in the shells.

Paul Stillwell: Some kind of incendiary?

Commander Harralson: Yes. I ran back in and, of course, I realized I couldn't stay in. I ran back out. And I just ran. I finally got around, up to the top of the tunnel, and jumped in the walkway with the rest of them.

Paul Stillwell: Did you get the equipment destroyed?

Commander Harralson: That wasn't my job.

Paul Stillwell: Oh, I see.

Commander Harralson: That was the section that stayed. That's what I wanted to do. If they had just shelled for another hour, maybe even a half an hour, I would have been on watch and the other ones would have been outside.

Paul Stillwell: I understand now.

Commander Harralson: We got up there and, God, there were bullets flying everywhere. We could hear our rifles crack, and we could hear a lighter crack, which was the Japanese 7 millimeter, and ricochets, tracers, all over the place. We sat there, crouched with our guns at the ready. We couldn't see anything; it was pitch black. We stared into that blackness. There was a war going on out there, but we couldn't see anything to shoot at. We stared so hard our eyeballs ached. And then it began to get light.

I looked to my left, to a ridge--kind of a spine--and up there I could see soldiers firing down the other way. So I climbed out. I thought, "I'll go up there and help." I ran up the hill, and I jumped in a shell hole. There was nobody to my right. To my left, 15 feet or so, was a machine gun. I think they were Marines. Well, I know that the line was

Marines, but there were a lot of plug-ins with Army clerks and sailor yeomen and that sort of thing. But you couldn't tell by the uniform; everybody had some weird, nondescript clothing on. Our helmets were the World War I type, those flat helmets.

Paul Stillwell: Tin pots.

Commander Harralson: Yes. I had two hand grenades stuck in my pocket and the two bandoleers. The machine gun was firing; it was a Browning water-cooled, and it would go choonk, choonk, choonk, choonk. They would fire back with a much lighter-sounding machine gun. Its cadence, or rep-rate was irregular; it would go faster and then slower.

To my right, and slightly ahead, was the end of a small, undeveloped airstrip. There were no buildings or anything like that. There was a road that came from the other side, around, and went past, right in front of us and went on towards Malinta Tunnel. It was down, maybe ten feet below us. I fired down into the ravine. I could see things now and then, and I fired. But I never got a real clear shot at anything or anybody. But I fired anyhow. In fact, I fired so much that I burned my hand putting another clip in the gun.

Then the Japanese started dropping little mortar shells. They were falling all over the place. They put one right into the machine-gun nest. I think it was a Marine--of course, it clobbered everybody there--but I remember this Marine staggering down the hill backwards, fighting to stay on his feet. The firing would get real intense, and then slack off, then get real intense, you know. I began to wonder about where I could get more ammunition. I could see that as being a problem. In one of the slack periods, I saw the top of a white flag, just over the corner of this airstrip, see. I climbed out of my shell hole and started jumping up and down. I hollered, "They're surrendering. They're surrendering." The flag moved on, and I saw a meatball in the middle.

So I climbed back down in my hole. The flag came farther, and I saw that it was sticking up from a tank. It came around the road and it stopped, what, 10 feet below, 15 feet. It was right down there, about 20 feet to the right. I tried to shoot in the slit above the barrel. It was really a little tank. I'd heard that if you could put a shot inside, it would ricochet around and do a lot of damage. So I shot a lot of rounds, trying to put it in there, but I didn't, I guess.

Then I did a ridiculous thing; I threw hand grenades at it. I threw them at the tracks. I thought maybe I could knock the tracks off. One of them detonated, and the other one didn't. Neither one went anywhere near where I was throwing. So I crouched down, back in my hole. I guess Rambo or John Wayne would have run around and got a log and jammed under the sprockets or something like that or climbed up there and stuck his rifle barrel in there, but that's John Wayne and Rambo. That wasn't me.

Anyhow, we were being enfiladed. They started firing right down that line, and they got another machine gun, down at the end. Then the tank went on. We saw him going down the road and around the corner. Then things just went quiet. We sat there for a while and wondered, "What's next?" The word came up the line, "Everybody back to base. General Wainwright has surrendered the island."[*] I sat there for quite a while, kind of dazed, I guess. Then I got up and walked back down to the tunnel. They were throwing all kinds of guns and material over the side, into the water.

I walked inside the tunnel and found a great big chaotic mess in there. I found a box that I had built to keep valuables--soap, pipe tobacco, stuff like that, and maybe 100 pesos. I got a pack of Dobie cigarettes, and then I just threw the box on this pile of rubble. All I kept were the Philippine cigarettes. (Anything Philippine was referred to as "dobie," as in dobie cigarettes, etc. I believe it comes from the word adobe--used to make bricks for houses. It was not especially derogatory; it just implied that something was native made.) We sat around there, just milling. There was nobody ever in charge. There was no leader, because we were all chiefs or first class. And we were expert communicators but lousy soldiers.

The FRU unit had been taken out by submarine sometime before, so the curtain had come down and we saw the other half and could see concrete stairs up one side of the tunnel. The stairs went up to a steel door. There was a big iron bar, locking the door. Well, we were milling around down there, and there came this bang, bang, bang at the door. We just ignored it for a while. It banged and banged again. So finally I felt I needed a resolution to this situation; it was impossible where we were. So I went up, and I opened the door.

---

[*]Lieutenant General Jonathan M. Wainwright, USA, was the senior U.S. Army commander in the Philippines following the departure of General MacArthur.

There was a tiny Japanese soldier. I don't think he was over five foot tall. His clothes were kind of a blue-gray, worn khaki. He had a leather belt with pouches on it. He was standing there with his rifle at rest, gun butt on the ground. His helmet had a net and was full of branches and twigs. He was standing there, nonchalant, at ease. We stood there looking at each other for a little bit, and then he waved me on. Their wave is like this--means come. And he pointed.

Paul Stillwell: It's kind of a horizontal wave you're showing me.

Commander Harralson: Yes. So he motioned me out and pointed to where he wanted me to stand. So I went out. As I passed him, he handed me some of their ration, a piece of what I would call hardtack. So I went over and stood there. Everybody was out. They put us in a line. Of course, there were other Japanese soldiers there too. We started down this path. We passed a bunch of bodies by the side of the path. They were Philippine Scouts. Their hands were tied behind their backs, and they had all been bayoneted through the throat. So that told us these people weren't playing.

I think we stayed on the rock for the next three or four weeks. There were some pretty nasty things done.

Paul Stillwell: Why did they keep you there that long?

Commander Harralson: I don't know. It might have been because they needed a way to get us in to the mainland there. That night they outlined where we were to sleep, and it was where there had been a searchlight, for air aids. It was layered with big, broken rock, and that's where we had to sleep, on that rock. And I tell you, I laid down and slept. The next day they took us down to Malinta Tunnel. I saw, in front of Malinta Tunnel, a pile of bodies. I would hate to estimate the size, but it looked enormous--just bodies. I guess they had been cleaned out from the hospital.

I don't know what all happened that day, except we slept that night on the railroad tracks. They picked out the railroad tracks for us to sleep. The next day, I had the misfortune to be selected, with three others--they were Army--for a detail. It had to be more than the next day, because the soldiers that took Corregidor were vets from China. They knew their business. But, all in all, they weren't too bad.

What came next was far worse. The occupation soldiers--a lot of them kids, teenagers--were vicious, mean as snakes. It was with one of those groups that the four of us were assigned, as a squad. We thought we were going to work, but they took us out past Monkey Point, into a little clearing and sat us down. They had a lot of smiles. They were jabbering amongst themselves. Finally, they signaled to two of our men, and about four of the Japs took the two down the side of the hill. Then we heard several rifle shots, and the soldiers come back up, without the two men. They took them down there and shot them. I looked at this other guy, and we thought we were next. I guess that as we were looking, our eyes were telling each other, "Should we run? What should we do?"

A Japanese officer appeared on the scene. You've seen pictures of aristocratic Japanese. They look different; they have a very haughty look. He appeared on the scene, and he barked at the soldiers in his Japanese, and those guys were scared. Finally, he turned around and told us, in English, to follow him.

We went up the road a ways, down to the beach. There were two other Americans there. The water, off of this beach, was almost solid with dead Japanese, where the Marines got them. They had sunk their landing craft. Our job was to retrieve certain parts of them that seemed to be necessary for records or what. What we had to do was take off a dead man's belt, which had the bayonet scabbard and bayonet, and one of his leggings. I think the leggings had identification sewed into them. I remember trying to get the belts off of these guys. I thought, "God, these guys are fat." Well, they'd been out in the sun and the water there, and they were bloated. We struggled and struggled, and finally we'd end up hitting the corpse--pow, right in the gut, to take that belt off. Then we'd unwrap the leggings. Then the officer would come down. He had a sword. It wasn't a Samurai sword; it was their issue sword, I guess. He'd cut off the left hand. He put the hand in a white neckerchief a certain way, folded it up, and set it aside.

We'd done a bunch of those, like that. The officer was sitting there on a rock, and finally he called me over. He had what looked to me like a German Luger, lying next to him on the rock. The soldiers were sitting, kind of like up on the bank. He gave me the sword. He told me to cut the hands off. That was not an easy job. I found you have to have a block of wood or something under that. So that's how we spent the rest of the day, taking off belts and leggings, and I was cutting off hands.

Paul Stillwell: Do you have any idea why you were cutting off hands?

Commander Harralson: Yes. Because the next day, there was a big ceremony up on this little airstrip, where they burned the American flag. I've seen pictures of that. We were there. They had soldiers, with this white neckerchief with the hand in it, tied around their neck, hanging around their neck. It was our understanding that those would be cremated and sent home to the people. But the thing was, it didn't seem to me like they had much paperwork down there to record who was who. First of all, we didn't bury them; we dragged the bodies up onto the beach. At first they had us trying to cover them with palmettos. Then, as the day wore on, they got less and less particular. When we left there, there were still hundreds of bodies out there.

Now, there have been estimates of something like 4,000 killed. I won't argue with that. But Baldwin put the estimate of Americans killed, I think, way too low. There were bodies all over the place. And the Japanese wouldn't let us touch them. They stayed there, rotted, and stunk. You can imagine what the island smelled like. Eventually, the Japanese themselves came around and with gasoline or kerosene or something like that. They poured it over the bodies and set them on fire. That's what they did with the bodies outside the Malinta Tunnel. That's why I was perturbed. I thought that was a terrible, terrible thing to do to soldiers that died in battle--to leave them lay there and rot in the tropical sun. But, you know, I saw pictures of Okinawa. I saw how we treated the dead Japanese soldiers, and it wasn't any better. So I guess that's part of war.

The next thing I got into was a working party. We were like pack animals. They had a whole bunch of material they had saved from the sunken landing craft--ammunition and equipment--and they wanted to move it up to Bottomside. I would guess that it was about a mile and a half or two miles away, or something like that. There was maybe a dozen of us. We were under the charge of an older man, who told us he was a schoolteacher. He wore glasses and had like a shoestring that tied his glasses on his head.

He was a kind old guy. He was always worried whether we had enough to eat. He was always giving us our own C ration cans, you know. So I had built up a bunch of them I carried stuffed in my shirt.

The main problem was water. We were coming along the road there one day, and somebody discovered a gun emplacement with a shield of canisters that the powder came in. They had set them upright and filled them with sand, for protection of a gun position. One of them wasn't full of sand; it was full of water. So we all took our turns; we ladled the water out and filled our canteens. Everybody took a good drink. We got down to the bottom, and there was a dead rat. So we all threw the water away.

Paul Stillwell: I'm not surprised.

Commander Harralson: You know, when we came up from all this body work we did on the beach, my hands were bloody. But, you know, I sat down and ate a can of C rations with a bent lid.

Paul Stillwell: The bent lid was your spoon.

Commander Harralson: My spoon. So we weren't particular. We went on for two or three days, working for this old schoolteacher.

Paul Stillwell: Did he speak English?

Commander Harralson: Yes, he had a little English. Happiness was a cigarette and a yasumai, which was a rest by the side of the road, and a canteen full of water. But he got through with us and turned us into the big compound that was down where the seaplane hangars were. I was turned loose in there. I finally found a kind of makeshift tent, where there were some people I knew, radiomen and so forth. I went in and stripped down, putting my clothes in the corner. Maybe I had eight or ten cans of C rations there, covered by my clothes. Then I went down to the beach to take a swim in the seawater, which was just filthy. When I came up from there, my cans of C rations were gone. See, there were no provisions to feed all of us in this compound. So I didn't know what to do. I was able to get on another working party, and I built up another small horde of C rations. I wouldn't let them out of my sight. Then I got on a working party, hauling C rations.

That's what disgusted everybody. Here we were, starving to death, and all the food they took off of that island, we couldn't believe it; just case after case after case of these C rations.

Paul Stillwell: Evidently the American forces had planned to be able to hold out a lot longer than they actually did.

Commander Harralson: Well, you read about it. Supposedly the food was getting short. And then, when you think about it, 10,000 people eat a lot of food. Even if it's just a little bit, it takes a lot. So I really don't know what to say, except that there was an awful lot of food that went out of the laterals off the tunnel.

This one working party I got on was hauling cases of C rations. When we came back through the gates, into the compound, they shook us down. They found me with all of these C rations I had saved, so they accused me of stealing them. They worked me over with rifle butts. I got back in there, and here I was with no food again. The water situation was terrible. There was one tap, and the water coming out was not much more than a trickle. And here was a tremendous long line of soldiers. There weren't too many sailors on Corregidor. What made it worse, not only that the line was long, but that the Army would put a guy in the water line, and then everybody would drape him with their canteens. So here was a guy standing there with countless canteens hanging around him or some guy with a five-gallon can. So I really don't know how I ever got a drink.

The Army was coalescing into groups, and you got an inkling of what anarchy can be like. There was nobody in charge. It was small groups that seemed to band together. But, other than that, it was chaos in there.

Paul Stillwell: Are you speaking of the Japanese?

Commander Harralson: I'm talking Americans.

Paul Stillwell: Okay. Well, would the Americans have enough freedom to be able to organize themselves?

Commander Harralson: Well, inside the compound we were on our own.

Paul Stillwell: Oh, I see.

Commander Harralson: Yes.

Right up above the compound, the Japanese had the bulldozers that had been ours. They dug a great, big, long trench and filled it with dead bodies.

I question Baldwin's account of fatalities. It looked to me like there were an awful lot of dead Americans there. But I don't guess they know. I know that when I was working on the land wire, with Malinta Tunnel, I would get these long lists of Army transfers: by name, company to company, regiment to regiment, and that sort of thing. I thought, "What in the world are they doing here?" It finally dawned on me that, well, the only answer that I could think of--these are casualties, deaths and wounded. And they were so long, and the Army operators were so lousy, that finally they sent Hooper down there. Hooper was a good man with a bug. Hooper and I worked together real good and cleared that traffic fast. But that gave you an indication that there were a lot of people dying.

Paul Stillwell: So your life was saved, probably, by the fact that that aristocratic officer showed up when he did, rather than, say, five or ten seconds later.

Commander Harralson: Absolutely. Absolutely.

Paul Stillwell: Did he communicate in English?

Commander Harralson: I heard him say a few words in English, but I think he preferred to not disclose his English.

Paul Stillwell: How did he communicate what he wanted you to do, in connection with the Japanese corpses?

Commander Harralson: It's amazing, in a situation like that, how well you can understand what some points and snarls and threats, waving a sword at you.

Paul Stillwell: You understood threats.

Commander Harralson: You understand, yes. And a few sign motions.

Paul Stillwell: Well, he could probably pantomime what he wanted you to do with the bodies.

Commander Harralson: That's what he did. I got a block of wood, though, and put it under the wrists.

Paul Stillwell: What a grisly job, though. My goodness.

Commander Harralson: And you know, it didn't bother me. You get numb.

Paul Stillwell: That would have to be it.

Commander Harralson: Yes. And things were getting desperate down there in the compound. I was beginning to starve. Apparently I was getting a little water somewheres. Then I buddied up with a guy. I forget now who it was. Somehow we got ahold of dried lima beans, a little sack full of them. We decided if we could get them in water, and soak them, and then get some wood, we could cook them. But, see, all that stuff was very scarce. We weren't having much luck. We were in this draw, and the rainy season began that night. One of the most miserable sights I ever saw was that camp after the downpour that night. They were the most beat, gaunt people I ever saw, including myself. Everything we owned was sopping wet. There was no food. We wondered what was next.

About 10:00 o'clock that morning, they told us they were going to move us off the island. They brought up, that day, three old cargo ships and anchored them just off the beach. I can't recall how we got out to them.

Paul Stillwell: Would this be, now, about the middle of May?

Commander Harralson: Yes. Well, let's see. The island fell 6 May, and I think it was three weeks later. So it would have been just at the end of May. As I recall, it took two days to get us on the ship. But everybody perked up a little bit with the idea of getting the hell off of this terrible place. They jammed us aboard these three ships. I spent the night sleeping on the ship's rail. Well, it was wood; it was about that wide.

Paul Stillwell: Six or eight inches wide.

Commander Harralson: Yes. I slept on my back. I thought I was lucky, because it was a mass of humanity on the deck. Then they steamed in and anchored just off of Dewey Boulevard in Manila. We got in landing craft that hauled us toward the beach and dumped us out in about six feet of water. We got ashore. They got us all in ranks. This was a long, tedious process of moving men.

They got us in ranks and eventually we got moving. Then we were a parade. They paraded us all through Manila. There were Filipinos trying to give us rice balls and water, risking their own lives. They had Japanese officers, I guess they were, on horses. They kept riding up and down. This officer would go by, and here'd come a Filipino, charging out with one of those five-gallon tins full of water--ladling it out and everybody trying to get some, you know. Then he'd run back when the officer was coming back. Some of them would come out with rice balls and, of course, there was a mad scramble for rice balls. They marched us all over town and eventually to Bilibid Prison. There we got the first food issued by the Japanese, a little bowl of rice.

Paul Stillwell: Do you have an estimate of what you weighed at the time that you went over to Corregidor?

Commander Harralson: I got a lot skinnier. [Laughter] I would guess 130-135.

Paul Stillwell: So you were not heavy even before the war started.

Commander Harralson: No, no, I was about 155, about what I am now.

We stayed in Bilibid, I think, about a week. They had a real interesting latrine there. It was a big water trough, and they had a barrel. I met the guy that invented it there. He was a warrant officer, chief warrant. It had a big 50-gallon drum, and it had water going in it. It was pivoted so that water filled it from a little pipe; then at a certain point, it lost equilibrium and tipped over. When it dumped its water, the weight was on the bottom again and it flipped back up. The flow rate of the water dumped it and just periodically flushed this trough, which had a lot of use. There was a lot of dysentery.

Then they put us in boxcars. They jammed us in, so you couldn't fall over. We went up to Cabanatuan. I had hit it off with an Indian from Forest Hill, above Auburn. I knew his sister in high school. She was Juanita, and he was Dick Porter. He was a year behind me in high school, and he was Army. He and I hit it off for a while. We shared. That helped a lot, to have a buddy that you shared things with, like share a piece of cigarette together. We started to hike out to Cabanatuan, to the prison camp, which was quite a ways out from the town where we got off the train. I remember he and I sharing a canteen full of water. Both of us were very careful and made it last.

We were hiking along, and we passed by a calesa. As I passed, this hand came out, with a package wrapped in banana leaves. It came out right in front of me, and I reached up and grabbed it. As I brought it down, a big hand came over my shoulder and grabbed at it. I kicked backwards and took care of that. I opened the banana leaves while I was walking. Inside was a rice ball, and in the center was a big lump of brown sugar. Dick Porter and I shared that together. It was an old lady in the calesa that did that.

We passed a house. There were a lot of guys suffering from thirst. There'd been no provision for water or anything. I forget now how Porter and I had this canteen of water, but we did, and we made that do. As we were passing this little farmhouse, three soldiers broke from ranks and raced in, looking for water. Of course, the guards immediately got them. They didn't get any water. Their hands were tied, and they kept marching. We eventually got to Cabanatuan, and they took these guys out to a shed, where there were posts, and they had them squat down. Then their hands were tied behind their backs, around this post. Those poor guys sat out there for what must have been two or three days. Then the Japs took them and shot them. They claimed they were trying to escape.

In Cabanatuan there was an awful lot of dysentery. Another bad thing was tropical ulcers. They'd start out with a blister. We called it a Guam blister. It would break and then fester, and it just would keep getting bigger and bigger. You'd see guys with holes in their legs, all the way to the bone. I had one developing on my neck. I couldn't get it; it just kept getting bigger.

My old buddy Lauer had been on the Genesee. That's a story I didn't tell you. He was an airdale, and he expected to go to PatWing 10. He didn't; he went to the Augusta, made the trip to China with us, and came back. Well, he made a mistake. He went to Jimmy Fernald. He told Jimmy that he was sent to the Augie by mistake, that he was qualified in air, and he was supposed to go to PatWing 10. Well, you didn't tell Jimmy things like that. So Jimmy gave him a transfer, but instead of PatWing 10 he went to the Genesee, a small tug, [Laughter] which berthed not far from Cavite. We made a lot of liberties together.

But the reason I bring Lauer into this is that his Genesee was one of the small craft that was anchored right below Monkey Point, and the Japanese tried to sink it by shelling. Well, when the rock fell, he was one of the five that stayed on the boat to scuttle it.* Before he did, he raided the medical locker. He got a big bottle of sulfathiasol pills, which was a new antibiotic at that time. And he managed to keep them. Well, up at Cabanatuan, he was looking at this on my neck, and he said, "Here's how we'll fix it."

We got a canteen cup of hot water from the galley, and he got some saltwater soap, and we scoured it out real clean. He took tweezers and picked out some of the flesh. It made a big hole there, about as big around as a dime, I guess, or something like that--pretty deep. Then he ground up the sulfathiasol, which was in pill form, and he packed it into the

---

*The "rock" is a reference to Corregidor.

hole. Then we tried to put a bandage on it. I tried to keep it there and left it alone, and it healed.

The big thing about it--of course, he was my buddy, but if anybody had anything there, you didn't let go of it without a price. But he asked absolutely nothing in return. And it wasn't just to me; he gave it to other guys. He guarded it carefully, but when he saw somebody that needed it, he would give it to them. It would stop diarrhea. That was a terrible thing. He gave me another pill later, for diarrhea. If you got diarrhea and went across the road, you didn't come back. There was no treatment for it.

The benjos were a terrible place.* The flies were beyond description. The Japanese, in an attempt to curtail the flies, had put out a reward for them. They would give a biscuit for an empty milk can full of dead flies. There were biscuits because the Japs had taken a lot of flour. Some cook had figured out a way to make a dough that rose, a kind of sourdough yeast agent. They built an oven, so they could make these biscuits. Well, they were more than biscuits; they were a leavened bun-like. And, of course, to us they tasted like cake. Well, the Japanese controlled who got them. A reward for a milk can full of dead flies was a biscuit.

So there was a lot of ingenuity out there, to capture flies. One guy made himself a great big fly swatter. Then he got ahold of a piece of rotten flesh. He threw it out there by the benjo, the flies would swarm on it, and he would hit them with the fly swatter. That was one way. Another guy, of all things, cut up a mosquito net he had and made a trap to put over one of the benjo holes there. But he had no way of getting the flies out. Then another guy took charcoal that he got from the galley, ground it up fly-size. He took a can, filled it within about a half-inch of the top with charcoal, and then put a few flies on top.

Paul Stillwell: [Laughter] So if we're again thinking about fate, that conversation that Lauer had with Fernald also helped save you, indirectly.

Commander Harralson: Yes, right. I never thought of that, but, you know, there are so many ways it could have gone different. But that's what war is.

---

*Benjo is a Japanese term for a ditch that serves as a toilet.

Paul Stillwell: That's right.

Commander Harralson: Ninety percent luck and ten percent ability of some sort.

Paul Stillwell: Well, I'm sure that proportion varies with individuals.

Commander Harralson: Yes. And, of course, darn cliques developed, mainly on the Army side. There was a guy, Pinky Covert, a radioman second class from Cavite.[*] A lot of true natures came out. They had Army truck drivers going in and out of Cabanatuan. These truck drivers had access to dealings. There were always Japanese guards that could be dealt with, with people that had something to deal with. A lot of these truck drivers became sort of princes. They would make deals and do deals for people in camp, and extract their portion and that sort of thing. That developed more and more as we stayed there.

Well, Pinky Covert, in our barracks, got ahold of things. I think he started with cigarettes. He got some canned fish, and he promoted some of these buns and made sandwiches. Then he sold them for other items like cigarettes--cigarettes was a medium of exchange--a lot of different, very valuable things. He built a sandwich empire. He got to the point where he didn't do any of the selling; he was just the manager. He had guys going around selling these sandwiches. Their pay was a sandwich for them. They had working parties that went out to cut wood for the galleys. When they'd come back from a wood cutting, each one was given one of these biscuits. That's where a lot of swapping and dealing went on.

I went on a wood-cutting detail once. Another time I was on a work party that was hauling camotes. Camotes were our staple. They're like a great, big yam or sweet potato. We hauled them in sacks. I really put myself in jeopardy; I snitched a couple big camotes and tried to hide them in my shirt. I got away with it. But then I had the camotes; what do you do with camotes, wild camotes? So I figured if I could get them cooked, I could eat them. Well, I could get them cooked, but it would cost part of the camotes. Anyhow, it got into a big, involved deal, and I ended up with a small portion of the camotes.

---

[*]Radioman Second Class Lawrence W. Covert, USN.

Oh, what the heck was the Marine officer? He had a pet dog, a little dog. Hogaboom.* I think his father was a high-ranking officer too. But, anyhow, Hogaboom had this dog, and the dog disappeared. The dog ended up in the soup.

Paul Stillwell: Well, did you have any purpose, or were you just marking time here in this camp?

Commander Harralson: Marking time, trying to stay alive.

Paul Stillwell: But they didn't give you work details, other than, say, fetching the wood or whatever?

Commander Harralson: No. We Navy men were all together, along with a few Marines, in this one barracks. Oh, incidentally, we were divided into ten-unit-men groups. If anybody escaped from that group, they would kill all of the group. There were lots of ideas of escaping then. And we all said, "If you're going to try to go, tell me; I want to go with you."

Paul Stillwell: What were the barracks like? What sort of place did you have to sleep?

Commander Harralson: It was sort of basic everywhere we went. There was a platform, six feet in; and up above it, another platform. Just a straight platform. That's the way it was in Japan. In Japan, there were tatamis on them.†

Paul Stillwell: So this was just like sleeping on the bare wood?

Commander Harralson: Yes. Fortunately, in September, they notified 300 of us--mostly sailors, Marines, and a few soldiers--that we were going to Japan, as guests of the

---

*First Lieutenant William F. Hogaboom, USMC, had been stationed in the Philippines as part of the 4th Marines. He was killed 19 December 1944 when the POW ship in which he was riding was sunk off the Philippines.
†A tatami is a type of straw matting used as a floor covering in Japanese homes.

Emperor. You know, I think that there was a basis of truth in it, although it was a mockery. But I think that's kind of the way the soldiers looked at it. I don't know if we were the first to go north, but we could have been. I think we were the first taken out of Cabanatuan number three. They put us on the train--jammed us into boxcars--and we went down to Manila. It's not too far to Manila.

That afternoon, we boarded an old cargo ship. It was the <u>Lima Maru</u>. They put us up on the foredeck, the forecastle area. The next morning, we got under way and out to sea. It was nice. The air was clean, and we were outside.

Paul Stillwell: It reminded you of being a sailor.

Commander Harralson: Yes, it did. We went up to Taiwan. I don't know the name of the port we put in, but it was on the south end, I'm sure. Waiting for us when we got off the ship was a string of passenger cars. We thought, "Wow, we're really living now." But the passenger cars turned into instruments of torture.

The seating in the cars was like you put a bench athwartships, and then you put a back straight up in the middle of it. Two people sat facing one way, and two people sat facing the other way. And these were very close together. So to sit, your knees interlaced with those of the man opposite. And there was no padding; it was plain board. We sat in there for quite a while. Eventually the train got under way. We traveled north. By the hour, the bench got harder and harder. You couldn't change your position. It turned to just outright torture.

We arrived somewheres in the middle of the night and parked. The next morning we saw that it was a village. Well, more than a village--a town; paved streets, cobbled streets, nice buildings. They brought aboard, for breakfast, something that was more like a tea than it was a soup. So we had tea and a piece of bread, kind of like a bun, that tasted real good. We enjoyed that tea and the bread.

Then we got off the train, and they paraded us all over town. The streets were lined with little children, all dressed the same: white midis for the girls and blue skirts. Everybody had a little Japanese flag, waving it, but nobody was smiling. We never saw a smile anywhere.

Paul Stillwell: You were sort of a curiosity.

Commander Harralson: Yes. They marched us out to the edge of town. And there was another train. This was a narrow gauge, with flatcars. We piled onto these flatcars, and we took off. There were rice fields all around; it was fun. We went zooming over the landscape, quite a ways out of town. Then we marched a ways and came to several barracks with thatched roofs. They bivouacked us there. There was an interpreter, who was the most sorry-looking person I ever saw. His English was pure book English. You know, the Japanese have trouble with L's. For example, "Honoruru." The Chinese have trouble with R. They make an L out of an R. But in this case, he put up a sign that he had made, that said, "Dairy routine."

We're going to work in a dairy. Everybody had visions of milk. [Laughter] But he meant daily.

Paul Stillwell: Oh, darn.

Commander Harralson: A really interesting episode occurred. They had marched us out to our work. Now, there was a levee right next to camp on one side and a rice field on the other. We marched along this levee, then went up over the levee, and down to a very wide riverbed. Way over, at one side, there was a small river. But this was obviously full of water in the rainy season. There was a railroad trestle nearby. The guards marched us out there and sat us down. And they even offered us some smokes, and they were all smiles. They had a bunch of bamboo poles and a bunch of baskets and a bunch of the straw-rice rope. We sat there. We were joking, and they were joking with us. Everybody was smiling.

So they started to put these poles and the baskets together, to make yoho poles. Then one of the guards got under the pole, baskets on the ground, while another guard filled each basket full of dirt and rocks. The guard picked up the yoho and trotted off a little ways with it. baskets swinging. Then they called up one of the sailors. They filled his baskets and wanted him to lift it and trot off with the guard. He couldn't lift it.

Paul Stillwell: He wasn't strong enough?

Commander Harralson: He wasn't strong enough. Now, some of that was probably acting. But he made a valiant effort at it. At least he was a good actor; he struggled with it. They took a little bit of the dirt off, but they were beginning to get a little bit angry with us. They called up some more sailors and loaded them down. And they struggled and they struggled. And they took a little off, but not much. Finally, they began to get real mean. They made the guys shove off, you know, staggering down the road under this load. We were to take it, I would say, about the length of two football fields and dump it by this railroad track. I think what they wanted to do was build some kind of a platform out there by the railroad tracks.

But I think more than that, it was a make-work type of thing, because, as it turned out, we were there for quarantine purposes, really. When the POWs showed up at the tracks, half of a load would be gone; somewhere along the road they dumped half of it.* Well, the guards got mad. Then there was a lot of rifle butts swung around--hollering and threats. The guards would go back and fill the baskets and send them on, but they would never get there full. They tried to station people along to stop that, but they'd stop it one place, and it would occur at another, see. Finally, they eased off on that. Sailors were arriving with baskets half full. They decided, I guess, "We're going to have to live with that."

But then, what got them next, is here came two guys with a pole between them and one basket.† Partway there, they had re-rigged things. Well, there was a lot of bashing going on about that. But people persisted. We were more than they could deal with, really.

Paul Stillwell: Evidently, you were not in fear of these people.

---

*POWs--prisoners of war.
†The norm for the Japanese on a yoho pole was one man with two baskets.

Commander Harralson: Well, what can they do to you? So you get hit with a rifle butt. We won. And within a week, that was the standard--two men, one basket, half full.

Paul Stillwell: Of course, if it's a make-work deal, it doesn't make any difference anyway.

Commander Harralson: No, so we worked it that way for a while.

There was a turkey wondering around in camp that disappeared mysteriously.

Then one morning, we didn't go to work. We saw two sedans drive up. Out stepped two naval officers in dress whites, swords and all. We were called to line up, to muster in the compound. They lined us all up, standing at attention. We stood there and we stood there and we stood there. People begin to sag, including the guards. Then pretty soon a sergeant would come around, and the guards started hollering. Then we were all up at attention again. We'd been there, I don't know, two hours maybe.

Finally, here came the interpreter and one of the Army officers--not one of the naval officers. They called out the name of one of the radiomen. Then they went off with him, disappeared around the corner. We began to sag. They called us to attention again; then we sagged. The mosquitoes were biting too. Every once in a while they'd show up again and call out a name. This kept going on. It became late afternoon, and we were still standing there. Then they called my name. I was marched around the corner, into an office by the gate. Here were two naval officers, sitting down. So I stood there while they talked to each other in Japanese. Finally, one turned to me and said my name. Then he said, "You're a radioman?" They talked like they were from LA--I mean, just like us.

I said, "Yes."

He said, "Do you know any codes?"

I said, "Yes."

"Hmm, what are they? Can you tell us about them?"

I said, "A's a dot and a dash. B's a dash." [Laughter] I got to C, I think it was. He blew up. Finally, he explained to me what he was talking about. I said, "That stuff? I don't know anything about that stuff," which was absolutely true. So they told me to be off, and I was taken back to the barracks, and here were all these other guys. About the same thing took place with them.

Paul Stillwell: And that's the reason the U.S. Navy took Wimpy Anderson out of Corregidor, so that the Japanese could not get what he knew.

Commander Harralson: Yes, exactly. One of the first things the Japanese did there--I missed this when we were talking about Corregidor. They had a roster of the FRU unit, and they called out the names.

Paul Stillwell: That is amazing.

Commander Harralson: Yes, they did, everyone in the FRU unit. Then what blew their minds was when they got no answers. I think somebody tried to tell them that they were gone. Then they proceeded to call our names out, right down the list. I wondered, "Did they find that somewheres or something?" I don't think so. They had sources.

You see, this is the one thing that causes me to wonder sometimes about espionage back here in the States. I want to tell you, there were all kinds of Japanese that just happened to be in Japan when the war broke, and they wouldn't let them come home. We had an interpreter in camp--I'll tell you now, Okimoto. He was white-haired and talked like you and I. His favorite thing to do was to ask one of the prisoners where he was from. If it was from a city, he'd tell him the name of the big hotel there; tell him about the city. He claimed to be a traveling salesman, tennis rackets. He was 20 years in the United States. Now, I don't think his main purpose was selling tennis rackets. Fuji's Bar in Cavite--of course, that was in the Philippines, but I think we had counterparts in the States. I'm sure we did.

Paul Stillwell: Well, at Fuji's Bar the Japanese could pick up a lot just from stray sailor talk.

Commander Harralson: Oh, drunk sailors, yes. Loose mouths.

Paul Stillwell: Well, you were speaking of Envoy Kurusu before. He had an American wife. They had a son. I think he was killed as a pilot for the Japanese, during the war.

Commander Harralson: Gosh. You know, there's a book out, The Gods of War, and it's about a mixed Japanese-American family.* They were involved in State Department business. It was a Caucasian wife and a Japanese husband. The wife was caught in Japan, in Tokyo, and suffered through all that bombing. Now, this is fiction, supposedly. But let's see--characters in the story become prisoners of war. There's a relation there, but I forgot it. But what was remarkable to me was their description of prisoner life, Cabanatuan, and the misery and what happened over there across the road. It was too real, too authentic. It just seems, what you're saying here is like the book. And in it, I think, that they have a son that's killed. I wonder if that could be the basis for this story. Now, what burns me up is, I lent that book to somebody, and now I've forgotten exactly who it was, The War of Gods. I forgot the name of the author, but whoever it was, knew what he was writing about.

Paul Stillwell: Yes, there's frequently a lot of truth in fiction.

Commander Harralson: Oh, yes, for sure.

Paul Stillwell: What was your attitude day-to-day? Did you figure, whatever happens is what happens; you're not going to fight it?

Commander Harralson: I don't think I had an attitude. [Laughter]

Paul Stillwell: You had to think about something. You had plenty of time to think.

Commander Harralson: Yes. Well, really, that's a very difficult question.

---

*John Toland, The Gods of War (Garden City, New York: Doubleday & Company, 1985).

[Interruption for change of tape]

Paul Stillwell: Where did you go next?

Commander Harralson: In Taiwan, we went back down to the port, whose name I've forgotten, where we were put aboard the Dai Nichi Maru. This was a little different, in that there were already 200 soldiers from Hong Kong aboard. We were jammed down into an after hold--extremely crowded, congested. Then the ship got under way for Japan.

We were fed twice a day. They lowered food down in a box--rice and little else. The only time we got on deck was for the benjos, or latrines, that were Chick Sales-type affairs, rigged out over the ocean. There was always a long line there, because there was a lot of diarrhea rampant, and the food in our voyage was not helping it--and possibly because it was our only chance to get out in the fresh air.

It was bad enough for the first three days, and then the weather worsened. It was so bad down below that I found a place up among the boards of the hatch cover. I sneaked in a corner there, where I was unobserved, and I slept the first three nights. But then we hit bad weather--in fact, it was a typhoon--and I had to get below. Then they boarded the hatch over--covered it over--and we were sealed down below. Now, this was with 500 men with dysentery. You could still go to the head--there was an outlet for that--but you had to climb up this long ladder. This was not a place for a bunch of men with dysentery. It was so crowded in there that you barely had room to sit.

Then we got into the typhoon. The ship heaved. There was seasickness. It became indescribable. In fact, it's sort of a blank in my mind.

We eventually arrived at Moji, Japan, and were off-loaded. It was Thanksgiving Day, 1942.

Paul Stillwell: Which island is that on?

Commander Harralson: That's on Kyushu, the southern island. From there, we were put aboard a ferry and traveled across the straits to Shimonoseki, on the island of Honshu. I would like to say this about the trip: how terrible it was, but I can just imagine the horror, being in the same situation and being under attack by American submarines or American aircraft. We had many cases, later during the war, of that happening. I can't imagine a more frightful situation than that.

We got to Shimonoseki, where they put us on railroad passenger cars again, and we started north. These were decent cars that had decent seats. I forget what time of day it was, but we got our first meal. When the train stopped, they issued each man a little wooden box of real thin wood, something like they used to use to make strawberry boxes. It was about an inch deep and maybe four inches by four inches. It had a little wooden partition, catty-cornered, across one corner. Rice was in the large part. At breakfast, there was a small slice of orange in the little compartment. For the noon meal, it was the same thing, only in the small compartment were some pickled daikons. For the evening meal, again the rice, and in the compartment was a small piece of beef. That's what the regular passengers on the train were getting. To us it tasted very good; it was not enough, but it was good.

The trip took us two days. We arrived at Yokohama, got off the train at the big depot there, and marched around to what was to become our barracks. It actually was a very large concrete warehouse, all open in the middle, with two levels of wooden platforms and a passageway down the middle. They were back-to-back with other platforms. But these platforms had tatami mats on them. They had a little shelf across the back. Sitting on this shelf were a large shallow bowl, a large rice bowl, a smaller bowl in it, and then a smaller bowl in that. Each man had that set. On the tatamis was a stack of five blankets, thick looking blankets. So it looked like it wasn't going to be too bad.

We were issued clothing. We were issued a pair of light cotton pants, an arrangement that tied around the ankles, and it tied around the waist. I guess that was considered underwear drawers. And then there was a shirt that had no collar but was a decent shirt. Then with that we had a padded army coat and padded army pants. In addition was a suit made out of a cloth that very closely resembled burlap--what they make gunny sacks out of.

We were to go to work at Mitsubishi shipyard, which was around this small bay, within Tokyo Bay. The first day we went to work, I put on the underwear--that is, the drawers that tied around your ankles and the shirt. Then I put on the work coat and pants that were made out of burlap, and we went to work.

Paul Stillwell: What did you have on your feet?

Commander Harralson: I had on my feet my Marine shoes; very much worn, a sad state of affairs.

We went out to the shipyard, and the shipyard, of course, was right on the bay there, a cold wind blowing off it. It blew through the clothing like it wasn't there. That first day I almost died from the cold and misery. After that, I did like everybody else; I put on everything I owned. It was seven kilometers to work and seven kilometers back. And we went out there every day, seven days a week, except that on every second week we stayed in on Sundays.

Paul Stillwell: You had to walk 14 kilometers each day?

Commander Harralson: That's right, yes. Oh, in addition to the clothing, we got a large, heavy overcoat. It would look like we were well equipped, except that the blankets had no warmth and the coats had no warmth. I think they were made out of wood or something. [Laughter] That was true. Most of us did have an army blanket that we were able to keep with us. There was more warmth in that one army blanket than there was in those five blankets that we had.

Paul Stillwell: How did the Japanese treat you during this period?

Commander Harralson: I can honestly say they didn't treat us too bad. I think that we were fortunate to be, possibly, the first. I don't know of any others that preceded us up that way. I think we were sort of a demonstration bunch. We were expected to work in the shipyard, but we were given what was considered by them adequate food and lodging. And I think they had somewhat of a case there. The Japanese had a very Spartan type of living; substandard by American standards, but not so substandard to Japanese. The thing is that the situation deteriorated as the war went against them.

The first months there, of course, we were a curiosities. We got a lot of staring and in the yard, a lot of attention. But we began to be part of the scenery. It finally got around to where I don't think people paid any attention to us.

Paul Stillwell: Probably just as well. That's what you wanted.

Commander Harralson: Yes, yes. Our only complaint about the food was that there just wasn't enough of it. It was very basic. We got a bowl of a mixture of barley and rice, about 50-50, to begin with. On Tuesdays we got four little sardine-like fishes. On Thursday we'd have soup with some pork fat in it. I understand it was about ten kilos of pork fat for the 500 of us. But it made the soup greasy, and that was a welcome thing. Sometimes you might even find a tiny hunk of pork fat in there. We craved fat. But as time went on, the little fishes disappeared and the pork fat disappeared. Then our soup was made out of water, a miso paste, and sliced daikons. We had to eat the daikon tops before we got to the daikons.

Paul Stillwell: Is that like a radish?

Commander Harralson: A daikon is a great, big white radish. It used to appear in my nightmares. [Laughter] In the spring, they were small--only a foot, foot-and-a-half long. By fall, they were six feet long. They were monsters. [Laughter]

Paul Stillwell: Well, that says something about your state of mind.

You've described yourself as not being a church person. Did you resort to prayer during this period?

Commander Harralson: No, I didn't. I'm not an atheist, but I don't pray. But I think about our Maker, and why we're here, and I always have. There have been times when I've had waves of religious feelings, but I've become cynical in a lot of ways, against what occurs as religion today. I think about world events and how religion is involved in so much of our strife. It's the man part of religion that I don't want any part of.

Paul Stillwell: Well, the TV ministers and their money grubbing would add to your cynicism.

Commander Harralson: [Laughter] Yes.

Paul Stillwell: Well, after a while, did you sort of settle into a routine?

Commander Harralson: Yes, it became very routine. You got up at daybreak, and, let me tell you, one of the worst sounds I have ever heard in my life is a Japanese bugler blowing reveille at 5:30. It just freezes your blood. The first winter there, we were miserably cold; there was no heat.

Oh, we got a Red Cross issue. It was dried pears and shoes, from South Africa. Of course, like everything, there wasn't enough for everybody to get shoes. And everybody didn't need shoes in an equal degree. I had my Marine shoes, but they were in pretty bad shape. I had developed a bad blister on my heel. I was worried about it. That was at a time when you walked or else.

Paul Stillwell: Or you died.

Commander Harralson: Exactly. So when I went up to get a pair of shoes, they spotted this hole that I had cut in the heel so I could keep walking. They were horrified at that; they had a great big, long discussion. It appeared to me that they couldn't understand why a man would cut a hole in his shoe. So I explained that if I hadn't cut that hole in my shoe, I wouldn't have been able to walk. And if I couldn't walk, then it was curtains. Suddenly the light dawned on them, and I got my shoes. Of course, they were two sizes too big. They had hobnails and leather heels and all, but those shoes lasted until the end of the war. I threw them overboard, and I wish I had kept them. [Laughter] They had been patched; they had patches on top of patches. The heel wore very quickly, completely--cut diagonally across the heel. Because they were too large, the front ends turned up like skis. The soles wore just at the bottom that touched the ground; they were thick at the top. They looked like something a clown would wear.

Paul Stillwell: Please tell me about the sabotage efforts.

Commander Harralson: Well, I would like to make clear that these were not sabotage committed by an organized group, where we sat down and said, "Hey now, if we do this, we can do this. Now you keep a watch over there," or any planned thing. These were the targets of--what do they call it?

Paul Stillwell: Targets of opportunity?

Commander Harralson: Yes. We were all patriots and good sailors, but I have to say that probably our prime motive was revenge against the little bastards. When opportunities popped up, we did it. We didn't talk about it before. We didn't talk about it afterwards. There were informers in camp. We just did it and went on. I can get more worried now, thinking about the experience and what we did to one ship. Had our Navy not hit it with rockets, further damaging it, the Japanese might have figured out what happened.

Paul Stillwell: Well, please tell me what you did to it.

Commander Harralson: Well, I got transferred to the kojus. The kojus can be roughly translated to riggers. In the riggers I was put in a squad of four; we were all sailors. Our job was to push a little flatcar on railroad tracks. We'd push it over to the machine shop--a very large machine shop. There it would be loaded with fittings for ships that were in being worked on--valves and bearings and all sorts of machine parts. Then we would push this flatcar over to the dock, alongside the ship they were for, to be unloaded. Our honcho was a workman we dubbed Smiley. Smiley didn't have all his marbles. He was smiling all the time, and he didn't have anything to smile about.

We pushed the flatcar over to the dock one day when we first started. We were loaded with some large bearings--shaft bearings, I guess they were--and Smiley was trying to get a crane to take the material off. So we decided to help Smiley out. We pushed the first half bearing off, so it fell with the soft-metal bearing up. Then we pushed the second half off, and we pushed it so it fell into the first one, and put a big gouge in it.

In doing this, we made a big scene about how hard we were working; we were struggling and we were arguing. Smiley was quite happy; we were helping him. The crane operators were a haughty bunch. Smiley couldn't get much action out of them. So we helped him; we off-loaded the parts and pushed the flatcar back to the machine shop. Nobody said anything to the others. We didn't discuss it. But after that, we always helped Smiley off-load.

We found other ways to do things. They had a piece of a machine part. The best way I can describe it is a very large doughnut, maybe a foot and a half in outer diameter. It had an inner diameter. It was like a big doughnut, only the edges were square. It had valves on the outer periphery, handles. We rolled that off like a wheel. Things bounced off it, like the handles to the valves. Big valves, themselves, we would dump them off upside down. We did all this with a great bit of acting. Pretty soon we began pushing parts back to the machine shop for rework.

Now, it just seems to me that anybody in his right mind would say, "Well, certainly some foreman is going to notice." But the place was not that well organized. I mean, I think one part of the yard didn't know what the hell the other side was doing. No gang knew what the other gang was doing. The ones that got the parts aboard ship must have thought that the dumb people up in the machine shop screwed up, or something.

Anyhow, we did that. We didn't damage every part. We didn't want to look like saboteurs. And we had to maintain our credibility as clumsy oafs. But we did that for about two months, maybe a little longer.

Paul Stillwell: Well, it probably helped you that Smiley didn't have a clue what was going on.

Commander Harralson: He didn't. He didn't. We were all actors, and there was no dialogue between us, with regard to what we were doing. We just were terribly inefficient and got in each other's way.

Paul Stillwell: Well, it sounds like you made a game of it.

Commander Harralson: We did. We did. We didn't like those people. Then they took us off of the flatcar. I don't think it had anything to do with what we were doing; just every once in a while they changed gangs around.

We ended up on this ship. It had started out as a tanker. When we first arrived at the yard, they had six middle-size tankers on the ways. They were in varying degrees of construction. Let's see, it must have been late 1944 when the first one came off the ways. They decided to make an escort-sized carrier out of it. They had it alongside the dock, fitting out, putting the machinery in and all. There was an awful lot of work yet to be done on it.

We were put aboard there, under a honcho, to clean bilges. And believe me, the bilges needed cleaning. There was a lot of sand, muck, and corruption down there. But the honcho would put us down there and then go off. Now, many times we'd get a bucket full of muck and then sit around and do nothing. Usually the ship was very noisy, because they were putting in the boilers, lagging boilers, and so forth. There was a lot of work going on. But one day we were down there cleaning, so to speak, and suddenly the ship became quiet. Well, we knew what that meant. That meant that the yardbirds had gone off for their noon meal.

So we thought we'd better go up there and get ready to go for ours. We climbed up out of the bilge and started across the engine room floor. There was this big chief machinist's mate, Bull Campbell, in the lead. I was right behind Bull. He stopped abruptly. He looked up, and right above his head was a pipe, perhaps eight inches in diameter. The open end was right above his head. He looked down to his right, and there was a piece of wood, maybe three feet long, maybe three by three or four by four. He reached down and picked it up, and he shoved it in the pipe. He gave it a mighty shove. It went back up into the pipe. He picked up his bucket--we were all carrying this bucket of muck--and we started on.

We went by this huge mound of machinery, which I understood to be the turbine and the reduction gears. And the reduction gear housing was bigger than the turbine. That surprised me. As we went by, I climbed up on this reduction gear housing and was sweeping around with a broom. I looked around and there was nobody around. There was a pipe sticking up that had a piece of wood, like a cork, in the top of it. The pipe was maybe three-quarters of an inch, or maybe an inch. So I pulled the plug, and I put in more than two, less than five, handfuls of this muck. I had to coax it down the pipe. I wiped the pipe off and put the plug back. Then I slid off. The others were sitting down on the deck, over at one side, and I went over and sat down with them. We were waiting for our honcho to come get us and take us, because he was supposed to do that, to where we ate our noon meal.

We sat there and talked for a while. I asked Campbell what the pipes were since he was a machinist's mate. I was a radioman, and I didn't know anything about engine rooms. He told me that the big pipe, that he had shoved the wood in, was the main steam line, not fully connected. He told me that the pipe sticking up from the reduction gears was the bearing vent pipe. And he added that on American ships that pipe is curved back down, to keep anything from falling into it. We waited some more, and eventually the guard showed up and we went off to our meal. I never thought any more about it. We never talked about it. Shortly, we were taken off that job and went on to another one, and I never thought any more about it.

I guess perhaps a month later, they took the ship out for a sea trial in Tokyo Bay. The next morning, it was anchored about 400 or 500 yards out from the Mitsubishi yard. There were motor launches carrying workman back and forth. We asked one of the riggers there, Japanese, what was the matter with the ship. He said, "Oh, they've got problems," or words to that effect. But we went on to a new job.

Then about the 17th of March--for some reason that date sticks in my mind.

Paul Stillwell: Was this in 1945?

Commander Harralson: Yes. It was an eventful day. We started out to work and had gone maybe four or five blocks when all the sirens everywhere sounded off. The guard stopped us and turned us around, and we went double-time back to the compound and into the compound. The guards all ran into their air-raid shelter, which was a deep trench with about three feet of earth covering it. We had some trenches, about three feet deep, no cover, that we could have gone to. The trench would have been better than standing around, but we didn't go there. We were wondering what was coming off.

Then, all of a sudden, here came these U.S. Navy airplanes. Boy, they were swarming everywhere, seeking targets. One attacked this carrier anchored off the yard, with rockets. We'd never seen rockets before. I stayed on the ground, but there were some that climbed up on top of the roof. I thought they were damn fools, because we looked like Japanese ourselves. The planes couldn't tell from afar.

Paul Stillwell: Especially with those clothes on.

Commander Harralson: Right. But they said that this plane dived with rockets and hit it, and that it was sinking. The next day, we went back out to work and when we got to a point where we could see it, why, it was still afloat, but it had been hit. It was down by the stern and had a real severe list on it.

Thinking about it in later years, that attack might have been a good thing for us, because I think the engineers, when they really got into the problems, they might have found that wood in the steam line or the material in the bearing. They could have tracked it back to us, I suppose, but that didn't happen.

Paul Stillwell: Well, when that Navy air raid came over, that must have been one of the happiest moments of your life.

Commander Harralson: Oh, you bet.

Paul Stillwell: Did you stay in Yokohama, essentially, from November '42 onward?

Commander Harralson: I was there until about April '45. I know it was April, because it was April 13th that Roosevelt died.* They told us. We marched out to the yard and assumed we were going to work. At the yard we were told that we would no longer work at Mitsubishi and that our President Roosevelt had died.

Paul Stillwell: Did you believe them?

Commander Harralson: Oh, yes. And when they said Truman was President, we said, "Who is Truman?"† [Laughter]

Paul Stillwell: A lot of Americans in the States were asking that same question.

Commander Harralson: Yes, that's what I hear. But the bombing began in November 1944. Now, I have a picture of me as a POW that I think was taken in 1944. The reason is that later, in the late winter or early spring of 1944, I wasn't in too good a shape. Dr. Price--a little British doctor from Hong Kong, a feisty fellow--got me transferred to Shinagawa, which was supposed to be a hospital for POWs. I was there, at Shinagawa, until maybe October or November. I remember that, because the first B-29 we saw was at Shinagawa, just before I left.‡ It was way up, with contrails. I don't think the Jap fighters could get up there. Of course, that was a shot in the arm. One of the Jap guards pointed to it and said, "Tomodashi," which means friend. And what he was telling me was that that was my friend up there.

    I went back to the camp, and it was after I got back that I was put into the kojus, and this business with the flatcar and the ship all occurred.

Paul Stillwell: Did you learn much Japanese in the process?

---

*President Franklin D. Roosevelt died at Warm Springs, Georgia, on 12 April 1945, which was the 13th in Japan, on the other side of the International Dateline.
†Harry S. Truman served as President of the United States from 12 April 1945 to 20 January 1953.
‡The U.S. Army Air Forces's Boeing B-29 Superfortress was the most advanced bomber of World War II. It had four 2,220-horsepower engines that gave it a top speed of 365 miles per hour at 25,000 feet. It had a maximum range of 5,830 miles. It was armed with eight .50-caliber machine guns, a 20-millimeter cannon, and could carry a bomb load of up to ten tons.

Commander Harralson: We were not inclined to want to learn, but we had to learn certain words. We had to learn to count very fast, because when we fell in ranks, we had to bango, which meant count off. And we stayed there until we got it right: ichi, ni, san, shi, go, roko, shichi, hachi, ku, ju, ju ichi.

Paul Stillwell: They gave you some incentive.

Commander Harralson: Yes, they did. [Laughter] Also, your shipmates gave you incentives too. [Laughter] You'd better get it right.

Paul Stillwell: Well, did you have a sense, as these years passed--'42, '43, '44, '45--of how the war was going?

Commander Harralson: A little bit. A little bit. They had an interesting situation. It wasn't in our camp, but I was trying to think how we got word. In another camp they got ahold of a Japanese newspaper. There was a Chinese POW that could read the Japanese and an Englishman that could understand Chinese. So they were able to get it that way. [Laughter] But, of course, it was controlled press. But when we started seeing these planes coming over, we figured that it wasn't going too good for the Japs.

Paul Stillwell: Right. I think George Washington's birthday, in late February '45, was the first U.S. carrier raid on the Tokyo area.

Commander Harralson: Well, I have to tell you what else happened. I've left out the B-29s, the big raids there. Before we quit at work, we went out there one day--I'm trying to think, probably in March; it wasn't too far past the carrier raid--and we just got out to the yard when the air-raid sirens went. The guards chased us to some shallow trenches, on the edge of the yard there, and then they disappeared. We sat in these trenches for a half an hour or maybe an hour, and we were wondering what was coming off.

I was sitting there, looking one way, and facing me the other way was this little Irish kid. Gee, all of a sudden his mouth fell open, and I saw him staring over my shoulder. I turned around, and the sky was full of airplanes--big ones, B-29s. They were very, very low, and they flew right over us. We saw fighters dive on them and get blown up. The B-29s dropped silvery stuff. We didn't know what it was at the time. It was window or chaff for radar countermeasures. The AA burst far above them.* They flew right on over us and on up north, towards Tokyo. Then we could hear the bombs. That's the day the sky was real black up that way. We thought those big planes were invincible. What else? They were at something like 5,000 feet, maybe less--low. So we thought they were invincible.

Then one night the air raid alarm sounded in camp, about midnight. We all bailed out and went outside. The guards went down into their air-raid shelters. Then here came the B-29s, flying right over us. There was a railroad adjacent to the camp, and these big planes were flying--it looked like--single file. They would fly over us, dropping their bombs real close. Soon, the whole place was lit up by fire. We could see the planes. "Gee," we thought, "they're really taking it to them tonight." We were jubilant.

And then one plane went by, and we could hear another, different sounding engine. We saw tracers come up behind it, and they were like little sparks, real close together. Then we'd see the B-29 fire back, its tracers looking like the balls of a Roman candle. I saw a B-29 start burning in one of the engines, on the starboard side. I think it was the inboard engine. You could see a little glow start, and then the thing would disappear, on fire, into the murk.

There was one that they got that way, just the same way. But instead of going straight, he swung out, putting him out over the bay. He came around, a 360, and he went in, just across the railroad tracks from us, and just wiped out two city blocks. We saw one we assumed was hit by antiaircraft just completely blow up. We were counting them, beginning a tally. I heard figures like 20 and 19 shot down.

Paul Stillwell: Did you have a fear for your personal safety during those raids?

---

*AA-antiaircraft.

Commander Harralson: No, because they were our friends.

Paul Stillwell: But your friends could still hurt you. You were talking before about the fear of being in a POW ship that got attacked by Americans.

Commander Harralson: I don't know. I don't remember much fear at all. I remember jubilation.

Paul Stillwell: Well, that would be understandable, of course.

Commander Harralson: Of course, we were real put out when we saw those planes shot down.

There was another funny occurrence, though. This happened all about the same time. After we had knocked off at Mitsubishi, we stayed in camp. We got a new camp commander who was a real congenial person. You could stay up all night. They had hot water in the galley. Some people had tea. People gambled. There was always a lot of gambling, for half bowls of rice, or quarter bowls of rice, or cigarettes.

Paul Stillwell: And the gambling also provided some entertainment, undoubtedly, something to pass the time.

Commander Harralson: Oh, yes, sure, sure.

We went for three or four days, and we didn't do anything. Everything was real relaxed. Then they formed us up, early one morning, and we started out on a long hike. I think it must have been close to 15 kilometers we marched. We came up to a beautiful golf course, on rolling hills. I remember the beautiful pine trees that had lightning rods in the top. There was beautiful turf. They gave us picks, and our job was to cut this beautiful turf up, roll it up, and take it to one side. The course was going to become victory gardens, for growing vegetables. But it didn't seem to be a high-priority job, because the guards were indifferent as to how hard we worked. We were always testing, to see just how much we had to do to make them happy.

Paul Stillwell: How did you test them?

Commander Harralson: By doing less and less, until they began hollering. [Laughter] We spent a lot of time looking for wild onions. They were about the size of a marble, and we were eating them. Also, we started collecting a bunch to take back and throw into the soup.

We were out there one day, and here came two Navy airplanes, flying in over the course. They went over us very low. We were jumping and waving and hollering, and the old Japanese sergeant was hollering at us. He was trying to tell us that we looked just like them, and that the next time around they were going to strafe. We realized he was right. The key word there was onaji, which is the Japanese word for same. We could understand him, and we all hit out for low places. But the planes didn't come back.

Paul Stillwell: What was the mortality rate among the people in your group?

Commander Harralson: The first winter there, 50 men died out of 300. It was real high. Old Doc Price blamed it as aftermath of the trip on the ship.

Paul Stillwell: Well, I've also heard that in some situations like that, it can be that some people just give up; they no longer have the will to live.

Commander Harralson: That's true. You hate to put that on somebody. But yes, there were guys. The first sign was that they were giving away their rice; they didn't want to eat it. And, boy, you'd better eat it. When I say rice, I mean the stuff they served.

Paul Stillwell: Did you ever have a problem with rice with rocks in it that broke your teeth?

Commander Harralson: I don't remember much in that way. I remember rice with rat turds. You tried to pick them all out, but you knew you didn't.

Paul Stillwell: Did the mortality rate go down as time passed?

Commander Harralson: Yes, it eased off greatly.

Paul Stillwell: Because then you had gotten down to the real survivors.

Commander Harralson: Yes. It's hard to judge that. I don't know what the key factors were, but I almost went down. We started getting different people in there. Some Australian merchant sailors showed up from a ship that was sunk. I was on the verge of giving away my rice. I felt, sort of, "What's the use?" Then a kid named Gordon Mutton, from Toowoomba, Australia, gave me a can of tobacco. It was a small, flat-type can. That so moved me that I decided to shape up. But I didn't smoke the tobacco, which was very valuable. I traded it to a British officer for a pair of woolen socks. It sort of started me back the other way.

Paul Stillwell: When did that occur?

Commander Harralson: Oh, about '43, somewheres along in there. I had trouble there the first year. I hadn't cut my hair. I had the wildest mop of hair; it was getting longer and longer. And I was in bad shape. They had a sick bay there, with this old Dr. Price. He didn't have anything to treat anybody with, but he still had a sick bay. Sometimes he could persuade the Japanese to let them stay in, instead of going to work. I have a letter from him down there, if you care to see it.

I finally got to see him. He took one look at me, and he said, "I'm not going to talk to you or do anything until you come back here with your hair cut." Well, I was sort of in a situation there. I was so damned ornery that my friends steered clear of me, I guess. So I tried to cut my hair myself. [Laughter] But I ended up getting some help, and I got my hair shorn down to clipper sides. And I went back. But, like I say, he couldn't do anything but try to boost your morale.

Paul Stillwell: Did you find yourself daydreaming about things back in the States?

Commander Harralson: Oh, absolutely. Everybody had his thing. Now, a weird part of it was the making of menus. We had men in there that never cooked in their lives, and knew nothing, but they were dreaming up menus that were loaded with fat and sugar and rich things. For example, a banana dipped in egg batter and walnuts, stuffed with peanut butter and fried in deep fat. But you know what, when I went to bed, I always dreamed of owning a 40-footer and where I was going. But I'd always end up involved in loading the boat with food and supplies. I never got much farther than loading it with food.

Paul Stillwell: Food seemed to be the common element in these dreams.

Commander Harralson: Oh, it was. Girls disappeared completely from the conversation. They were gone long ago. And the topic of conversation was food, all the time. We said very, very little about other things.

Paul Stillwell: I heard some of the Vietnam POWs built imaginary houses in their minds.

Commander Harralson: Yes. People had different things that they thought of. My friend Hooper, who was there, got me into his kind of dream. His dream was a one-acre, self-sustaining farm. We were always finding ways to save space and to produce more food. The house would be built on stilts and all the chickens and pigs would be underneath, a la the Filipinos. Around our fence would be grape vines and berry vines, all around the periphery. Then we'd have this kind of fruit tree and that kind of fruit tree.

Paul Stillwell: It's surprising to hear you say that the girls disappeared from your conversations.

Commander Harralson: Sex was a non-issue.

Paul Stillwell: You had something more basic to focus on.

Commander Harralson: Yes. The acquisition of a smoke became very, very important because we found out that after you'd finished your meals--we said rice, but it wasn't rice--it always relieved a void that you felt if you could drag on a cigarette, maybe just two or three drags.

My friend Hooper was in a gang that worked a moving crane. They moved different things around. They were working a pile of poles one day. The poles rolled, and one of them rolled on Hooper's leg and broke it. So they put his leg in a cast. They let him stay in camp for two weeks, and then they took the cast off. He was happy to get it off, because of the cooties. I hadn't told you about the lice. [Laughter] Anyhow, the lice got into his cast and drove him crazy. He was getting sticks or anything he could find to try to scratch it. They took the cast off, and after that, poor old Hooper limped terribly going out to work. When he got back to the States, they found that his one leg was two inches shorter than the other. They re-broke it and reset it for him.

The lice were something. The first winter there, we could see it coming down the line--the scratches. It got down to us, and then soon it was everywhere. You could feel the lice as they fell from one place to another inside your clothes. What was terrible was to have them fall on your hair. We fought and fought--we washed what we could. But that was an ordeal because if you washed something, that meant you had to go to work not wearing it. So that was a real problem. But we finally got the upper hand. And you know how we did it?

Paul Stillwell: No, please tell me.

Commander Harralson: When we went to bed, we hung our underclothes out, and they froze. Now, if you put them on the same way you hung them out, it wouldn't work. You turned them inside out and hung them out to freeze, and then you turned them inside out again. By that alternating inside and out, I guess you confused them to death. [Laughter]

Paul Stillwell: But when the solution to the problem is to wear frozen underwear, that's not a good idea, either. Not too enjoyable. [Laughter]

Commander Harralson: We got a bath once a month. They had a washroom with a boiler nearby. There was a big wooden tub. The way it was supposed to work was that they had a bunch of little tubs, and you came in, stripped down. You got a little tub full of water, and you washed yourself off good. Then you climbed into the big tub. And you could sit there for a while. And, of course, that couldn't accommodate too many at a time, so we went a squad at a time. To make everything fair, they rotated the sequence. If you got towards the last, you got pretty murky water. Sometimes you wondered whether you were worse off coming out than when you went in. But sometimes it felt so good, for the warmth that seemed to penetrate.

Let's see, there was something else. Oh, I had a situation in the spring. Going out to work, I noticed just outside the gate we passed a fig tree. Every day, as we went out, I noticed little figs coming. The little figs were getting bigger and bigger. One day, as we went by, I reached over and snagged one, which I put in my mouth and ate. I was amazed to find that it was sweet and ripe. I concluded that this was a variety of green fig. I didn't tell anybody or say a word. But every day, when I went by, I'd yank a fig. Well, pretty soon I had that side cleaned off, and I was getting desperate. And here was the other side, over there, loaded.

So one day, as we passed by, I darted around and grabbed a fig from the back side, then came on around and back into the line. I did that once and got away with it. But about the second time out I tried it, I darted out and the guard caught me. He started swinging the rifle butt at me. I turned to dodge his swings. This was coming in that I got caught. When we fell in, I had to be in the right rank in order to pass next to the tree. That was always a problem, trying to get into the right rank. But, anyhow, the guard caught me and started jabbing at me with his rifle butt. I marched the rest of the way into camp backwards, trying to dodge his rifle butt.

When we got in, of course, I was in the front rank, because I had wanted to be there to go by the tree. I see the little fink going up to the CO and blabbing. Here they came, to me. The CO came up and stood in front of me. He looked me up and down. Then he reached up and grabbed the bill of this little hat that we wore and pulled it down over my nose, and turned around and walked off.

Paul Stillwell: You got off easy.

Commander Harralson: I did. I did.

Paul Stillwell: What did you observe of the Japanese civilians, during your comings and goings?

Commander Harralson: Well, I worked with some at the yard. My first job out there was in this great big shed, with the overhead crane. I worked with two young boys, not quite old enough yet for the army. They were pretty nice kids. And the old man was all right. We had a certain amount of work that had to get done. The only thing was, I was so slow that I would get up to where the crane hooks were about the time the kids had the load hooked up. So I spent my time just walking back and forth.

Then we took a lot of breaks. They had a little sawdust-burning stove. We'd go over there and stand around the stove and shoot the breeze and that sort of thing. He was a reasonable human being, and so were the boys. I worked with them for quite a while. But in this big shed--down the sides of the shed were these huge machines, made in England, maybe Birmingham.

Paul Stillwell: Could well have been. That was a steel center.

Commander Harralson: Yes. They all worked on this flywheel principle. You had an electric motor driving this great, big flywheel, and whatever it was going to do--shear, or punch holes, or whatever--then a trip lever was set by foot or hand, and a plunger would catch a pawl and drive the shears or punch. One of the machines punched rivet holes in the big steel plates that made up the hull of the ship. They had rivet holes all down the sides and ends--quadruple holes in double rows. These big sheets of steel came over from the pattern shop, all marked out with white chalk, with a stamp, where the holes were to be.

They were moved over to the bed of a punch machine that had two movements, longitude and lateral, controlled by the operator that sat in front of this machine. It had these great big hand wheels. One wheel controlled one movement and one, the other movement. The operator had a sight and would position this big plate right under him. When it got to the spot he wanted to punch, he'd press the foot pedal, and the plunger would punch that hole. Here's this big plate, with these countless holes on it, and that's the way they put them in. The thing was that the operator was about a 14 year-old kid. And when those sheets came out of there, a lot of those holes weren't where they were supposed to be. They'd get the plates up alongside the ship and then try to find holes that matched, to get a bolt through. They had to ream almost every hole, with a big reamer, so that they could get a rivet in.

There were two Scotsmen there that had worked on the Queen Mary in the shipyard.* I asked them one day, how did they do it when they were building the Queen Mary--how about these holes? They told me, "Very seldom did you find a hole that didn't match." The reaming was just very infrequent. They didn't like to do that. That wasn't conducive to strength. It allowed for slipping, because it elongated the hole.

Paul Stillwell: Right. That makes sense.

Commander Harralson: Yes. These Japanese reamed every hole, automatically. And some they couldn't get the reamer in because it was that far off. Then they'd have to call for the drillers.

Paul Stillwell: What do you remember about receiving Red Cross packages?

Commander Harralson: [Laughter] That was always a subject of rumor, scuttlebutt. We were always going to get a package. It went on and on and on and on. I don't even need all the fingers of one hand to count the Red Cross packages. We never did get a whole package per man. It was always a package for two, or two for three; that was a good deal. But that brought up the problem of how you divided it. This was the old American Red Cross issue; it was a box about like that, about that deep. All told, I think we got maybe four issues, partial parts of boxes. And that brings up another thing.

---

*RMS Queen Mary was a large British passenger liner converted for use as a fast troop transport in World War II. She was built by John Brown & Company, Clydebank, Scotland; her first voyage as a commercial ship was in August 1936.

Somewheres midways through our stay there, they broke this big warehouse up into sections, so that it broke up the bigness of it--the coldness of it, I guess. We were put into smaller areas, almost like rooms, with two tiers of tatamis on one side and two tiers on the other side. We were divided into squads. The men that occupied one side comprised one squad. Then on the other, the other squad. I think there were about 40 men in a squad. Now, on one side was all sailors, mostly radiomen, and we were all first class or chief. Those that weren't had promoted themselves. [Laughter]

Paul Stillwell: What did you promote yourself to? [Laughter]

Commander Harralson: I didn't. I always put myself down as first class. They were always giving us questionnaires, but they were filled out with myths and daydreams.

On the other side was a squad that was mostly Marines. There were a few sailors in it. Now, on our side, we were democratic; we elected a squad leader, we elected the guy that dished out the grain and things like that. We argued about it loud and long and hard. We had a lot of disagreements--a true democracy. [Laughter]

On the other side, there was this Marine gunner. He took a look around, and he said, "I think I'm senior here. Okay, I'm the squad leader." And that's what he was, Ray Steele. He was about six-foot-four, real gaunt. We watched in awe how he operated over there. He was absolutely fair, absolutely. When they got something to share, they had a system where one man would face one way, and another man would face the other way. One man would look at the item to be shared, the part of the portion, and say, "Whose part is this?" And the man looking the other way would call out a number. We all wore numbers. That's what the receiving man would get. So the guy saying who got the part had no idea what it was like or its size.

We used to have tenko every night--muster. We were supposed to sweep down ten minutes before muster, and the guards used to get quite nasty about it. Certain prisoners had this poker game going on in the middle; the damn fools were gambling with rice. We had guys there that owed a whole month's ration of rice. Our prisoner CO--Major Tisdale, a British officer--had to declare a moratorium. Well, they gambled with rice, and cigarettes, and about anything else of value there. This darn game would start the minute we got back, and it would go on almost to tenko. It was beginning to interfere with the sweepdown that we were supposed to do. So Ray Steele told them, "You guys have got to knock off ten to." But they kept creeping into the sweepers time. Finally, Ray Steele walked in there one evening, and he said, "I told you ten minutes before." He grabbed this table and he just flipped it over. Cards and all kinds of stuff went flying by. That put an end to that.

One of the kids there--O. B. Harris, a sailor--looked like a teenager when you saw him from 30 or 40 feet away. You'd get up close to him, and you'd see in his eyes and his face that he was no teenager. Well, out at the yard one day, he did something one of the honchos didn't like. The honcho picked up a piece of wood and came at him. He took the wood away from the honcho and beat the honcho down, and they took the honcho to the hospital. This caused a very tense period. The interpreter, Okimoto, talked to Steele, a leader who was looked up to.

Paul Stillwell: By both sides, apparently.

Commander Harralson: Yes. He told Steele that tensions were high, this was a very serious thing, and that at work we should datsibo, tip our hat, every time we saw one of these honchos. So Ray Steele did what he was told. He got up in front of the camp and told us what the interpreter told him, that he suggested we all datsibo. And then when he got through, he said, "Now, that's what he told me to tell you. I'm going to tell you what I'm going to do. They can go to hell. I don't tip my hat to anybody." Nobody did.

The Japanese gave O. B. Harris 30 days in the guardhouse. And you have to know what that guardhouse was like. It wasn't big enough to lay down. And he had to go out to work each day. He got one rice ball; that was his food for the day. It came out of the galley, the Japs gauged it, and it started out as a little rice ball. In the middle of the night, the guards would get O. B. out of the doghouse there and have him do calisthenics. I think it would have killed an ordinary person, but he hung in there. Then pretty soon the cooks were trying to make that rice ball bigger and bigger, and the Japanese began to let it get bigger and bigger. That guy survived, and he was held in pretty high esteem, because they really put it to him.

Paul Stillwell: What would be in these Red Cross care packages that we talked about?

Commander Harralson: The big thing was a can of Klim, which was powdered milk. Another was a quarter pound of American cheese, Kraft cheese. There was a can of liver paté. There was a can of corned beef. I think there was some soluble coffee.

Paul Stillwell: Any chocolate?

Commander Harralson: Yes, there was chocolate. Of course, that was highly prized. [Laughter]

Paul Stillwell: You told me earlier that there was more to the story of Ernie Clark. If you could put that one on the tape please?

Commander Harralson: All right. Somewheres during our stay in Yokohama, the Japanese told us that a selected few prisoners would be allowed to participate in a broadcast that was intended to be received back in the States. Those that were selected to make this broadcast were to submit what they were going to say, on paper, to be censored. It was decided that they should stick to naming names of other prisoners and so forth, and addresses. I told you about Ernie Clark, who had gone out to Cavite on a merchant ship and was left there. He made one of the broadcasts. He put my name in it when he broadcast. I guess it was copied by a lot of different places back in the States, and his wife got it in Denver. I don't know whether she heard the broadcast directly or not, but anyhow she got the word. So she notified the different people that were on Ernie's list.

Paul Stillwell: The relatives?

Commander Harralson: The relatives, yes. So she sent my mother word that I was alive and well. My mother corresponded with her then, off and on, for the rest of the war. Ernie had told us that his wife was Chinese, and that she had gone out to Denver to get away from the coast. After the war was over and I was home, my mother got a letter from Ernie's wife, telling her that she had passed through Applegate. She debated whether or not to stop and see my mother, but she decided she shouldn't, that she should tell her now that she was Japanese. She felt there might be some resentment.

Paul Stillwell: She was a Nisei?*

Commander Harralson: Yes. Of course, that wouldn't have made a bit of difference with my mother. My mother wrote back and told her she should never have done that and so forth. Then, later on, after I came back and got married, my wife corresponded with her off and on for several years.

Paul Stillwell: I take it the reason she was in Colorado was she had been taken out as part of that internment process.†

Commander Harralson: Right, right. I think back in Colorado they were allowed some freedom around, as opposed to out here. But I'm not sure about that.

Paul Stillwell: She must have had a degree of freedom if she could carry on that kind of correspondence.

Commander Harralson: Right. I think she actually was doing work. I don't know how much control they had over her. I get a lot of different descriptions of how they were treated and handled.

Paul Stillwell: Well, it is unfortunate she didn't stop and visit, because she had become a friend of your mother already, just by correspondence.

---

*A Nisei is a native-born American of Japanese ancestry.
†Shortly after the attack on Pearl Harbor in 1941, Japanese Americans on the West Coast were interned in camps in the interior of the country.

Commander Harralson: Yes. But there was a lot of bad feeling around Japanese, and a lot of people couldn't distinguish between a Japanese from Japan and an American of Japanese origin.

Paul Stillwell: And that led to a great deal of injustice, as those people were sent away and their property was lost.

Commander Harralson: Yes, it did. I have a lot of trouble with that, because I talked to Suzanne's father.

Paul Stillwell: Suzanne is your daughter-in-law, we should explain.

Commander Harralson: My daughter-in-law, who is third-generation Japanese ancestry, an all-American girl, a registered nurse, a graduate of the University of California, Irvine; a lovely person, all around. I've had long talks with her father, and, of course, he's very bitter about it. The thing that to me was bad about it was the taking of their property, to the gain of other Americans. I think that's where the real injustice is.

Now, the truth of the matter, of course, is that--judging from what I'm told by my brothers and my mother and my father--that that was the best place for them, in internment camps, for their own protection. Because people don't realize the fear that went up and down this coast after Pearl Harbor, near panic in some situations. Because we didn't know. And the truth was, we were in terrible shape, militarily.

Paul Stillwell: Yes.

Commander Harralson: That's something that the later generations don't understand. We were isolationists. Our Navy was small, really. Our Army was small, ill-equipped. The Marines were well trained, but they were not very many. And here we had a war on two sides. There were a lot of scared people.

Paul Stillwell: Well, what happened during the summer of 1945?

Commander Harralson: Okay. After this terrible bombing, and after about two or three weeks out on the golf course, they told us we were moving. We put our stuff together, and they put us on a train. We headed towards Tokyo. What we traveled through was an utter desert of debris, just the most desolate-looking destruction you ever saw. We'd be traveling along and see a building in the distance. Somebody would say, "There's one they missed." Then, when we'd get alongside, it would be a hollow shell. It was one that just didn't fall down. The Japanese guards told us that many, many Japanese had dug air-raid shelters under their houses. When those firestorms hit there, they were baked alive.

We got off the train and were marched through the streets. We saw bodies from the recent raid, I guess. They marched us over a bridge, onto a little sandy island, to a camp called Omori. It was considered POW headquarters camp. They put us in their standard barracks. They kept us away from the rest of the camp. The rest of the camp worked in a railroad yard. From what we were able to learn, they had pilfering down to an art. They knew what was in every freight car that went through there. For those cars that had material they wanted, they took it. They had guards bribed; all kinds of Japanese workmen bribed. One of their big threats was, "If I go, you go." And it would have been harder on the Japanese than on the POW, I think. They had a kingdom set up there. They had all kinds of goodies--sugar, raw rice, better rice.

Then over in a barracks, kept separate from everybody else, was a whole bunch of aviators that had been shot down. There was a general there. Somebody said that he was the youngest general in the Air Force. He had been shot down in a B-29. They marched them out every day to work, carrying shovels and rakes, to clean up some of the destruction. But I don't know how big a dent they would have made.

While we were there, there was an air raid again. I don't know what in the world they could have been bombing. But I saw one of them make a run. I was laying up in the top pad--we didn't have any place to go--where there was a window. I watched outside, and I saw this B-29 lay a stick of bombs that came right towards the camp. It approached on the other side from the island, but the stick of bombs stopped right at the water's edge. I felt then that they really knew that we were there, that this was marked as a POW camp.

Paul Stillwell: Pretty good bombing, I would say.

Commander Harralson: Yes.

Paul Stillwell: Did you have any means of marking the camp yourself, so it would be identifiable from the air?

Commander Harralson: No, no. I think there were marks.

Paul Stillwell: I've seen some pictures of signs on roofs. But maybe that was after the surrender.

Commander Harralson: I think it was. I think it was. They took us out of there. We knew we were just there for a short while; I think three weeks was all. They put us on a train again, and we went north, again through all of this terrible destruction. Finally, we left it behind and climbed up into the mountains. One of the scenes I remember vividly is the train going around a big curve on the side of this mountain. The curve embraced an apple orchard that was in full bloom. It was such a pleasant sight, and it had been so long since we'd seen anything so beautiful, it just took our breath away.

We were on the train--gee, I don't know how long, up in the mountains. We ended up at a place with the name of Wakasenen, which was a very small town. We were to work in a pig iron foundry, as we called it, though it wasn't actually a foundry. It was really a smelter that made iron ingots for further fabrication. We worked in this mill, and lived not far outside in a camp that was made out of wood. It had cracks a half-inch wide in it. There was no heat in it. Of course, it was getting into summer, and the weather wasn't bad, but we understood that the snow got six or seven feet deep in the winter. So we hoped this war would be resolved before winter, which it was.

At the mill, I was put into a group that made the carbon that they used for the big electric furnaces in this smelter. I worked over in this plant, where we mixed some kind of oil and baked coal in a big mixer--like a cement mixer. We put in so many buckets of oil, or tar, and so many buckets of coal. It would churn in there and become viscous. Then we'd dump it out onto a big metal plate, and people with shovels put it in forms. So that you ended up with a block, say, 18 inches long by 10 inches wide by, say, 6 inches deep.

Of course, like I said, the coal had to be baked. Now, they had a smaller electric furnace there, where they baked the coal. The bin for this coal that was to be baked was adjacent to the bin where it came out of the furnace. A couple of us were over there one day, shoveling this baked coal into these five-gallon tins, with wire handles, to carry over to the mixer. A new guy had been assigned there. All I can remember is that he was a chief electrician. I can't tell you a name. There are several names that have drifted through my mind, but I'm not sure. Anyhow, he was there, and he was shoveling into a bucket. But he was shoveling the unbaked coal. I told him, "Hey, we're supposed to use the baked coal here."

He said, "So?" And he went on shoveling the raw, unbaked coal.

And I thought, "Well, why not?" [Laughter] So after that, every mixture received some amount of unbaked coal in it. This went on for three weeks, maybe four. Then they started having breakdowns in the big furnaces. That was serious business. These chunks we made were dumped into the top and heated. They formed the center core of the electrical furnace--the electrode. But through impurities, or some other strange reason, these electrodes developed big cracks. When that happened, why, the furnace broke down. So they had to shut down and unload the furnace itself and also put in a new shot of the material for the electrode. The sad part was that my good friend Lauer was one of those guys that had to go to work there, to unload this thing and to help fix it. It was brutal. Years later I told him about what we were doing. He hadn't known, because, there again, we just did it; we didn't talk about it.

A funny thing: we'd get a stack of these blocks, and periodically we'd push a little loaded flatcar, again on tracks, over to the furnace. We were pushing a load one day, and there was something on the tracks; we couldn't go. So we simply climbed up and sat on the pile of blocks. We were sitting there, perfectly happy, and here came a Japanese with a hard hat and a suit and a tie, and he said, in very good English, "You fellows shouldn't be sitting up there. You're liable to contaminate these blocks. We have to keep them clean." We had a hard time keeping a straight face. [Laughter]

One day we went out to work. At noontime we all ate in this one building. We'd finish a rice box and put our heads down, most of us, to catch a short nap. This one day I did that, and when I woke up, I realized that a much longer period than 15 minutes had passed. It seemed to me it must be midafternoon. It was. We looked around; everybody looked around and wondered, "What's going on here? We should be working." Here came the guards. They told us we were going back to camp. They marched us down the street of the town. Here were people hanging out of windows and just boxes sitting out on the curb, with radios on them. Everybody just stared with a complete poker face, I guess you'd say, completely devoid of any emotion. We got back to camp, and they didn't tell us anything.

The next day, we didn't go to work. There was a detail in camp that emptied the benjos. They dipped it out and put it in buckets, and with a cart hauled it up the road. I don't know what they did with it, but that's how we took care of the benjos there. The benjos were full. These guys asked the sergeant what to do with the benjos. And the sergeant said, "Dump them in the air-raid trenches." That was the significant. We knew then that this war was over.

Paul Stillwell: That there were going to be no more air raids.

Commander Harralson: Yes. That was another thing; when we first arrived in camp, they told us there wouldn't be any air raids in there, but there were. They didn't do much damage, though.

[Interruption to change tapes]

Paul Stillwell: We just took a break here, to change tapes. And you mentioned during the break that you left out a harrowing experience at Shinagawa. So let's cover that, please.

Commander Harralson: Shinagawa was a hospital camp. The difference was that at a hospital camp, you didn't have to go to work. You got less food because you didn't have to go to work, but the lack of food was why you were there. So it was sort of a Catch-22 situation. But midway through my stay there, for some unaccountable reason, I and another guy were singled out and told to go over and report to what turned out to be a laboratory. We had been told not to eat breakfast, which we didn't.

We went over there. We were sat down. We were given a bowl of something that seemed like rice water and drank it. Then we were made to swallow a rubber ball on a tube. Then periodically they would pump out some of the contents of our stomach. We sat there for about two hours, doing that. Then they pulled the tube and the little ball out. I was taken into a room and put on a table. I could see them getting ready with a syringe that looked like something you used on a horse. It had needle on it that looked like a six-penny nail. It was full of some kind of white, milky fluid. They injected that, intravenously, in my arm. I would say within less than a minute, probably less than 30 seconds, my face, my hands, everything started to swell up like balloons. They then gave me a shot of something that I believe was adrenaline, and the swelling gradually subsided. Then they let me go. I often wondered what the white stuff was. I had no idea.

But after the war, I have read that there was this doctor in Shinagawa who was injecting all kinds of bad stuff--they named some things there that are terrible--as some kind of crazy experiment. I figured that I was quite fortunate, in that what they gave me apparently didn't do any permanent damage. I have no idea what it was. Now, I think the so-called doctor was Tokuda, but I'm not sure about that. I learned later that there was a Tokuda in the Philippines that killed a bunch of POWs with some of his weird experiments.

Paul Stillwell: Well, you were fortunate, also, that he gave you the remedy.

Commander Harralson: Yes.

Paul Stillwell: What was your worst moment as a POW?

Commander Harralson: Oh, think that ship trip was the worst.

Paul Stillwell: With the dysentery and the seasickness.

Commander Harralson: Yes. Locked down in the hold.

Paul Stillwell: And the air must have been just noxious.

Commander Harralson: Yes, it was.

Paul Stillwell: What was the process by which you were repatriated?

Commander Harralson: Well, after the sergeant told them that they could dump the benjos in the air-raid trenches, we thought for sure the war was over. The next morning, we congregated out in the compound. The camp commander showed up in full military uniform and told us that the United States and Japan had come to an agreement, and that the war was over. He turned and he walked out the gate. The old sergeant there went over and banged his head against the side of the guardhouse. He did. [Laughter]

Paul Stillwell: He took it hard.

Commander Harralson: He did. Of course, there was jubilation of all kinds--not as much as you would think. It was just a tremendous feeling of having survived. It took a while for it to really sink in.

Now, one of the deals they were required to do was furnish us with a radio receiver, so we could tune in on the Missouri.* And that they did. It sat on a chair out in the compound, with a long extension cord. It was tuned to the Missouri and we all listened. And they kept telling us to, "Stay where you are. Don't try to come in."

Paul Stillwell: So you heard the broadcast of the surrender ceremony, with General MacArthur on this radio?

---

*The battleship Missouri (BB-63) was the site of the Japanese signing of surrender documents in Tokyo Bay on 2 September 1945.

Commander Harralson: I don't recall hearing that. I really don't. But they kept repeating over and over: "Stay where you are. We'll come get you. Don't try to come in by yourself." And we did that. We stayed there quite a while. I'm not sure how long it was. But, of course, one of the big things we found out was about the atomic bomb.*

Paul Stillwell: What was your first news of that?

Commander Harralson: I think it was by radio there. And, of course, I don't know if I heard it directly, but anything coming over got around camp almost instantly. We decided that we needed security, so we appointed a security guard. Then we went on liberty. We started walking out into the town and around. In fact, one place we were invited in. We went in and had tea and watermelon. [Laughter]

Paul Stillwell: This in a civilian home?

Commander Harralson: Yes.

Paul Stillwell: Where were you geographically, by this time?

Commander Harralson: There's a port north of Tokyo, Sendai. We were inland from that, up in the mountains. It's kind of hard to judge, but I don't think we were more than about 30 or 40 miles from Sendai, to the west and perhaps a little bit north. There were pretty rugged mountains around us.

Paul Stillwell: With 50-some years since then to think about it, what are your views on the U.S. use of the atomic bombs?

Commander Harralson: [Laughter] That's easy. The bomb was here, whether we used it or not. I think that is absolutely true. Scientific breakthroughs of that size are known

---

*In the first combat use of atomic bombs, U.S. B-29 bombers hit Hiroshima, on the island of Honshu, on 6 August 1945 and Nagasaki, on Kyushu, on 9 August.

throughout the science community. There couldn't be any secret about it. So the bomb was here, like it or not. The use of the bomb saved--I can say--a million lives. I truly believe it did.

I've read articles on what they planned. The name of the operation was called Olympic.* They had some basis for their calculations from Okinawa--the cost to go ashore there, the cost to our side, and the cost to the Japanese. I think you have every right to believe that the Japanese people would be fanatical in their defense. I have just read an interesting story in the Naval History about the kamikazes--how effective they were, the damage they did, the ships they sank, and the advantage they had; where they could come from behind the mountains real quick, giving the operators and gunners very little time to zero in, in defense.† Things like that. I believe that the casualties would have been enormous.

Paul Stillwell: Including yourself, probably.

Commander Harralson: Including myself, because it was absolutely true the Japanese did not plan to turn us over; if it ever got down to the nitty-gritty, they would kill us. And they did, in some cases. They have written proof of that order, I believe, in the Philippines.

Paul Stillwell: How long did it take before you were liberated?

Commander Harralson: There was quite a while. The only date I can come up with--I think it was August 15, wasn't it?

Paul Stillwell: That's when the hostilities ceased.

Commander Harralson: All right. I remember taking off from Guam at noon on October the fifth and arriving in Honolulu at the same time, October the fifth, due to crossing the dateline.

---

*Operation Olympic was the code name for the Allied invasion of the Japanese island of Kyushu, scheduled for 1 November 1945.
†D. M. Giangreco, "The Truth About Kamikazes," Naval History, May/June 1997, pages 25-29.

Paul Stillwell: Oh, were you in an airplane?

Commander Harralson: Yes, a C-54.[*]

I'm just trying to work back from knowing that date. After we left the camp, we went down to Sendai and went aboard an AKA.[†] Then we went down to Tokyo and anchored there. I could see that carrier that I was telling you about. When I went up on the bridge and looked with binoculars, I could see that carrier, still afloat, over to one side.

Paul Stillwell: The one that you sabotaged?

Commander Harralson: Yes. And then I looked the other direction, into Tokyo Bay, and all I could see were these huge carriers. It just looked like a vast armada. It was. We stayed there one night, I believe, and then went on down to Guam. So let's see, that puts us into September. I think four weeks we stayed in camp. We rode a train into Sendai and saw some good old Americans--big, fat ones. [Laughter]

Paul Stillwell: Do you remember the name of the AKA?

Commander Harralson: No, I don't. I wish I did.

Paul Stillwell: You said you weighed about 155 at the beginning of the war. What did you weigh at the end of it?

Commander Harralson: Well, the time I got weighed was in Yokohama. This old doctor, Dr. Price, one day when things were slack around there, he borrowed the scales that they weighed the grain out in the galley. He got it over to sick bay, and he started weighing

---

[*]C-54 was the Army Air Forces designation for the Douglas-built DC-4 commercial airliner. The four-engine propeller plane had a top speed of 281 miles an hour. It was 118 feet long, wing span of 94 feet, and gross weight of 65,000 pounds.
[†]AKA--a Navy attack cargo ship, a type filled with landing craft for use in supporting amphibious assaults.

prisoners. I weighed in there at 44 kilos. That works out to about 98 pounds. And I think that's what I was, roughly, at the end. Because the food never got better.

Paul Stillwell: What do you remember of the voyage from Japan to Guam?

Commander Harralson: Not much. I remember going through the chow line, and the mess cook saying, "You like ham?"
    I said, "Yeah!" And I think he put about four big slabs of ham on my plate.

Paul Stillwell: Could your system accommodate rich food right away?

Commander Harralson: Well, we had been kind of building up, because they had dropped food to us.

Paul Stillwell: Oh, I see.

Commander Harralson: And, of course, our cooks took over the galley, and we had all of that food. Oh, we made the Japanese bring us a cow. We slaughtered the cow, so we had meat in our soup. So we had begun building up. But I think maybe we should have been a little more careful about eating. I ballooned up. Let's see, that would be October. The following spring, I weighed 215 pounds.

Paul Stillwell: [Laughter] You certainly did balloon.

Commander Harralson: I couldn't understand what was happening.

Paul Stillwell: You were making up for a lot of lost time.

Commander Harralson: Yes. Eggs and milk and all that stuff.

Paul Stillwell: Well, please proceed from Guam. How did you manage to get air transportation back to Hawaii?

Commander Harralson: Well, I wanted to tell you something. When I got on the ship, they told us we could write a message home; it would go by the Red Cross. So I filled out the blanks they gave us and turned it in. Then we got down to Guam. There was a tent there, where they told us we could send a message home, so I went over and I sent a message home to my mother again, telling her I was in Guam and coming home. We were there two days, I think. And then my group was put on a C-54, and we flew to Honolulu.

We landed there and went up to the big hospital. And I couldn't believe the food they served in this hospital. Gosh, all the milk you wanted and salads. Unbelievable. And I went to the USO show.* Oh, gee.

Paul Stillwell: What can you say about the psychological reaction to having all this freedom, after being deprived so long?

Commander Harralson: Almost overwhelming. We landed at Oakland Airport. The plane from Guam to Honolulu had bucket seats and the like. But from Honolulu to Oakland, we had padded seats and carpets. We flew in over the Golden Gate and landed at Oakland. We got out, and we were kind of milling around, wondering what next. A former POW came over and said, "You know, if you go over there and ask that girl, she'll give you coffee and a doughnut."

I went over there, and they gave me coffee and a doughnut, and I thought, "Man, this is living." [Laughter]

Paul Stillwell: All you have to do is ask now.

---

*USO--United Service Organization, a group of civilians who put on entertainment programs for service personnel and provided hospitality for them in many parts of the world.

Commander Harralson: They took us up to Oak Knoll, and I ran into a whole bunch of other guys I knew.* There was a little bit of unhappiness, because they had been there some time and were anxious to get going. They were being delayed in process.

While I was there, I asked around, what rate I was. I wanted to buy a uniform. We were still in these awful clothes. People kept assuring me that I was a chief petty officer. So I went downtown, and I bought a chief's uniform. You know that lousy gray uniform they had?

Paul Stillwell: Right.

Commander Harralson: Well, that's what I bought, and a fore-and-aft cap that they wore. And when I got to the tie, I didn't know how to tie a necktie. [Laughter] But, anyhow, I got a uniform, of sorts, and I went down to Greyhound. And Greyhound was on strike. So I went over to the railroad depot, and I found out there'd be a train to Sacramento at 9:00 o'clock that evening. So I bummed around and had a few beers and got on the train that night. It was just jammed with people. It took four hours from Oakland to Sacramento, a trip that should have taken two at the most. When I got to Sacramento, it was after midnight. I thought, "Well now, I'll go get a room in a hotel. Then I can get up in the morning, clean up and shave, get myself a good meal, and go on home."

So I headed out and found a hotel. I walked in and said to the clerk, "I'd like a room."

The guy looked at me, and then he pointed to the lobby and said, "You're free to sleep in there anyplace you can find." The place was just littered with bodies--sailors and soldiers. So I walked around town, drinking coffee until I was overflowing. Finally, daylight came, and I thought of another bus line. I went out there, to the bus line, and I was about to buy a ticket that would get me to Roseville. That was a little closer. I thought about hitchhiking, but I didn't like that. Being a chief petty officer in uniform, I didn't want to hitchhike.

---

*Naval Hospital Oakland was commissioned 1 July 1942 on the site of the former Oak Knoll Golf and Country Club, on the hills on the east side of San Francisco Bay.

Then I remembered I had an uncle that might be living in Sacramento. I looked in the telephone directory, and, sure enough, he was listed. I called him. Of course, he got all excited. He came down and picked me up, and we went out to his house. The two kids and his wife climbed in, and they took me up to Applegate.

He drove in the driveway and stopped. He told me, "We'll stay here. You go on in." So I went in. I walked in the back door, calling for my mother. She had been asleep on the bed, because she worked nights. She woke up, and I almost gave her a heart attack from the shock. Then I found out she had received no word about me at all. They had gotten this stream of POWs coming back, and then it was petering out every day. She had given up. She hadn't gotten either one of the messages.

I was home, I think, about a week, and here came a message from the Navy, advising her that, "We are happy to advise you that your son is alive and well, and will soon be home." [Laughter] But I went back to Oak Knoll. I had to go back; I was AWOL.*

Paul Stillwell: Oh, from the hospital?

Commander Harralson: Yes. I went back, and then they processed me and gave me 90 days' rehabilitation, and I went home.

Paul Stillwell: Did you get a big chunk of back pay?

Commander Harralson: Yes, it was quite a bit. I think I had around $5,000, or something like that, which, at that time, was . . .

Paul Stillwell: It was a small fortune.

Commander Harralson: Oh, yes.

Paul Stillwell: You could buy a house for that.

---

*AWOL--absent without leave. The Navy equivalent for this term is UA--unauthorized absence.

Commander Harralson: Don't I wish I'd bought some stocks--been smart. But did I? I bought a used car. [Laughter]

Paul Stillwell: Well, had you, in fact, been advanced to chief petty officer?

Commander Harralson: Yes, I was. I got terribly bored at home and was glad to come back to Oak Knoll. When I got back, they told me one of my tests had proven positive, that I had amoebic dysentery. So it meant I had to stay around for two more months for treatment. I had been going over to San Francisco, to a bar called the Westward Ho. A lot of radiomen congregated there, and it was a fun place to go--you know, a lot of good talk and everything. But I was drinking too much, which we'd been warned against. So, as I was going out the gate, I noticed on the right there was a shop. It was occupational therapy. So I went in, and there were a couple of WAVES working there.* One of them became my wife.

Paul Stillwell: Well, please tell me about that.

Commander Harralson: Well, I wanted to make a leather purse, is what I wanted to do. And one of them didn't think I was up to making a purse until I'd made a belt. So we argued about that. But she also poured me a cup of coffee. So I asked her out. I had dated a couple of nurses, but the truth was, they were too fast for me; I couldn't handle them. [Laughter] But this WAVE was different. We made liberties over in San Francisco and down to Fisherman's Wharf, when it was truly a fisherman's wharf, where the main occupation was catching fish, and a little restaurant on the side. The food was unbelievable. And we went to plays and movies.

Paul Stillwell: What was her name?

Commander Harralson: Naomi Winkler.

---

*WAVES--Women accepted for Voluntary Emergency Service.

Paul Stillwell: What was her rating?

Commander Harralson: She was a seaman. But I think she got gypped because she had a college education; she had a B.S. degree in home economics. They had sent her back to Hunter College, in New York, for training in occupational therapy. I think she was supposed to get something out of it but didn't. But, anyhow, we got along great and decided to get married. But we decided to wait until she was separated from the Navy. Then I eventually was cleared from Oak Knoll.

Oh, there was something to do with paperwork on me. A discrepancy there showed up; it became apparent that I had been AWOL. So they sent me over to the master-at-arms or someplace, to see if I was on a list of AWOLs. I wasn't, so they forgot about it.

For my next duty I wanted the communication office at the foot of Broadway in San Diego, but too many other people had already seized on that. So they sent me out to the Naval Electronics Lab on Point Loma. I stayed there until Naomi got out of the service. Then we were married in Long Beach.

Now, Long Beach back then was known as Little Iowa. It was full of Iowans.

Paul Stillwell: Which she was.

Commander Harralson: Yes.

Paul Stillwell: Why did it have that nickname?

Commander Harralson: A lot of people from Iowa lived there. Now there's a lot of people of Japanese ancestry that live there.

Paul Stillwell: Did the Navy do an interview or interrogation or a debriefing, to find out about your POW experiences?

Richard A. Harralson, Interview #2 (5/16/97) – Page 245

Commander Harralson: No, no. They didn't do anything. They brought us back and checked us out at the hospital, and that was it. It was incumbent upon us to get back in shape, straightened out.

Paul Stillwell: Well, here I am, on behalf of the Navy, doing it 50-some years later. [Laughter]

Commander Harralson: Yes.

Paul Stillwell: So they pretty much left you on your own after that?

Commander Harralson: Yes, they sure did. No big deal. Well, there were a lot of men that had it rough out there--taking all those islands.

Paul Stillwell: Including the ones who were not prisoners.

Commander Harralson: That's what I'm talking about. A lot of them didn't come back. So what's one guy that made it back, you know? The attitude was, "You guys, you were lucky. You didn't get killed. Welcome home."

Paul Stillwell: Well, please tell me about the job there at Point Loma.

Commander Harralson: Well, that was kind of a farce. The Navy was, as far as I could tell, thrashing around, most men counting numbers. It was while I was there that I got married.

Paul Stillwell: What was the date of that?

Commander Harralson: April 20, 1946. I went up to apply for Navy housing, and the girl there said, "Well, we have a long waiting list." She said, "Please fill out this form." So, in the place for months overseas, I said 72 months. I filled it out, and I gave it back. She looked at me, "What do you mean, 72 months?"

I said, "Well, that's how long I was out there." Then I told her I had been a POW. Then she said, "Wait." She went in the back room, came back shortly, and told me I had an apartment in Navy housing.

But I guess I couldn't stand good luck, because we moved in there and were real happy. I was having trouble with this car I bought. I sold it, and I had to hitchhike from the base of Point Loma out to the point. It wasn't very far. I usually rode with scientists. They had a lot of genuine Ph.D. scientists out there. That was a lot of fun. But there wasn't much to do. I set up an office in one building that had all kinds of gear in there, everything you'd want. Nobody knew what was in there, so to do something, I undertook an inventory. I was engaged in my inventory there, because I was always keen on Title-B equipment. I was serious about that. That's serious business, accountability for Title-B equipment.

Then I was up at the personnel office one day, and I saw that they were asking for volunteers to go to ET school at the Great Lakes.* I realized, at that time, that there was this break in ETs and radiomen. I didn't want to be a radioman ignorant in the technical side--all this new stuff such as radar and ultra-high frequencies. So I asked them at the personnel office if they would take a chief there. They said that they would ask. So they sent a letter in. What came back was a set of orders to the ET school.

Paul Stillwell: Had your skills as a radioman atrophied during the four-year layoff?

Commander Harralson: Oh, not to the extent they wouldn't have come back. You don't forget the code when it's driven into you like it was.

Paul Stillwell: Sort of like riding a bicycle?

---

*ET--electronics technician.

Commander Harralson: Yes, that's right. I have a speed key; I can still send. I have a telegraph sounder, and what I find is I can go real good for about two or three minutes, and then my wrist begins to cramp up.

Paul Stillwell: But you've still got it in your mind.

Commander Harralson: Oh, yes.

Paul Stillwell: So how long were you in that Point Loma job?

Commander Harralson: March, April, May--about three or four months.

Paul Stillwell: Sounds like it was mostly make-work.

Commander Harralson: It was. It was. And I was real happy with the home life, but I felt I was not achieving anything as a chief. I was real proud. I liked my chief hat. I felt I was a competent chief petty officer, but I wanted the other part. I was kind of upset about it. How could I be a radioman, which I liked very much, and yet still be able to do all this technical work too?

So we moved out to Great Lakes, where I entered a class with all these other rates. I was doing real well on the tests. Of course, my wife was with me there. Housing was terrible. There just wasn't any. We were living out of rooms and having to eat in restaurants. She got sick one three-day weekend, when we found the restaurants closed, all but a greasy spoon. I feared I wasn't taking care of my wife. I got the idea of a house trailer and found a used one for $1,000. I didn't have a car to pull it, but part of the agreement was that they would tow it out to a trailer park. What was the name of that? Murphy's Shamrock Grove. They towed it out there and set us up. I undertook a loan to pay for this, from a loan company.

In the meantime, we were getting along, situated out there. They called me over to the school office one day and asked me if I was interested in being an officer. I said, "Sure." So I filled out some papers and went on and forgot about it. In the meantime, my transportation, by bus, didn't work out too well. I was having a lot of problems getting to school and back. So I bought a real old Chevy, two-door sedan. It had a nice paint job. It was enough to get me back and forth, but that was about it. Then one day, they called me over to the Ninth Naval District headquarters. They said, "Chief, we have two letters of appointment here. One is a radio electrician and one is an ensign. Which do you want?"

I thought about it. I thought, "A radio electrician is supposed to be smart; an ensign--nobody expects anything out of an ensign." [Laughter] That was really my reasoning, so I said, "I'll take the ensign."

The clerk said, "Fine." But then she added, "We have to swear you in first as a W-1." So they did; they swore me in as a W-1, and then turned right around and swore me in as an ensign.

Paul Stillwell: So how many minutes were you a warrant officer?

Commander Harralson: Not more than five, if that long. That's true. I've got the letters of appointment in my files. So I went back home, and I thought, "Gee, my wife will be happy. I'm an officer now, a gentleman." I had to get my crow taken off, and a gold stripe on my sleeve, and get a new hat device.* I thought, "Well, now they're going to send me to some indoctrination course. You know, some kind of place where they'll tell me how to behave."

Paul Stillwell: When was the date of your becoming an officer? Was that in 1946?

Commander Harralson: Yes, October the sixth. But I was wrong. What I got was a set of orders sending me to Portsmouth, New Hampshire, to be the officer in charge of the radio station. I didn't know whether to be happy or cry.

---

*"Crow" is the nickname for the sewn-on design of an eagle that appears as part of a petty officer's rating badge. The nickname is particulary apt when a sailor is wearing his white uniform. In that case, the eagle is a dark blue, nearly black.

So I went home. Here I had a trailer and a car that couldn't pull the trailer, much less get halfway to Portsmouth. I had this trailer loan on which I'd made one payment. I realized right away that I had to get rid of the trailer, and I had to get rid of the car. So I advertised the trailer in the paper. I didn't get any bites, and I was getting scared. I had this old clunker car. I didn't want to sell it until the last minute. But on that trailer it got very, very close. I was desperate. One day, a guy showed up that was interested. He was an older person. He sounded like he was going to take it. He asked, "Do you have it financed?" So I explained to him that I did and who it was with. He said, "Bad news. Bad news." I thought he had decided that he couldn't do it. But he said, "Let's go down and talk to them."

So we went down to this loan company in Waukegan and talked to them. They were not about to let me off the hook. So we walked back out to the car and climbed in. I was thinking, "Oh, Lordy, what am I going to do now?" We sat there for a while.

Then he said, "You stay here," and he went back in. He came back out a while later and said that he had bought my trailer. So all it cost me was that one month's payment.

Paul Stillwell: Gee, that was a good deal.

Commander Harralson: I got out of it. Oh, it really took a load off. Then I went down and sold the car at the place where I bought it, for what I paid for it.

Paul Stillwell: So you just sort of borrowed it from them. [Laughter]

Commander Harralson: Yes, that's right. I couldn't believe that. We took a train to Boston, and then a train from Boston to Portsmouth, New Hampshire. Then a taxi. We found a nice house in Kittery, Maine. It was an old, old house but pretty well kept. The landlord, Mr. Russell, lived in one half, and we lived in the other. It was so close to the base that I could walk home for lunch.

Paul Stillwell: Were you stationed at the naval shipyard?

Commander Harralson: No, I was a component of the naval base. The naval base office was a brick building that was built way, way, way back. I'm talking John Paul Jones, I think. Way, way back. It had a cupola. It was two-story, very cubicle in proportions. The lower half was the OD's office and so forth, but the admiral's offices were topside, up in the northwest corner. The radio station was in the northeast corner. The chief of staff was in the south side, and there were other offices around there. The coding room was in the southeast corner.

Well, I arrived and reported in to the OD, which was down below. I was taken in to meet Admiral John Brown, submarine dolphins, big medals.[*]

Paul Stillwell: Navy football player in about 1912.[†]

Commander Harralson: [Laughter] I can't tell you anything about that!

Paul Stillwell: Babe Brown was his nickname.

Commander Harralson: He was a huge man, and very distinguished looking--academy ring, of course. He had a chief of staff; there were two while I was there. One was Captain Moseley.[‡] The other one was Captain Griggs.[§] All of them were submariners. They had an operations officer, submariner, academy. They had an admiral's aide, a Lieutenant Commander Jarvis.[**] Jarvis was a football hero. He was a huge man, with shoulders that wide, medals galore, dolphins. Now, I don't know anything about a submarine combat pin or device. Is there such a thing?

Paul Stillwell: Yes.

---

[*] Rear Admiral John H. Brown, Jr., USN, Commandant Portsmouth Naval Base.
[†] Brown graduated from the Naval Academy in the class of 1914. For his play during the 1913 season he was selected as a guard on Walter Camp's all-America team.
[‡] Captain Stanley P. Moseley, USN.
[§] Captain John B. Griggs, Jr., USN.
[**] Lieutenant Commander Benjamin C. Jarvis, USN.

Commander Harralson: Did they have them in World War II?

Paul Stillwell: Yes.

Commander Harralson: Well see, that's how ignorant I was. But I knew they had the dolphins. And, of course, Portsmouth is a submarine base. The last one on the staff was Ruth Rothberg, lieutenant (j.g.).*

So I checked in. I had six radiomen; four of them were chief petty officers. [Laughter] It was a very small station. The transmitters were right there in the radio room. I had a big low-frequency transmitter, an ET-8019 Collins that we used most of the time. There was one other. Teletype was the main source of traffic. But we were the end of the NTX system.† We had no stations to relay farther to or anything like that.

Paul Stillwell: This must have been quite a learning experience for you, because of all the changes that had occurred since 1941.

Commander Harralson: Yes. Right, right, it was. It was. But I was a good radioman. I could match any of those chiefs. It didn't take me any time to learn about the NTX system. I latched right on to that. Oh, the chief clerk's office was the big problem. It was located between us and the office of the admiral's aide. The chief clerk had an office and a big room for the people that worked for him. I learned at Portsmouth about chief clerks, the power behind the throne.

It wasn't too long before my troubles started. The electronics in the front end of one of my receivers burned out. To get it fixed, I went over to shop 67. The officer that I talked to at shop 67 was a lieutenant commander, a mustang who spoke my language.‡ He said, "Sure, bring it over. I'll fix it for you." So I had it sent over. He had it put back in order, and we were back in operation. Then, I think it was about a week or two, another one went out. So I sent it over to Shop 67. He told me, "I'll fix this one, but no more until I get a job order."

---

*Lieutenant (junior grade) Ruth L. Rothberg, USN.
†NTX--Navy teletypewriter exchange.
‡"Mustang" is Navy slang for a former enlisted man who has risen through the ranks to become an officer.

I said, "Well, how do I get a job order?"

He said, "You don't know?"

"No."

He said, "Well, you get one written up on your account."

I said, "What account?"

He said, "Your money. You've got money up there."

"I haven't got any money."

He says, "Oh, yes you do. You get an allowance to run that station." He said, "You go over to the shipyard accounting office and ask them where that money is."

So I went over to the shipyard and found out that the money went to the chief clerk. That's why the chief clerk was happy to give me paper and materials. So I told the shipyard, "That belongs to the radio station. I'm officer in charge of the radio station. I want the money allocated to me, in my control." And they were quite willing to do that, no problem. They signed it over to me. They set me up and showed me how to write job orders and everything. So I went back real happy.

The next day, the chief clerk stuck his head in my office and said, "Well, I hope you're happy, now. But remember this, don't come to me for paper or any supplies whatsoever. You're on your own."

Great. So about the next thing, I needed some message blanks. I filled out an order, with a sample, and sent it down to the First Naval District in Boston to print so many. I ordered a whole bunch.

The next day, the chief clerk stuck his head in again. He was always bringing me bad news; he delighted in that. He said, "You've done it now. You've overextended your allotment. That's a no-no. You're in deep trouble." So I called up the printing office in Boston, and I was able to stop the blanks for incoming messages, but I was too late for the outgoing blanks. I had spent just about all of my money. So the next day the chief clerk stuck his head in and said, "You've done it now. What are you going to do for message blanks?"

I said, "I'll do something." So I called up supply. I found that for $50.00 I could get a huge amount of paper, the kind of paper I wanted. I knew that the prison, which was a component of the base--Portsmouth Naval Prison--had a big printing shop. So I went over there and saw the executive officer, who was a Navy commander. The CO was a Marine colonel. I got in to see him, and I had samples of what I wanted. I asked him if he could print me up the message blanks if I'd get him the paper. There wasn't anything to them. It was a half sheet of the right kind of paper, with two red lines and U.S. Naval Communications Service. That was it. Those things from Boston cost two cents apiece. [Laughter]

So he said, "No, I can't. The union down there has stopped us from doing any work in the printing room. They're very strong. I'm sorry." But as he was telling me why he couldn't, he was making himself mad. And he began to shout. Finally, he said, "Get me the damn paper. I'll print your blanks." [Laughter] So I sent a truckload of paper over to him. They had it over there just a few days, and he called me. I sent the truck over and picked it up. To get it into the basement, where we stored supplies, you had to back the truck right up to the main entrance to the building. As the men were unloading it, taking it down to the basement, I looked up and saw the chief clerk looking at me.

Paul Stillwell: Very unhappy.

Commander Harralson: Well, I think he was. As far as I know, they might still be using the blanks out there I had printed.

Paul Stillwell: Well, you had kind of punctured his bubble there. I wonder what was happening to the excess of the allotment, that you hadn't been calling on.

Commander Harralson: Well, you can't help but wonder, you know. He was living like a fat cat.

I had a civilian, Mr. Cook, who was the dispatcher. He was a real old guy. I was getting some crazy phenomenon on the squawkbox--I'd get an S5 signal on the squawkbox, when I opened up on the transmitter. We could pull a two-inch arc off of the low-freq antenna switch. Then another receiver burned up. So I was getting worried; something was wrong. I got to talking to Mr. Cook one day. He told me about the counterpoise, the ground system they had here; how they laid this copper wire out. He said, "You know, they dug trenches back and forth across that many, many times. This station was old. It went back to the very beginning of radio. You can tell by its call sign, NAC." So I began to suspect that we were floating at some unknown distance above ground, which can give you all kinds of weird phenomena.

So I had a real problem, and what to do about it? So I sat down with a communications typewriter and wrote a letter to the officer in charge, radio stations, First Naval District. Signed it, folded it, put it in an envelope, mailed it. Quite a while later, two weeks or so, Ruth stuck her head in one day and asked, "Did you write a letter?"

"I've written a lot of letters."

"Did you write a letter to Boston?"

"Yeah."

"Oh, boy. You are in trouble."

Paul Stillwell: You had a series of people telling you that you were in trouble. [Laughter]

Commander Harralson: [Laughter] I was. I had just sandbagged the admiral. It took a while before I got the story. But the letter went to Boston, to the officer in charge of radio stations, First Naval District, a commander. It was an unusual letter; it didn't have an official look about, and it was signed by me. The commander really didn't know what to do with it. It sat in his circular file for a while, see. Then some guy showed up from Washington. I don't know whether he was a naval officer or an engineer; I'm not sure about that. But he was standing at the corner of the desk, talking to the commander. While he was talking, he was looking down, and he did a double-take on my letter. He picked it up, read it, and shook his head. He asked if he could have it, and he took it back to BuShips.

It got to CNO.* CNO called for an inspection. That's when Admiral Brown found out. There was a big inspection coming to Portsmouth. The inspection party consisted of a captain, commanders, and engineers. And here the admiral knew nothing about my letter. All my information of what was going on came from Ruth. The inspection party arrived, but they didn't invite me to go along. As a result of what they found, they decided

---

*CNO--Chief of Naval Operations.

that it was urgent that this station be brought up to date. They went back to the CNO with that recommendation.

Now, money was very tight then. But they dug into some contingency funds. They took an existing building, that was about a quarter mile down the road from us, and refurbished it, put it in good shape. They gave me a whole bunch of transmitters in the refurbished building, and big diesel emergency generator, frequency meters, and the whole schmear. They gave me new receivers. But the admiral was very much hurt, and the last thing in the world I'd wanted to do was rock the boat. I was a real strange officer amongst these naval officers of distinction. I'm sure I must have really shocked them. But I think they cut me a lot of slack. I really do. Captain Moseley seemed to be very understanding.

Paul Stillwell: Did you tell him that you were an ensign and you weren't supposed to know anything? [Laughter]

Commander Harralson: [Laughter] No. Well, the fact was, I wasn't an ensign; I was a jaygee. My appointment to ensign was backdated--though not for pay purposes--back to 1944 or something like that. So I was only there two months and was promoted to jaygee.

But I'd had other troubles. Ruth and I were the coding board. Ruth was from Boston. She knew all of the Celtic basketball players. I think she went out with them, so she was anxious to get back to Boston every weekend. So here I was, living just outside the gate, and I had a new baby by then, Joseph. She thought that there was no reason why I couldn't stand by for coding duty on weekends. We didn't have too much coded traffic, but one of us had to be available over the weekend. So when it was her turn, she would say to me, "How's to take the coding board this weekend?"

I'd say, "Okay." Well, that got to be a little bit much. It's not that I had any great thing to do, but I was beginning to resent her assumptions that I would. Then one day, a Thursday now, she was going go to Boston, and she asked me--sort of didn't ask me, she sort of told me to take the weekend coding board availability. I said, "No." What really made me mad is she began to question why I should say no. I didn't think it was any of her business. And we got into a great big, fat argument. It got louder. That's when I come up with, "The worst thing the Navy ever did is drag women into it." She really hit the fan then. I had to run for cover. [Laughter]

Paul Stillwell: What was her rank?

Commander Harralson: She was two months senior to me.

Paul Stillwell: So what was the outcome of that?

Commander Harralson: Nothing. I just didn't take her duty anymore. The only thing ever said to me, after the business of the letter and subsequent inspection, was shortly after they had determined to update the station. The operations officer, a commander, walked in. I can't remember his name. He walked right by me and over to the window. He stood there for the longest time, looking out the window. I thought, "He's a hit-man." Finally he said, "Harralson, can you remember the initials FDR?"
    "Yes, sir."
    "Well, remember this. F for facts, D for discussion, R for the request. The next time you write a letter, remember those initials." Then he turned and walked out.

Paul Stillwell: So that was one lesson you learned.

Commander Harralson: Yes. In the meantime, I was losing men. There was a shortage of radiomen. Then they started sending me radiomen from submarines that were in the yard. But I would get different ones almost every night. They didn't know anything about running the place, the NTX. It got to be very difficult, very problematic. Oh, and the new transmitters had the Collins auto-tune system. Theoretically, we were supposed to be able to dial our frequencies, and it would shift the transmitters, and we'd be all set. But the auto-tunes were terrible, because they had a backlash. You never could stay on frequency, on tune.

So I was going down to the transmitter building all the time, to touch up these transmitters. It became a real pain in the neck. Actually, it was a bad bill of goods. What should have been a nice new station, and right on frequency, became a big problem.

I had a diesel generator for emergency power. It sat there idle. I decided to test it periodically, so I set up a schedule for testing. I'd go down there and start it. To start it, you had an air-cooled, two-cylinder gas engine. You revved it up, and then you threw the lever and got this big, old diesel going. So I was starting it up periodically, and would run it for a little while, and then shut down. Then one morning it wouldn't start. I called for a diesel mech, out of the diesel shop. Two guys came over, and we discussed the problem. They told me I was doing the worst possible thing I could do--run that diesel engine with no load. They said you have to work them. So they cleaned it up--the injectors, or whatever they did--and got it running again. So I knocked off the tests.

Paul Stillwell: You were learning a lot of lessons there.

Commander Harralson: Yes, I was. Then I had some bad luck with Mr. Cook. His wife worked in the chief clerk's office. He'd been a dispatcher there for many years. Well, we didn't have too much radio traffic, and one of the most vital and important pieces of traffic we occasionally had were diving and surfacing reports, of submarines out on sea trials. When they were down, supposed to come up at a certain time, and were late, there was very little time before going to a certain condition. You had to notify a whole bunch of people and start a whole bunch of wheels rolling.

One day a surfacing report got lost. Bells began to ring, and all kinds of hell broke loose. The fault came back to the radio station, and I traced it to Mr. Cook, the dispatcher. He was slower than the seven years' itch. He smoked all the time, and everything had to take a back seat while he put his cigarettes in a holder. He had a little jar he put his ashes in. The whole procedure of taking the jar and unscrewing the cap, and then tapping off the ashes, and then screwing the cap back took him a long time. He was definitely the responsible party for this delay. I was able to placate most people on that event and assure them it was being corrected. Then the darn thing happened again. I figured I had to do something.

So I set up another desk, to one side, and I made up a new job for Mr. Cook. One Friday, I said, "Mr. Cook, we're going to try a new arrangement here." I said, "Come Monday, I want you at this desk over here." And I outlined some jobs for him to do. Then I said, "I want Chief Umpty-ump to take over this desk, as dispatcher."

He said, "All right, Mr. Harralson."

I guess he went home and talked to his wife. Came Monday, he was sitting at the dispatcher's desk. I said, "Mr. Cook, I want that new arrangement to go into effect this morning."

He said, "Mr. Harralson, I decided not to do it."

"Mr. Cook, you can't decide not to do it. I'm officer in charge here; that's where I need you, and that's where you're going to go." There were a few sharp words, and he got up and moved over there. The chief stepped in, and things ran real smooth for about two months. And by that time, he was the only chief I had left, and I think the only really experienced radioman I had. Then he had a terrible emergency at home, and he had to have emergency leave. He had to go. I didn't want to put Mr. Cook back there. So I sat in myself.

Captain Moseley called me in to talk to me about it. He said, "Harralson, you can't win." I stuck it out for about a month, but I had so many other things I had to attend to that I gave up.

Paul Stillwell: So did Mr. Cook go back to being the dispatcher?

Commander Harralson: Mr. Cook went back. But I thought I had proved a point.

Paul Stillwell: Is there any good news to report from that billet?

Commander Harralson: Well, my son was born there.* My home life was very happy. Naomi's mother and father came out from Iowa one Christmas. The snow was real deep, and we had Christmas, a real nice time. After Christmas, they told us, "Why don't you two take a break and leave us to take care of the baby?" So I went down to the travel office and

---

*Joseph Henry Harralson was born 30 January 1947 at the Portsmouth Naval Hospital, Kittery, Maine.

arranged for a trip to New York. I think it was about a three-day trip. It was over New Year's. We rode the train down to Boston, and at Boston we got on to what I think was actually a famous train in its day. It had luxury coaches. Instead of two seats on each side, they had one big swivel seat on each side. Great big windows. So we rode down to New York in luxury. We had a reservation at a hotel.

The first night there, I thought, "Gee, we ought to see a show." So I went down to the lobby, where they had a ticket counter, and I walked up to the lady. There was some musical that we wanted to see. I forget what it was. I told her, "I would like two tickets to that."

She says, "For what night?"

"Tonight."

She tried to cover her laughter. Then she said, "We're booked solid for three months."

I thought, "Gee, I'm naive." I turned and started to walk away, and she called me back. There was a guy that had come up and turned in two tickets, right there, for Finian's Rainbow.

She said, "I just happen to have two tickets for Finian's Rainbow. Would you like to see that?"

"Yes, yes." And they were first-rate seats, only a few rows back, right in the center.

Then New Year's Eve, I thought--kind of late, I suspect--I ought to try to get a reservation somewhere. I called around and not a chance. I finally called a smorgasbord place, and they said, "Well, yeah, we can accommodate you, but you have to be out by [I think it was 11:30] because we have a whole new show again." So I took them up on that. We got there. It was a real nice place. They had a tremendous, big smorgasbord. But I knew nothing, really, about smorgasbord. We sat down at the table, and the waiter came around. I ordered smorgasbord and a big steak. [Laughter]

He said, "I suggest, sir, that you have the smorgasbord. Then if you're still hungry, you can have a steak." So we took him up on that. When I got to the smorgasbord, I saw what he meant. For some reason, I thought it was a table full of tasty little appetizers.

While we were sitting there eating, a man came around. He was dressed in a tux and looked like a maitre d' or something. He started talking to us. He chatted with us a while and went on. After the meal, when we were having drinks, there was a big fanfare. This man went up to the mike and started talking. He said he wanted to introduce Mr. and Mrs. Harralson, from Kittery, Maine. "They're here while grandma and grandpa are taking care of the kid." He told our life story. Then he went on to other people. We thought over what we'd talked about, and we didn't know how in the world he knew all that he said. We didn't remember telling him.

Paul Stillwell: And what New Year was that starting?

Commander Harralson: It was 1948. Our social life was practically nil. Naomi did go to teas. She tells me Mrs. Moseley told her that babies grew up in spite of what the parents did.

Paul Stillwell: There's a lot of wisdom in that. [Laughter]

Commander Harralson: Yes.

Mrs. Harralson: Did you tell about when we were in New York, going to visit that doctor?

Commander Harralson: Oh, Dr. Clayton?

Mrs. Harralson: Yes.

Commander Harralson: Oh. Dr. Clayton was at Shinagawa. He was a POW. I don't know how we found him. Oh, we got a Christmas card, didn't we? Yes, we looked him up, and we went up to see him. The only problem was that he'd been out the night before--this was New Year's Day, and he looked a little worse for wear.

Mrs. Harralson: But they had a baby. She was a nurse, remember? And you and I felt so experienced. They were all worried about that baby.

Commander Harralson: Yes. Here's a doctor--

Mrs. Harralson: And a nurse.

Commander Harralson: And a nurse.

Mrs. Harralson: And a little, newborn baby.

Commander Harralson: And we were telling them how. Our baby was 11 months old, wasn't he?

Mrs. Harralson: Right.

Paul Stillwell: So you had a lot of experience.

Commander Harralson: Yes, we were experts. [Laughter]

Mrs. Harralson: But they were very hospitable. They were really worried about that baby. And we were old, experienced people. [Laughter]

Commander Harralson: As it ended up, we had a real good trip.

Also I want to tell you about an experience when my wife's father and mother were out with us during the Christmas period. I thought it would be a good thing if a farmer from Iowa could see down in a submarine. I wanted to see it myself; I'd never gone down inside of a submarine. So I made a few calls around and arranged for the crew of a submarine in there to take us around. I don't mean dive, but I mean simply down and show us around inside. And, of course, her father was very pleased, very happy to do that.

We had a first class submariner that was showing us around, and it was very interesting to both of us. We came to the head. I mentioned something about hearing stories about heads--when you go to flush them, not doing it in the right sequence or something and you get a backfire, so to speak. He laughed and said, "No, that doesn't happen here." Then he started turning valves and things, and the thing blew water way up in the air. [Laughter]

Paul Stillwell: Well, please tell me, how did somebody from California adjust to living in Kittery, Maine?

Commander Harralson: It was difficult. I had a worse time adjusting to Iowa. But I found the secret, see. I went to Iowa wearing California clothes, and went around shivering and shaking, with the natives laughing at me. Then I finally figured out what the problem was; they had a lot more clothes on than I did.

Paul Stillwell: That's right. Well, you'd had a little conditioning to prepare you, by the time you spent in Japan.

Commander Harralson: Yes. It snows in Tokyo. It snows in Yokohama. Yes, we had about a foot one time.

Paul Stillwell: Did you ever square things away with Admiral Brown, or was that just not mentioned?

Commander Harralson: Not mentioned. I don't believe I ever talked to him again, or had the opportunity. I don't feel like they gave me any bad time or anything like that, deliberately. I got 30 days' leave, and we went out to the farm. When I came back, Lieutenant Commander Jarvis, the aide, called me in. He said, "You had a mutiny while you were gone."

"Oh?"

He said, "The communications officer issued a bunch of orders that changed a lot of things in there." I think, at that time, I only had about four regular radiomen. They absolutely refused to do these things. Commander Jarvis talked to me like he was blaming me for the darn mutiny.

Paul Stillwell: What was the outcome of that?

Commander Harralson: Nothing. When I got back, everything went back to my old way.

Paul Stillwell: Did you have any other connection with the prison, besides getting those message forms printed?

Commander Harralson: No, that was the only thing. I applied for LDO and took the test.[*] It was one of those deals where you line up according to your performance on the test. I didn't get into it; I wasn't into the area that made it, although they said to reapply in the next year or so. But I did some rethinking about LDO, because LDO obligated you to 30 years.

Paul Stillwell: I did not know that.

Commander Harralson: Yes. By the time it came around to take it again, I didn't take it. I tell you, I think I was getting kind of sour. With all my troubles there, I was very, very close to throwing in the towel, saying, "This is beyond me," and that sort of thing. I really longed for my old chief's hat. I felt very comfortable in a chief's hat. But I lasted out the two years there. Oh, Admiral Brown wrote a letter, trying to eliminate the job of OinC of the radio station.

Paul Stillwell: That showed a lot of confidence in you, didn't it? [Laughter] What was your designator at that point?

---

*LDO--limited duty officer, a former enlisted man whose duties are limited to the area of his enlisted rating specialty.

Commander Harralson: [Laughter] It started out just straight 1100, but somewheres along the line--I don't know what date it was, but I have a copy of a letter that put the 2--made 1102--and defined it as "an unrestricted line officer, not an aviator, whose permanent status is enlisted." And I think, had they decided to revert me back, I would have gone back to W-1. But I applied for the electronics maintenance school, which was for officers, at Great Lakes. They sent me there.

Paul Stillwell: What year was that, 1949?

Commander Harralson: Yes, all of 1949, starting in January and winding up in December. There I was with people that I knew. We had pinstripes, chief warrants. We didn't have any ensigns, I don't think. We had jaygees--I was a jaygee--lieutenants, and a few lieutenant commanders. We had some Marine captains, and we had some foreign students. That was the class I was in.

Paul Stillwell: That was probably a confidence builder, after this experience in New Hampshire.

Commander Harralson: Yes, it was, it was. But there at the school, the name of the game was study, study, study. I worked real hard. We all did. The Marines told me that when they were sent there, their duty was to learn, and their fitness reports depended on their grades. So we really knuckled down. We did have a break. There was a lieutenant there, Paul Kenney, an Irishman from Boston.[*] He would come out to the house and babysit for us. Oh, that was when Arthur, my second son, was born.

Mrs. Harralson: In June. He was born in June.[†]

---
[*]Lieutenant Paul G. Kenney, USN.
[†]Arthur Frost Harralson was born 13 June 1949 at the Great Lakes Naval Hospital.

Commander Harralson: Every Friday there were tests. One Friday we'd have three, and the other Friday, two. They were very difficult, difficult subjects. They wrung you out. It was sort of the procedure then, having finished the test, to go over to the warrant officers' club, which had a much more congenial atmosphere than the big O-club. We'd all sit there and drink a beer. I can remember that first beer--well, the only beer, really. I could just feel it going down and relaxing my arms and legs. I had to fight a very strong desire to stay there and have another. But I couldn't, because my wife was out in the country; we only had one car.

Paul Stillwell: So how did you do in the course, overall?

Commander Harralson: Middle of the class. They had a lot of smart people there.

Paul Stillwell: What did this course enable you to do that you hadn't known before?

Commander Harralson: Well, as a radioman, I had known that the only thing to use vacuum tubes for was radio receivers, transmitters. A direction finder was just a radio receiver. I knew the circuitry and how it worked. But when the radar came on the scene, they introduced a whole bunch of new kinds of circuits. How did they generate these VHF and UHF signals? The limitation of vacuum tubes was getting any power at the ultra-high frequencies, or very high frequencies, that they needed for radar. That was solved by the magnetron--a British invention in which some Americans at MIT were involved.[*] It worked quite differently from a regular tube. All of the electronics that was behind radar made it much more sophisticated and complicated than transmitters and receivers. That's what I wanted to stay in, that aspect of it.

Paul Stillwell: Any other highlights to mention from that year?

Commander Harralson: No, it was pretty cut and dried. We didn't have any other duties. I think we had a few personnel inspections, and that sort of thing. We had a big party, a

---

*MIT--Massachusetts Institute of Technology.

graduation party. After that I drew the Sicily.* I knew it was in Boston, but it was to be redeployed to San Diego. So I sent Naomi and the two kids out to the farm.

Paul Stillwell: Where was the farm?

Commander Harralson: In north Iowa. So after she left, I was home alone. One morning I got up and discovered that I had a flat tire. I changed it, and it made me late but there was no problem resulted from that. About two or three weeks later, I was late again. That time I simply didn't get up--alarm or something--and I was late. They didn't tolerate that, so I got a memo from the OinC, Commander Clarke, telling me to explain to him why I was late.† So I wrote a letter, and I told him that I was remiss and that I would take steps to change and that sort of thing. It seemed to satisfy him.

Now, Paul Kenney, who lived down at the BOQ, came in late, and he got a note from Commander Clarke, telling him to explain why he was late.‡ Paul took the defensive, saying something like, "I was only ten minutes late." It wasn't a very good excuse.

He showed it to me, and I said, "Paul, don't do it." But he went ahead and sent it, and it bounced back--"Unsatisfactory. Better explanation is needed here." Do you know, he was still writing explanations at the end of the semester. [Laughter]

Paul Stillwell: The Navy system for you.

Commander Harralson: Yes.

Well, when I finished there, I went to the Sicily, in the Boston shipyard. Here again, I was in new territory. The last ship I was on was the Augusta, and that as a radioman second. And here they are, putting me to stand OD watches, in port.§

---

*USS Sicily (CVE-118), a Commencement Bay-class escort carrier, was commissioned 27 February 1946. She had a standard displacement of 10,900 tons, was 557 feet long, 75 feet in the beam, an extreme width of 105 feet, and draft of 31 feet. Her top speed was 19 knots. The ship was originally armed with two 5-inch guns and could accommodate approximately 33 aircraft. She was eventually decommissioned in 1954.
†Commander Frank Herbert Clarke, USN.
‡BOQ--bachelor officers' quarters.
§OD--officer of the deck.

Paul Stillwell: Because you had a straight line officer's commission.

Commander Harralson: Actually, and I was a jaygee. I took the spy glass, and I walked like a man that knew what he was doing.

Paul Stillwell: That's a big part of it. [Laughter]

Commander Harralson: I realize that. And I thought about, "What would Hornblower do?"[*] [Laughter] But I want to tell you something. The captain was Captain Duerfeldt.[†] Not too long after I'd been aboard, a Marine orderly appeared, snapped a salute, and handed me a memo. I was invited to the captain's cabin for coffee and doughnuts at 1000. So, promptly at 1000, with a clean shirt and trousers and hat cover, I knocked on the door. He told me to come in. We sat down. We had coffee and doughnuts. He was a very easy man to talk to. We talked trivia. I was beginning to wonder, "Am I supposed to end this, because we can't go on forever, talking like this."

But he got around to the point he wanted to drive home. He got real serious. He said, "You know, it used to be that electronics were an aid to navigation, an aid to accomplishing your task. But it's reached a point now, where it's no longer an aid; it's a necessity. I have to have my electronics working in order to do what I am supposed to do. I am depending on you to keep it that way." And, boy, that really charged me up. I went out there--God, I was going to give it hell.

I was just the assistant. Henry Weber, a lieutenant commander, was the electronics maintenance officer.[‡] He was a mustang too. He'd come up in through the aviation world, which was quite different; through CNaTechTra, I think, or something like that.[§] He was a good egg, old Henry.

Oh, you know, we were talking about carrying out orders?

---

[*] Horatio Hornblower was a fictitious naval officer from the age of sail. He was the protagonist of a series of popular novels by British author C. S. Forester.
[†] Captain Clifford H. Duerfeldt, USN.
[‡] Lieutenant Commander Edgar Henry Weber, USN.
[§] CNaTechTra--Chief of Naval Technical Training.

Paul Stillwell: Right.

Commander Harralson: Whether you knew they were legal or not. The operations officer stopped me one day and said, "I found us a VK-8," which was a new radar repeater. He said, "Can you install it?"

I said, "Commander, it's not on our equipment list."

He replied, "I didn't ask you that. I said, 'Can you install it'?"

I said, "Yes, sir."

He said, "Do it."

"Aye-aye, sir."

Paul Stillwell: So you carried out orders.

Commander Harralson: Yes.

Paul Stillwell: Well, you said you went out all charged up after talking to Captain Duerfeldt.

Commander Harralson: Yes. Oh, I learned about the ship, got acquainted. And I liked being an officer aboard ship. I bunked in a room with three others. I found out that sailors didn't have to go over the side to scrape the ship hull anymore. Instead, the shipyard personnel sandblasted it, and they put on a coating that lasts a long, long time, compared to the old method.

I found a lot of good restaurants in Boston. Prince's Spaghetti House was one of my favorites. Boston's a very interesting city and all. I think we were there a month or two after I arrived. We got under way, headed for San Diego. We stopped in at Norfolk and anchored in Hampton Roads. Early one evening, the weather began to worsen. There was a real gale blowing out there, and they were on the verge to canceling small boating. But they wanted to get the liberty party back, so they were sending in boat officers. I got tapped as boat officer about midnight--the last run. I thought, "My God, what do I know about boats? I'm way over my head."

When my time came, I put on my Mae West and jacket, and I went down and climbed in the launch, and we started out. It seemed to be a launch, if I remember right. Anyhow, the coxswain headed straight in and then turned and went along the front of the wharves. We were approaching where the boats were coming out from the landing see. I watched and saw that he was going to go past the end, up real close, blind. I thought, "That's not the way to do it. You don't know what's coming. It's like going through an intersection when you can't see." So I got up next to the coxswain, and I said, "Get this boat out, where you can see what the hell's coming." And he did it with no argument. He got out there. There wasn't anything coming, but I got to thinking about it, and I thought, "What the hell am I doing, telling him? He probably has years of experience." But I felt that basically I was right, that I used proper judgment, and that he was creating a dangerous situation. So that gave me a little courage--maybe I did know something.

Paul Stillwell: Well, you'd ridden a lot of boats back there in your cruiser days.

Commander Harralson: Yes, I had, and made a lot of liberties. I rode a lot of boats in Manila Bay. The San Felipe was the ferryboat, but lots of times, late in the evening or something, they'd run a 680 boat, which was much, much smaller. I think one of the wildest rides I ever had was on Manila Bay in one of those 680 boats.

The Sicily left Norfolk and headed down to the Caribbean. We were crossing the Caribbean when this navigation radar repeater went out. I cannot remember its nomenclature. We had an SG-1B surface-search radar, and they had this radar repeater that gave you a rotating sweep. But it also gave you a sweep on X-Y coordinates. Not polar plots but where you measured out from a start line with the main bang, and that gave you distance. It was very accurate; they claimed 20 yards plus or minus. They used that when they were in sight of land for navigation.

It was very dependable, but it crapped out there. Of course, everybody got excited, so I rushed down to combat. I broke out my screwdriver, and I was lying on the deck there, trying to open the panel to get at what I thought the problem was. I looked up, and here was a second class ET, one of my people, glaring at me. Suddenly it dawned on me,

"What am I doing here?" So I stopped right where I was, and I got up, adjusted my shirt, and said, "Is this your equipment?"

He said, "Yes, sir."

I said, "Well, let's get it fixed." [Laughter]

Paul Stillwell: Sort of sheepishly you said that.

Commander Harralson: Yes, indeed.

Paul Stillwell: I remember talking to a warrant who was our EMO in the New Jersey, and he said that was the hardest thing for him to do was break himself away from repairing things himself.*

Commander Harralson: Oh, yes. I was so anxious to get my hands into it, but I learned real quick that that was not my job. In fact, a big part of my job was explaining the capabilities and limitations of the equipment.

Paul Stillwell: To whom?

Commander Harralson: To the navigator, to the operations officer, and even the captain. They had some weird conceptions about some of that gear.

Paul Stillwell: Well, that suggests that you learned it pretty quickly.

Commander Harralson: Yes, I knew the instruction books and what they were supposed to do. We went ashore in Colon, Panama, and I went with a bunch of fellow officers up to a so-called wholesale place, where they poured us drinks. They had soft cushion seats to sit on while they sold you all kinds of junk because you were half-drunk. [Laughter] But I was wary. I bought a bottle of Chanel Number Five and let it go at that. I knew about

---

*EMO--electronics material officer.

guys buying these beautiful carved chests and a month after they'd get them, the chest would develop a great, big crack down the middle and stuff like that.

Paul Stillwell: Chanel Number Five was a good choice.

Commander Harralson: Channel Number Five. [Laughter] We got up to San Diego, and my wife and her mother and my two kids were there to meet me. My wife and her mother and the two kids had come across in our Studebaker Commander. I guess it was a rough trip with the smallest one. We met them, and we got set up. We obtained Navy housing, lived out towards what used to be Mission Beach. We lived not too far from the end of Lindbergh Field.* At that time they were retro-fitting the B-36--putting on four more engines--four jets--a double jet pod way out on each wing. It already had six engines.† It would take off and come over our house at full bore. I'd be in shaving, and glasses would bounce around and fall on the floor.

We were real happy there. We bought our first bit of equipment. There was an icebox, and Naomi was worried about Arthur's milk getting sour. So I went down and bought a Crosley refrigerator. That was our first big investment, other than our car.

Paul Stillwell: You mean people still came around and delivered ice in 1950?

Commander Harralson: Yes.

Paul Stillwell: I didn't realize that hung on that late.

Commander Harralson: Yes, it was delivered, wasn't it, Honey?

---

*Lindbergh Field is the name of the commercial airport in San Diego.
†Consolidated Vultee, based in San Diego, built the Air Force's B-36 bomber, known as the Peacemaker. The B-36D model was equipped with four J-47 jet engines in under-wing nacelles and six piston engines that drove propellers. The jet engines enhanced the plane's maximum speed from 376 miles per hour to 435 miles per hour.

Mrs. Harralson: Yes.

Commander Harralson: You had a sign, and it had 25, 50, 75, and 100 on the four corners. Whatever number you hung up was what the iceman brought you.

My brother and his wife came down to see us, stayed with us. One Sunday I had the duty, and I invited them aboard for dinner. I guess it was the evening meal. And that's when the Korean War broke.* Commander Schoenweiss, our exec, came in and told us.†

Paul Stillwell: Had Captain Thach taken command by that point?‡

Commander Harralson: Yes, yes.

Paul Stillwell: When did he relieve?

Commander Harralson: Shortly after the ship arrived in San Diego.

When we came into San Diego, they had a great, big reception for us. There was a fly-over with F9Fs, early jets. I remember standing at quarters there with some of the ship's officers who were pilots. They were amazed at all the air traffic, contemplating the dangers and everything of flying in and out of San Diego.

Two days after the exec told us about the Korean War, we were headed for Guam. We were loaded with aviation spares. Nobody seemed to know just exactly what we were going to do. We got out to Guam and off-loaded all these spares, and then headed up to Yokosuka. You call it Yo-kuss-ka or Yo-ko-su-ka?

Paul Stillwell: Yo-kuss-ka.

---

*The Korean War began on 25 June 1950, when six North Korean infantry division and three border constabulary brigades invaded the South Korea. The troops were supported by approximately 100 Russian-made T-34 tanks. In New York that same day the United Nations Security Council adopted a resolution condemning the invasion.
†Commander Carl W. Schoenweiss, USN.
‡Captain John S. Thach, USN, became commanding officer of the Sicily in June 1950. The oral history of Thach, who retired as a four-star admiral, is in the Naval Institute collection.

Commander Harralson: We ended up there and took the Marine squadron, VMF-214.*

Paul Stillwell: What kind of an air group had you had prior to that, ASW?†

Commander Harralson: Yes, that's right. That's what we were. We were an ASW carrier, by virtue of having a QSV sonar; that was the only difference.

Paul Stillwell: Was that part of your responsibility also?

Commander Harralson: Yes, yes. That belonged to us.

Paul Stillwell: Was that mounted in the bow?

Commander Harralson: No, back from the bow. I think one of the things that increased our draft was the depth that we had to allow for its housing. I think before this Korean thing, we went out from San Diego several times on ASW exercises. But that happened pretty early. I think we were the first ship out of San Diego after the war started. We hightailed it out. I was going along merrily there. I was wondering why I didn't have to stand any watches under way. I thought, "Well, that's because they need me to look after the equipment." I should know better than that. [Laughter]

Paul Stillwell: They just had forgotten you.

Commander Harralson: Yes, I was forgotten. When we got out there, we picked up the Marines, and then we headed around to Sasebo. I think we had to take on something at Sasebo. And we went into Sasebo at night for the first time with this radar repeater. The radar operator was calling out the letters they had as reference points. A lot of little islands stick up from the entrance, and it's a dogleg affair going in. I thought it was quite remarkable to take that ship in at night. These young men down there calling for, "Give

---

*Marine Fighter Squadron 214, known as the Black Sheep Squadron in World War II, was made up of F4U Corsairs.
†ASW--antisubmarine warfare.

me Able, give me Baker, give me Cast"--you know, taking cuts from the radar repeater and plotting them on the chart.* We went right in and anchored, like we knew where we were going.

Paul Stillwell: That must have boosted your confidence greatly.

Commander Harralson: Oh, yes, sure.

Paul Stillwell: Did you have any shakedown period after you came out of the yard, before you came around to the West Coast?

Commander Harralson: I don't think so. Not unless you can call the trip from Boston to San Diego a shakedown.

Paul Stillwell: Then it must not have been a major yard period, maybe just a shipyard availability.

Commander Harralson: I really don't know what they did.

Paul Stillwell: Well, that's typical after a yard overhaul--to have a shakedown.

Commander Harralson: Sure. I know that. But I don't recall any kind of shakedown. I think we lit out of there. That doesn't sound quite right, though, does it? To take a ship out that's had serious work done and not test it. I guess they could have sent a message back, "Hey, I'm coming back," or something.

Paul Stillwell: Maybe that's one of the few things that hasn't lodged in your memory.

Commander Harralson: [Laughter] Yes, that's always a possibility. That was very important for the submarines. Everybody was on edge. You know, the Squalus was very

---
*"Able," "Baker," and "Cast" were the first three words in the phonetic alphabet of the era.

much on people's minds at Portsmouth.* That had a lot to do with updating the radio station. Another thing was that Truman had a meeting up there somewheres near, and there was such a flood of correspondents and traffic that the station actually broke down, failed. And that's why, when my letter went in, there was already on the books an allowance, equipment allowance, that was triple what existed there. It was because of that experience. The only reason they hadn't put it in was because they didn't have the money. That wasn't the top of the priority list until this crazy-looking letter.

Paul Stillwell: Well, you probably didn't stay long in Sasebo then.

Commander Harralson: No, we didn't. I'm not sure just what we did there, but we got out to the operating area, on the Yellow Sea side there, and started sending in strikes. It was early on there that they discovered that I didn't have any watches. They dragged me into CIC, and I can't think of the name of this lieutenant commander who was the CIC officer. He sat me down at the VK-8 and said, "You're going to be an air controller, and here's how you do it. You got two planes up there that are 'Goosebump One' and 'Goosebump Two.' [We were "Goosebump.] And you send them up to angels ten, and you intercept any bogeys that come by."

See, what I had going for me was the CREI course I took before the war. It was loaded with these vector problems I was telling you about. So I understood vectors very well, and that's what you're dealing with when you run intercepts and ship movements. So I was okay there. The main thing was to keep talking, keep talking back and forth. I had to watch against too much silence. Our altitude information was not very good. We had SP radar that was fighter director, they called it. But we had a lot of problems with it, and it wasn't too accurate.

Paul Stillwell: That was not a particularly new radar at that time either.

---

*The USS Squalus (SS-192) sank in 243 feet of water while conducting exercise dives on 23 May 1939 off Portsmouth, New Hampshire.

Richard A. Harralson, Interview #2 (5/16/97) – Page 276

Commander Harralson: No, I guess it wasn't. Oh, we had three radars. The other two were the SG-1B surface search and the SK-3 air search. Now, that was an old one. It had a great big parabolic mesh; it must have been 18 foot in diameter.

Paul Stillwell: The SK-2 had that. Was there also an SK-3 that had it as well.

Commander Harralson: The one we had was an SK-3. It had a 60-cycle, I believe, rep rate, which was very slow. It had a long main bang. Its resolution was very poor. But we got phenomenal ranges. And in the Yellow Sea, for some reason, anomalous propagation is the norm. We had trouble on the SK-3 with second-sweep echoes. We were getting back echoes after the next bang. These would put us somewheres unknown on the sweep, so you couldn't measure it. It really confused us when we first ran into it, but then we figured out what it was, and there was nothing you could do about it but recognize it.

Paul Stillwell: Was this caused by atmospheric conditions?

Commander Harralson: Yes, the prevailing atmosphere. Actually, I get mixed up a lot as to whether it was during my first time out there as assistant electronics maintenance officer and the second time, when I was the electronics maintenance officer. I get mixed up to which trip this happened on. But on one of them we had left Sasebo, heading out again, and I heard this word I used to dread: "Now, the electronics maintenance officer, lay up to the bridge immediately." So I went up there, and here were the navigator and the captain, and they were very much concerned. They hadn't raised Wolmi-Do on the SG.* I said, "How far is it, do you think?"

They said, "It should be about 30 miles."

We had a thumbnail way of estimating the range to expect by adding the two heights--the height of the antenna and the height of the object you were pinging on. You added those two in feet, and then you took the square root. And that would give you the distance in miles, approximately. So I applied that rule of thumb. This was a very

---

*Wolmi-Do is an island at the approaches to Inchon, South Korea. U.S. Marine troops made a dramatic behind-the-lines amphibious assault at Inchon on 15 September 1950.

low-lying island. It came out at 20 miles, so I said, "You should expect it at 20 miles." Well, they wouldn't buy it.

They said, "We usually raise it at 30 miles. Something's wrong with the SG. Check it."

So I called down to combat and said, "Take a ring time on the SG." That was the way you could measure whether your radar was up. They did, and it rang normal. The navigator kept thinking something was wrong with the SG-1B. But it wasn't. It was simply that the range wasn't as good that night. The SG was working fine, but the atmospherics, propagation characteristics and everything, were different. Everything worked fine from then on, but it was not long after that, when I saw an Electron magazine, which the Navy put out monthly. On the cover it had a memo that looked like it was attached with a paper clip. It said, "Captains, please read." It was about anomalous propagation, and it talked specifically about the Yellow Sea, the fantastic ranges they were getting out there. So I showed it to the operations officer, and I suggested maybe the captain may like to read it. He tossed it back, and he said, "That's what we got you for."

Paul Stillwell: What do you recall about the Inchon invasion in September 1950?

Commander Harralson: Just a lot of ships, and I think we had a weather problem, possible typhoon brewing. There was a lot of questions as to whether we were going to proceed or not. It was decided to go ahead with the invasion. And, of course, the Marines--I'm not sure just how they figured into it--air support, I suppose. But there wasn't much resistance. It went off pretty slick.

Paul Stillwell: Well, you started telling me before about your experience as an air controller. There were two experiences that you wanted to mention--one case where the pilots shook your hand and one where they didn't.

Commander Harralson: Yes. Well, the CIC officer came in and sat me down and gave me a 15-minute explanation of terminology. He said I was an air controller, and I had a CAP up there.* I started talking to them, and I eventually ran a few intercepts that were nothing consequential. But I got into it, and I enjoyed doing it--the lingo and everything. I was doing fine.

They ran strikes all day long, and they always came home late at night, when the sun was going down and the weather making up. There was a certain time when the CIC wanted CAP to come in, and I would talk them in. This one time I thought I'd done a good job, a professional job. All the planes got down safely, and I secured my position. I was talking to the CIC officer when the two pilots appeared in the doorway of CIC, dressed in their flight gear. They wanted to know where the air controller was. I was pointed out. They came over, and they wanted to shake my hand. I was thrilled. I got a great boost from that, and it gave me a lot more confidence in what I was doing.

Some months later or so--over on the other side of Korea, on the Japanese Sea side, on the east side--we had the same situation. Strikes coming back, sun going down, and getting dark, weather closing, and a lot of clutter on the scope. The SK always had a lot of clutter overhead. I brought the CAP in, and I thought I had them up above. The CIC officer asked me where the CAP was. I told him, "Overhead, angels five," or something like that. He looked at me, walked over, and looked over my shoulder. He saw two fuzzy blips way out at the edge--20 miles, I guess it would be, maybe farther. He said, "What are those?" I knew right away that it might be the CAP. So I gave them a right turn, and the two blips turned. So then I gave them a steer home and brought them back. They landed safely, but that was a scary experience for me--not to mention them.

Paul Stillwell: They didn't shake your hand.

Commander Harralson: No, they didn't come in and shake my hand. To this day, I hate to think about it, because, you know, in just a few more minutes they would have been off the scope. Now, I could have gone to a longer range, but I didn't know of any reason to do so. I thought they were overhead. I just wasn't experienced enough or alert enough to have

---

*CAP--combat air patrol, a force of fighter planes deployed in the air to intercept incoming air raids headed toward a naval force.

caught them. I was a little bit complacent, I guess. The result very nearly could have been disastrous.

Paul Stillwell: Well, please tell me about what kind of man Captain Thach was.

Commander Harralson: Everybody liked him. He was very considerate of the crew. There was a situation on the supply of fresh water. The usual procedure when you're short on water or worried about having enough for your boilers is to put water hours on washrooms and do things like that. But Captain Thach came on the speakers and laid out the water problem: "We have so much water, we can make so much a day, we use so much a day for boilers. We have to have that. We're not getting ahead on the water," or words to that effect. "I would like to have each man to conserve water, as much as possible, and see if we can avoid water restrictions." That got results. They didn't waste it in showers, and they didn't have to put on restrictions.

It wasn't that way on the Lexington. They simply locked up the washrooms, and that took care of that.

Paul Stillwell: That was Genial John.

Commander Harralson: [Laughter] Genial John. I never heard the "Genial."

Paul Stillwell: Well, that was a sarcastic nickname.

Commander Harralson: Yes, right. You told me about that.

Paul Stillwell: What other examples do you remember about Captain Thach?

Commander Harralson: Well, my admiration stems a lot from the support I seemed to have from him, although I didn't talk to him directly very much. It was always through the operations officer or the exec. Another time I remember, they called me to the bridge, and here were the captain and the exec. They were in an argument about the range of the QHB sonar. As soon as I got up there, why, they asked me if its max range was 10,000 or 12,000 yards. I said, "Maximum range is 6,000 yards." They didn't believe it. I assured them that it was. And I added, "But that's under the most ideal conditions. The practical range of the QHB is more like 2,000 or 3,000 yards. It depends, of course, on the water salinity and temperature."

I didn't try to lecture them on that, but I was trying to point out that even 6,000 yards was very questionable. Then there was a limitation put on it by the screen, an interference limitation. They were very doubtful, and I finally had to go get the instruction book and show them. To me it indicated, again, that there was a kind of a gap in some commanding officers' knowledge of the capability of what electronics could do. And, of course, I doubt if that's the case now, because electronics have become so integral. But there was that transition period of the electronics from an aid to a necessity.

Paul Stillwell: Well, you had a couple of other stories about the captain. One was when you had to run this antenna wire, and also when you had to go through BuShips.

Commander Harralson: I can't quite place the exercise, just how it fit in the sequence of my time on the Sicily, but at one point they required us operationally to communicate on low frequency. We couldn't even raise a ship that was in visual distance. We got gigged on it, a serious failure on the part of the ship, because we wouldn't communicate low frequency. I think it was the first time since I was aboard that the ship tried to communicate low frequency. After this inspection, some people came aboard. I can't remember just where they were from. They investigated everything and decided that we needed three more transmitters.

I was shocked at their findings. I told the operations officer, and I'm sure he told the captain, that our problem wasn't transmitters. Our problem was antennas. I tried to explain about Marconi antennas--when they go on low frequency, because the wavelength was so long they go to what they call a grounded Marconi, a grounded antenna. Actually, it's supposed to be one quarter wavelength long. Well, when you get in those very low frequencies, a quarter wavelength is quite long. They were trying to do it with whip antennas. You can do it up to a certain point by loading it with inductance, but you reduce the efficiency of the emission. All they had for the low-frequency transmitter aft was this whip that was laid in a horizontal position when we had air ops, which made it absolutely useless then.

They had a transmitter in the radio room that had a low-frequency side, and it fed the whip antenna just forward of the bridge. The lead was a coaxial cable. To me, that didn't make sense for what was essentially supposed to be a quarter-wave antenna. So when the captain wanted to know what we could do to get through this emergency, since we were able to beat back all these extra transmitters, I suggested we go through the skin of the ship forward and come up under the whip, to mate directly to the whip with quite a long lead. What it did was increase the length of the antenna electronically, making it approach quarter wavelength in actuality. We didn't feed it through a coax, which is a whole different problem. So the captain said, "Go ahead with it."

When we were in Pearl Harbor the next time, on our way out, we did that. We did it on a weekend, and I think something like eight or nine different shops were involved in overtime and double overtime. I should have known, but I was amazed by the number of shops that got involved in just going through the insulation and then the steel hull and installing that lead through. We did it. We accomplished it, and the next time we tried it, it worked beautiful. Loaded up fine, the antenna. We did it, but then, after that, we never used it again. [Laughter]

Paul Stillwell: What's the story you remember about Captain Thach and the wives of the Sicily officers?

Commander Harralson: The story I remember comes to me directly from my wife. Captain Thach was relieved from the Sicily sometime in the summer of 1951 and went back to San Diego. In the meantime, Mrs. Thach held a tea at her house for officers' wives, and Captain Thach was there. As each wife came in, Mrs. Thach introduced her as the wife of So-and-so officer. Captain Thach recalled the name and had an interesting anecdote about each one, which was quite remarkable. And it was something nice to say.

Paul Stillwell: Absolutely. Anything else you remember about that first deployment over to Korea?

Commander Harralson: Yes. We put the Marine squadron ashore at Hungnam, over on the east side of Korea, and we beat it down to Guam. The scoop was that we were going to do ASW exercises out of Guam and then go back to the States. Well, we had just got down to Guam when the Chinese broke through.[*] We immediately turned around and beat it back up get the Marines out of there. We went in to Hungnam to pick up the ground personnel and equipage. It was a bit dicey, because the area was supposed to have been mined. Although they had a channel through there, it was still pretty shaky.

Paul Stillwell: Well, they evacuated through Hungnam right around Christmas of 1950.

Commander Harralson: Yes. We made a big sign and hung in the hangar deck, "Welcome back, you Marines." They had a big meal--steak and all sorts of goodies. And, of course, this was for the ground personnel. The pilots had landed aboard. That was one time the Marines were sure glad to see the Navy.

Paul Stillwell: I'll bet.

Commander Harralson: Yes.

Paul Stillwell: So then you came back to the States. And what happened before your next deployment?

Commander Harralson: Well, we came back. In order to give each man ten days' leave, the rest of the ship had to go into a two-section watch. And unless you've been a watch stander in three-section watches, why, you can't appreciate what it means to go to a two-section watch for 20 days. It doesn't sound too bad, except when you start figuring in

---

[*]On 25 November 1950 some 300,000 Chinese Communist regular troops entered North Korea, largely undetected initially by United Nations forces.

that you also had to do your normal day's work. You didn't go home until after 4:00 o'clock, and you had to be there at 8:00. These extra watches were on top of all that. So that you got practically nothing at home, just in order to get ten days's leave. Everybody had his turn.

Then the ship took off on ASW exercises, and also an ORI inspection.* There was an event there I thought was rather remarkable. We were doing quite well, and we had to make a radar anchorage in an assigned area south of the island of San Clemente. We had an anchorage assigned, and we were something like 20 miles to the south. The captain called down to CIC on the squawkbox and said, "Combat, for all practical purposes, you have the conn. Give us course changes and speed changes to deliver us to anchorage Baker [or whatever it was]."

The radarmen picked out three points on San Clemente that were easily recognizable on the radar. This third class radarman sat there at the DRT, and he would call out, "Give me a cut on Able. Give me a cut on Charlie. Give me a cut on Baker."† Then he'd say, "Recommend come right two degrees." The CIC officer was standing next to the plot table. He'd pass the word up to the bridge. This kid recommended, "All engines two-thirds, one-third, all engines stop." Put us right in the anchorage. This was a third-class radarman doing it. Everybody else was just observing.

Paul Stillwell: Very impressive.

Commander Harralson: Yes, it was. It was.

Paul Stillwell: When did you get a new captain?

Commander Harralson: You know, I can't remember when. But when Captain Thach was relieved out there, things didn't change much. The new skipper was Captain Schoech.‡ I can't remember anything in particular about him.

---

*ORI--operational readiness inspection.
†DRT--dead reckoning tracer.
‡Captain William A. Schoech, USN.

Paul Stillwell: Well, your job changed. You relieved Weber as EMO.

Commander Harralson: Oh, yes, that was back in the States, before we ever left on our second deployment.

Paul Stillwell: I see.

Commander Harralson: When we got back after the first trip out, Weber was relieved. It was his time to go. They just made me the electronics maintenance officer--division officer and all. By that time, we were getting reservists called up, coming back. The first trip out, we had something like 25 ETs, and the second trip out I had 40.

I had an interesting shore leave in Yokosuka. The ship was in there to pick up parts or something. I went ashore with three other officers, and they wanted to go to Yokohama. I went with them, and there was O-club up in the top of about an eight- or ten-story building. So we went up to this O-club and got a booth sitting next to a window. I was sitting there drinking, and I looked out the window. What do I see but Mitsubishi shipyard? I saw the cranes. I got to thinking about it and drinking more than I should have. I guess I got into a blue funk--sort of morose, "What am I doing out here again?" and that sort of thing. My friends had departed. I guess I was no longer good company.

Paul Stillwell: This was an exception to your pattern of being a happy drunk.

Commander Harralson: That's right. That's right. I was rather morbid, I guess. Anyhow, somewheres about 11:00 o'clock, why, I decided to go. I went down the elevator, went out the front, and climbed into a pedicab. I started hollering at the pedicab man in my dockside Japanese. We went along for several blocks that way while I was telling him to, "Hurry up, hurry up. There's no resting around here. Turn right and turn left." Finally, he stopped, and he got off and came back and looked in at me. "Nonda?" He wanted to know what was going on.

So I told him about Mitsubishi. I you could see a light dawning on his face: "Ah." So he climbed back on and started pedaling off. We rode for quite a while, then pulled up in front of some houses. He beckoned me to get out and follow him. And I did. We went around and went in the back door. Here was a room with one of those charcoal braziers in a hole. Sitting around it, I would say, were six, seven pedicab drivers. We moved in and sat down beside them. We sat there by this fire and started this game we used to play--tosha ika su. Something about, "How old are you?" They asked me, and I would give them some ridiculous age. They would laugh, and then I'd ask them, and they'd tell me a ridiculous thing. It was a very childish sort of game, but it was banter.

We were getting along fine, and pretty soon here came a Japanese girl. She had two big plates of food. It had a base of noodles and a lot of vegetables and stuff on it. She started delivering and working her way around. When she got around to us, she gave me a plate and chopsticks. I was sitting there, and the others were digging in. But my pedicab driver didn't get one. I asked him where his was, but he didn't want me to worry about it. I insisted, and he insisted. So I got the girl to bring in another plate. By this time, they were all watching. I measured this food out with my chopsticks very, very carefully. I made a great, big act out of measuring it exactly. I very carefully cut to the center, divided it, and slid half over into his plate. That was the right thing to do. They got a big kick out of that.

We finished the meal, and then they called me away and showed me a bedroom with a Western-style bed. They wanted me to sleep there. So I climbed in and went to sleep. They woke me up the next morning. I dressed, went down, and climbed in the pedicab. He hauled me off to the railroad station, and he wouldn't let me pay.

Paul Stillwell: Why was he so hospitable?

Commander Harralson: I don't know. Former enemies are like that sometimes. It happens all the time. Guys that go back to Vietnam, and they hug one another. I've seen that.

Paul Stillwell: So had the pedicab man been a shipyard worker?

Commander Harralson: I don't know. I don't know. But apparently he knew about the war.

Paul Stillwell: What was your observation on how much the city of Yokohama had been rebuilt in those years?

Commander Harralson: I don't recall seeing much damage. Of course, I was in the shipyard, so I never got to walk around where we used to work.

We left Yokohama. The only big raid, other than the Navy strike, that did damage right in Yokohama was that one I described with the B-29s. I don't know what happened there afterwards.

Paul Stillwell: How did your second deployment to Korea in the Sicily compare with the first?

Commander Harralson: Well, of course, I felt like I had a lot more weight on my shoulders. I didn't have an assistant. All I had was a couple chiefs, and that was it. We had one headache. At the last minute, the operations officer told me they were going to bring a PO trailer aboard, and that I had to get what material I needed to make it operative. I didn't even know what a PO trailer was. But it turns out it had the equipment in it to receive a radar signal from a plane and put it on our scopes. It required the proper coaxial cable and a special antenna. To bring the lead from the antenna down required RG-18U, which was a large-sized coaxial cable.

I spent almost a weekend running down I forget how many feet of this big cable and getting it to the ship. Then I only had one ET that had any training with the PO trailer. We put it in one corner of the hangar deck and cabled it down and secured it for sea. When we were around Japan they wanted to try it, to send a plane up with radar and be able to receive its signal, containing antenna reference and the video info. It was a long time before we got to try it, and we got results only once, to where we had any kind of signal decent.

It was a lot of work and a lot of trouble, and the PO trailer in the hangar gave us a headache. It was always in the way; somebody was always grousing about it. So, finally, in Sasebo the operations officer wanted me to go over to the base and have the base there take our PO trailer and take care of it. So I went over to see them, and the commander laughed at me. He says, "Why should I be bothered with your problem?"

So I went back, and I told Commander Schoenweiss. He thought I had goofed it up. So he sent me back with a Lieutenant Commander Somebody that was supposed to be able to talk to him a lot better than I did. We got in there, and we were thrown out of the office. He didn't see why he should have anything to do with that. That was out of his province, so finally I think the exec went over. He found a place where it could be stored. Then he told me to get a crane. So I went over and got a crane. Coming back with the crane to pick up the trailer and take it in, I got to talking to the Japanese crew on the crane. We had tea up front, and they gave me some green tea as a going-away present. They picked up the PO trailer and took it back.

Paul Stillwell: Sounds like it didn't give you much of an operational advantage.

Commander Harralson: No, it didn't. I don't know whose idea it was but somebody on there--probably the operations officer--talked them into letting us use it. But it was not a good idea.

Paul Stillwell: Were you pretty much still in the vacuum tube era at that point?

Commander Harralson: Yes, it was vacuum tubes. The only solid state that I knew of was some of your big rectifiers. I didn't run into solid state until I got to Glynco, Georgia. They were using it a lot there in some of the new equipment they were putting in. That was CNaTechTra equipment--not BuShips. Vacuum tubes are very temperamental.

Among the first things I learned out there, was when we came into Sasebo--having been operating for 40 days or so--there was a lot of routine maintenance that needed to be performed on the equipment, so I shut everything down. When we got under way again and fired off, I had breakdowns all over the place. For about three or four days, we were running around like mad, stomping out fires. Then the equipment finally settled down, and we were all right. But what happens, you come in, this equipment's been hot for a long time. When you shut it off, it gets cold. Electrical equipment takes the biggest shock when you put the juice to it, because all kinds of surges go on in the equipment. That's when you get most of your breakdowns.

The magnetron for the SG-1B was supposed to have a 200-hour life. But by keeping the thing fired up all the time, never shutting if off, we were getting a service life of 700-800 hours.

Paul Stillwell: Wow.

Commander Harralson: And that's what I learned about tubes. If they're in there working for you, leave them alone.

Paul Stillwell: Well, that tour of duty was a real learning experience for you.

Commander Harralson: It was. It was. I learned a lot. And I feel like I learned to be an officer.

Paul Stillwell: What specifics would you cite in that case?

Commander Harralson: Oh, my dealings with the men. I think I had some of the right ideas about leadership. I'm not talking leadership where you charge ahead of them in battle, but the sort of the low-key leadership where you get the men working for you.

Paul Stillwell: Well, and working together as a team.

Commander Harralson: Together--yes, absolutely. I respected them, and they respected me. I tried to encourage that as much as possible. I took every opportunity to praise in public, but it had to be sincere. It had to be something that was worthy of praise. And I was very careful to chastise in private. Those are very basic fundamentals. I also never threatened, because you should never threaten unless you're fully prepared to carry it out. I also steered clear of, "That's an order." I think you can avoid the necessity or any need to say that, simply by the way you talk to your men. I tried not to engage in frivolous talk or banter too much. I tried to keep a certain formality--for my sake, as well as theirs, I mean.

Paul Stillwell: Well, if they do have genuine respect for you, then you don't have to come through with that, "That's an order."

Commander Harralson: No, you don't. No, you don't. And just by the tone of your voice, the way you say it and all, they know it's an order.

Paul Stillwell: Well, part of the division officer's responsibility is helping out with personal problems and family concerns. How much of that did you get into?

Commander Harralson: Well, not very much, because we were overseas so much. I had a problem in my family, in that when this Korean thing started and I went overseas, they wanted my family out of naval housing in San Diego, because it was for shore-based personnel. I went into a kind of tizzy out there. I sent a message back home, told my wife to buy a house. I sent her my power of attorney. She set out to buy a house and found out that there was a lot of problems. For instance, we had no credit, because we always paid cash. So she went out and deliberately started some small credit accounts to establish credit. She was able to buy a little house in Claremont, which was a beautiful location. I think it cost $10,000. Can you imagine a nice little house in San Diego overlooking Mission Bay for $10,000 these days?

Paul Stillwell: Not today.

Commander Harralson: But it was difficult for her, and we had another child in that period. I can't leave my daughter out. Helen K. Harralson was born 11 January 1952 at a private hospital. I wanted Naomi to see the same doctor every visit, which would not have been the case at the naval hospital in San Diego. Helen was born about two months before I was relieved on the Sicily.

I wasn't aware of any of the men's problems so much. I had a chief, a reserve, that was called back. He was concerned about his house up in Maine because you can't leave a house empty in Maine through the winter. All sorts of terrible things happen to it, and he was trying--from way out there--to get somebody to move into it. I had some good men on there. I only had one ET that had any experience with the PO trailer, though.

Paul Stillwell: Do any memories of the air operations come to you?

Commander Harralson: Oh, yes. Seemed like they were always taking off and landing, taking off and landing.

I had to inventory the narcotics. I had a big safe, and I knew the combination. Monthly I had to go there and inventory everything. In the inventory were something like 48 little two- or four-ounce bottles of real good brandy and a couple of big bottles of brandy. All I did was count what was there and put it on my report, but that brandy kept going down and being restocked and going down. The doc on the ship was giving it to these Marine pilots when they came back--for medicinal purposes.

Paul Stillwell: Well, that's legitimate.

Commander Harralson: Yes. Oh, they worked hard. Oh, one time in Sasebo I had the deck in the evening watch, the 8:00 to 12:00. Liberty was up at 11:00 o'clock--2300--on the dock. About 2315, a Mike boat pulled up to the gangway.* And who got out but the exec? He came up and said, "This boat has hardly any men in it. When we left at 2300, there was no <u>Sicily</u> personnel on the dock. We took everybody who was there." He said, "Therefore, everybody that comes aboard from now on is over leave. Put them on report."

The next boat that showed up was loaded with Marines. As they came over, the boatswain's mate was taking their liberty cards. I was standing there, and I felt this hot breath on my neck. I turned around, and here were the silver leaves of a Marine lieutenant

---

*Mike boat is the nickname for an LCM, a landing craft mechanized, because Mike is the word for the letter M in the phonetic alphabet.

colonel. He was breathing fire. He wanted to know what in the hell I was doing with taking these Marines' liberty cards. I said, "They're over leave, Colonel."

"How in the hell are they over leave?"

I said, "Well, the last boat left the dock at 2300 and took everybody there and was half empty when it arrived here. Therefore, everybody that comes after that boat is over leave."

He said, "I'll see about this." And he said, "I'm going to see that you put every sailor that comes aboard on report." And that's what we did. We put everybody on report. It was the only way. Of course, I knew that it would never get anywhere, which it didn't.

Paul Stillwell: Why not?

Commander Harralson: Well, now, that's not too practical a thing-to put about a couple hundred men on report.

Paul Stillwell: Oh, it was that many.

Commander Harralson: Oh, yes. Eleven o'clock in the evening is just getting started for a lot of people.

Paul Stillwell: Who was the lieutenant colonel?

Commander Harralson: He was a squadron commander.

On one of our trips I think it was the squadron CO that was killed. When he was approaching on a landing, he lost power or something and slammed into the stern and was killed. There were several accidents. There was a 20-millimeter, I believe it was, that went off in the hangar and killed a couple guys. But I found the excerpt from Captain Thach's story most interesting--how they operated over there.[*]

---

[*]John S. Thach, "Right on the Button: Marine Close Air Support in Korea," U.S. Naval Institute Proceedings, November 1975, pages 54-56.

Paul Stillwell: How were you accepted in the wardroom as a mustang? Was that any problem?

Commander Harralson: Absolutely not. And I'll tell you, here and now, that I never ran into any problem because I was a mustang. Now, I might have not been aware of undercurrents; I don't know. But I know simply that I did not feel inferior or put upon or anything by my credentials--even on the Mississippi, which was the most formal, I guess, of ships that I was on. And, of course, on the Sicily, when I first went aboard, electronics maintenance was in the engineering department. Electronics maintenance seemed to be a pain to shipboard organizations. They didn't know quite where to put us. But we ended up in operations. Going into operations, I became the only black shoe in with a bunch of brown-shoe officers.* I had no problem there; I got along great. I made a lot of shore leaves with them, and I found them to be on the wild side. [Laughter]

Paul Stillwell: They had that reputation.

Commander Harralson: Yes, and I can remember going into Sasebo there was a place where they hung out, way up on a hill. I had found that when I was out at night drinking that, if about every other drink I would eat a bowl of rice, and so I'd have the girl bring me a bowl of rice and chopsticks, and I'd sit there and eat the rice. I could stay pretty sober during a long night. I put a lot of the airdales in a cab of some description to get them back, and I helped them down a hill.

We had a lot of trouble with shoes. A lot of the places you went into you stepped out of your shoes. If you were one of the later ones coming out, then you might not find your own shoes there.

Paul Stillwell: Do you have anything else to say to wrap up on the Sicily?

---

*In the early days of naval aviation, the aviators wore brown shoes with their khaki uniforms and green uniforms. They thus acquired the nickname "brown shoes" to distinguish them from the traditional surface ship officers, who were known as "black shoes."

Commander Harralson: No, we had a hairy experience putting a new direction finder antenna right up on top of the mast. Ours went out. We were using it for an antenna to get weather reports from a recon plane that was flying around the edge of China.* It was quite a distance, and the radio room wanted to know what was best to use. So I took them into air plot, and they tied into this direction finder. It worked beautifully. We were able to copy this plane and get the weather reports. But it went out. We lost it somewheres, and we were able to trace it back to the antenna itself.

The next time we were back in the States, we ordered a new one. When we got to Pearl Harbor, on our way out again, my crew put it up. This antenna sat right up on top, the very top. It was the topmost part of the mast, bolted down to the top flange. I had an ET that wasn't afraid of heights. He went up there and unbolted it. Then a floating crane lifted it off and lifted a new one on. But right in the middle of all of this, here went a tugboat charging out, leaving a great, big wake. This crane started bouncing around, and up there this kid was hanging on. I guess he was scared, but I was scared to death he would fall. But he got a bolt in and got it on.

Paul Stillwell: Well, we've put close to nine hours on tape today. I think that's a pretty good record.

Commander Harralson: Okay.

Paul Stillwell: Why don't we wrap up the rest of your career tomorrow morning?

Commander Harralson: Great.

Paul Stillwell: Thank you. Many thanks.

---

*Recon--reconnaissance.

Interview Number 3 with Lieutenant Commander Richard A. Harralson, U.S. Navy (Retired)

Place: Commander Harralson's home in Shingle Springs, California

Date: Saturday, 17 May 1997

Interviewer: Paul Stillwell

Paul Stillwell: Well, after our marathon session yesterday, we're ready to cover the rest of your career this morning. After you had been on board the Sicily, you reported to the Technical Training Unit at Great Lakes. Could you tell me about that tour of duty, please?

Commander Harralson: Yes. I was assigned to the Electronics Maintenance School, which was a component of the Service Schools Command at Great Lakes. It had an officer in charge, a lieutenant commander or a commander. When I first arrived, they sent me to instructor training school for about a month, where I learned how to be an instructor, supposedly.

Paul Stillwell: Was that useful?

Commander Harralson: Not really, [Laughter] because when I finished that, they put me down in the laboratory for a short while, where we were supposed to train reserve officers doing a two-week annual cruise--equipment familiarization and so forth. I looked forward to a good teaching job, because in teaching, you learn. However, I moved from there up to technical training officer. The easiest way to describe it is to say it was sort of like a low-level executive officer to the officer in charge. The officer in charge sat in his big office and thought big things, and I had to see that everything got done. I didn't get to teach, but I had several interesting experiences.

The Uniform Code of Military Justice had just been put into effect, and I was assigned to a court-martial board at Great Lakes, Ninth Naval District.* Prior to that, I had

---

*The Ninth Naval District comprised 14 states, ranging from Ohio in the east to Wyoming in the west. The district headquarters was at Great Lakes, Illinois.

to go to two weeks' instruction in the Uniform Code, from two reserve officers doing their active duty, who were lawyers from Chicago. They had many interesting tales to tell about Chicago and the crooks and so forth, and big trials that occurred there. But I did learn a lot, I believe. It was all very interesting, as was my tour on the court-martial board.

Paul Stillwell: You told me an interesting tale before, when the tape recorder wasn't running, about their discussion of giving and obeying illegal orders.

Commander Harralson: Yes, they spent a lot of time on that subject, starting with the Nuremberg Trials.* The idea was that a person, regardless of being subject to orders of a superior officer, was still responsible for acts that involved morality. When they got all through, it was still a very cloudy area. Because, as they pointed out, for a military unit to function, the subordinates have to carry out the orders of the superior. You don't always have time to discuss it or argue about it. Yet, if you carry out an illegal order, you can be in deep trouble later on. I don't think they'll ever have a clear answer to it. It's all a matter of judgment.

Paul Stillwell: Well, you had an interesting example, regarding martial law and shooting somebody.

Commander Harralson: Yes, they brought up a hypothetical situation, where martial law was declared in Chicago and an officer and one of his soldiers were going down the street. The officer sees this man run out of a building, and he tells the soldier to shoot the man. The soldier does. As long as martial law exists--is held in effect--the soldier and the officer can't be prosecuted. But when the martial law is rescinded, then the relatives can come back and sue--and very likely win--for killing the man and it being unjustified, for some reason.

---

*In the wake of World War II, the Allied Powers tried a number of Germany's wartime leaders in war crimes trials held in Nuremberg, Germany, in 1945 and 1946. As a result of the trials, a number of Germans were executed, and others served prison terms.

Paul Stillwell: What conclusions would you have, as a long-serving Navy man, on the Articles for the Government of the Navy versus the UCMJ?

Commander Harralson: Oh, I think they're tremendous. I'm not sure I'm correct, but I have always seen it as every bit as just as civil law. It's very similar. I see no conflict. I was called to jury duty in which it had to come out that you were retired from the service and that you had sat on court-martials. In my particular case, I was asked by the judge if I saw any reason of conflict between the civil law and the military courts; would I have any trouble? I saw absolutely no problem. Because, as I understand the Uniform Code of Military Justice, it has all the protections of civil law.

The one article, which if I remember correctly was Article 115, was kind of an exception. But its inclusion was due to the fact that it had existed in military law from the time of the Romans. That's the general law that says you can be court-martialed for spitting on the sidewalk, or anything that's against the good of the military service.

Paul Stillwell: If they can't find anything else to get you on, they'll get you on that one. [Laughter]

Commander Harralson: Right. [Laughter] But it was to be used with discretion.

Paul Stillwell: Did you have any trouble adjusting to this? Some people thought the old way was better than the UCMJ.

Commander Harralson: No, I don't, because I did believe--and I vaguely believe there were instances where the CO said, "I want that man found guilty. I want to get him." And the court-martial board had to do it. I think there were actual cases of that; I can't cite them. But under the new Uniform Code, there was little likelihood of that happening.

In fact, before we started sitting on this general court-martial--there was a whole series of general court-martials before we started hearing cases--the legal officer for the Ninth Naval District got us all in an auditorium and talked to us about it. He advised us that in sentencing, if you're going to give a man a six-month sentence, they have to subtract time already served. That meant that he would stay in the local brig, where he couldn't get the attention he would get if he went to one of the large prisons. So he was implying that you should, maybe, make it a little higher so you would be sure that he would go on to prison for six months. He got in a lot of trouble with that. I think he was removed, but I'm not sure of it.

Paul Stillwell: Are there any of these court-martial cases that you particularly remember, that were interesting?

Commander Harralson: Most of them were very boring, usually desertion. We had one young man, though. He was a handsome young fellow. And, of course, they come in in nice, clean dress blues and look very upstanding. He was accused of desertion. We found him not guilty of desertion, but guilty of the lesser included offense, of being absent without leave. Then, of course, we entered the sentencing part. The defense stood up and said, "I have matters of mitigation." He told about this young man's poor aunt that lived in Milwaukee, and on and on about that, and got through.

Then the prosecution stood up and said, "I have matters in aggravation." That kid had been in the Navy four years, his enlistment was about up, and I think the Navy got two months of useful work out of him. He had been court-martialed before and been to captain's mast so many times.

Paul Stillwell: Unfortunately, there are a few bad apples that come in.

Commander Harralson: Oh, yes. Oh, another thing, though, that impressed me was that the lawyers were Navy lieutenants. They don't call it prosecution; they call them the defense counsel and the trial counsel--two lieutenants. They would go after it, hammer and tong. You would think they were mortal enemies. They insulted each other. They put on a show. But after one trial, I had a car problem and needed a ride to Forrestal Village. I knew this one lawyer lived over there, this one lieutenant, so I asked him for a ride and he said, "Sure." He said, "I've got another ride, we have to wait for." So we waited there, in the car. Pretty soon, the other lawyer showed up.

Paul Stillwell: The one he'd been insulting?

Commander Harralson: Yes. [Laughter] These guys were bosom buddies. They lived next-door to each other.

Paul Stillwell: They were just doing their jobs. [Laughter]

Commander Harralson: Exactly. No offense.

Paul Stillwell: Well, I would expect a lot of those are pretty much cut and dried; the facts are clear-cut and so forth.

Commander Harralson: Yes. Desertion is a little hard to prove, because it involves intent to stay away forever. But there were certain things that could be taken into account, like getting rid of all uniforms, and destroying ID cards, and living under an assumed name. You'd begin to suspect he didn't intend to come back. [Laughter]

Paul Stillwell: Well, the Navy rather arbitrarily sets 30 days' absence as constituting desertion.

Commander Harralson: But that alone doesn't do it. You have to prove that the man intended to stay away permanently.

Paul Stillwell: I see. Were there any cases that involved what would be crimes in civilian life?

Commander Harralson: I can't recall any.

Paul Stillwell: So that was just, more or less, an interesting sidelight to your regular job.

Commander Harralson: Yes. I did that for six months. And then they tagged me for security watches under the provost marshal for the base there. That was exciting at times.

Paul Stillwell: Well, please tell me about it.

Commander Harralson: Well, of course, Great Lakes is not too far from Chicago. There's a lot of bad things going on up there. I had to make midnight patrols--I had a truck with a radio in it--an unscheduled tour. In fact, I was supposed to make two of them in my watch, from 1600 until the next morning. We had a bunk. I slept there, in the building where security was based. On these trips I never had any trouble with gangsters or anything like that. The big source of problems was family matters, family spats.

I got a call in the truck one night about a family quarrel going on, a fight, there in Forrestal Village. So I drove over and knocked at the door. This woman came to the door, and she'd been crying. I could see inside, spaghetti on the floor and all. She said her husband caused her all kinds of trouble. I asked her, "Are you having any physical trouble right now?" That was my only concern.

And she said, "No."

So I said, "Where is your husband?"

She said, "He's gone away. I don't know where he is."

"Well, you call us if he comes back and starts trouble. That's my concern here." So I got in the truck and drove off. A call came from the base saying they had a chief petty officer in there. He was all beat up. Well, they didn't tell me that then, but they had this chief petty officer, and he had been in a fight with his wife. So I told them to hold him and that I was coming right in.

So I got in. They sent the chief to me. And here was this little, bitty chief, all beat up. He had a bloody lip and bruised eyes, and he said, "Sir, I just couldn't stand it anymore."

Paul Stillwell: Was he the husband of the spaghetti woman?

Commander Harralson: Yes, he was the husband of the spaghetti woman, and she had beaten him up. [Laughter] So I called over to the chiefs' barracks and asked them there if they could put him up for the night. The next morning, I called the chaplain and told him about it. He knew the couple.

Paul Stillwell: It would be interesting to know what happened after that.

Commander Harralson: I don't know. I had another one with a U.S. Navy man who he was a Guamanian, a Chamorro. I was really scared there. There was physical violence, and we took him in.

Paul Stillwell: Was this between a husband and wife?

Commander Harralson: Yes. I had two security men with me. I impounded a car and threw a guy off one night. And I didn't know whether the provost marshal would back me up or not, but he did, all the way.

Paul Stillwell: Why did you impound the car?

Commander Harralson: Well, the patrol found a civilian over there by the WAVE barracks, where he shouldn't be. They brought him in, and he gave me a whole bunch of lip, that I couldn't do this and I couldn't do that. He claimed to be Navy, but he didn't have anything to prove it to me; he was in civilian clothes. So I told the men there to escort him to the gate. He said, "I have to get my car."

I said, "Your car is impounded. Throw him out." I wasn't too sure that I could do that, but I did it. And the provost marshal backed me the whole way.

Paul Stillwell: Well, usually if something works successfully, they have a good reason to back you up. [Laughter]

Commander Harralson: Yes. I had a bad time one night with a retired chief warrant officer. The old guy had really been through the battles. But he went over to the warrant officers' club and just raised hell. The shore patrol brought him in, and he was belligerent.

Paul Stillwell: What happened to him?

Commander Harralson: Well, I turned him over to the OD, at the Ninth Naval District, up at the administration building. I tried to reason with him and everything.

Paul Stillwell: What was his problem, too much to drink?

Commander Harralson: Too much to drink, yes. He was drunk. And you can forgive them for that, and you can let a lot of things slide. But you get to a point where, you know, you can't let it go anymore. He had overstepped his bounds.

Paul Stillwell: So did he get to sleep it off in the brig?

Commander Harralson: He did, but I think he was in trouble. It was interesting duty there. I think I stood a watch every seventh or eighth day.

Paul Stillwell: So this was a collateral duty, from teaching?

Commander Harralson: Collateral, yes.

Paul Stillwell: Well, please tell me about the teaching.

Commander Harralson: Well, of course, I wasn't able to teach; I was the technical training officer, in charge of the teaching.

Paul Stillwell: I see.

Commander Harralson: There was this one class of 30, and 18 of them were foreign students. At one time there, we had 12 different nations involved. We had a Yugoslavian, by the name of Dabovich. Dabovich couldn't speak English when he first came. Over the Christmas break, somebody apparently really went to work on him, because when he came back, he could speak. [Laughter] And we used to have some real good parties.

It was customary for the graduating class to throw a party, to which all of the staff was invited. We had one memorable party, where they went over from an organization that provides--special services. And they had a bunch of tickets in there for the Schlitz brewery up in Milwaukee. So they hired a bus. And we all climbed in the bus, early one evening, and rode up to Milwaukee.

They put us out at the Schlitz brewery, and we were escorted down into a basement rathskeller. The beer started flowing, in pilsner glasses--tall. Actually, there wasn't much beer in each glass, but they kept them coming. It was the best beer I ever drank. Everybody got noisy and happy and full of fun. They had a small combo band there. We had music. There was a big fanfare. They rolled tables in, loaded with all kinds of good food, and we ate. Then we drank some more. At times they would stop the dancing and make everybody change partners. They'd mix everybody up.

Paul Stillwell: Where did the girls come from?

Commander Harralson: They were wives and girlfriends that came up. This went on till about 1:00 o'clock in the morning. Then we all went out and climbed in the bus, singing and happy as larks, and went back to Great Lakes. The wonderful thing about it is, we woke up the next morning with no hangovers.

Paul Stillwell: Sounds like a great time. [Laughter]

Commander Harralson: I don't know what kind of beer you can do that with, but that's true; that's what happened.

Paul Stillwell: That's your story, and you're sticking to it. [Laughter]

Commander Harralson: Absolutely. And my wife will back me up. [Laughter]

Paul Stillwell: Well, please tell me about the training. What was the content of the courses, and what did it qualify men to do?

Commander Harralson: It was engineering level. It was evaluated by the National Association of Colleges as being worth 44 units. It included basic electricity, physics, optics--which was my nemesis, when I was a student--mathematics. We got up into calculus. When I was a student, I learned how they derived equations; all these equations I'd had to memorize. I'd always wondered where some of the constants had come from.

Paul Stillwell: Why was optics part of it?

Commander Harralson: It was part of the physics course, really. It wasn't a course in itself. I suppose it stands out in my mind because I had so much trouble with it.

Paul Stillwell: What were the applications envisioned from this training?

Commander Harralson: Oh, that you would be an electronics maintenance officer; that you could go out and be able to tell technicians what to do, and know what they were doing. As I found out later, as far as repairing equipment, that was not my job. [Laughter] But it helps to know what your ETs are doing, and why they're doing it or why they're not doing it.

Paul Stillwell: Well, did this presume a certain skill level going in, that people had already been ETs?

Commander Harralson: Yes, it did. It would have been terribly hard for somebody that didn't have some kind of background. I don't think they could have made it.

Paul Stillwell: Was there any hands-on component?

Commander Harralson: Yes, there was. One of our projects--as a student, now; and, of course, I was involved in it as technical training officer, but one of the projects was to build a five-tube superheterodyne receiver. If you wanted to graduate, it had to work. There was a laboratory. We learned how to handle frequency shift keying equipment, loran, tune transmitters, repair, trouble-shoot.*

Paul Stillwell: It's interesting, some of this went back to what you did as a kid, when you were involved with homemade radios.

Commander Harralson: Yes, it did. But, you know, in the final analysis, I don't think I was as technically inclined, or had the natural talent. Or what I'm trying to say is, my natural talent for the hands-on part of it was mediocre. I could have studied that stuff and worked on it till the cows come home, and I never would have achieved the abilities of some men I've known, to understand and get in and do things. I had to wing it, so to speak.

Paul Stillwell: Would you say your talent was more as an operator?

Commander Harralson: Well, yes. I thought I was on the road to becoming a real good operator, but the whole business became obsolete, it almost seemed, like within the space of a couple years. Radio teletype moved in. And contrary to what the radiomen argued, radio teletype, properly tuned, could do better than the best operator.

Paul Stillwell: Certainly faster.

Commander Harralson: Oh, yes.

---

*Loran (long-range aid to navigation) is a system of electronic navigation that involves the reception of pulse signals transmitted simultaneously by paired stations ashore.

Paul Stillwell: And, presumably, fewer mistakes, because it doesn't depend on the mind interpreting something.

Commander Harralson: True.

Paul Stillwell: So CW really became a sideline, or a backup, at that point?

Commander Harralson: It did. It did. It seemed like the next thing I knew, my area of expertise was obsolete.

Paul Stillwell: So you had to adapt.

Commander Harralson: Yes. Well, I had moved into an area where I didn't have to use it anymore. But still, I felt sad about it.

Paul Stillwell: What do you remember about family life there in Forrestal Village?

Commander Harralson: Very pleasant. We got a very nice apartment. They were brand new. It had an upstairs and a downstairs. It was all Navy, of course. I had my three children by then. My daughter was a baby. Very pleasant. We went to parties. It was a good, close-knit school--the staff.

     Commander Clarke was transferred, and our new CO was Lieutenant Commander Reggie Brown, who was an interesting case.* He had been a student in there when I was. Of course, I think he was a senior lieutenant at that time. But his history was quite interesting. He was from Alabama and never went beyond the fourth grade. He had to go to work in the fields and joined the Navy when he was very young. I think he was 17 when he went in. By the time of Pearl Harbor, he was a warrant officer. He went on to become a commander, and he had some interesting duty over in Italy, in connection with the State Department. I don't know just what his job was. Then, when he retired after 30

---

*Lieutenant Commander Reginald O. Brown, USN.

years as a full commander, he went to work for the California Department of Motor Vehicles. And he rose to a pretty high position in that.

Paul Stillwell: He must have been a very capable gent.

Commander Harralson: He was. He had something about him that was reassuring to people. He had a slow drawl in speaking. He had a homespun quality about him that I think made people trust him. A very nice person. It was a privilege to be a friend of his.

Paul Stillwell: As the time went on, with you in the role, did you get more confidence in your ability to run it?

Commander Harralson: Yes. I was feeling pretty sure of myself. [Laughter]

Paul Stillwell: Typically, when you get to that point, then the Navy transfers you somewhere else.

Commander Harralson: That's right. That's right. We had a bad winter. My wife had tonsillitis, and we had to put our kids in day school while she was in the hospital, there at the naval base, to have her tonsils out. When she got out, I took leave; I think it was for 15 days. We took the kids and we headed straight south from Great Lakes, down to Louisiana. We didn't stop in New Orleans; we went by it and over to Florida, and eventually to Daytona Beach. We rented a little cabin on the beach and had a wonderful time. We went in and saw different places--the Cypress Gardens. There was a new one starting up--Crystal Springs. We did the whole bit.

The time was approaching when we'd have to start back, and then our son became sick. This was on a Friday. We took him in to the doctor, who said he had the measles. The doctor gave us some medicine and some instructions and said that he was going to be all right. We went back to our cabin. The owner came up and said I had a call from Great Lakes. So I called back, and it was Reggie Brown, the commander. He said I had orders there to go to Washington, to BuShips, and that he wanted me to come back right away, as soon as I could. So we called the doctor, to ask about our boy traveling. The doctor said, "Bring him in tomorrow morning, and then I'll tell you." So the next morning, we took him in, and he looked him over and checked him out and said, "He'll be all right, and go ahead."

So we took off for Great Lakes. On the way, I think the first day out, why, our daughter broke out in measles. Now, we couldn't see any on our son, but she got the measles. I didn't want to stop at a motel with a child with measles, and I was supposed to get up to Great Lakes. So what I ate some No-Doze pills, my wife took care of the kids, and I drove. It was quite an ordeal, but we made it back.

Paul Stillwell: What month and year would this have been?

Commander Harralson: It was early in the year--February, March, late winter or early spring of 1954.

Anyhow, I went to Washington, to BuShips. I spoke to a commander there. They had a job for me in Turkey. He wouldn't tell me too much about it, but that it was way out in the sticks and that it was a voluntary job. He said there might be a little danger in it, that it was strictly voluntary, and that I had 48 hours to decide whether I wanted it. If I didn't want it, why, no problem; just go back like it never happened. But I began to see visions of adventure, and this original desire that put me in the Navy took hold again. I said, "I'll take it."

He said, "You don't want 48 hours to think about it?"

I said, "I'll take it." Then I went home and told my wife, and she was very unhappy with me. She was a very good Navy wife, supported me in all respects. But she felt like I'd left her out of a major decision. I felt bad about it. Because I know that she wouldn't have told me to not go, but she felt like I hadn't taken her into my confidence. I think she was justified. But I'd done it; I was committed. And she could stay where she was, where she knew people. She wouldn't have to move, since this was temporary additional duty for a year.

The orders came in. I had to go to Washington to be briefed more. Then they sent me to Bell Telephone Labs, in Murray Hill, New Jersey. It was a huge building on the top of a grassy knoll--just acres and acres around it of grass neatly cut. I drove up in a taxi, got out, and went into the reception room--a beautiful, big place, soft music coming out of the walls somewhere, and beautiful receptionists. They escorted me to a room where there were two of their scientists, two doctors. One was Dr. Tyrell. It was a little room, sort of like a schoolroom, that had a blackboard.

They began to tell me about what we were doing over there, and that we had a problem. But they soon got into an argument. For most of the morning, I sat there and listened to them argue about things that were far beyond my ken. So when I came out of it, I didn't know much more than when I went in. But I enjoyed listening to them. Then we went to lunch. We had lunch in a beautiful dining room, with potted flowers and plants everywhere, and music. It must have been a beautiful place to work.

I went on from there. I caught the plane at Springfield, Illinois. It was no longer NATS but had become MATS; it was no longer the Naval Air Transport Service, but it had become Military Air Transport, in which it was a joint operation, I guess.

Paul Stillwell: What had been the point of this visit to the Bell Telephone place?

Commander Harralson: To educate me about the station I was going to and its problem.

Paul Stillwell: Did it succeed in that regard?

Commander Harralson: It did not. [Laughter] I had a vague idea of what I going to be doing, but I really didn't know what the problem was. I caught the plane at Springfield, a DC-6, a four-engine plane, and the seats all faced aft, in case it crashed, I guess. It was heavily loaded. We took off and got into the air. A big hand came over on my shoulder, and I heard this voice behind me saying, "Where you bound, son?"

I turned around, it was a Navy captain. I said, "For Turkey, Captain."

"What are you going to be doing there?"

"I really don't know."

There was a pause, and then he said, "Oh, one of those kind of jobs." [Laughter]

We landed in Argentia, Newfoundland, and took off from there in a snowstorm. I always get nervous when we take off. I listen to those engines real careful, you know. I don't want any of them coughing. [Laughter] We got in the air and landed in Prestwick, Scotland. We stayed there two hours and took off to Tripoli, Libya--Wheelus Air Force Base. We flew over Paris at night. I went up and was talking to the pilot, and I saw this vast sea of lights below us. I asked him what it was. He said, "Paris." We landed in early morning, at Wheelus. There was a sedan there, to meet the captain, and the captain invited me along. So I got in the car with him and a commander that was accompanying him. And we started for officers' quarters, or dining hall.

The captain said to the driver, "You know, I need a bath. Where can we take a shower?" And so the driver took us over to what I guess was a BOQ. We all were able to take showers and shave. Then we had breakfast in a real nice dining hall. Our next leg was in a DC-3 that was red carpet--pretty plush inside--and flew to Rome.* We flew right over Sicily. A beautiful day; the Med was just beautiful. We landed at the Rome airport and found out we were going to have to stay there for a couple days. So we went into Rome and stayed at the Hotel Nord. Again, I was with the captain and the commander.

I went out to see Rome on my own. I was in uniform. I didn't want to go wandering around Rome in uniform, but it was the first time I'd been there, and I thought, "I'd better do it; I won't get back here." I went anyhow. I found all the old ruins. While I was in Washington, I had seen the movie Quo Vadis. So all those old ruins were very interesting. Coming back, I asked at the desk, in the hotel, about restaurants. I wanted not a tourist restaurant, but I wanted a real good restaurant. Then I went up to my room. I had just cleaned up, came out, and met the captain as he came out. He asked me where I was going to eat. So I told him, and he said, "I'll go with you."

Paul Stillwell: Do you remember who this man was?

Commander Harralson: No, I don't. I wish I did.

Paul Stillwell: Were you a lieutenant by this point?

---

*The Douglas-built DC-3 carried the Navy designation of R4D and the Army Air Forces designation C-47.

Commander Harralson: I was a lieutenant. I wasn't used to going to dinner with captains. [Laughter] I remember the name of the restaurant. It was Biblioteca Bali. And it was truly for the Italians. It was in a basement. The walls were lined with wine. I found out it was real wine; it was not empty wine bottles. They had a stringed orchestra. The lights were low. And the food was beyond description.

Paul Stillwell: I hope that means good.

Commander Harralson: Exactly that. Exactly that. It was excellent. Everything about it was top-notch. I sat there and I listened to this music. We had wine. I looked over there and I thought, "My God, why don't I have a beautiful woman over there? I've got this captain." [Laughter]

Paul Stillwell: Well, let me also make one observation--you were a long way from Milwaukee.

Commander Harralson: Yes, I was. [Laughter] We caught a DC-3 out of there. This was not red-carpet DC-3; this was bucket seats and freight. We were headed for Athens. We got over Athens about 11:30 and started flying in circles. The captain wanted to know what the hell we were doing. They told him that if they could stay up there until past midnight, they would get another day's per diem. [Laughter]

We landed. And again, I went with the captain and the commander. Oh, and we'd picked up another one in our entourage. He was an Army lieutenant. I think he was a dentist. He was an American of Greek ancestry, and he spoke Greek fluently. So he became part of our crowd. We got in the car and headed in for Athens. We arrived at this great, big hotel and checked in. The captain said, "I'm hungry." The clerk told him about the big dining hall. The captain said, "I don't want to go in there and listen to music and dancing and all that." He says, "I'm hungry. I want to eat and I want to go to bed."

So we got in a taxi, all four of us. The Greek lieutenant talked to the driver. The driver took off, and we went down into the native section, around back alleys and such.

The driver stopped and went up and knocked on a door. The door opened. He beckoned us, and we went in. It was a little eating establishment, everything was bare boards--scrubbed boards and benches. We sat down to a meal of cold roast beef, olives, goat cheese, beer, and bread. It all tasted very good. Then we went back to the hotel and went to bed.

Paul Stillwell: It was quite a travelogue, just getting there.

Commander Harralson: It was. We stayed in Athens a few days--the captain, commander, and I. I think the lieutenant had other ideas. He went somewheres else while we started walking the streets. It was showery, and it started to rain. We saw this big building and a porch, or a portico, outside. So we ran up there to get out of the rain. While we were standing there, a woman came out and started talking to us in English and invited us in. It was a museum. We had a little tour of the museum, but we also got an earful of the countries that had robbed Greece of their treasures, mainly England. Then we were up to the Acropolis and saw that.

Then, from there, we caught another DC-3. We flew to Izmir. We didn't stay there. Then from Izmir, to Ankara, Turkey. At Ankara, Turkey, I reported in. My orders called for me to report to the Chief, Navy Group, Joint Military Mission for Aid to Turkey. It was known as JMMAT.

Of course, I went to the desk of the Navy group, and I met Commander G. E. O'Neil, a submariner.* As officer in charge of project X-31, he was my boss. He explained some of the things I would be doing. It turned out that I was going to Amasra, which is on the coast of the Black Sea, almost directly north of Ankara, and opposite the Crimean Peninsula. What we had there were hydrophones out in the Black Sea, that came in on a binaural system. And we recorded sea sounds. Nobody ever told me that we were recording to obtain submarine signatures, but I could not figure out any other reason that we would be doing this. That was what we were doing.

Paul Stillwell: Was there a direct wire link to the hydrophones and where you were?

---
*Commander Guy E. O'Neil, Jr., USN.

Commander Harralson: Yes. A cable came in from the two hydrophones. I don't know how far they were separated. The signals came in, and each one had its own amplifier. It was recorded on a long-playing tape that had a reel, perhaps ten inches in diameter. I forget how long it would go. But we were to record constantly. Also, the building, which was built by the Navy for this job, had a window that gave you a good view of the Black Sea. We kept a log when we saw any ship movements out there. We had a good set of glasses, so we used to pick them up hull down.

I had to stay in Ankara for about two or three weeks. The commander said, "They're building a dossier on you. Keep a low profile." I turned in my uniforms at JMMAT; it was civilian clothes on the site. I'd been told that.

Paul Stillwell: So did you bring a supply of civilian clothes with you?

Commander Harralson: Yes, purely casual--dungarees and sport shirts. I had a sport coat too.

I holed up in a fairly decent hotel, right on the main street, Ataturk Boulevard, in Ankara. I had two weeks to kill. Commander O'Neil advised me to stay on Ataturk Boulevard, eat in only the best restaurants, and keep a low profile. So I started my two weeks.

I received a Turkish driver's license. It was a hard two weeks in Ankara--very boring. I bought some magazines at the PX at JMMAT.[*] I ate one meal a day in a restaurant. The rest of the time I snacked on Cheese-Its, potato chips, and other junk food I had bought at the JMMAT PX.

Paul Stillwell: Who was building the dossier on you?

Commander Harralson: The Turks. At that time, Turkey was much more authoritarian--it wasn't quite as democratic as I think it is now, from what I have read and seen. It was supposed to be a democracy, but it was tightly controlled.

---

*PX--post exchange.

Finally my time was up. And I met the courier, a Navy lieutenant named Clymer. We climbed into a carryall. We had a new man, Cronin, for the station. He was a first-class engineman, a submarine man. We took off over some of the wildest country I have ever seen. Lieutenant Clymer told Cronin there wasn't room for him. He would have to go later. But Cronin begged to go, because he had had enough of Ankara. Clymer told him he had to ride in back. Clymer was trying to be Barney Oldfield or something.* He drove like a madman.

Cronin was my senior petty officer out there and a hell of a good sailor. He rode in back, and the dust just swirled up and around. The truck was canopied, but whoever rode back there just ate dust. I guess we'd gone about three-quarters of the way, and I felt so sorry for him, I let him ride in front and I climbed in back. I just went a third of the way that he did, but I don't know how long I could have stood it back there.

Anyhow, we went through the town of Barton. It was in the mountains. And out of Barton, we descended down some pretty steep grades, down to Amasra. Amasra was an ancient town that went back to the Greeks, and then the Romans. The Romans called it Amastris.

Paul Stillwell: Antiquity.

Commander Harralson: Yes. We found the station there. I met the officer I was to relieve, a lieutenant. I had about three or four days to learn the ropes. Then the courier departed with the lieutenant, and I had it. I had six men. This one engineman, the new man, was senior, and became my leading petty officer. The building in which we were housed had three major sections. Across the front was the lab, where we had our recording equipment and a certain amount of batteries and other items that we needed. The next, perhaps the largest room, had a bathroom at one end. That was where we slept. The only amenity that I had, being an officer, was the fact that I had a single-level cot that occupied one corner. The others slept in double-deck bunks in the other three corners. I wondered about maintaining my position as an officer and gentleman.

---

*Barney Oldfield was a racecar driver early in the century.

Paul Stillwell: It's a very democratic situation you were in.

Commander Harralson: Yes, it was. But I think I did good. Because at heart, I was a swabby, really. [Laughter] But I held my own. There never was any doubt who was in charge, who was running things. O'Neil was the officer in charge, but he was in Ankara. I was there. It was my station.

Paul Stillwell: Well, that's the good thing about the Navy system too--there's a hierarchy that people recognize.

Commander Harralson: Yes. Out in back, we had two Chrysler industrial six-cylinder engines cranking 15-kilowatt generators.

Paul Stillwell: You were not hooked into regular electrical power?

Commander Harralson: This little town was primitive. There was no electrical power. Of course, one of the generators had to run constantly, and we alternated them each day. We had a backup on a trailer that we could use. The problem was interference. Adjacent to us was a Turkish hotel. Now, this was not your normal kind of hotel. This was a government-owned hotel for miners from Zonguldak, where each summer the miners and their families could come for recreation. Their source of power was an old German generator, a 25-cycle generator. They closed the hotel down during the winter, but when they opened it up in late spring, they fired up this generator. It caused such extensive noise that it blocked everything we were trying to receive. So, as long as it was running, why, it destroyed all of our work--prevented us from recording.

We packaged these tape reels that we used. When the courier departed, he took them with him, and they went back to the Bell Telephone lab, where they were analyzed. I think I'd been there a few months before the noise came on. The hotel activated the generator, and it was just blocking out everything.

Paul Stillwell: And, of course, the people running the generator had no idea what you were doing.

Commander Harralson: No. No, I don't think the Turks really understood. Now, up in the hills, back of us, there was a Turkish naval station. Of all things, they stored torpedoes there. They were supposed to deliver torpedoes to submarines that came into Amasra. This was a developing situation. The commander back at JMMAT had tried to get them to establish their storage somewheres else. He told them that to tote those torpedoes down that torturous road, which was not paved and full of chuckholes, wouldn't do the torpedoes any good. But they built the station up there anyhow.

This noise really worried me, because there were all kinds of ideas proposed to rectify the situation, none of which, to me, seemed plausible. Ones like rewiring the hotel. I didn't think I was capable of doing that, provided the Turks give me permission to do it, and provided I had the material. Somebody else thought the trouble lay in the big fish pond, which had underwater lights. So they were really concerned about it, because it was destroying all of the effort that had been put into the place.

Paul Stillwell: Had you gotten any feedback from the Bell people, on the quality of the tapes you were sending?

Commander Harralson: We were told, from time to time, that the tapes were okay, keep up the work, and all of that.

Paul Stillwell: But this was not any word from them that led you to try to deal with this generator problem?

Commander Harralson: No. They were aware of it. I mean, they were the ones that kept saying we had to do something about it. That's what I was supposed to have learned at the Bell Telephone lab--about this problem and any ideas they might have to rectify it.

Paul Stillwell: Oh, so it existed even before you got over there?

Commander Harralson: Oh, yes. It had been a thorn in the side since the very beginning, the first summer there.

Paul Stillwell: Let me just interrupt a minute. Where were the hydrophones? Were they in international waters or Turkish territorial waters?

Commander Harralson: I think they would be called international waters. Now, I don't know how that applies in the Black Sea. Is there a 3-mile or 12-mile limit? I don't know.

Paul Stillwell: Well, that's been the big question for many years, but the United States, back then, recognized a three-mile limit.

Commander Harralson: That's right.

Paul Stillwell: But if they had Turkish permission, then they could run the wires through that territorial sea.

Commander Harralson: This whole operation was a high-level, off-the-record type of project. We had no security classification. We were told, "You don't talk. Nobody knows about it." They said not even the rest of the Navy knew; it was a very, very clandestine operation. And I suspect it wouldn't make any difference, the 3- or 12-mile limit. They just did it.

Paul Stillwell: Right.

Commander Harralson: But I don't think it was that. It couldn't have been any farther than, say, about six miles.

Paul Stillwell: But the Turks had to know about it, didn't they?

Commander Harralson: They knew we had an operation there. This Turkish station up in the mountains was supposed to look after us and make sure we didn't get in trouble with the local people--the police or anything like that.

Paul Stillwell: I see.

Commander Harralson: And they helped us.

Paul Stillwell: In what ways?

Commander Harralson: Well, I had a lot of problems out there. Let me get to that. [Laughter]

Paul Stillwell: Okay.

Commander Harralson: I sat in a wicker chair that was sort of my position in the lab. I spent a lot of time there, just reading books. But with this noise going on, I was worried sick about it, that I was going to have to do something beyond my capability. And I didn't believe in these ideas that that they were proposing. So I was sitting there, with this interference that had been going on about a week, at that time. And, of course, there was just a short period during the day where you could get a few signals all right. But for this thing to be effective, it had to be 24 hours. That was my feeling.

Paul Stillwell: Well, that makes sense, of course.

Commander Harralson: So I was sitting there one day, just thinking about it. I don't know how I ever came to do what I did. I don't think it was the result of a thought process; it was just almost automatic. Now, each of these amplifiers, I had found out, was balanced to ground. And they had an adjustment on the front, in which you could balance the noise input to ground, which theoretically should take out the noise. We had tried balancing, and we had a meter, which was common to both amplifiers, that would show a balanced situation. And, of course, you could do it with your ears, for there was a speaker on the system.

I got up and started to balance one amplifier, to balance out the noise. But this time, I did something I'd never done before. I reached over and switched off the other amplifier. I hit a beautiful zero on noise--just completely out, and a pure signal in. But only one amplifier. So I turned off that amplifier and balanced the other one, the same way. It came right up to zero--no noise, a good signal. I flipped the first one on; I had a beautiful signal feeding in, with no noise. Now, it's that simple, the answer to the problem that they had been fretting over since the very beginning actually.

Paul Stillwell: So you just sort of stumbled across it.

Commander Harralson: Yes. And it was so basic, so elemental, that I knew there was going to be some embarrassment. [Laughter] So I thought, "How am I going to play this?" I finally decided, "Let's play it with some class." I had to keep a log and write a routine report. I just wrote, "Have eliminated the noise by revising the tuning procedure. We seem to be getting a clear signal now." That's all I said. If I had to, I could call JMMAT on the telephone, but they didn't like me to. Also, they broadcast to us, I think, once a week on radio. It was a one-way deal. We tuned in at a certain time. They usually told us, in cryptic words, that the courier was on the way or something like that. So I just wrote it in the log like that, and we went on like nothing had happened. When the next courier came, why, I had all these tapes. He asked about the noise, and I said, "That's taken care of." I never heard anything about it.

Paul Stillwell: It's interesting. You'd think that the Bell people would at least tell you that they were getting a better signal.

Commander Harralson: Well, they told us that everything was all right. Yes, eventually, it came back that the tapes were good and we were doing all right.

Paul Stillwell: Did you have a sonarman, as part of this small group?

Commander Harralson: Yes, we did. Yes, we did. His name was Brown, and he was a source of a lot of my problems. [Laughter]

Paul Stillwell: Do tell. [Laughter]

Commander Harralson: The sonarman was a redneck. Can I say that?

Paul Stillwell: By all means. You've already said it. [Laughter]

Commander Harralson: I got along great with the men, but he was an acey-deucy player. We all were. One day he got into a argument with the rest of the ETs--all of them very smart--on doppler, what doppler was, how doppler worked.* And he was absolutely wrong. But of all people, a sonarman should really understand doppler. He argued and argued. And the argument got louder and louder. Finally, no one would talk to him, and the only person that would play acey-deucy with him was me. So I started playing with him, and he brought up the subject of doppler. I tried to explain it to him. It was like talking to a wall.

Then we got word that we were going to have visitors: some scientists from Bell Telephone Lab and Commander O'Neil from JMMAT. They were coming out to pay me a three-day visit. They arrived on station. This sonarman couldn't wait till he got one of these Ph.D.s at our dinner table and wanted him to explain to him how his theory of doppler--how it worked--was right, and that we were wrong. So this doctor tried to explain to him how doppler worked. And he argued with the Ph.D. [Laughter] Finally, one day I was sitting in my wicker chair, reading. The engineman had the watch, and Brown had the battery duty--checking the battery levels and all. It was just a minor chore that we had to do. He had been late on it, and the engineman told him, "Let's get the batteries checked out; get them up to date."

---

*Doppler is an apparent change in the pitch--that is, frequency--of sound or a radio wave caused by relative motion between the source and the listener.

Commander Harralson: The sonarman came back with some vulgar words. He said something like, "You take a flying leap."

I heard that, and I'd already just about had too much of Brown. So I said, "Brown, that's enough. Pack your gear. Be ready for the next courier." Brown had the watch, and this engineman had come in and was looking at the batteries. I told Brown, "You're relieved. Sign your log over to me, and be prepared to catch the next courier." He tried to argue, but I wouldn't have any of it. He was very disruptive.

Subsequent to that, and before the courier, which was about a week away, we woke up one morning to hear this terrible moaning, out on the beach. We got up and raced down the beach, where we saw a whole bunch of Turks crowded around. One of them was holding a child--I would guess about three--and they were beating him on the back. The engineman and I rushed down there. We came up to the crowd, and we didn't know what to do. I thought, "Gee, they're not doing right." But I didn't know what to do. Then here came Brown, charging down the hill. He bowled everybody aside, took that child out of the Turk's hands, laid him out on the sand, checked his mouth and tongue, and gave him artificial respiration; not the mouth-to-mouth, but the old kind we used to do, very gently. The child came around.

So I went back and wrote a letter, to go with the other letter explaining why Brown was coming back early.

Paul Stillwell: So they could sort of canceled each other out.

Commander Harralson: Yes. And I suggested that he be awarded some kind of lifesaving medal.

Paul Stillwell: Well, he earned it.

Commander Harralson: But they never did. I was upset about that. Yes, one letter of condemnation and another of commendation.

These darned scientists brought a bunch of sonobuoys with them. They wanted to take those sonobuoys to sea and try to record them. They had the equipment with them.

I'm not sure what their intent was, and I'm not sure it wasn't just having fun. They wanted a way to signal to the boat. Now, we had bought, with mess funds, about a 14-foot boat, a double-ender. I had sewn sails for it, and we stepped the mast. It had no keel, so I made leeboards. So we could take the sonobuoys out and place them, but we wanted a way to signal. Do you know what they wanted to do? They wanted to go on the hill back of the station and send smoke signals. They were going to burn my engine oil. [Laughter] I objected to that. They ended up burning some old tires to send their smoke signals.

So Costa, one of the men, and I headed out to sea, out past the breakwater, with our boat. But with our sail and our leeboards, I couldn't tack very well against the wind. So we rowed; we rowed and we rowed. We got way, way out; could just barely see the place. Then we started dropping these sonobuoys. We had smoke signals arranged, but I don't think they ever got the fire started. [Laughter] We stayed out as long as we thought we ought to, and then we had all this distance back. I was kind of worried about it, the fact that we couldn't beat to windward.

Paul Stillwell: Well, the wind should have been helping you on the way back.

Commander Harralson: That's exactly what happened. We had a tailwind there and we hoisted sail. That was quite a ride. They had had all kinds of trouble with their equipment, and the sonobuoys didn't work or couldn't be received.

Paul Stillwell: Did you get a good replacement for Brown?

Commander Harralson: Well, I had another problem. There was a guy named Fisher who was a first-class ET. He had worked for the Office of Naval Research, where they had the Vandergraf machine. He was actually a terribly smart, intelligent man. He knew his electronics. I'm just glad, for my own sake, that I was the one that figured out how to defeat the noise, because I had to hold my position with some very, very, very smart young men.

Well, one day I was coming back from town, and I saw Fisher walking arm in arm with a Turkish girl on the beach. So that evening I called Fisher aside, and I said, "Fisher, when you came over, when they interviewed you for this job, which was voluntary, they advised you that you had to stay away from the girls." I said, "We're in a vulnerable position here, and I can't have that. So, from now on, you steer clear of that young woman." And I reminded him he was married and he had a kid at home.

About two days later, a young Turkish man came to the door. He told me to tell Mr. Fisher that if he gave up alcohol and became a Moslem, he could marry his sister. [Laughter] I called my man in and said, "Fisher, you put a stop to this, one way or the other. If you don't, you're going back to Ankara, and you will not have my blessings." He did. He knocked it off.

Then, the replacement I got, Robinette, was a disaster.

Paul Stillwell: Worse than Brown?

Commander Harralson: Yes, for different reasons. Now, when I first arrived, the officer that I relieved was an accountant; he knew bookkeeping. He had set up a system of double-entry bookkeeping for the mess fund. He was going to turn it over to me. The first thing I said was, "That won't be my job. That belongs to one of the men."

He replied, "They won't take it." So we held a vote. We asked the men, and they would have nothing to do with it. Nobody wanted anything to do with it. So it ended up I had to take it. But I knew nothing about bookkeeping. I hate the stuff. I should not be allowed around books of that kind. He showed me the double-entry system. And, by gosh, it began to work out, where at the end of the month, they were supposed to balance. And each man had an account. He could put money in as he needed to, any amount, and we kept a record. It was beautiful. Gee, it was fun. I'd get the biggest thrill at the end of the month, when the book came out exactly balanced.

Then, when our tourists arrived, the engineers and the commander, I had to pick them up on the mess. I tried to do it and keep it going like it was, so that when they got ready to leave, I told them how much money they owed. But at the end of the month, the book didn't balance. So I looked around real quick, and I put some money in the kitty. And from that time on, it never balanced. I was either putting a little in or taking a little out. [Laughter]

Paul Stillwell: So much for your accounting career.

Commander Harralson: Yes.

Then Robinette, the new ET, arrived on the scene. One of the first things we found out about him was that he snored. My God, he snored. And, of course, we were all in the same room. [Laughter] Guys were swearing in the middle of the night. They'd get up to turn him over. It didn't make any difference. Then one day I was working on the mess accounts, and Robinette came in and stood there watching me. He said, "Who audits your books?"

I said, "No one."

He started quoting Navy regs, the supply manual, or something. I said, "Robinette, nobody knows we're here. I don't want this job, but nobody else will take it." He suggested maybe he could. I said, "You talk to the men. If they vote to have you take the mess accounts, that'll be fine by me." So they held a vote. The only vote for him was his own. So I kept the books. But the snoring got so terrible. And he questioned everything that we did there, rather arrogantly. So one day I told him, "Robinette, you need a break. You're going to Ankara for two weeks." What I really meant was that the rest of us needed a break. So I sent him to Ankara. I wrote a letter to explain why he was coming back to Ankara. He stayed there two weeks. I intimated that he could stay longer if he wanted to. [Laughter]

There were six men that stood the watch. But when he left, that put us back to five, so I took the watch. But they sent him back at the end of two weeks. When he got back, he wanted to know about how many lira he could put in the mess fund. We used gold, or American money, when we bought things from JMMAT that came up with the courier. Now, we also bought a lot on the local market, and for that we used lira. So we used lira and gold, and I observed the official exchange rate. But the black market rate--I forget the figures on it, but the lira was a lot cheaper.* Well, Robinette began challenging how I determined who could pay in lira and who could pay in gold. When I wanted gold, I asked

---

*The official rate was 2.8 lira to a dollar in gold. The black market rate was anywhere from 5 to 7 lira for a dollar in gold.

somebody who was low in his account, "Can you give me some gold, here, for the next courier trip?" Or, if I was low on lira, I would ask somebody to put in some lira for our next trip to market. But he wanted to pay everything in lira, and he wanted everybody else to put in gold. So I asked the engineman, "Why does he want to do that?"

Cronin laughed. He said, "When he went to Ankara, he bought a whole bunch of black market lira. And now he's got to get rid of it, because when he leaves Turkey he can't take it with him." So he was trying to contribute into the messing fund with very cheap lira.

So I figured out how much lira, each month, we spent and how much gold. Then I made a quota. I took myself out; it didn't make any difference to me. I said, "Each man will be allowed to contribute this much lira. Now, you may exchange your allowances as you care to." And the rest of the men, who never before cared one way or the other, now demanded their share.

Paul Stillwell: So Robinette was not popular.

Commander Harralson: No, no, he wasn't.

Paul Stillwell: Was the engineman there to look after these generators?

Commander Harralson: Yes, to maintain the generators, which were getting an awful lot of wear. He was also my leading petty officer. And he stood his watches. He told me that the inserts for the valves, after so many grindings, were wearing down, and they were going to have to be replaced. That represented a major problem. I told Ankara about that. Fortunately, I saw it as a major problem--when it had to be resolved or else--was beyond my time. But I was going to make sure that they knew this was pending.

We had other problems. We needed parts. It took three months to get parts from the States for these generators. And Mustafa Batman, our landlord--the old Turk that owned the land we were on, quite a character--told us that in Zonguldak there were all kinds of parts houses. Zonguldak was a big mining town, right on the Black Sea. We thought maybe we could go there.

So Cronin and I set up a trip to Zonguldak, in our Jeep. Zonguldak was about 60 miles away, but to get there you had to go over high mountains, very steep mountains as you descended down to the sea-level. So we set up a big checkoff list of spare tires, extra cans of gasoline, extra oil, everything we could think of, to get us there. We started out one morning, when we could barely see--daylight just beginning. We had a rough map of how to get to Zonguldak, because the roads were not marked. We finally got up to the top of the mountain, where the road led down. It was beautiful scenery, very rural, undeveloped. We wound down this road, into Zonguldak, and started looking around.

We zoomed down into Zonguldak, which was nestled up against the mountains--a real mining town--and had no trouble finding a parts house, Mopar. We took our sample parts, my English/Turkish dictionary, paper and pencil, and we walked in and put the parts on the counter. The Turk clerk took one look at us and said, "Yok," which meant no. We tried to explain. Again he said, "Yok," no. So we walked out, and we found another place. The same thing happened there. In fact, the place was crawling with parts houses. Everywhere we went, we got the same reaction. We were about running out of parts houses. We went into one, and the guy said, "Yok." I tried to explain. And he said, "Anglaise," and I said, "Yok, American."

Oh. A big light. He came around, grabbed us by the arms, took us around in back, and set us by the stove. Then he hollered a bunch of orders. A Turk brought in tea. We sat there drinking tea while he took our parts and brought in new parts.

Paul Stillwell: What did they have against the English?

Commander Harralson: Well, don't you remember Gallipoli?*

Paul Stillwell: Oh, yes. That was a long time before.

Commander Harralson: Oh, yes.

---

*The Gallipoli Peninsula is a narrow tongue of land that extends southwest from the south coast of Turkey. It was the scene of an ill-fated amphibious landing by Allied troops, mainly Anzacs, on 25 April 1915. The campaign, which also included naval bombardment of Dardanelles forts, was ultimately unsuccessful. The last Allied troops withdrew in January 1916.

Paul Stillwell: They had long memories.

Commander Harralson: You know, the English are disliked in a big part of the world.

Paul Stillwell: And you found that out.

Commander Harralson: I like the English. The French and English fight like cousins.

Oh, we had a nice conversation, and got all the parts we wanted, exactly; Mopar parts. We went back to the Jeep, put them in the Jeep, and then looked for a place to eat. We found a restaurant, went in, and ordered. Before they brought the meal, they brought out a plate full of peppers. They were shaped something like an okra--a long, green pepper. I'd been eating those peppers ever since I'd come to Turkey. They were very good and mild. So I picked up one and chomp, chomp, chomp--nearly the whole thing. My mouth was on fire. I had never had that kind of pepper burn, of that magnitude, before. Water didn't do any good. They said salt helps. That didn't do any good. In fact, it paralyzed my mouth, and I couldn't eat my meal. Now, at the time, I didn't know what to think. Now I think they thought I was an Englishman, and they sabotaged me. [Laughter] Anyhow, the engineman saw my reaction and he didn't bite in.

Paul Stillwell: Smart man.

Commander Harralson: We did some shopping. The grocery stores, or markets, seemed to have some interesting things--bananas for one, and oranges--that we didn't have too much of. So we bought things like that, then took off for home without any further problem, the trip being a success.

Paul Stillwell: Except for your mouth.

Commander Harralson: Yes. The next day, the lieutenant from the Turkish naval base dropped in to see me. He could speak English, after a fashion. He had gone to submarine school in the States. We had a good relationship. We talked a little bit, and then he got down to why he was there. It was to tell me that if I wanted to go somewheres else, I had to clear it with him. He said that our trip had upset the whole Turkish security system and caused waves all the way to Ankara. He wasn't telling me, exactly, that I couldn't go; he was saying, "Please let us help you go." I took notes, but I had the parts I needed.

On one of the courier trips Commander O'Neil came. He did that once in a while, made the trip himself instead of Clymer. On this trip he told me that just in front of our lab and to the left was an old Roman breakwater that extended out into the bay, perhaps 50 to 75 yards.

Paul Stillwell: Made out of stone?

Commander Harralson: Yes, and it was in bad condition. He told me that the Turks were going to build it up and extend it out farther, and put in a T-like wharf there, to on-load torpedoes into submarines. He wondered about our cable. We were able to figure out that if they did that, they were going to pile big rocks--as they built out--on our cable. We were going to have to do something about it. So he left me with that problem.

My solution called for raising the cable. There was a boat that I chartered on occasion. It was, I would say, a 40-foot Turkish boat owned by an old guy. He had a young kid as a bow hook. The boat had a little in-board engine. I hired him from time to time for various jobs. So I hired him for this. We were able to get the cable up. My idea was to get it up and bring it in, over the top of the breakwater. We dug a trench across the breakwater. Then I had a 4-inch diameter pipe in the back of the station that was at least 16 feet long. I took it up to the naval base, and they cut it in two--sliced it lengthwise--and welded large nuts along the side so that I could bolt it together. My idea was to lay the bottom half in this trench, bring my cable over and lay it in the pipe, then bolt the top half on. So they did that for me; they welded these ears on the pipe.

The Turks were already hauling rocks. The problem became urgent. So we went out there one night, all hands, with a generator-powered light.

Paul Stillwell: Was this a clandestine operation on your part?

Commander Harralson: No. We went out at night because that's when the trucks weren't running. We had a small generator that gave us light. We used levers and crowbars and all kind of prying, because some of these rocks were big, and we managed to get a trench dug in. But my pipe wasn't really long enough. We put the cable in, then we put the top half on. We went to bolt it together, and I discovered a principle--that if you're going to bolt two parts together, you don't want threads in the top part. And I had threads in both lugs, which meant that I could pull it no tighter than it was when the bolt went into the second half, because it had threads in the first half. But we got it together, more or less, in pretty good shape. We got it covered back in time for the big trucks that were coming. We were doing fine. We thought we had solved the problem, although the cable actually came out of the water and was draped over some of the rocks at the side.

Well, I thought all the work was going to be out at the end of the breakwater. They started widening it, and great big rocks rolled down and pinned the cable. We were out of commission. So I hired a boat again and tried to break it loose. My idea now was to roll up the cable and relay the inner part. We had a great, big Bell Telephone drum and extra cable, so I thought, "If we can get that end out, we can splice this extra cable on, and then bring it out around the end." It looked like a fearsome job, but we had to give it a go.

We couldn't break the cable loose with this boat. Well, that's where the Bim Bashi entered the scene. Up at the naval base, the CO departed. When he left, he was replaced by the next highest officer. He was a commander that we called Bim Bashi. When he took over, the place relaxed and everybody became quite friendly.

The Bim Bashi came to the station one day. He wanted to put a truck bed, with a canopy, in my back yard. He intended to use if as sort of a summer tent for himself, his wife, and his baby--as well as some other Turks. I really didn't want him there, but I wanted him as a friend, see. So we finally figured out that if he put his truck up on the side of the hill there, it would be all right. And I agreed to run him an extension cord out there--it was maybe 100 feet long--so he could have light. Oh, he was happy as a lark.

Well, he hadn't been in there more than a week than he came to the door one day. His baby was sick and would not eat. He was very worried about it and asked if I had any milk. Now, we were the only one place that had refrigeration in the whole area there. We had some Klim, which was powdered milk. I mixed up a careful formula of Klim. I measured it all carefully. And having helped raise some kids myself, I knew a trick. I put a little Karo syrup in it. I made up a batch of formula for him. He filled his baby bottles and he went back. The baby just ate it up. So, from then on, we kept formula in our fridge. And I'd mix up batches of formula for him. [Laughter] So he was a friend.

Well, I went to him. At that time, there was a Turkish ship--something like an AKA, an ex-States ship--that had a motor launch. It was a regular Navy motor launch, a 50-footer. There were a bunch of dependents on this ship. It looked like they were on some kind of a vacation--Turkish people, women, children, sailors. And they were riding around in this motor launch. He went over and commandeered the motor launch and kicked the people out. He came over with the motor launch, and we tried that. That's got a pretty hefty engine, but we couldn't break the cable loose.

Finally, the ship was using a barge that was developed during the war, I guess. It had what was essentially an outboard motor, a great, big diesel engine with a stern drive. They were hauling clinkers out to sea with this barge. He went over and commandeered that for me. We got that thing over there and broke the cable loose. Then we got the bitter end. We would have to splice an extension on the inboard end.

We put this great, big Bell Telephone cable drum on the barge and tied it down as best we could. My idea was then to head to sea, with the men taking up the cable as we headed out to sea. The cable drum was on jacks that supported an axle so the drum could be rotated. I was going to go out, just to the end of the modern breakwater, and then come back in, paying out as far as it would go, on a new course that would take us past the projected end of the new breakwater they were building, with plenty of leeway. We already knew where the station end was. Then we would splice in what we needed for the additional distance and cut out what had been damaged.

So we started out to sea, and I was at the helm. The men were rolling up the cable. We got it rolled up to the harbor entrance. And then I started back, unrolling it. I had made a chart of the bay there, and I knew how I wanted to come in. I had established landmarks. We were backing as we did this. We rolled it in, going forward, and then laying it out, we were backing down. The water was clear, so I could see that great big propeller there working away. We were doing it slowly and carefully. Everything was going fine.

Then I got past the end of the new breakwater, where I had to make my turn. As I was looking down, I saw some great, big rocks. That big prop was missing those rocks by six inches or something. So I altered course a little bit more to the right and started in, right straight towards the station. Then we come to the end of the cable. We tied a buoy on the end of it. Then we took the barge back. That was a terrible job, though--that big drum. We got the drum off and turned the barge back to the ship.

Then I used my two best men for the rest of the job. They were Costa and Gowdy; I have a picture of them. They took our boat out and spliced in the cable extension. Now, splicing was a very long and tedious job. But they did it successfully, and we got back into commission. And I owed the Bim Bashi. [Laughter].

Paul Stillwell: You talked about standing these watches. What was involved in that?

Commander Harralson: Simply making sure that the take-up was running. You had to change the tape. And you also kept a log. You kept a good description of anything going on out at sea. We used to pick up these propeller noises, and then pick up ships hull down--the smoke first, the stack, and you'd see them come up. There were a lot of weird optical events, distortions and reflections.

Paul Stillwell: Was the cook one of your six men?

Commander Harralson: No, the six men took turns cooking.

Paul Stillwell: I see.

Commander Harralson: Yes. And nobody complained. The penalty was you had to cook.

Paul Stillwell: Well, did you feel you did some good, during that year out there?

Commander Harralson: Yes, I did. I tell you, when I got back to Great Lakes, the captain wanted to see me, Captain Williams, service school command. I went up there and, he says, "Harralson, what the hell did you do out there?" He says, "Your fitness report is very good."

Paul Stillwell: Who wrote it, the commander back at JMMAT?

Commander Harralson: It was signed by the admiral at JMMAT. I suppose it was written by the commander. That made me feel good.

Paul Stillwell: It should.

Commander Harralson: But he wanted to know what I was doing, and I wouldn't tell him. I've often wondered if I did right. I told him I couldn't tell him. [Laughter] That took a lot of guts, to tell a captain that you can't tell him, especially one that you were under.

Paul Stillwell: Yes, it did. Well, that was a TAD thing. Did that end your assignment to Great Lakes, at that point?

Commander Harralson: That's right. Now came one of the payoffs. The commander at BuShips had said, "Now, there's no guarantee here, but when you get back, you can go over to the lieutenants' desk at BuPers and talk about where your next assignment will be. They'll probably listen to you with sympathetic ears."

So I did that. I went over to the lieutenants' desk. I brought up the subject, and the man there told me, "Well, yes, we can do that." He was looking at some papers there, and he said, "However, if you want to get promoted, you better go to sea." So I thought about that.

Paul Stillwell: What had been your inclination up to then?

Richard A. Harralson, Interview #3 (5/17/97) – Page 332

Commander Harralson: Oh, I saw some more good shore duty. I was becoming a family man, and I'd been away. So I thought about the time when I was back at ElMaint. I remembered some guys talking about building 128, the Mississippi, tied up in Norfolk.* It never went anywhere, so it was called building 128. So I said, "How about the Mississippi? Have you got a billet there?

"Yes, communications officer. You want it?"

"Sure." So I went to the Mississippi, the most seagoing ship I was ever on.

Paul Stillwell: Oh, really? [Laughter]

Commander Harralson: It never went anywhere, hardly, but it went to sea all the time.

Paul Stillwell: You mean, it didn't go far, but it went often?

Commander Harralson: Right. Every week out to sea. And it was not a happy ship.

Paul Stillwell: Why not?

Commander Harralson: They had a crazy exec. They had a martinet for a captain, it seemed to me.

Paul Stillwell: Who were these people?

Commander Harralson: I don't remember the name of the crazy exec. It's a name to forget, anyhow. The captain was Martell.† When I went aboard, Amory was the lieutenant

---

*Effective 15 February 1946, the old battleship Mississippi (BB-41) was reclassified as a miscellaneous auxiliary with the new hull number AG-128. During a yard period that year, she was converted to a gunnery development ship. Three of her four 14-inch gun turrets were removed to make room for new guns and as sites for testing new ordnance developments. She subsequently lost the last turret and was reclassified EAG-128.

†Captain Charles B. Martell, USN, commanded the USS Mississippi (EAG-128) from 9 July 1954 to 13 August 1955.

I was relieving. Amory took me up to meet the exec. He knocked on the door, and this voice said, "Come in." We went in and here's this commander, sitting with his feet up on the desk, eating grapes.

Amory said, "Commander, this is Lieutenant Harralson, my relief."

"Yeah, yeah, yeah. Okay."

Paul Stillwell: He waved you off?

Commander Harralson: Yes. So that was a bad start. Then we started inventorying Title B. Amory had a different idea about Title B than I did. I wanted to see each and every piece. I wanted to see the serial numbers, and I wanted to see the card that said where it was assigned. Amory didn't think that was necessary. But I did, and what I thought counted.

Paul Stillwell: That's right.

Commander Harralson: So we struggled there for a good week, and it slowed his departure. He was unhappy. But I insisted. We saw everything, except one piece. I think it was a Japanese war relic that was on Title B. It was some kind of optical spyglass, mounted on a stand. We couldn't find it, and we couldn't find it. So Amory wanted me to sign him off anyhow. I told him, "I'll sign it off with a disclaimer statement." And that's what we finally had to do. He departed. Shortly after he departed, I found out that the chief engineer had had this eyeglass all the time, and he knew Amory was looking for it. But the chief engineer was not a nice guy. [Laughter] I don't remember his name.

But the exec was a madman. At liberty call, he'd get up on the quarterdeck there, and with what appeared to me to be no provocation whatsoever, start tearing up liberty cards.

I had two divisions. I had the signal division and the radio division. Each one had a division officer, so I was sort of a half-baked department. I was required to attend all department head meetings. But I was under the operations officer and in the operations department. We would go into a noon meal and sit down, and over the speakers would come, "There'll be a meeting of all heads of departments immediately, in the executive officer's cabin." So we'd get up. By the time we got back, our meal was cold and ruined. He ranted and raved and was just a jerk.

I wondered why he was that way. I wondered if the captain had his spurs in him. Because the captain was a very small man physically. But he was either on the list or had made it; he was on the verge of becoming an admiral.

Our major job, of course, was testing various things. Our biggest project was the Terrier missile.* The big guns, of course, had been removed and this missile launcher installed forward.

One day I went by the bulletin board that had the watch list posted, and I saw my name for OD under way. I thought, "They're out of their minds." I turned around and headed for the navigator, who made up the watch list. I was going to tell him, "You've made a mistake." But then I thought, "I'm an unrestricted line officer, a senior lieutenant. I've faked it this far; let's not quit now." [Laughter] So I turned around and went back to my room.

Incidentally, I had luxurious quarters. The Mississippi had admiral quarters, and I guess they didn't expect any admirals aboard. So the captain moved into the admiral's quarters. The exec had the captain's quarters. The operations officer moved into the exec's. I moved into what, I guess, was the operations officer's cabin. I had a large porthole. I had a desk. I had a file cabinet. I had a table. And I had a rug on the floor. Because when the captain moved into the admiral quarters, he had the rugs removed and new carpet laid. Then the carpet that came out of there was divvied up, and there was enough left to go into my room. Now, the chief engineer had his own room, in another part of the ship, so I don't know about him. But, anyhow, it was a real nice place. I had a typewriter of my own. I enjoyed that aspect of the Mississippi tremendously.

---

*The Terrier, a radar-beam-riding surface-to-air missile began in the late 1940s as an outgrowth of the Talos supersonic test vehicle. Its first shipboard launch was in 1951. Operational testing on board the Mississippi began in July 1954. The missile first went into fleet use on board the cruiser Boston (CAG-1), which was recommissioned on 1 November 1955 after conversion to a guided missile ship.

So, having found out that I had the watch the next morning, the 8:00 to 12:00, I went back to my cabin, and I tried to read up on the Rules of the Road, The Bluejackets' Manual, or anything I could find--helmsman's orders. I tried to cram it all in the night.

I reported to the bridge the next morning. We were under way. We were at the outer end of the channel, I guess. I reported at quarter to 8:00 and received the status from the officer of the deck: course, speed, and pertinent data. We faced the captain, and the fellow I relieved said, "I have been properly relieved, sir."

I told the captain, "I have the conn, sir."

"Carry on."

So I stood there, scared to death, with my glasses--the badge of office. Pretty soon, "Mr. Harralson," from the captain. When they put a "mister" in front of your name, look out. I thought, "Oh, God, what have I done?"

He said, "You see what's going on out there?"

I looked out there, and, my God, way in the distance there was a trawler crossing. I said, "Yes, sir."

He said, "Do something!"

"Aye-aye, sir. Right standard rudder."

"Blow the god-damned whistle!" So I pulled the cord and heard, "Booooo." So I gave the helmsman a new course, I think 20 degrees to the right of our established course. When I thought we had gone far enough, I gave two blasts on the whistle and ordered left standard rudder. Then we resumed our original course. But I--Boooo, Boooo. I get confused, this difference between the international and inland orders. I guess in international waters your whistle tells other ships your rudder signals.

Paul Stillwell: It's information. Whereas in inland waters, you have an exchange and get an agreement on proposed course corrections.

Commander Harralson: We steamed on. But I'm telling you, it was nerve-wracking up there. There were two situations that were just terrorizing. The exec would wander around. I guess the captain told him when he wanted this to happen. When he saw the right place and felt the time right, he'd give a signal. A Marine would rush out with a dummy and throw it overboard, and the exec would start his stopwatch.

Paul Stillwell: A man-overboard drill, of course, was something you had zero experience with.

Commander Harralson: Zero. But I had been warned and told about it. [Laughter] If he threw him over to starboard, then the first thing was, "Right full rudder," with the idea that you were supposed to kick the stern away from where the guy fell. I don't think it could ever happen that fast. But that's what you were doing. Then you were to execute a Williamson Turn.* Did you ever hear of that?

Paul Stillwell: Sure. I met Williamson once, the guy who invented it.

Commander Harralson: Oh, God. [Laughter] Anyhow, I think the turn has to fit the ship, but I came right 57 degrees. Then the order was, "Shift your rudder." And you came around. Then, let's see, "Left standard rudder, meet her," and you'd come back. If you did it right, you came back on your own track.

Paul Stillwell: You're on the reciprocal of your original course.

Commander Harralson: Right. And as you come back onto your reciprocal course, you had to spot the Franklin buoy, that supposedly some character had had sense enough to release. Then you had to worry about bringing the ship to a halt. It took forever to stop the ship. I had to give, "All engines two-thirds, all engines one-third, all engines stop." But on top of all of this, you had to worry about the JOD, and the lifeboats, and the lifeboat mustering. They were holding muster to find out who fell overboard. Oh, God, it went on and on and on and on.

---

*Early in World War II, Ensign John A. Williamson, USNR, devised the man-overboard turn that came to be named after him. It involves turning about 60-65 degrees in one direction, then reversing the rudder so as to go down the reciprocal of the ship's original course. His description can be found in U.S. Naval Institute Proceedings, October 1979, pages 89, 92.

Then the other terrorizing thing: they had electrical steering and steam steering. With the electrical, the helmsman operated a controller. At one time, in shifting to steam steering, somebody fouled up on the sequence of orders, and the rudder jammed. So we had periodic drills in changing from electrical to steam and steam to electrical. And you never knew when the captain was going to tell you, but you had to get it right. That was a headache.

We'd go out to sea and fire the Terrier missile at drones. Somewhere over at Chincoteague or Assateague was an airfield. Two chase planes and a drone would take off. The drone was a full-sized obsolete aircraft that could be remotely controlled. We would try to shoot it down with the Terrier. There was a lot of timing and failures involved in this; a lot with the drone, and getting off the ground and everything.

But come evening, we'd head towards land and anchor at the 20-fathom curve, somewheres off Chincoteague, so that the captain could go down to his quarters. He'd leave his sea quarters and go down below, where he could have a better meal and watch the movies. But the OD stayed up on the bridge. The watch was maintained on the bridge, for good reason. Because the 20-fathom curve was near the major sea lane for the merchant ships coming down the coast. You'd be up there, and our defense was the saluting battery. [Laughter] We had a crew on standby for the saluting battery. And when he got within a certain distance of us and it looked like a collision, we were to fire the saluting battery. [Laughter]

Paul Stillwell: And warn him off.

Commander Harralson: Yes. Well, you'd pick these guys up on radar, 20 or 30 miles north. And you'd watch them. You'd keep on them, "What's their bearing? What's their bearing?" And, you know, when a thing's coming down at you from that distance, a bearing doesn't change very much. You'd begin to pray for--I told you I didn't pray, yes I did. [Laughter] I used to pray for, "Just give me a degree, just give me a degree." [Laughter] Oh, we had some near misses. They'd come by. We'd put the glasses on them. It looked like the bridge was empty.

Paul Stillwell: They'd be on Iron Mike.*

Commander Harralson: Iron Mike.

Paul Stillwell: No wonder they weren't changing! [Laughter]

Commander Harralson: But, you know, this crazy exec we had was transferred; a regular change of duty. And we got a new exec, who was the antithesis--Commander Spear.† I think his father was an admiral, but in the Supply Corps. Do you know any Supply Corps admirals?

Paul Stillwell: Well, not any named Spear.

Commander Harralson: Oh, what a beautiful officer he was. He came aboard. I was down in the spaces below, and this Marine came up, saluted, and handed me a memo. The memo said, "There will be a meeting of department heads in the executive officer's cabin at 1000, for coffee and doughnuts. You are cordially invited." I went up, had coffee and doughnuts, and we had a very amicable, businesslike meeting. This Commander Spear was a true gentleman. Not only that.

See, when we were coming in late Friday, at dusk, into Hampton Roads, up that channel, traffic heavy as hell, visibility poor--it was a madhouse on the bridge. We always had a senior officer at the conn. It was always tense. And my special sea detail was a little radio room, right aft of the bridge. I had voice radio position there. Usually I had a Marine up there, for a radio operator. But, anyhow, I was always on the bridge when we were coming in. And the door was always open, and I could see everything.

Paul Stillwell: A chance for you to learn.

---

*Iron Mike is the nickname for an automatic steering system that keeps a ship on a constant course until changed.
†Commander Louis P. Spear, USN.

Commander Harralson: Yes, sure was. I'm telling you, it was a terrible place, really--the tension up there. But when Commander Spear brought us in the first time, he was so on top of everything. He spoke so softly. He was truly a wonderful officer. I have other reasons to say that. But he had one habit that kind of indicated that maybe internally he wasn't quite as calm as he appeared. He smoked a lot, and he always had a cigarette in his mouth. And sometimes the darn thing would burn down till it burned his lip.

One time, when we were anchored out at the 20-fathom curve, I had the early evening watch. I was up there. Everything was calm, no problem in sight. Then the phone rang. The boatswain's mate answered and he said, "Sir, the executive officer would like to speak to you."

"Officer of the deck speaking, sir."

"Who is this?"

"Lieutenant Harralson, Commander."

"Mr. Harralson, do you read the plan of the day?"

"Yes, sir, I do." A long pause.

"I find that strange. If you read the plan of the day, why didn't you call away the 8:00 o'clock reports at 7:00? Because it says that in the plan of the day, which is out of the normal routine." There was a long pause there. "How do you explain that? There must be some explanation."

Paul Stillwell: Was this Spear that was doing this?

Commander Harralson: Yes, yes. And he had that way about him. You'd done something, and you were a first-rate officer, you knew what you were doing--it was probably that he didn't understand. "Therefore, would you please explain?" And I saw him do that to an ensign that was the OD when we were at anchor. I really felt sorry for that poor kid. The commander was not somebody that you wanted to do something wrong in front of.

Paul Stillwell: So how did you work that one out? Did you explain that this may have been one time you missed it? [Laughter[

Commander Harralson: I didn't have a real good explanation. I hemmed and hawed and gasped and stumbled around.

Paul Stillwell: Which, of course, he knew from the beginning.

Commander Harralson: Absolutely. But I tell you one thing, I always checked that plan of the day after that. [Laughter]

Paul Stillwell: Well, you said you had some other reasons to admire him. What were they?

Commander Harralson: Well, that was one. That was one. It's just in these meetings we had, and how considerate he was of you. One time I had the evening watch. We were, again, anchored at the 20-fathom curve, and the navigator came up. I didn't know what he wanted. He was looking around, and he said, "What's that light over there?"

I said, "That's the Chincoteague light, sir."

He says, "How do you know that?"

"The guy I relieved told me." Wrong! So all the ODs had to take a lesson in determining what the periods were for the lighthouses.

Paul Stillwell: The pattern of flashes and so forth.

Commander Harralson: Yes, the periods. I anchored the Mississippi at the 20-fathom curve. I couldn't miss. That was a nice experience. But that was under a new captain, Ruckner.*

Paul Stillwell: Were your fellow officers of the deck helpful to you, in teaching you some of these things?

---

*Captain Edward A. Ruckner, USN, commanded the USS Mississippi (EAG-128) from 13 August 1955 to 17 August 1956. The oral history of Ruckner, who retired as rear admiral, is in the Naval Institute collection.

Commander Harralson: Oh, yes, sure. And it was towards the latter part of my stay there that the promotion came out, to lieutenant commander.

Paul Stillwell: Well, so going to sea had paid off, as the detailer suggested.

Commander Harralson: Yes.

Paul Stillwell: Please tell me about Captain Ruckner.

Commander Harralson: I don't remember much about Captain Ruckner. He was a much milder man. There was one commander on there, and I can't remember what he was. He came up one day. We were engaged in some operation, and he was reporting to the captain. He had a chief's hat on. He was a full commander, and here he is with a chief's hat. The captain said, "Commander, you ought to take a look at your hat." [Laughter] He had been somewheres and had just grabbed the wrong hat.

One day--speaking of chiefs--in my opinion, chief petty officer status had ebbed, or receded, after the war. They didn't have the authority or status that I had known about before the war.

Paul Stillwell: What evidence or manifestation did you have of that?

Commander Harralson: A very good one. One of the chief radiomen came up to me one day. He was very mad and shaken. He had a report slip. And he said, "Mr. Harralson, will you sign this report slip?"

I said, "What happened?"

He said he had sent this radioman up to clean up the UHF room. "And Commander Ennis, the operations officer, while wandering around up there, had found him asleep back of the transmitter. And he called me up and bawled me out."[*]

---

[*]Commander William W. Ennis, USN.

I said, "Well, Chief, you can sign it yourself." He didn't seem to know that. I said, "But before you do, why should we pass our troubles on to the captain? Why don't we take care of it ourselves?" He thought I meant some kind of punishment. So I said, "No, we can't punish. That's the captain's prerogative. But the good book says that your man can't go ashore until he gets his work done. Now, has he got his work done?" You could see a light going on in his mind.

Paul Stillwell: You were doing a training course on him, the way the exec did on you.

Commander Harralson: Yes. [Laughter] You could see lights dawning. So he wandered off with his paper. So I went on. I think it was about five days, maybe a week, later that the chaplain called on me. He wanted to know what I was doing to this radioman striker. So I told him what transpired. You could see that he understood. But the guy had come to him with a sad story. I had to tell the chief, "Don't run the thing in the ground. Be fair about it, you know."

Now, the chiefs that I knew when I was a seaman and a third class and all that--oh, man.

Paul Stillwell: They understood these things.

Commander Harralson: Oh, they did, they did. Sometime later the JAG Journal came out with an article about this division-level action, which couldn't be considered punishment, but it was a way of taking care of minor problems like that.

I was summary court officer on the Mississippi. And that was interesting. I had a case where the chief engineer caught a man reading a comic book when he was on watch for the water-level indicator in the auxiliary steam room. He had put him on report. The man was awarded a summary court, and it was given to me. As I understood a summary court, I was to represent the Navy and to represent him; I was to look out for both sides.

Being an old watch stander myself, I took a dim view of anybody reading a comic book on watch. Now, his defense was that he was sitting right in front of the water-level indicator and could see it very easily. My rebuttal was that his attention was on reading the book, and the possibility existed that he could be absorbed in something he was reading at the very time when he should see a problem. And so I found him guilty, and I hit him hard, which wasn't really very hard, but toward the upper limits of what was prescribed. I also wrote that, in my opinion, this was a case that wasn't necessarily a summary court. There were other ways--for example, extra jobs and extra education on standing a watch--to accomplish the purpose.

The ship's legal officer disagreed with me. He thought the man, because he was sitting there in front of the glass, shouldn't have been adjudged guilty. But from there on, they went with me.

Paul Stillwell: What do you remember about those missile shoots? Could you describe them, please.

Commander Harralson: No, because when they fired the missile, everybody was below a certain level, secured in. I take it back. I did see some shots. They were misses. But I don't remember very many successes. I remember a lot of failed attempts, either getting the drone in the right place, or the range fouled--that was a problem--and missile problems or computer problems. They had a lot of trouble.

We had a lot of other jobs there. We were a target for the Petrel missile.[*] It was something they flew out low-level and dropped, I think. The wings fell off it or something. Different things like that.

Paul Stillwell: You probably had a smaller crew than the ship had had as a battleship.

Commander Harralson: They had a lot of missile people on there, but I imagine it was smaller, because those big guns took a lot of men.

Paul Stillwell: What do you remember about the physical condition? This was, by far, the oldest ship you'd ever served in?

---

[*]The Petrel was developed in the mid-1950s as a torpedo-carrying missile, designed for use against surface ships. It was canceled soon after it entered service because submarines were the primary Soviet naval threat.

Commander Harralson: That's right. I don't think it was too good. It had suffered in a hurricane that it got caught in. It went through the eye of the hurricane, as I understand it. They had the hurricane condition in Norfolk, and, of course, the ships took out to sea. The <u>Mississippi</u> headed north, not too far from the coast, then decided everything was clear, turned around, and headed back down. But the hurricane changed and came in on them. The <u>Mississippi</u> ended up passing through the eye of the thing. It took green water over the bow, broke the hatch that led down to the chiefs' quarters, which were flooded. The electrical wiring got soaked. It was the start of a whole series of electrical fires. They had an awful lot of problems after that with the electrical system.

Paul Stillwell: Were you still having those problems when you were there?

Commander Harralson: Yes, they had slowed down, though. But we went into the shipyard, up the Elizabeth River, a couple times.* I don't know how serious the problem was. I remember I was acting operations officer the last time we went in. It was customary, in passing the degaussing station, to call for calibration. There were certain things to do. Being acting operations officer, I asked the captain about proceeding with that. They were worried about a lot of other things, and they didn't want to mess with it. There were major engine problems.

Paul Stillwell: Well, more on material condition--what can you say about how it looked?

Commander Harralson: Oh, of course, it looked fine as far as upkeep. I mean, everything was painted. No, there wasn't any streaks or rust or any of that. Outwardly, cosmetically, it looked great.

Paul Stillwell: Did you get down in the engineering plant at all?

---

*This was the Norfolk Naval Shipyard, Portsmouth, Virginia.

Commander Harralson: I think I saw it once, but I know very, very little. This thing took a mile to stop from, I guess, 15 knots. It had a backing-down turbine, which gave you one-third the power that you had ahead. It took forever to stop it. That's why we always overshot on the man overboard.

Paul Stillwell: What do you remember about the camaraderie and the experiences in the wardroom?

Commander Harralson: Oh, I enjoyed the wardroom there. Although the food wasn't so great, the ambience was something else. I thoroughly enjoyed the evening meal. The talk was always pleasant and non-controversial. And the table was set with linen and silverware--the gift from some distant benefactor. There was a light, formal air about it. We had our own napkin rings, and we were served by mess attendants. We could all see where the mess attendants, the stewards, ate. And, of course, their ration money went into our food money.

Paul Stillwell: The wardroom mess.

Commander Harralson: Yes, the wardroom mess. And, of course, then they could eat our food. We thought they ate a hell of a lot better than we did. [Laughter] They would be eating T-bone steak, and we'd be eating spaghetti. After I left there, there was a big scandal in Norfolk, that had to do with chiefs and chandlers. I think our wardroom procurer was involved in it--kickbacks, supposedly receiving supplies that we didn't.

There was two forces apparent in the wardroom. The married men, of course, were concerned about the wardroom mess bill. And the bachelors, that lived aboard, wanted to eat better. So we had that conflict.

Paul Stillwell: Well, you at least got to spend time with your family on weekends, I take it.

Commander Harralson: Oh, you'd be surprised how many weekends are disrupted. We would come in late Friday, sometimes Saturday morning. Of course, every third weekend you had the duty, which was the whole weekend. The truth was, it seemed to me like I wasn't getting very much time at home.

Paul Stillwell: Even though you'd asked for this semi-shore duty?

Commander Harralson: Exactly. Exactly. Here's a hearsay story: Of course, Captain Martell was a very proud person, as he should be. This was before I was aboard. They were coming in, and they dropped the hook before they should have. The ship still had too much way on, and they lost the anchor and 10 or 20 fathoms of chain. So at his going-away party, he was presented with a silver-plated anchor and 20 fathoms of chain, in small scale.

Paul Stillwell: In miniature.

Commander Harralson: They say that he reacted very poorly. [Laughter]

Paul Stillwell: I'm not surprised, given what you've said about what kind of man he was.

Commander Harralson: From the Mississippi he went to the new missile cruiser Boston.[*] I realize now, we were at the beginning of the missile age, and the beginning of the end of the big guns.

Paul Stillwell: The Mississippi had been his training ground for the Boston.

Commander Harralson: Yes.

Paul Stillwell: I presume the Mississippi didn't deploy at all, anywhere?

---

*Captain Martell commanded the Boston (CAG-1) from 1 November 1955, the date of her recommissioning following conversion, to 3 July 1956.

Commander Harralson: While I was aboard, we made two trips to New York, for recreation. In a lot of ways they were big headaches. I remember going up there one time, and they woke me up in the middle of the night, to get up on the bridge. We were still a long way from Ambrose Light, where we were to pick up the pilot. They wanted me up on the bridge because the TDZ, RDZ, UHF transceiver that they used couldn't raise Ambrose Light. I asked, "Well, how far is it?" I think it was something like 50 miles.

I tried to tell them that it was too far. But I had made a mistake one time up there. They were having trouble communicating, and here I was, the communications officer, which, of course, communicating is my problem too. But their equipment wasn't working right, so I pulled out a little screwdriver in my pocket, and I peaked up the transmitter and the receiver. There was a way you could do it, because it had this auto-tune system, and you got a lot of backlash. I peaked them up, and then communication was fine. I was doing ET work.

Paul Stillwell: And they expected that from then on.

Commander Harralson: That's right, whenever they had TDZ, RDZ trouble, why, they called me up. And that's what they did this night. So I did my little job, and that still didn't do it. But I was awake, and I stayed in my little communications office and watched everything. They called and they called. And it was getting foggy. Things were getting real tense on the bridge. Finally, when we were quite close, boom, here came the Ambrose Light in on the radio, loud and clear; no sweat, no problem. We got alongside. It was daybreak, the fog was getting patchy then, and we began to see a few things. Here came the pilot. The JOD went down to escort him to the bridge. The pilot came up to the bridge, stepped in, and said, "Good morning, Captain."

Captain Martell said, "Good morning, Captain. Do you think we'll make it?"

The pilot looked around, and says, "Captain, you have enough men up here to row us in." [Laughter]

Paul Stillwell: Was the reason Martell was asking because he was concerned about the fog?

Commander Harralson: Yes, I guess. It was a patchy fog.

Paul Stillwell: Did you ever steam in company with other ships when you were in the Mississippi?

Commander Harralson: No, always alone. We would steam quite a ways out in the Atlantic, and we got caught in a real good storm one time. That was a real thrill, to be up on the bridge and see that.

Paul Stillwell: Well, please describe it.

Commander Harralson: Oh, everybody that's been on the bridge of a ship at sea is awed by the enormity of the waves, wondering if the bow is going to dig out in time for the next one.

Paul Stillwell: Did it dig quite deeply in?

Commander Harralson: Yes, it did. Yes, it did. We got a little green water. One time out there, we were just going real slow, for some reason. The sea was real calm. And out there were whales--and I'm talking hundreds, big whales. It was like some gathering, seminar, or something out there.

Paul Stillwell: [Laughter] Seminar!

Commander Harralson: They passed word over the speaker, "All hands observe to starboard, a large number of whales." I used to like to write the deck log up there and use nautical language in describing things. Then when you had to report to the navigator's office to sign your smooth log--the navigator was always after ODs, "Get down there and sign the smooth log," you know, to delinquents. But I always liked to go down, to see if they bought what I said. [Laughter]

Paul Stillwell: Did you have any special electronics on board to support the missile system?

Commander Harralson: Oh, yes, yes. But I knew nothing about it, then.

Paul Stillwell: That wasn't under your purview?

Commander Harralson: No.

Paul Stillwell: Who ran that?

Commander Harralson: Well, they had a missile department. I think the top man in it was a lieutenant commander who had been navigator on the Missouri.

Paul Stillwell: Please put that story on the tape. You didn't tell that when we were recording.

Commander Harralson: Well, the roster of officers came out every month, and we used to scan it over and see who's who; standard procedure, I think. One evening, I was up topside, leaning on the rail, talking to a shipmate. The roster of officers had just come out. I had noticed that Lieutenant Commander So-and- So--I don't remember his name--had been a lieutenant commander for an extraordinarily long time. So I said to my friend beside me, "Who did old So-and-So punch in the nose?"

He laughed and said, "Don't you know? Don't you know that he was navigator on the Missouri when it ran aground in Portsmouth?"*

Paul Stillwell: That answered that question.

---

*USS Missouri (BB-63) ran aground on 17 January 1950 in Thimble Shoal Channel, en route from Hampton Roads to the Atlantic. The commanding officer, Captain William D. Brown, USN, was relieved of command, court-martialed, and convicted.

Commander Harralson: That took care of that.

Paul Stillwell: Well, how modern was the radio equipment that you were in charge of?

Commander Harralson: It was the standard equipment. They were coming out with receivers now that were much, much smaller than the old ones that I knew. They weren't into solid state that much yet, but receivers were getting a lot smaller. In fact, one of the receivers aboard was there for evaluation. While I was aboard, there came out a CinCLant order, to electronics officers, that laid out a by-the-numbers testing of all vacuum tubes, on a rotational basis.* This applied to the electronics maintenance people. Periodically, they were to take the vacuum tubes out. And, of course, they were to stagger this, so that it didn't mean all tubes out of all equipment on the same day. But they were to take all the tubes out of certain equipments, put them through the tube checker, and throw away the bad ones, replace them with new ones. Now, to an experienced electronics maintenance man, that is sheer madness; that is disaster.

Paul Stillwell: Because if it's not broken, don't fix it.

Commander Harralson: Right. Now, vacuum tubes were eccentric. You could put a tube in, and it would work beautifully for a long time, no problem. You put the same type tube in, brand new, and it would upset the calibration, crap out one week later--things like that. Of course, the tube testers they had didn't tell you a whole lot about the tube. They gave you some basics, but it was nothing to rely to that extent. Of course, they rescinded that order very, very quickly. But that was sheer nonsense. That showed the old Navy, by-the-numbers type of thinking when it was strictly no go.

Paul Stillwell: What I'm getting essentially, though, is even though this was a very old ship, they kept her up to date in electronics.

Commander Harralson: Yes, yes.

---

*CinCLant--Commander in Chief Atlantic Fleet.

Paul Stillwell: Well, they'd have to, to be able to keep operating.

Commander Harralson: Yes.

Paul Stillwell: Did the ship fire her guns at all while you were on board?

Commander Harralson: I can't think of any guns she had. I really can't. I think they took them all off. They had Marines aboard, a detachment, with a lieutenant and a captain. I got in pretty good with them, because coming in one night--it was the night of the big Marine Ball, you know, the celebration, and we were late. I was able to arrange, through the port director, a special boat that came out and picked the Marines up. I worked with them. They would send a Marine up to stand the radio watch, up on the bridge with me. I had to teach every one that came up. They rotated it around, but we got along fine.

But what I wanted to tell you about is--they went over to this big party. They, of course, had a blast, and came back in the wee, small hours of the morning. They were still full of the Old Nick. They got into a horsing-around affair in their compartment, and tore their compartment all apart. The lieutenant and the captain were standing in the door, watching them. Then when they were exhausted, at about the usual breakfast time, and it was apparent they had spent themselves and it was all over, they had a very, very exacting field day. [Laughter]

Paul Stillwell: Remedied the problem they had created.

Commander Harralson: They sure did.

Paul Stillwell: You said that you were in charge of the signal bridge also. Do you have any memories of visual signaling?

Commander Harralson: Very little. And I was very scared of that job. [Laughter] I trusted my signalman.

Paul Stillwell: Since you had little choice.

Commander Harralson: Yes. [Laughter] But they were good, very dependable at getting the right flags up when we were doing the right things.

Paul Stillwell: Well, but if you weren't operating with other ships, there wouldn't be that much need for them.

Commander Harralson: No, but you know, you always have to fly some kind of flag or hoist. They were always on top of it.

You know, early on, I realized if I was going to do my job, I had to rely on the men under me. And I did everything to encourage and promote that feeling toward them.

Paul Stillwell: Of course, that's good in any job.

Commander Harralson: That's true. That's true. But, you know, I've seen officers that don't do that. And I think they're kind of dumb. They don't understand their job. I've picked that up in the some of the letters I've read in the Naval Institute--that these men really don't understand what their job is as officers.

Paul Stillwell: What do you remember about coming to the end of the operational period, and then preparing the ship for decommissioning?

Commander Harralson: Well, we got the word there was some kind of breakdown in the engines, and they decided that it wasn't worth fixing. We were all sad about that. It brought up a whole series of problems. I was also the postal officer, and I had a lot of highly classified material that was in my custody, and a lot of post office headaches. But I had an assistant postal officer, an ensign, academy graduate--in fact, I had two academy graduates, and they were my best. I have to say that, because they were; very good, very respectful, and they really took hold of their jobs. There's an awful lot of paperwork involved. Somewheres down below, I've still got paperwork on that--receipts for classified material turned in.

I remember being called up to the captain's cabin. There was a bunch of dignitaries and VIPs there. The captain gave me a whole bunch of letters that I had to take down and get canceled in the post office. The state of Mississippi was inquiring about getting the Mississippi as some kind of a memorial or museum piece. The reply they got advised them of all the costs and what was required to maintain it. The Navy didn't want one of their beloved old ships rusting to pieces in some backwater; they would rather see it cut up in scrap. When the state of Mississippi found out the cost of keeping one of the these old behemoths, it didn't go any farther. We took it in and left it.

Paul Stillwell: Well, this was not a ship that was going to be mothballed, so what steps did you take? Did you strip ship at that point?

Commander Harralson: I got off before any of that started. We had a decommissioning ceremony, and as far as I was concerned, that was the end of my business. And I had orders.*

Paul Stillwell: What do you remember about the ceremony?

Commander Harralson: Not much. It was dress whites again, and all that; quarters, listening to people read some of the history of the Mississippi.

Paul Stillwell: So strip-ship occurred after the decommissioning?

Commander Harralson: Yes, yes. I had absolutely nothing to do with that.

Paul Stillwell: Well, I presume that the Navy would take, for example, that up-to-date radio gear and redistribute that.

---

*The Mississippi entered the Norfolk Naval Shipyard 26 May 1956 for inactivation overhaul and was decommissioned there on 17 September of that year.

Commander Harralson: Oh, certainly, certainly. They would never leave that. I suppose there was a lot of equipment that was not so antique.

Paul Stillwell: There were signal flags and many other things.

Commander Harralson: Somewhere down in the basement I have a 48-star flag and a halyard that came from the Mississippi.

Paul Stillwell: You must have a real treasure trove.

Commander Harralson: I've got some things; not objects, but letters and pictures.

Paul Stillwell: Well, where to from there?

Commander Harralson: From there I went to the CIC school at the Naval Air Station, Glynco, Georgia, which was just a few miles north of Brunswick, Georgia. On the way, I had 30 days' leave, delay in reporting in. By that time, I had a one-wheeled trailer, with a box on it and a sloped back. We had an assortment of gear and equipment that my wife wanted to take along. When we moved and were in a transitory situation, she carried a little sewing machine amongst that. But we made this a camping trip. We camped out in the Smoky Mountains and got caught in the backlash of a hurricane and nearly drowned.

We reported in and found the housing situation difficult. We went over to St. Simons Island, opposite Brunswick. It was across the bridge, over the inland waterway and swamps and reeds and so forth, onto this sandy island. It was a beautiful little town there. We found a house and rented it, right on the beach, for $125.00. A nice house, a modern house, three bedroom. We were quite happy until I found out that there were three months in the summer when the rent became $125.00 a week. So we enjoyed it for a month, and then the best I could find was a little, bitty clapboard house, two bedroom, very tiny.

But some of our happiest days were spent there. The island was a wonderful place for kids. It seemed like kids would wander around there in the utmost safety. I can see my three kids--well, they're a little older than they were there. [Pointing to a photo in the interview room] Joe was ten, Arthur was seven and a half, and Helen was five. There was two and a half years' difference between them. We'd go fishing and end up bringing home fish, crabs, mussels, all kinds of things. Then we'd put a bunch of newspapers on the table. We'd steam the crabs, and we'd sit there and eat them.

Another thing we enjoyed doing there was going out for rides--my three kids, my wife, and I. On one of them I remember pulling into an ice cream place, a drive-in. I went over and I got us all ice cream cones. I came back, sat in the car, and was looking down the side. Towards the rear, was a sign sticking out that said, "Coloreds." And the whole idea was that if you were black, you had to go down there; you couldn't go up in front and get an ice cream cone. I thought that was terrible. I realized at the time that if I had been a black soldier in the war, a pilot, any of those, I would have been outraged at having to do that.

But I understand the southern approach. My father was from North Carolina, my mother from Tennessee. Back when I was a boy about--I think I was about eight--I had a good friend at school named Knowledge. He was a black boy. I went to Knowledge's house after school several times, and we played. Then one day I brought him home. I brought him in the front door, and I introduced him to my mother and my father. And they said, "Hello, Knowledge." Everything was fine. We went out in the back and played.

Then, when Knowledge went home, my father pulled me aside and said, "There are black people and there are white people. The black people have their place, and the white people have their place. And we shouldn't mess with that," words to that effect.

But you know, even then, at eight years old, I felt that that was wrong. I didn't buy it. And for that reason, I think that this racial bias is something that has to be taught to young people.

Paul Stillwell: You're exactly right. It's not something that you're born with.

Commander Harralson: No, I think most children, normal children, are very fair-minded in that respect. I'm preaching. [Laughter]

Paul Stillwell: Well, that's a valuable sermon.

What else do you recall from Glynco?

Commander Harralson: I bought a five-horsepower, used outboard motor. There was a place you could rent boats. We'd go out fishing. It was this life that I didn't want to leave when my tour was up. That's the reason I asked to retire.

Paul Stillwell: Well, before you get to that, could you tell me about your actual job at Glynco?

Commander Harralson: It was a good job. I liked it. The front end there was the offices and the captain and all of that stuff. Next down were all the classrooms. Then down in my area was all the equipment. I had 80 men, mostly ETs. I had some electricians, I believe. I had two warrant officers--a pinstripe and a W-4. I had several chiefs. The place was mine to run as I saw fit, which was a great experience. They wanted me to take care of things down there and don't bother them. I saw an opportunity to apply some of the things I felt should be done--the way things should run. I tried to reestablish the chain of command through the ratings. We had the men divided up into different maintenance groups. I had senior men in them as group leaders, assigned to specific equipment.

One of the first things I did was jack up the security down at that end, and the watch that we had down there. I had many chiefs, but not enough that I could have a chief for the senior petty officer on watch. So I dipped down into my senior first class, so that they would have enough men to give a decent rotation. Then I said I wanted a watch list that you could look ahead for a year and know when you were going to stand a watch. I didn't mean that you couldn't make swaps, but we had an official list that would apply. I wanted the group leaders to be the approving authority of any special leaves, or special requests of men under them. And the next layer up, a chief, should go with the group leader's recommendation. If he had a disagreement, if he thought it was wrong, he should not openly go against it, but call the man aside and explain why he disagreed, and then next time make it different.

I didn't want anybody putting anybody on report. Of course, that excluded acts of moral turpitude and all of that. I had cases of men coming in a little bit late for our quarters, which I tried to make as formal as possible, and as reliable as possible. But if a man was late--and we had a few cases--what he got was the extra job of cleaning the cable deck. Above us was a cable deck, about five feet of head space in there, where all this tremendous amount of cable was. It was never properly cleaned up, as far as odds and ends and construction debris. So when we needed a nasty job, why, it was the cable deck.

Paul Stillwell: That provided plenty of motivation, I'm sure.

Commander Harralson: It did. It did. [Laughter]

Paul Stillwell: Who were the students in this school?

Commander Harralson: Prospective CIC officers and air controllers. There was a huge mass of electronic equipment in the building.

Paul Stillwell: Did you have simulators?

Commander Harralson: Oh, yes.

Paul Stillwell: Repeaters and so forth?

Commander Harralson: Yes. We had a room full of VK-8 repeaters, which were the leading instrument at the time, which they used for air control practice. In order to use them, they had a large room full of synthetic target generators. All of the target generators were from the Air Technical Training Command's design, and in no way met BuShips standards for electronics. The installation of them was by a private contractor. They no more than got these target generators installed, than they realized their max speed was too slow for the planes that they were dealing with. They had to be able to cope with 1,000-knot closure rates, and the simulators couldn't produce the speed.

A contract was let for modification that would give them this speed, and that's what was going on at the time I entered the picture. It was a tremendous job. It was the beginning of solid state electronics. The job went on and on. It was beginning to be behind time, and we were getting a lot of pressure from up front to get the job done. They needed it. So I was on this young engineer, from the contractor, to get the job done. One day he came in and was happy to advise me that they had the first unit working, and would I care to observe it?

So I went in, and they went to demonstrate it. It wasn't working. They fooled and fiddled, and they pulled out drawers and they changed cards. I spent about a half an hour waiting for them to fix it, but they didn't fix it. So I walked away. I said, "Call me when it's fixed."

I was sitting in my office and this Maddux, this young engineer, came in, and said, "Mr. Harralson, we've got to do some more work on it, but we're going ahead on the rest."

"Wait a minute." I said, "You can't modify the other units until you get this one going." He walked away.

He came back a little later and said, "Mr. Harralson, I don't want to be disrespectful here, but actually it's not between you and us; it's between Savannah and us. We asked you in merely as a courtesy."

I said, "Fine, I understand that, but understand this: availability is my prerogative. There are no more units available to you, until you've shown me that the first one will work"--words to that effect. So he walked out, and I went on about my business.

Pretty soon, here came the captain and the training officer--we had a Naval Reserve commander there that was head of the training--and several other officers and an engineer or two more. The captain walked up. I stood up. The captain said, "Harralson, what's going on here?"

So I told him, as briefly as I could, that the contractor couldn't make the first unit work, and he wouldn't get any more available until he showed me that the first one worked. The captain turned around and said to the others, "You heard the man," and walked out.

Paul Stillwell: And you felt great.

Commander Harralson: Yes, that did it.

Paul Stillwell: Did you have any input or responsibility in the curriculum, or were you just providing the electronic support?

Commander Harralson: Strictly electronic support. I had nothing to do with the training itself.

Paul Stillwell: Did this job, sort of, fall into a routine after a while?

Commander Harralson: It never did get routine. There was always something. There was an economy kick. The CO of the air station there was concerned with that. We had an enormous air-conditioning system because of the amount of concentration of vacuum tubes. Consider this. I think this one room had 24 VK-8 radar repeaters; a large, upright piece of equipment. I counted the tubes in one, and there were 80 vacuum tubes. And, of course, the vacuum tube is a heat generator. When you multiply 24 times 80, you get a lot of vacuum tubes and a lot of heat. Now, that's just this one room. We had all kinds of other rooms. The dissipation of heat was extremely important. But the captain, the CO of the air station, wanted to economize and run the air-conditioning only from 0800 to 1600. I was horrified.

    I went to my captain and explained this. I convinced him of this heat problem. He went to work on the air station captain. I guess they went to battle over it. The final result was a compromise. It had to be shut down eight hours. That was during the night. I thought that was a false economy, shutting that huge equipment down and letting--not a lot of heat, but some heat build. And it had to work that much harder the next day to bring it down. But that's what we had to live with.

    We had an interesting episode. A man came in one day, and he was from the agency that had to do with putting a satellite into orbit. I don't know what they called it then. But they had a tracking station that wasn't too far from us; just where, I'm not sure.

He was concerned about spare parts. He wanted to know what kind of spares we had and if they would be available. We were under a new spare-parts consolidation, and we had a pretty good system. So I took him over and showed him. We figured out that he could get parts there. But the thing that I remember--now, this was just before Sputnik, and there was a lot of talk going on about the United States putting one into orbit.* He told me what they were planning, vaguely. I remember my words to him, as he departed, "Do you think they can do that?" [Laughter] To me, it didn't seem possible.

Paul Stillwell: It turned out they could.

Commander Harralson: Yes. He said, "Yeah, I think they can." It wasn't too long after that when Sputnik arrived.

Paul Stillwell: How did this naval career of yours come to an end, after 20 years of active service?

Commander Harralson: Well, I was happy as a lark over there with my family. We were doing all these neat things. We belonged to the church. The people were very, very friendly on St. Simons Island. We joined the church. It was a very nice Presbyterian church. It was just nice living. It appeared to me to be the kind of living a civilian could have, until his kids grew up.

Then, as my tour at CIC was getting towards the end, when I knew I'd be getting orders, I began to think about my next duty, which I figured would be sea duty. My instinct told me I was due for a big carrier in the Med. The idea of going off like that, for another long tour didn't appeal to me. See, I'd had that year in Turkey, and then the time on the Mississippi; those were not conducive to good home life. And I had my 20 years in.

Also, at that time, we had a lot of reserve officers, most of them pilots. They came in during World War II. At the end of World War II, they went out of active duty but stayed in the reserve. Then they were called up during the Korean War. By the time the

---

*On 4 October 1957, the Soviet Union launched Sputnik I, the first artificial earth satellite. It caused great uproar in the United States, which had expected to be first in space.

Korean War was over, they took a look around and realized they had quite a bit of active duty time, and they were beginning to get up in years. It would have been more difficult for them to find a job. They all had those considerations. So a lot of them decided to make a full career of it. At that time they could, so they stayed in. Gee, I think some of them might have had something like 12, 13, 14 years in. Then, all of a sudden, they were being pushed out of active duty during cutbacks. I knew this commander who had played a big part in the school, as head of instruction, and he was going to have to leave. Boy, that really threw a chink in the works. I knew a lot of these guys, and it really was a curve. I felt sorry for some of them.

But I had my 20 in, and I was still a temporary; that's what I'd remain. The Navy was always rediscovering that I had no formal education, like somebody overlooked that somewheres. That was a big drawback. All those things added together, so I submitted my letter.

Paul Stillwell: Did you feel any pangs of regret, taking off the uniform after 20 years?

Commander Harralson: You bet I did. Sometimes I would think, "Oh, my Lord, what have I done? Am I doing the right thing? Did I do the right thing?" Yes, I had a lot of second thoughts. I really liked the Navy.

Paul Stillwell: Well, obviously, in much less detail, maybe you could give me the highlights of the 40 years that have ensued between then and now.

Commander Harralson: Well, we came back out to California. I had no trouble getting a job at Aerojet General Corporation, which manufactured jet engines, rocket engines.

Paul Stillwell: Where was that?

Commander Harralson: In Sacramento, California. We bought a home in Rancho Cordova, not far from the Aerojet plant. I hired in at a salary that, added to my retirement pay, equaled almost to the dollar what I was getting on active duty, with full base pay and longevity and the other allowances. I thought that was pretty good, if I could make this transition and not take a cut in money.

I had an interesting job at Aerojet. I worked first in logistics, which covers about anything. I had to do with ground support equipment for the Titan missile engines. We made only the engines, liquid rocket engines. I wrote up field changes. When they submitted changes to ground support equipment, they came to me, and I drafted the description of the change for the contract. Then I had to send a team in the field to accomplish the job.

At Aerojet, they had all these different projects going. When a project petered out, you had to go out and seek a new job, hopefully within the plant, and carry on without any loss. That happened with the ground support. Originally, different projects came to us for support equipment. But pretty soon they'd begin to think, "Let's do our own ground support." So the ground support equipment department died. I got into the Titan engine program, doing the same thing; drafting up call contracts. We were involved also in configuration management. It was very hectic at times. I had over me a young man who was a good boss, a very good boss.

Then I got into the Apollo program. We made the service module engine for the lunar landing effort. The service module engine was the engine that had to fire to bring them home. They were concerned about reliability.

Paul Stillwell: Understandably. [Laughter]

Commander Harralson: That was a job that was boring and then frantic, at times. But all this time, I was fighting a stomach ulcer. Most people thought it was due to the stress, but I didn't think it was. I thought it had to do with my allergies. But I would be going somewheres and fall flat on my face. I had a stomach ulcer that didn't hurt much, but just started bleeding. It would be bleeding, and I wouldn't know it. I would fall over, and they would haul me off to the hospital. That caused a problem. I wrestled with it for about 10 or 11 years. It made me quit smoking, which is the best thing I ever did.

I had in about 9 years, 11 months. When I was hired at Aerojet, the population there was about 4,000. Those were boom times: government contracts, cost-plus-fixed-fee type of things--like the gold rush. The population rose up to almost 24,000. Then after it peaked, there was a while, and then it began to decline. When it came down to 4,000 again, I had 9 years, 11 months, and they were going to lay me off. It had gotten down to where it was only me and my boss, and he had told me, "The next one that goes is going to be you. It's either you or me, and it's going to be you." [Laughter]

But he asked me if I was interested in the retirement system, and I said I was. Well, if you have ten years in, you have a vested interest in the system they had. And I definitely was interested. So he was able to get me three more months, and put me over the hump. I was laid off, but I had a vested interest in the retirement, which has proven quite worthwhile.

I tried to get a job around Sacramento, even a lesser job, but I couldn't find one that I felt was adequate. I found a job in the South Bay area, with Dalmo Victor. They made the radar for an Air Force fighter--F-111.[*] This is one that has a radar in it, and it goes in low level. The radar takes it up and over the hills, and that sort of thing. But, anyhow, that's what it was. Then my ulcer struck again, and they hauled me off to a hospital. When I finally recuperated enough to go back to work, I got out on the freeway and into terrible commuter traffic. It took me an hour to go 20 miles. By the time I got there, I was a nervous wreck. I walked in and I said, "I quit." It was a limbo period, downhill. I went into a blue funk. It seems like that part of you that has to do with courage had melted or disappeared. But I had a strong wife, fortunately, and she stayed with me.

She took a job teaching. She hadn't taught for quite a while. She taught the third grade, and I stayed home as chief cook and bottle washer for the house. My kids talked me into going to college. I think it was the last year of my GI eligibility, but I got in on that.[*]

Paul Stillwell: When was that?

Commander Harralson: In 1969. I went to a junior college for two years, got all my general ed requirements. Then I went to California State University, Sacramento, and

---

*The F-111--originally designated TFX--was a controversial fighter plane that Secretary of Defense Robert McNamara tried to develop in the 1960s for use by both the Air Force and the Navy.

received a degree with two majors, Spanish and art. [Laughter] The college was for therapeutic purposes. In the meantime, I'd bought two acres up here and had started the house.

Paul Stillwell: Well, please tell me about what it was like to mix with that era's college students?

Commander Harralson: It was a wonderful experience. I found some of the young students very hostile, but one the whole young people were very nice. I concluded it depended on what kind of relationship they had had with their father. It was the age of the hippies, the flower children, Vietnam, all the turmoil of that era. It was very interesting. Generally, I had no problems with instructors, or really with any of the students. I did run into one that--we seemed to clash. He seemed to wonder what in the hell I was doing there. It was a wonderful, wonderful experience.

It took me five years. I graduated with a pretty good average. I was invited to go to Burgos, Spain, with my Spanish on a master's program. I was on the verge of becoming fluent. But I was committed to the house, and it was taking all of our money. I couldn't afford it. I couldn't afford the time. So my wife got an apartment in Sacramento, and I began to go to work up here in earnest.

Paul Stillwell: Doing what?

Commander Harralson: Building the house with my own hammer and saw. With the exception of some of the foundation work and the cinder block basement, I did it all myself.

Paul Stillwell: And from my last three days' observation, it's a very pleasant, comfortable house.

---

*The GI Bill, officially the Servicemen's Readjustment Act of 1944, provided educational assistance and other benefits to all veterans honorably discharged with six or more months of active service after 16 September 1940.

Commander Harralson: Well, I thank you very much.

Paul Stillwell: One other question that occurs, and this may tie in with the ulcers, did you ever have any evidence that your imprisonment had an effect on your physical condition?

Commander Harralson: No. I think it had nothing to do with it. And recent findings support that. Ninety percent of the ulcers, now they believe, are caused by bacteria. And the treatment is with antibiotics.

Paul Stillwell: Could you comment, also, on your observation concerning the former POWs who harbor a hatred and those who don't?

Commander Harralson: I feel sorry for them. I've known several that were full of this bitter hatred. I know how they acquired it. And I know that there are a lot of them that went through worse things than I did. Some of the camps, especially those that remained in the Philippines, had a much more brutal experience. So I can see why some men would have a hatred that couldn't be let go of. But it was really to their own advantage. I give myself credit, because I realized that if I harbored hatred, it would eat at me. So I made a conscious effort to let go of it. I was very fortunate in the wife I found and the children we had. It's been a tremendous help to be in the normal life, without all of this hatred baggage.

I have a quote in one of my folders in the basement. It's by one of the movie stars. It has to the effect that your soul is made up of your life experiences, to be baggage for the rest of your life--or ammunition. And I like that.*

Paul Stillwell: Well, please tell me about your children.

Commander Harralson: I have two boys and a girl. My oldest, Joseph, has just had his 50th birthday--the big 5-0. He's a professor of mechanical engineering at the Sacramento

---

*The quotation is from Audrey Hepburn: "Your soul is nourished by all of your experiences. It gives you baggage for the rest of your life--and ammunition, if you like."

State University, California. He's a hands-on type of professor. He's at home at a lathe and other machinery. He designed and built the patterns for a racing engine that has been a success, although the vehicle that it is in has not. But it's a tremendous engine, 450 horsepower, and it's his and his alone, as far as design. He learned to be a pattern maker. He made patterns for the castings for this engine, which requires accurate and extensive woodwork. I hold my son in awe.

He, his wife, my daughter, and her husband jointly own 15 acres of grapes: Chardonnay, Zinfandel, and one other type I can't spell. That takes a lot of their extra time. He's been a wonderful son. I am extremely proud of him. My other son, Arthur, is a professor of clinical pharmacology at the University of Pacific. He, too, is a wonderful son, I hold in awe.

All my children have been good. We revel in the fact that they gave us no serious problems. We had the usual. They're all successful professionals. My daughter Helen is a RN, and is especially trained in neonatal intensive care. She's checked out and runs what they call an ECMO machine, which has to do with preemie babies that can't breathe very well. She works very hard, and I'm proud of her.

It's my children that have made my life these years--my wife and I--we realize we have been extremely lucky. Because we know that having children and raising them is a hard job, and there's a lot of just plain luck involved in it. And we were lucky.

Paul Stillwell: How many grandchildren?

Commander Harralson: I have six grandchildren, five granddaughters and one grandson. We have enjoyed them. All of my children live in our vicinity, and our grandchildren have come and gone. We have watched them grow, and we have been delighted with them. We are on the best of terms with all of them. They love us dearly. We love them.

Paul Stillwell: Well, please describe your current life, here in Shingle Springs.

Commander Harralson: Until Mr. Stillwell showed on the scene, it was very placid, uneventful. [Laughter] And he has cured me of telling sea stories. [Laughter]

Paul Stillwell: Well, then let me describe it. You've got two acres of woodland here: a bucolic setting, a relaxing environment, occasionally punctuated by the sounds of a crowing rooster, a barking dog, and a braying burro.

Well, I just want to say, after having heard your tales, I'm most grateful to you for putting these on the record. You have a gift for story telling, and your memory is superb. Your service to your country is one legacy, and this oral history is yet another legacy. And I thank you.

Commander Harralson: Those are very kind words. I thank you.

Index to the Oral History of Lieutenant Commander Richard A. Harralson, U.S. Navy (Retired)

Advancement in Rating

For junior enlisted men in the aircraft carrier Saratoga (CV-3) in the late 1930s, advancement depended on the initiative of individual sailors, 39, 42-43; advancement was difficult in the late 1930s because there were so few openings, 60-61, 80; value of correspondence courses in 1940 to prepare an individual for advancement exams, 130-131

Aerojet General Corporation

Jet engine manufacturer for which Harralson worked after leaving active duty in 1957, 361-362

Aircraft Battle Force, U.S. Fleet

In the late 1930s the flag allowance radio gang performed various duties on behalf of the staff, 58-60, 147-148; setup for flag radio in the late 1930s on board the aircraft carrier Lexington (CV-2), 61-62, 64, 66-68, 79; in the late 1930s Vice Admiral Ernest J. King served as the type commander, 63-64, 71-72; in 1939 Captain John Hoover, AirBatFor chief of staff, laid down tough rules for the squadrons at North Island, 84-85

Air Force, U.S.

The B-36 Peacemaker bomber was noisy while going through tests at San Diego in 1950, 271

Alcohol

When young sailors wore civilian clothes while on liberty in the late 1930s, they weren't asked for proof of age if they could pay for their beers, 28-29; in early 1939 the crew from the aircraft carrier Lexington (CV-2) went ashore for beer and baseball at Guantanamo Bay, Cuba, 69-70; American sailors' drinking habits during liberty in China and the Philippines shortly before World War II, 114-115, 122, 138-139; in 1937 the crew of the cruiser Augusta (CA-31) got drunk during a visit to Vladivostok in the Soviet Union, 160; beer flowed freely at an early 1950s party in Milwaukee for students and staff from the technical training course at Great Lakes, Illinois, 302

Ankara, Turkey

In 1954 Harralson spent time in the city while waiting to report for duty at Amasra to collect submarine sound signatures, 311-312

Antiair Warfare

The antiaircraft guns of the heavy cruiser Houston (CA-30) had been beefed up before she took over in November 1940 as flagship of the Asiatic Fleet, 141-142; in the mid-1950s, the missile test ship Mississippi (EAG-128) fired Terrier missiles against drones, 337, 343

Antisubmarine Warfare
In 1954-55 Harralson had duty at Amasra, Turkey, in charge of a group that used hydrophones to collect submarine sound signatures from the Black Sea, 311-331

Army, U.S.
In 1941 operated radio communications from the island of Corregidor in the Philippines, 155-156; General Douglas MacArthur's lackluster response in December 1941 when the Japanese attacked the Philippines, 163-164; Army personnel held out on Corregidor until May of 1942 when it was captured by the Japanese, 173-192

Army Air Forces, U.S.
Clark Field and Nichols Field in the Philippines were hit by Japanese bombers at the onset of war in December 1941, 161-162; B-29 bombing of Japanese home islands late in World War II, 214-217, 230-231; in August 1945 B-29s dropped atomic bombs on Japan, 236-237

Asiatic Fleet, U.S.
In the 1930s Harralson's brother Bill served with the Marine Corps on the Asiatic station, 5-6, 93; work of the flag allowance radio gang on board the fleet flagship Augusta (CA-31) shortly before World War II, 92-93, 101-106, 124-125, 129-133; flagship visits to various ports, 93-97, 108-118, 121-122, 135-139, 159-160; composition of, 118-119, 135-136; flag transferred in November 1940 from the Augusta to the cruiser Houston (CA-30), 140-141; in the late 1930s and early 1940s enlisted men in the fleet often shacked up with Oriental women rather than getting married, 149-151

Athens, Greece
Harralson made an interesting tour of the city in 1954 while en route to duty in Turkey, 310-311

Atomic Bombs
Used against Japan in the summer of 1945, 236-237

Augusta, USS (CA-31)
Messing and berthing arrangements on board in 1940, 92, 126-128; activities of the Asiatic Fleet flag allowance radio gang in the period shortly before World War II, 92-93, 101-106, 124-125, 129-133; visited various ports in the Far East, 93-99, 108-118, 121-122, 135-139, 159-160; in early 1940 ran aground near Palawan in the Philippine Islands, 95-96; dry-docked at Subic Bay in the Philippines, 97-98, 101; a crew member killed himself shortly before World War II because he never had any relief from the ship, 114-115; shipboard environment in 1940, 119-121, 133-134;

gunnery, 134; relieved in November 1940 as fleet flagship by the heavy cruiser Houston (CA-30), 140-141

B-29 Superfortress
Bombing of Japanese home islands late in World War II, 214-217, 230-231; in August 1945 dropped atomic bombs on Japan, 236-237

B-36 Peacemaker
Air Force bomber that was noisy while going through tests at San Diego in 1950, 271

Barbados
In early 1939 served as the site of liberty for the crew of the aircraft carrier Lexington (CV-2), 73-74

Baseball
In early 1939 the crew from the aircraft carrier Lexington (CV-2) went ashore for beer and baseball at Guantanamo Bay, Cuba, 69-70

Bell Telephone Company
In 1954, at a company laboratory in New Jersey, gave Harralson instruction for duty he would be carrying out in Turkey to gather sound signatures from the Black Sea, 307-308; analyzed the tapes sent back from Turkey, 314-315, 318-319, 320-321; equipment supplied by Bell, 328-330

Black Sea
In 1954-55 Harralson had duty at Amasra, Turkey, in charge of a group that used hydrophones to collect submarine sound signatures from the Black Sea, 311-331

Blakely, Vice Admiral Charles A., USN (USNA, 1903)
In 1939-40 served as Commander Aircraft Battle Force, 79

Bombing
In December 1941 the Japanese bombed the Cavite Navy Yard in the Philippines, 165-169; bombing of Corregidor on Christmas of 1941, 174-175; of the Japan home islands late in World War II, 213-217, 230-231; in August 1945 U.S. B-29s dropped atomic bombs on Japan, 236-237

Bremerton, Washington
In the late 1930s the crew of the aircraft carrier Saratoga (CV-3) scraped and painted the ship's bottom at the Puget Sound Navy Yard, 45-46; as a liberty town in the late 1930s, 47-48

Brown, Rear Admiral John H., Jr., USN (USNA, 1914)
In the late 1940s served as the Commandant of the Portsmouth, New Hampshire, Naval Base, 250, 254-255, 262-263

Brown, Lieutenant Commander Reginald O., USN
In the early 1950s was in charge of the electronic maintenance school at Great Lakes, Illinois, 305-306

Bureau of Ships
In 1954-55 sent Harralson on a temporary duty assignment to Turkey to gather sound signatures from the Black Sea, 307-331

California, USS (BB-44)
Smashed a boardwalk while making a landing in the late 1930s at the foot of Broadway in San Diego, 32; sported an early radar antenna, 32-33

Cavite, Philippine Islands
In 1941 some of the enlisted men at the Navy radio station were unhappy because a married radioman started receiving an additional pay allowance, 78-79; operation in 1941 of the Navy radio station at Cavite, 106-107, 143-147, 149-158, 161; the onset of war in December 1941 meant that sailors didn't have to pay their debts, 136-137; in 1941 Pan American's Clipper planes operated in and out of Cavite, 145-146; disruption of the radio station when war started in December 1941, 161; in December 1941 the Japanese bombed the Cavite Navy Yard, 165-169; aftermath of the bombing, 169-172

China
Shanghai was attractive as a site for liberty for sailors who were part of the Asiatic Fleet flag allowance in the period shortly before the beginning of World War II, 93, 97, 108-112, 121, 135-136; at Tsingtao there were representatives from other nations, 97, 113, 116-118, 122-123; Tsingtao's liberty attractions for sailors, 113-117; Admiral Thomas Hart used the yacht Isabel (PY-10) for a trip to Chefoo, 123-124

Clark, Radioman First Class Ernest, USN
After being recalled from the fleet reserve, he went to the Philippines on board a merchant ship in December 1941 and was stranded there when war started, 162; as a prisoner of war, made a radio broadcast from Japan that included the names of fellow prisoners, 227-228

Clarke, Commander Frank H., USN
In the late 1940s and early 1950s served as officer in charge of the electronics maintenance school at Great Lakes, 266, 305

Codebreaking
In the late 1930s a radioman named Wimpy Anderson left the flag allowance of Aircraft Battle Force and went to Washington, D.C., to learn cryptography, 147-148; in the early 1940s Anderson wound up in crypto duty on Corregidor in the Philippines, 148-149; the crypto unit on Corregidor was evacuated prior to the Japanese capture of the island in May 1942, 184; in 1942 Japanese Army officers interrogated U.S. Navy radiomen to see if they had any knowledge of codes, 201-202

Combat Information Center Officer School, Glynco, Georgia
Training role in the mid-1950s for prospective CIC officers, 354-361

Communications
Harralson's early interest in the 1930s in crystal sets and ham radio, 3-4, 8, 10-13; Navy radio school in 1938 at San Diego taught Morse Code and radio procedures, 21-24; work of the radio gang in the late 1930s on board the aircraft carrier Saratoga (CV-3), 34, 36-37, 39-45, 49; in the late 1930s the flag allowance radio gang performed various duties on behalf of the staff of Commander Aircraft Battle Force, 58-60; setup for ComAirBatFor flag radio in the late 1930s on board the aircraft carrier Lexington (CV-2), 61-62, 64, 66-68, 79; visual signaling during a 1939 war game in the Caribbean, 71-72; work of the flag allowance radio gang on board the Asiatic Fleet flagship Augusta (CA-31) shortly before World War II, 92-93, 101-106, 124-125, 129-133; early radio tests were conducted in 1899 off New Jersey, 100-101; operations in 1941 the Navy radio station at Cavite in the Philippines, 106-107, 143-147, 149-158, 161; description of radio transmitters on board the Augusta, 135; radio setup on board the heavy cruiser Houston (CA-30) in November 1940 when she became flagship of the Asiatic Fleet, 142-143; radio broadcast from a prisoner of war camp included the names of American prisoners, 227-228; operation of the radio station at the Portsmouth, New Hampshire, Naval Base in the late 1940s, 250-263, 274-275; radio communications in the early 1950s by the escort carrier Sicily (CVE-118), 280-281, 293; by the early 1950s radio teletype had largely replaced CW, 304-305; in the mid-1950s on board the missile test ship Mississippi (EAG-128), 347, 350

Cook, Radioman First Class Louis, USN
Large man who told tall tales to his shipmates while serving in the heavy cruiser Augusta (CA-31) shortly before World War II, 127; skill in sending radio messages in Morse code, 131-132

Corregidor, Philippine Islands
In the early 1940s was the site of Navy radio codebreaking, 148-149; operation of Army communications, 155-156, 174; provided a temporary home for a number of Navy radioman evacuated from Cavite in December 1941 after it was bombed by the Japanese, 173-180; bombed by the Japanese on Christmas of 1941, 174-175; in May of 1942 the Japanese captured the island and took American prisoners, 181-192

Courts-Martial
Held at Great Lakes, Illinois, in the early 1950s, shortly after the Uniform Code of Military Justice went into effect, 294-298; in the mid-1950s on board the missile test ship Mississippi (EAG-128), 342-343

Covert, Radioman Second Class Lawrence W., USN
   After being captured by the Japanese in the Philippines in May 1942, he became a real entrepreneur as a prisoner of war, 196

Cuba
   In early 1939 the crew from the aircraft carrier Lexington (CV-2) went ashore for beer and baseball at Guantanamo Bay, 69-70

Dewey Dry Dock
   For many years prior to World War II was used at Subic Bay in the Philippines for maintenance and repair work on U.S. Navy ships, 96-98, 100-101

Disciplinary Matters
   Courts-martial were held at Great Lakes, Illinois, in the early 1950s, shortly after the Uniform Code of Military Justice went into effect, 294-298; in the mid-1950s on board the missile test ship Mississippi (EAG-128), 341-343

Duerfeldt, Captain Clifford H., USN (USNA, 1926)
   As commanding officer of the escort carrier Sicily (CVE-118) in early 1950, emphasized the importance of electronics, 267-268

Enlisted Personnel
   Recruit training in 1937 at San Diego, 6, 9, 13-20, 25-28; professional training for radiomen strikers in the late 1930s, 21-24, 28-31; in the late 1930s enlisted men in uniform were not always welcome at better places in San Diego, 27-28; after men got out of boot camp in San Diego, they rented lockers ashore so they could make liberty in civilian clothes, 28-29; interaction with older sailors, 31-32; for junior enlisted men in the aircraft carrier Saratoga (CV-3) in the late 1930s, advancement depended on the initiative of individual sailors, 39, 42-43; enlisted pilots made a spectacular save of a tangled parachutist in the late 1930s while operating from the aircraft carrier Lexington (CV-2), 53-54; advancement was difficult in the late 1930s because there were so few openings, 60-61, 80; in the early 1940s the Navy began paying an additional allowance to enlisted men who were married, 78-79; in the late 1930s and early 1940s enlisted men in the Asiatic Fleet often shacked up with Oriental women rather than getting married, 149-151; in 1954-55 a group of enlisted technicians on at Amasra, Turkey, used hydrophones to collect submarine sound signatures from the Black Sea, 311-331

Families of Servicemen
   In the late 1930s and early 1940s, few of the Navy's lower-rated enlisted men were married, 78; in the early 1940s some Asiatic Fleet sailors lived with foreign-born wives in the Far East, 122-123; housing was difficult for Navy families in the period right after World War II, 245-247; the family of Harralson's wife came to visit in New Hampshire in the late 1940s and enabled the couple to have a holiday in New York, 258-262; in 1950 Harralson's wife and family drove across country when his ship, the escort carrier Sicily (CVE-118), was assigned to San Diego, 271; in the

early 1950s Captain John S. Thach, commanding officer of the escort carrier Sicily (CVE-118), charmed the wives of the ship's officers, 281; when Harralson's family was ousted from Navy housing in San Diego in the early 1950s, his wife had to arrange to buy a house, 289; the Navy's role in the early 1950s in handling family squabbles at the Great Lakes Naval Training Center, 299-300; life for Harralson's family from 1952 to 1954 at Great Lakes, 305-307; life for Harralson's family in 1956-57 in Georgia, 354-355, 360

Fernald, Commander James M., USN
Demanding individual who served shortly before World War II as communication officer on the Asiatic Fleet staff, 93-94, 102-105, 194-195

Fighter Direction
Use of radar on board the escort carrier Sicily (CVE-118) in the early 1950s to provide vectors to fighter aircraft, 275, 278-279

Fleet Problems
In early 1939, the aircraft carrier Lexington (CV-2) and other ships of the Battle Force engaged in Fleet Problem XX in the Caribbean, 64-73

Flying Boats
In 1941 Pan American's Clipper planes operated in and out of Cavite in the Philippines, 145-146

Food
Messing arrangements on board the transport Henderson (AP-1) in 1939, during a voyage to the Far East, 87-90; available in restaurants in the early 1940s at Tsingtao, China, 113; in 1940 on board the heavy cruiser Augusta (CA-31), 126-128; on Christmas of 1941 cooks on Corregidor prepared a fine holiday meal, but the troops weren't able to eat it because of Japanese bombing, 174-175; slim rations thereafter, 175-177; meager food for American prisoners of war, 188-189, 191-193, 196, 198, 204-205, 207, 222, 227; in World War II prisoner of war daydreams often focused on food, 219-220; after being released from prison camp, Harralson ate a lot, 239-240; meal served to Harralson by a Japanese family in the early 1950s when he was in Yokohama on liberty, 285; Harralson enjoyed sumptuous meals in Italy and Greece in 1954 while en route to duty in Turkey, 310-311; in the mid-1950s the peppers served in Turkey were very hot, 326

Genessee, USS (ATO-55)
Auxiliary tugboat captured by the Japanese in the Philippine Islands in May of 1942, 194

Gold Star, USS (AK-12)
Cargo ship that operated primarily out of Guam while providing logistic services in the Far East in the years shortly before World War II, 90-91

Great Lakes, Illinois, Naval Training Center
Site of electronics technician school in the period shortly after World War II, 246-248; in the early 1950s was the site of electronics maintenance school, 264-266, 303-307; handling of legal and disciplinary matters in the early 1950s, 294-307

Greece
Harralson made an interesting tour of Athens in 1954 while en route to duty in Turkey, 310-311

Greenwell, Chief Radio Electrician Peter Albert Earl, USN
In 1938 served as officer in charge of radioman school at San Diego, 21

Guam, Marianas Islands
In 1939 served as a way station when personnel on board the transport Henderson (AP-1) were making their way to the Asiatic Fleet for duty, 90-92

Guantanamo Bay, Cuba
In early 1939 the crew from the aircraft carrier Lexington (CV-2) went ashore for beer and baseball at Guantanamo Bay, 69-70

Gunnery—Naval
Fired in 1940-41 by the heavy cruiser Augusta (CA-31), 134

Habitability
In the late 1930s berthing compartments on board the aircraft carrier Lexington (CV-2) were too hot for sleeping when the ship was in the tropics, 68-69; messing and berthing arrangements on board the heavy cruiser Augusta (CA-31) in 1940-41, 92, 126-128; in the mid-1950s the ship's officers on board the missile test ship Mississippi (EAG-128) enjoyed luxurious living quarters, 334

Haiti
In early 1939 served as a mediocre site of liberty for the crew of the aircraft carrier Lexington (CV-2), 72

Halsey, Rear Admiral William F., Jr., USN (USNA, 1904)
In 1939 was a carrier division commander during a war game in the Caribbean, 72

Harralson, Lieutenant Commander Richard A., U.S. Navy (Retired)
Boyhood in California in the 1920s and 1930s, 1-13; parents of, 1-2, 5-8, 13-14; siblings of, 5-7; in the late 1930s enlisted in the Navy and went through recruit training at San Diego, 6, 9, 13-20, 25-28; education of in California, 7-8; in 1938 attended radio school at San Diego, 21-24, 28-31; served in 1938 in the aircraft carrier Saratoga (CV-3), 33-37, 39-58; in 1938-39 was assigned officially to Scouting Squadron Three and for a time sub-assigned to the flag allowance of Commander Aircraft Battle Force, 57-86; duty in 1940-41 as part of the Asiatic Fleet flag allowance, 86-143; served in 1941 at the Navy radio station at Cavite in the

Philippine Islands, 143-172; spent the early months of 1942 on the island fortress of Corregidor in Manila Bay, 173-184; as a prisoner of the Japanese during the bulk of World War II, 185-235; Nisei daughter-in-law, 229; repatriation from Japan after being released from prison, 236-243; in 1945 met a WAVE named Naomi Winkler, who became his wife, 243-244, 247, 258-262, 266, 271, 289, 307, 363-365; in 1946 was stationed at the Point Loma Electronics Laboratory in San Diego, 245-247; in 1946 was a student in the electronics technician school at Great Lakes, 246-248; in October 1946 became a commissioned officer, 247-248; served from 1946 to 1948 as officer in charge of the Navy radio station at Portsmouth, New Hampshire, 248-263, 274-275; children of, 255, 258, 261, 264, 266, 271, 289, 305-307, 355, 365-366; in 1949 attended electronics maintenance school at Great Lakes, 264-266; from 1950 to 1952 served in the escort carrier Sicily (CVE-118), 266-293; duty from 1952 to 1954 as an instructor at the electronics maintenance school at Great Lakes, 294-307; served on temporary additional duty in 1954-55 on a Bureau of Ships intelligence-gathering project in Turkey, 308-331; in 1955-56 served as communication officer of the missile test ship Mississippi (EAG-128), 332-354; completed active duty by serving in 1956-57 as electronics maintenance officer for the Combat Information Center Officer School in Glynco, Georgia, 354-361; post-retirement activities, 361-367

Harris, Radioman First Class Kenneth L., USN
In 1941, while stationed at Cavite in the Philippines, got in trouble with the shore patrol in Manila, 152-153

Hart, Admiral Thomas C., USN (USNA, 1897)
Short in stature, 96; as Commander in Chief Asiatic Fleet shortly before World War II, imposed a restriction on fleet ships in Tsingtao, China, as the result of an international incident shortly before World War II, 117; made a trip to Chefoo, China, on board the yacht Isabel (PY-10), 123-124; interested in press news that came in by radio, 124

Henderson, USS (AP-1)
Transport that in 1939 carried naval personnel from the West Coast to duty with the Asiatic Fleet, 86-88

Hogaboom, First Lieutenant William F., USMC (USNA, 1939)
Was captured in the Philippines in 1942 and killed on board a POW ship in 1944, 197

Hooper, Radioman Second Class Harold E., USN
In 1939 was transferred to duty with the Asiatic Fleet in the Far East, 90; service in the flag allowance on board the flagship Augusta (CA-31), 95, 109; on liberty in the Far East, 114, 116; was stationed on the island of Corregidor in the early part of World War II, 174, 179-180, 190; as a prisoner of war in Japan, 221

Hoover, Captain John H., USN (USNA, 1907)
Relationship in the late 1930s with Vice Admiral Ernest J. King when Hoover was commanding the aircraft carrier Lexington (CV-2) and King was embarked, 64; in early 1939 secured the heads on board the Lexington because of a shortage of fresh water, 73; in 1939 he became chief of staff to Commander Aircraft Battle Force and caused unhappiness with a temporary ban of coffee in the flag radio spaces, 79; laid down tough rules for the squadrons at North Island NAS, 84-85

Houston, USS (CA-30)
In November 1940, at Manila, relieved the heavy cruiser Augusta (CA-31) as flagship of the U.S. Asiatic Fleet, 140-141; upon arrival in the Far East, the ship had an enhanced antiaircraft capability and a larger crew than the Augusta, 141-142; radio equipment capability, 142-143; atmosphere among crew members, 143

Hungnam, Korea
Evacuation of Marine Corps in late 1950s by the escort carrier Sicily (CVE-118), 282

Inchon, Korea
Use of radar in the early 1950s by the escort carrier Sicily (CVE-118) while approaching Inchon's Wolmi-Do Island, 276-277; invasion of in September 1950, 277

Inspections
In 1940-41 on board the Asiatic Fleet flagship Augusta (CA-31), 119-120

Intelligence
In 1954-55 Harralson had duty at Amasra, Turkey, in charge of a group that used hydrophones to collect submarine sound signatures from the Black Sea, 311-331

Isabel, USS (PY-10)
Yacht that served as a temporary flagship around 1940 for Admiral Thomas Hart, Commander in Chief Asiatic Fleet, 123-124; escaped to Australia when World War II began, 169

Italy
Harralson made an interesting tour of Rome in 1954 while en route to duty in Turkey, 309-310

Japan
In December 1941 the Japanese bombed the Cavite Navy Yard in the Philippines, 165-169; from 1942 to 1945 a group of American prisoners of war, captured in the Philippines, worked in a shipyard in Yokohama, 205-217, 219-229; attacks on the home islands by American bombers late in the war, 213-217, 230-231; prisoners worked to turn a golf course into a garden, 217-218; internment of Japanese-Americans in the United States during World War II, 228-229; in the summer of 1945 prisoners were transferred to a camp called Omori, 230-231; transfer of

prisoners in 1945 to a camp at Wakasenen to work in an iron foundry, 231-232; harrowing medical experiments on Americans in a prison camp at Shinagawa, 233-234; release of the American prisoners when the war ended, 233, 235-236; in August 1945 U.S. B-29s dropped atomic bombs on Japan, 236-237; in the summer of 1950 the escort carrier Sicily (CVE-118) stopped at Yokosuka and Sasebo en route participation in the Korean War, 272-274; in the early 1950s Harralson was in Yokohama on liberty and went to visit a Japanese family, 284-286

Japanese Army
In 1940 Japanese soldiers performed training maneuvers in Tsingtao, China, and sometimes got into hassles with Americans, 116-118; in May of 1942 captured the island of Corregidor in the Philippines and took American prisoners, 181-192; in 1942 conducted interrogation of American prisoners of war, 201-202

Japanese Navy
Maintained warships at Tsingtao, China, in the years just before World War II, 97, 116-118; perception of the capability of ships in Japan itself, 159

Jarvis, Lieutenant Commander Benjamin C., USN (USNA, 1939)
In the late 1940s served as aide to the commandant of the Portsmouth, New Hampshire, Naval Base, 250, 262-263

Joint Military Mission for Aid to Turkey
Had local control of Harralson's activities in 1954-55 while he was on duty in Amasra to do Black Sea intelligence collection on behalf of the Bureau of Ships, 311-331

Kenney, Lieutenant Paul G., USN
In the late 1940s was a student at the electronics maintenance course at Great Lakes, 264, 266

Kimmel, Admiral Husband E., USN (USNA, 1904)
His active naval career came to an abrupt end shortly after the December 1941 raid on Pearl Harbor by the Japanese Navy, 163

King, Vice Admiral Ernest J., USN (USNA, 1901)
Embarked in the aircraft carrier Lexington (CV-2) in the late 1930s while serving as Commander Aircraft Battle Force, 63-64, 71-72

Korean War
Soon after the war started in late June of 1950, the escort carrier Sicily (CVE-118) deployed westward from San Diego to take part, 272-274; the Sicily's operations in the Yellow Sea to provide close air support, 275; evacuation of in late 1950 of Marine Corps personnel from Hungnam, Korea, by the Sicily, 282

Lauer, Radioman Second Class Willard L, USN
  In 1939 was transferred from aviation duty to serve with the Asiatic Fleet in the Far East, 89; service shortly before World War II in the Asiatic Fleet flag allowance, 106-107; on liberty in the Far East, 114, 138; was captured by the Japanese in May 1942 after service on board the auxiliary tug Genessee (ATO-55), 194-195; as prisoner in Japan, 232

Leave and Liberty
  For recruits at San Diego in 1937, liberty involved visiting the local YMCA and patronizing merchants in the city's downtown area, 25-28; in the late 1930s enlisted men in uniform were not always welcome at better places in San Diego, 27-28; after men got out of boot camp in San Diego, they rented lockers ashore so they could make liberty in civilian clothes, 28-29; interaction with older sailors, 31-32; in the Puget Sound area in the late 1930s, 47-48; operation of liberty boats in the late 1930s by the aircraft carrier Saratoga (CV-3), 54-55; in the late 1930s sailors frequented a Long Beach amusement park known as the Pike, 55-56; in early 1939 the crew from the aircraft carrier Lexington (CV-2) went ashore for beer and baseball at Guantanamo Bay, Cuba, 69-70; in early 1939 in Haiti, 72; in Barbados, 73-74; in early 1939 in Norfolk, Virginia, 77; in 1939 in Honolulu, Hawaii, 88-89; in various ports in the Far East during the period shortly before the beginning of World War II, 93-99, 108-111, 113-118, 121-123, 135-139, 150-151, 160-162; in 1950 the escort carrier Sicily (CVE-118) visited Panama, 270-271; in the early 1950s Harralson was in Yokohama, Japan, on liberty and went to visit a Japanese family, 284-286; problems when crew members of the Sicily were late getting back to the ship in Sasebo, Japan, during the Korean War, 290-291; trip to Milwaukee in the early 1950s as the site of a party for students at the technical training school at Great Lakes, Illinois, 302; Harralson made an interesting tours of Rome and Athens in 1954 while en route to duty in Turkey, 309-311

Legal Matters
  Courts-martial were held at Great Lakes, Illinois, in the early 1950s, shortly after the Uniform Code of Military Justice went into effect, 294-298

Lexington, USS (CV-2)
  In the late 1930s enlisted naval aviation pilots from the ship performed a spectacular save of a man tangled up in a parachute, 53-54; setup for flag radio in the late 1930s, serving Commander Aircraft Battle Force, 61-62, 64, 66-68, 79; aircraft operations, 62-63; Vice Admiral Ernest J. King was embarked as ComAirBatFor, 63-64; in early 1939 traveled through the Panama Canal, 64-65, 68; berthing conditions on board, 68-69; in early 1939 members of the crew went ashore for beer and baseball at Guantanamo Bay, 69-70; involvement in early 1939 in Fleet Problem XX in the Caribbean, 71-73; scarcity of fresh water on board ship, 73; liberty ports following the fleet problem, 73-74; arrangement of the ship's hawsepipes in relation to the clipper bow, 74-75; Marines were part of the crew, 75-76; a planned visit to New York City in the spring of 1939 was cancelled because of the international situation, 76-78

Long Beach/San Pedro, California
Operation of liberty boats in the late 1930s by the aircraft carrier Saratoga (CV-3), 54-55; in the late 1930s sailors frequented a Long Beach amusement park known as the Pike, 55-56

Lyons, Radioman First Class Anthony J., USN
In the years just before World War II, he served in the Asiatic Fleet and married a Russian woman in China, 122-123, 151-152, 159

MacArthur, General Douglas, USA (USMA, 1903)
Was caught by surprise in December 1941 by Japanese attacks on the Philippine Islands, 163-164; took money from President Manuel Quezon of the Philippines to facilitate Quezon's evacuation, 164-165; mixed job of training Filipino soldiers prior to the advent of war, 177-178; in March 1942 was evacuated from Corregidor, 179

Magruder, Captain John H., Jr., USN (USNA, 1911)
In 1940 was commanding officer of the Asiatic Fleet flagship, the cruiser Augusta (CA-31), when she ran aground in the Philippines, 95-96; fondness for baseball, 132

Manila, Philippine Islands
Attractive as a site for liberty for U.S. sailors in the period shortly before the beginning of World War II, 93, 137-139, 152-153, 160-162; was declared an open city in December 1941 following Japanese attacks on the Philippines, 164; site of prisons that held captured U.S. military personnel during World War II, 193-198

Marine Corps, U.S.
In the 1930s Harralson's brother Bill served with the Marine Corps on the Asiatic station, 5-6; in 1939 Marines tended to ignore security rules at North Island Naval Air Station until a sentry fired a pistol near one of the Marines, 85-86; stationed in Shanghai, China, shortly before World War II, 135-136; some Marines were among the American contingent on the island of Corregidor in Manila Bay in the early months of 1942, 175-176, 178-183, 186; as prisoners during World War II, 197, 225-226; evacuation of in late 1950 of Marine Corps personnel from Hungnam, Korea, by the escort carrier Sicily (CVE-118), 282; in the crew of the Sicily during the Korean War, 290; in the mid-1950s had a detachment on board the missile test ship Mississippi (EAG-128), 351

Marine Fighter Squadron 214 (VMF-214)
In the summer of 1950 embarked on board the escort carrier Sicily (CVE-118) to provide close air support in the Korean War, 273

Martell, Captain Charles B., USN (USNA, 1930)
In 1954-55 served as commanding officer of the missile test ship Mississippi (EAG-128), 332, 334-335, 337, 346-348

Massachusetts, USS (BB-2)
In 1899 was used for early radio tests off New Jersey, 100-101

Medical Problems
Treatment of infections and other maladies among American prisoners of war in World War II, 194-195; during World War II, Radioman Harold Hooper suffered a broken leg while a prisoner of war in Japan, 221; harrowing medical experiments on Americans in a prison camp at Shinagawa, Japan, in World War II, 233-234; in 1945, after being released from prison camp, Harralson was treated for amoebic dysentery, 243; in the mid-1950s Harralson's wife had tonsillitis and his children had measles, 306-307; after beginning civilian work in the late 1950s, Harralson had stomach ulcers, 362-363, 365

Missiles
In the mid-1950s, the missile test ship Mississippi (EAG-128) fired Terrier missiles against drones, 337, 343

Mississippi, USS (EAG-128)
In the mid-1950s did a lot of local operating in the Norfolk area, 332, 345-346; inventory of Title B equipment, 333; communication department, 333-334; underway watch standing on the bridge, 334-340, 347-348; the ship's officers enjoyed luxurious quarters, 334; test-fired Terrier missiles against drones, 337, 343; had electrical problems as a result of going through a hurricane, 344; short on backing power, 345; fine ambience in the officers' wardroom for meals, 345; trips to New York City for recreation, 347; radio communications, 347, 350; once spotted a large gathering of whales, 348; Marine detachment once created a shambles of the berthing compartment and then had to clean it up, 351; visual communications, 351-352; steps leading to the decommissioning of the ship in September 1956, 352-354

Moseley, Captain Stanley P., USN (USNA, 1925)
In the late 1940s served as chief of staff to the commandant of the Portsmouth, New Hampshire, Naval Base, 250, 255, 258; wife of, 260

Movies
Some of the films of the 1930s featured Navy themes, 2; in 1940 the American element in Shanghai, China, got the film Grapes of Wrath withdrawn from showing, 109; special showing of Gone with the Wind for Navy personnel in Shanghai, 109-110

Mudge, Radioman Second Class Arthur G., USN
In 1939 was transferred from the battleship Arizona (BB-39) to duty with the Asiatic Fleet in the Far East, 89; died at Cavite in the Philippines shortly after World War II started, 91; as a married man, he didn't go ashore much in the Far East, 114

Music
    In 1940-41 Bandmaster Sid Zeramby's group did a wonderful job of entertaining the crew of the heavy cruiser Augusta (CA-31), 121

Nasworthy, Radioman First Class Robert W., USN
    Served in the early 1940s in the Asiatic Fleet flag allowance on board the fleet flagship Augusta (CA-31), 125

Naval Aviation Pilots
    Enlisted pilots made a spectacular save of a tangled parachutist in the late 1930s while operating from the aircraft carrier Lexington (CV-2), 53-54

Naval Reserve, U.S.
    In the mid-1950s a number of reserve officers who had been recalled for active duty for the Korean War had to leave the service without being able to finish their careers to retirement, 360-361

Navigation
    In the early 1950s the radar on board the escort carrier Sicily (CVE-118) was used as an aid to navigation, 267, 273-274, 283

News Media
    In the 1940s Navy radio stations transmitted to ships abbreviated news summaries derived from commercial news organizations, 124-125

New York City, New York
    In the spring of 1939 the U.S. Fleet was scheduled to visit New York, but the ships were sent back to the West Coast instead because of the international situation, 76-78; visited in the mid-1950s by the crew of the missile test ship Mississippi (EAG-128), 348

Norfolk, Virginia
    Because of local segregation practices, in 1939 black sailors had to sit at the back of streetcars, 77; visited briefly in early 1950 by the escort carrier Sicily (CVE-118), 268-269

North Island Naval Air Station, Coronado, California
    In the late 1930s operated a variety of aircraft, including flying boats, 30; in the late 1930s was the home base for Scouting Squadron Three and the flag allowance of Commander Aircraft Battle Force, 58-59; in 1939 Captain John Hoover, AirBatFor chief of staff, laid down tough security rules for the squadrons at North Island, 84-86

Nuclear Weapons
    In August of 1945 the U.S. Army Air Forces dropped atomic bombs on Japan, 236-237

Oak Knoll Naval Hospital, Oakland, California
  Site of treatment in 1945 for American prisoners repatriated from Japan, 241-245

Olongapo, Luzon, Philippines
  Site of liberty for sailors of the U.S. Asiatic Fleet in the period shortly before the beginning of World War II, 98-99

O'Neil, Commander Guy E., Jr., USN (USNA, 1937)
  In the mid-1950s served in Turkey, in charge of a project to collect submarine sound signatures from the Black Sea, 311-312, 314, 319, 327

Palawan, Philippine Islands
  Served in early 1940 as the site for liberty by the crew of the Asiatic Fleet flagship Augusta (CA-31), 95; in early 1940 the Augusta ran aground near Puerto Princesa, 95-96

Panama
  In 1939 Panama City served for a time as an anchorage for the aircraft carrier Lexington (CV-2), 75; in 1950 the escort carrier Sicily (CVE-118) visited Colon, 270-271

Panama Canal
  In early 1939 the aircraft carrier Lexington (CV-2) scraped her sides against the walls of Miraflores Locks while going through the canal, 64-65, 68

Pan American Airways
  In 1941 Pan American's Clipper planes operated in and out of Cavite in the Philippines, 145-146

Pay and Allowances
  Pay and pensions provided in the late 1930s for Navy enlisted men, 6; warrant officers in the late 1930s on board the aircraft carrier Saratoga (CV-3) were well paid, 48-49; in the early 1940s the Navy began paying an additional allowance to enlisted men who were married, 78-79; in 1945, after being repatriated from prison camp, Harralson received about $5,000 in back pay, 242

Philippine Islands
  Manila was attractive as a site for liberty for U.S. sailors in the period shortly before the beginning of World War II, 93, 137-139, 152-153, 160-162; the fleet flagship Augusta (CA-31) visited the southern islands, 94-95; in early 1940 the Augusta ran aground near Puerto Princesa, Palawan, 95-96; U.S. ship repair facility at Subic Bay, 97-98; the onset of war in December 1941 meant that sailors didn't have to pay their debts, 136-137; operation in 1941 of the Navy radio station at Cavite, 106-107, 143-147, 149-158, 161; President Manuel Quezon in 1941 paid General Douglas MacArthur to ensure that he, Quezon, would be evacuated in the wake of the Japanese attack, 164-165; in December 1941 the Japanese bombed the Cavite Navy Yard, 165-169; aftermath of the bombing, 169-172; in May of 1942 the Japanese

captured the island of Corregidor and took American prisoners, 181-192; in mid-1942 prisoners were held for a few months in prisons in the Manila area, 192-198

Point Loma Electronics Laboratory, San Diego, California
Didn't have much work to do in the period immediately after World War II, 246-247

Portsmouth, New Hampshire, Naval Base
Operation of the naval radio station in the late 1940s, 250-263, 274-275

Prisoners of War
In May 1942 Japanese soldiers on Corregidor captured a large number of U.S. servicemen, 185-192; meager food for American prisoners of war, 188-189, 191-193, 196, 198, 204-205, 207, 222, 227; in mid-1942 were held in prisons around Manila for a few months, 193-198; trip to Taiwan on board ship, 198; activities in captivity in Taiwan, 198-203; in late 1942 prisoners suffered during a voyage from Taiwan to Japan, 204-205; from 1942 to 1945 the prisoners worked in a shipyard in Yokohama, Japan, 205-217, 221-224; prisoners worked to convert a Japanese golf course to a garden, 217-218; survival rate among prisoners, 218-219; daydreams often focused on food, 219-220; problems with lice, 221; organizational structure among the prisoners, 225-226; radio broadcast from the prison camp in Yokohama included the names of American prisoners, 227-228; in the summer of 1945 prisoners were transferred to a camp called Omori, 230-231; transfer in 1945 to a camp at Wakasenen to work in an iron foundry, 231-232; harrowing medical experiments on Americans in a prison camp at Shinagawa, 233-234; release of the prisoners when the war ended, 233, 235; Japanese plans to kill U.S. prisoners if the home islands were invaded, 237; prisoners who harbored hatred after release, 365

Puget Sound Navy Yard, Bremerton, Washington
Site of scraping and painting of the bottom of the aircraft carrier <u>Saratoga</u> (CV-3) in the late 1930s, 45-46

Quezon, Manuel
As President of the Philippines in 1941, paid General Douglas MacArthur to ensure that he, Quezon, would be evacuated, 164-165

Racial Segregation
In 1939 local practices meant that black sailors in Norfolk, Virginia, had to ride at the back of streetcars, 77; in the late 1930s blacks and white went their separate ways on board the aircraft carrier <u>Lexington</u> (CV-2), 78; in the mid-1950s in Georgia, 355

Radar
Around 1940 the battleship <u>California</u> (BB-44) sported one of the first radar antennas in the fleet, 32-33; use of in the early 1950s on board the escort carrier <u>Sicily</u> (CVE-118), 267-270, 275-279, 283, 286-287; on board the missile test ship

Mississippi (EAG-128) in the mid-1950s, 337; used in the mid-1950s for training at the Combat Information Center Officer School in Glynco, Georgia, 357-359

Radio
Harralson's early interest in the 1930s in crystal sets and ham radio, 3-4, 8, 10-13; Navy radio school in 1938 at San Diego taught Morse Code and radio procedures, 21-24; work of the radio gang in the late 1930s on board the aircraft carrier Saratoga (CV-3), 34, 36-37, 39-45, 49; in the late 1930s the flag allowance radio gang performed various duties on behalf of the ComAirBatFor staff, 58-60; limited amount of encrypted traffic, 59-60; various commercial companies sold Navy men correspondence courses in radio operations and material maintenance, 60, 130-131; setup for ComAirBatFor flag radio in the late 1930s on board the aircraft carrier Lexington (CV-2), 61-62, 64, 66-68, 79; work of the flag allowance radio gang on board the Asiatic Fleet flagship Augusta (CA-31) shortly before World War II, 92-93, 101-106, 124-125, 129-133; early tests were conducted in 1899 off New Jersey, 100-101; operations in 1941 of the Navy radio station at Cavite in the Philippines, 106-107, 143-147, 149-158, 161; description of transmitters on board the Augusta, 135; equipment setup on board the heavy cruiser Houston (CA-30) in November 1940 when she became flagship of the Asiatic Fleet, 142-143; in 1942 Japanese Army officers interrogated U.S. Navy radiomen to see if they had any knowledge of codes, 201-202; radio broadcast from a prisoner of war camp included the names of American prisoners, 227-228; operation of the radio station at the Portsmouth, New Hampshire, Naval Base in the late 1940s, 250-263, 274-275; communications in the early 1950s by the escort carrier Sicily (CVE-118), 280-281, 293; by the early 1950s radio teletype had largely replaced CW, 304-305; in the mid-1950s on board the missile test ship Mississippi (EAG-128), 347, 350

Recruit Training
Conducted in 1937 at the naval training station in San Diego, California, 6, 15-20; liberty in downtown San Diego for the boots, 25-28; the art of sleeping in hammocks, 37-39

Religion
During his time as a prisoner of war in World War II Harralson did not pray, 207-208

Rochester, USS (ACR-2)
Old armored cruiser, a relic of the Spanish-American War, that in the early 1940s was at Subic Bay in the Philippines, 99-100; in 1899 was involved in early radio tests, 100-101

Rockwell, Rear Admiral Francis W., USN (USNA, 1908)
Served as the Commandant of the 16th Naval District in 1941 when the Japanese bombed the Cavite Navy Yard in the Philippines, 171-172

Rome, Italy
Harralson made an interesting tour of Rome in 1954 while en route to duty in Turkey, 309-310

Rothberg, Lieutenant (junior grade) Ruth, USN
In the late 1940s served on the staff of the Portsmouth, New Hampshire, Naval Base, 251, 254-256

Royal Navy
In the summer of 1941 the damaged British battleship Warspite visited Cavite in the Philippines while en route to the United States for repairs, 152-154

Ruckner, Captain Edward A., USN (USNA, 1932)
In 1955-56 served as commanding officer of the missile test ship Mississippi (EAG-128), 340-341

SBC Helldiver
Aircraft used by Scouting Three in 1939 for towing targets during gunnery practice, 81-82; VS-3 sent a detachment in 1939 to the world's fair at Treasure Island in San Francisco, 82-83; passenger hops around the San Diego area, 84

Sabotage
American prisoners of war committed sabotage while working in a Japanese shipyard during World War II, 209-213, 238; prisoner sabotage in 1945 at an iron foundry in Wakasenen, 232

San Diego, California
For recruits in 1937, liberty involved visiting the local YMCA and patronizing merchants in the city's downtown area, 25-28; in the late 1930s enlisted men in uniform were not always welcome at better places in San Diego, 27-28; after men got out of boot camp, they rented lockers ashore so they could make liberty in civilian clothes, 28-29; trainees interacted with older sailors on liberty, 31-32; around 1940 the battleship California smashed a boardwalk at the end of Broadway while making a landing, 32; passenger hops around the San Diego area in 1939 by planes of Scouting Three, 84; the Point Loma Electronics Laboratory didn't have much work to do in the period immediately after World War II, 246-247; during the early 1950s was the home port for the escort carrier Sicily (CVE-118), 271-273, 281-283, 289

San Diego Naval Training Station
In 1937 served as the site of boot camp for Harralson and his fellow trainees, 15-20, 37-39; in 1938 was the site of radio school for young enlisted men, 21-24

Saratoga, USS (CV-3)
Work of the radio gang in the late 1930s, 34, 36-37, 39-45, 49, 52; difficulty loading and unloading boats while the ship was rolling in harbor, 35-36; tactical maneuvers with other ships, 40-41; scraping and painting of the ship's bottom in the late 1930s at the Puget Sound Navy Yard, 45-46; recreation on board, 50; head and laundry facilities on board, 50-51; operation of ship's boats, 51-52, 54-55; in the late 1930s air operations were exciting to watch, 53; lost an anchor at Seal Beach, California, while preparing to host a visit from Shriners at Long Beach, 57-58

Sasebo, Japan
During the Korean War was used as a base of operations by the escort carrier Sicily (CVE-118), 273-274, 286-287, 290-292

Schoenweiss, Commander Carl W., USN (USNA, 1934)
During the Korean War served as executive officer of the escort carrier Sicily (CVE-118), 272, 287

Scouting Squadron Three (VS-3)
In the late 1930s operated out of the North Island Naval Air Station and did training flights nearby, 80-82; in 1939 sent a detachment to the world's fair at Treasure Island in San Francisco, 82-83; passenger hops around the San Diego area, 84

Shanghai, China
Attractive as a site for liberty for sailors who were part of the Asiatic Fleet flag allowance in the period shortly before the beginning of World War II, 93, 97, 108-112, 121, 135-136

Shipbuilding
From 1942 to 1945 a group of American prisoners of war, captured in the Philippines, worked in a shipyard in Yokohama, Japan, 205-216, 221-224; acts of sabotage, 209-213, 238

Shore Patrol
Necessary in Tsingtao, China, around 1940 because of the proximity of Japanese and American sailors, 116-117

Sicily, USS (CVE-118)
In the early 1950s, the ship's electronic equipment played an important role, 267-270, 273-281, 283, 286-288, 293; operation of ship's boats, 268-269; operations in the Caribbean in early 1950, 269-270; soon after arriving in San Diego in the summer of 1950, deployed westward to take part in the Korean War, 272; in the spring of 1950 conducted ASW operations out of San Diego, 273; air operations from the Yellow Sea in support of the Korean War, 275-279; evacuation in late 1950 of Marine Corps personnel from Hungnam, Korea, 282; period in between deployments to Korea, 282-283; inventory of the ship's supply of narcotics and

alcohol, 290; Marine squadron CO was killed in a landing accident, 291; relationship among wardroom officers, 292

Simulators
Used in the mid-1950s at the Combat Information Center Officer School in Glynco, Georgia, 357-359

Sonar
In the early 1950s was used on board the escort carrier Sicily (CVE-118), 279-280; in 1954-55 Harralson had duty at Amasra, Turkey, in charge of a group that used hydrophones to collect submarine sound signatures from the Black Sea, 311-331

Soviet Union
In 1937 the U.S. Asiatic Fleet flagship Augusta (CA-31) visited Vladivostok, 159-160

Spear, Commander Louis P., USN (USNA, 1939)
Fine officer who served in the mid-1950s as executive officer of the missile test ship Mississippi (EAG-128), 338-340

State Department
Communications in 1941 about Japanese envoy Saburo Kurusu visiting the Philippine Islands while en route to the United States, 155-157

Stoddard, Radioman Second Class Harry G., USN
Was present at the Cavite Navy Yard in the Philippines in December 1941 when it was bombed by the Japanese, 171-172

Subic Bay, Philippines
In the years before World War II, the U.S. Navy maintained the Dewey dry dock there for ship repairs, 96-98, 101; the former armored cruiser Rochester (ACR-2), was still there in the early 1940s, though stricken from the Navy list, 99-100

See also: Olongapo, Luzon, Philippines

Submarines
In 1954-55 Harralson had duty at Amasra, Turkey, in charge of a group that used hydrophones to collect submarine sound signatures from the Black Sea, 311-331

Taiwan
Site of prison camp for Americans held in captivity by the Japanese in World War II, 198-201

Terrier Missile
In the mid-1950s, the missile test ship Mississippi (EAG-128) fired Terriers against drone aircraft, 337

Thach, Captain John S., USN (USNA, 1927)
In the early 1950s commanded the escort carrier Sicily (CVE-118) and took her to war in Korea, 272, 279-280; charmed the wives of the ship's officers, 281

Torpedoes
Malfunctioning torpedoes posed a substantial problem for the U.S. Navy in the early part of World War II, 168-169; in the mid-1950s the Turkish Navy used the port of Amasra as a base for loading torpedoes into submarines, 315, 327-328

Training
Boot camp in 1937 at the naval training station in San Diego, California, 6, 15-20, 37-39; radio school at San Diego in 1938 taught Morse Code and radio procedures, 21-24; in the late 1930s various commercial companies sold Navy men correspondence courses in radio operations and material maintenance, 60, 130-131; in 1946 Harralson attended electronics technician school at Great Lakes, Illinois, 247; in the early 1950s Great Lakes was the site of electronics maintenance school, 264-266; 294-307; in the mid-1950s at the Combat Information Center Officer School in Glynco, Georgia, for prospective CIC officers and air controllers, 357-361

Tsingtao, China
Visited in the early 1940s, before World War II, by the Asiatic Fleet flagship Augusta (CA-31) and warships of other nations, 97; the culture represented a variety of nations, 113, 122-123; liberty attractions for sailors, 113-116; sometimes hassles resulted from the proximity of Americans to Japanese soldiers and sailors, 116-118

Turkey
In 1954-55 Harralson had duty at Amasra, Turkey, in charge of a group that used hydrophones to collect submarine sound signatures from the Black Sea, 311-331

Uniform Code of Military Justice
Courts-martial were held at Great Lakes, Illinois, in the early 1950s, shortly after the Uniform Code of Military Justice went into effect, 294-298

Uniforms-Naval
In the late 1930s tailors made alterations to Navy-issued uniforms so they would fit enlisted men better, 25, 56; in the late 1930s enlisted men in uniform were not always welcome at better places in San Diego, 27-28; distinctive markings of enlisted men in various categories in the Navy of the late 1930s, 31; enlisted working uniforms worn in the late 1930s on board the aircraft carrier Lexington (CV-2), 65; variety of uniforms worn in 1940-41 on board the Asiatic Fleet flagship Augusta (CA-31), 120-122; in 1945 Harralson bought a gray chief petty officer uniform after being released from Japanese prisoner-of-war camp, 241

Utah, USS (AG-16)
Gunnery training ship that on one occasion in 1938 provided transportation for sailors and Marines from San Diego to Long Beach, 33-34

VMF-214
    See: Marine Fighter Squadron 214 (VMF-214)

VS-3
    See: Scouting Squadron Three (VS-3)

Visual Signaling
    Use of flag hoists during a 1939 war game in the Caribbean, 71-72; in the mid-1950s on board the missile test ship Mississippi (EAG-128), 351-352

War Games
    In early 1939, the aircraft carrier Lexington (CV-2) and other ships of the Battle Force engaged in Fleet Problem XX in the Caribbean, 64-73

Warspite, HMS
    British battleship that in the summer of 1941 visited Cavite in the Philippines while en route to the United States for repair of battle damage, 152-154

Weather
    In the mid-1950s the missile test ship Mississippi (EAG-128) had electrical problems as a result of going through a hurricane, 344

Weber, Lieutenant Commander Edgar H., USN
    In the early 1950s served as electronics maintenance officer on board the escort carrier Sicily (CVE-118), 267, 284

Whales
    While at sea in the Atlantic in the mid-1950s, the men of the missile test ship Mississippi (EAG-128) spotted a large gathering of whales, 348

Yokohama, Japan
    From 1942 to 1945 a group of American prisoners of war, captured in the Philippines, worked in a shipyard in Yokohama, 205-216, 221-224; in the early 1950s Harralson was in Yokohama on liberty and went to visit a Japanese family, 284-286

Yokosuka, Japan
    In the summer of 1950 the escort carrier Sicily (CVE-118) went into this port to take aboard Marine Fighter Squadron 214 for duty in the Korean War, 272-273

www.ingramcontent.com/pod-product-compliance
Lightning Source LLC
Chambersburg PA
CBHW080622170426
43209CB00007B/1491